"Karen Jobes provides a beautiful portra
Testament on John's Gospel. Jobes' writ
pastoral and historical. This book joins Jobes depul and richness cultivated
by a lifetime of scholarship with her heart that cares for her readers' spiritual
growth. Whether a scholar, a pastor, a student, or simply an interested reader,
everyone will find something of deep value in this book for years to come!"

—Beth M. Stovell,
Associate Professor of Old Testament, Ambrose University

"Karen Jobes, long-time professor of New Testament and Greek at Westmont
and Wheaton Colleges, presents here the culmination of a career-long interest
in John's writings. Wearing her learning lightly, this very accessible commentary
majors on Old Testament backgrounds, the structure of the text, and the
significance of both for correctly understanding the gospel of John. Abreast of
the most recent scholarly literature, Jobes judiciously selects what readers most
need, and her interpretations almost always make the most sense. She even
sneaks in compelling life applications here and there as well. Short enough to
be manageable, but detailed enough to be deeply enriching. A wonderful book."

—Craig L. Blomberg,
Distinguished Professor of New Testament, Denver Seminary

"Karen Jobes skillfully explores John's reliance on the Jewish Scriptures,
whether in citation, allusion, or echo. She brings to her analysis a keen
understanding of John within the Second Temple Jewish context and shares
her insights in compelling prose. Accessible, clearly written, incisive. I heartily
recommend this book."

—Jeannine K. Brown, Bethel Seminary

"I enjoyed reading this book for the same reason that I love to go to Israel.
Both teach about the Jewish and Old Testament roots of Christianity and
the entire Bible. My eyes have been opened! The highlight boxes of 'Going
Deeper' and 'What the Structure Means' very much enriched the experience."

—Ken Jasko,
Pastor, Monmouth Worship Center, Marlboro, NJ

"Scholars usually notice the overt and allusive use of the Old Testament in
the Gospel of John. Karen Jobes, however, uniquely and comprehensively
uncovers the Jewish subtext of this gospel. Her careful exegesis and powerful
suggestions for application are a reliable guide to students, pastors, and
Christian leaders as they seek to listen to God's Word in the middle of
contemporary contextual realities. This creative book will become an
inseparable companion to standard commentaries on John."

—Carlos Raúl Sosa Siliezar,
Associate Professor of New Testament, Wheaton College

Through Old Testament Eyes
New Testament Commentaries
Series Editor: Andrew T. Le Peau

JOHN
THROUGH OLD TESTAMENT EYES

Karen H. Jobes

ANDREW T. LE PEAU
SERIES EDITOR

KREGEL
ACADEMIC

John Through Old Testament Eyes: A Background and Application Commentary
© 2021 by Karen H. Jobes

Published by Kregel Academic, an imprint of Kregel Publications, 2450 Oak Industrial Dr. NE, Grand Rapids, MI 49505-6020.

The Hebrew font, NewJerusalemU, and the Greek font, GraecaU, are available from www. linguistsoftware.com/lgku.htm, +1-425-775-1130.

ISBN 978-0-8254-4508-8

Printed in the United States of America

21 22 23 24 25 / 5 4 3 2 1

For My Doktorvater,
Dr. Moisés Silva

CONTENTS

SERIES PREFACE

The New Testament writers were Old Testament people. Their minds were populated with Old Testament stories and concepts. Their imaginative world was furnished with Old Testament images, motifs, metaphors, symbols, and literary patterns. When Jesus came and turned much of their conventional wisdom on its head, they largely had Old Testament tools to understand what was going on in order to explain Jesus to others and to themselves. So that's what they used.

For many Christians the Old Testament has, unfortunately, become a closed book. It seems long, mysterious, and boring with a confusing history full of many strange, unpronounceable names. And then there are those sometimes bizarre prophecies populated with strange creatures. Yet my consistent experience in teaching the New Testament is that when I turn the attention of students to relevant Old Testament passages, the proverbial light bulbs go on. The room is filled with "aha"s. Formerly obscure New Testament passages suddenly make new sense in light of the Old. Indeed the whole of each book of the New Testament takes on fuller, richer dimensions not seen before.

The purpose of the Through Old Testament Eyes commentaries is to give preachers, teachers, and other readers this same experience. This series opens the New Testament in greater depth to anyone who wants to see fresh ways that Scripture interconnects with Scripture.

Scholars have long known that the Old Testament influenced the New Testament (an idea known as intertextuality). In fact, over a millennia and a half ago Augustine famously proposed that we understand the relationship of the two testaments in this way: "The new is in the old concealed; the old is in the new revealed." Yet no commentary series is as devoted as this one is to seeing the richness of Old Testament allusions, references, echoes, and background to illuminate both puzzling passages and explain others in fresh ways.

Practices like baptism, meals, fishing, and fasting; concepts like rescue, faith, sin, and glory; and terms like wilderness, Sabbath, and Lord are just a few of the dozens of words in each New Testament book and letter with deep Old Testament resonances. Sometimes a narrative arc or an argument is also shaped by the Old Testament. An appreciation of this background enriches our understanding and helps us appropriately apply each passage.

In these commentaries you will find four repeating features which will enrich your encounter with the Scripture.

Running Commentary

Verse-by-verse or paragraph-by-paragraph commentary will include Old Testament background as well as other key information, to give readers an understanding of the text as a whole and to answer questions as they naturally arise.

Through Old Testament Eyes

Periodic summaries offer overviews of chapters or sections. These occasional pauses give the opportunity to step back from the detail to see the bigger picture of how Old Testament themes and motifs are being used by the New Testament authors.

What the Structure Means

New Testament authors often get their points across through the way they structure their material. The very organization of their writing conveys significant meaning in and of itself. How the events and teachings are linked makes a difference that, while not explicit, is an important part of the message. Again it is important to not take verses out of context as if they were timeless truths standing apart from their original settings, which affect how we understand them.

The authors of the New Testament also deliberately use, for example, repetition, contrast, hyperbole, metaphor, story, and other techniques so they can have the maximum impact on their readers. "What the Structure Means" will highlight these every so often and help us keep track of the overall flow of each book and letter so that the Old Testament background can be seen in its proper context.

Going Deeper

New Testament writers did not want merely to convey information. They wrote with the needs of the early church in mind. What should their attitude be toward family members who weren't Christians? How should they respond to challenges from Jewish or Roman authorities?

What about internal disputes within the church? These and many other issues were on their minds, and the New Testament addresses them and many more.

Through Old Testament Eyes commentaries will not only leave readers with an enriched understanding of the text but with enriched lives. In "Going Deeper" the authors will unpack the practical implications of each book and letter for Christians and churches, especially drawing from the Old Testament dimensions uncovered in the text.

As much as this series champions the importance of understanding the New Testament's use of the Old, two key points need to be mentioned. First, the Old Testament is not merely a tool for understanding the New. The Old Testament is important and valuable in its own right. It was the Bible of Jesus and the first Christians. They guided their lives by it. The Old Testament needs to be and deserves to be understood on its own terms, apart from the lens it provides for seeing the New Testament clearly. All the commentary authors in this series begin just here as they approach the text. In fact, our hope is that these commentaries will be a window into the Old Testament that will motivate many readers to look more deeply into what some have called the First Testament.

Second, the Old Testament is not the only interpretive lens we need to understand the New. Roman and Greek culture and history, for example, had a very significant influence on the New Testament era. So did the Second Temple period (from the start of rebuilding the temple about 537 BC to the destruction of the temple by Rome in AD 70). Where essential, these commentaries will reference such background material. But the emphasis will be on providing in-depth Old Testament background that readers too often overlook.

While these commentaries are grounded in solid scholarship, they are not intended primarily for an academic audience. For this reason many topics, approaches, and debates found in technical commentaries are absent. This series is for those who want to teach or preach, as well as any serious reader committed to understand Scripture.

The past is always present. The question is: Are we aware of how it affects us or not? The Old Testament was present with the New Testament writers. They knew that and treasured it. We can too.

—Andrew T. Le Peau
Series Editor

INTRODUCTION

The summer between my junior and senior years at college I made an adult profession of faith in Christ after reading John's gospel. I'll let you guess how many years ago that was! But throughout the intervening decades the fourth gospel has always held a special place in my heart. As a young adult who had encountered the reality of sin in my life, this gospel reminded me that Jesus loves me, and that the Father sent Jesus into the world so that through faith in Christ we might not perish because of our sin but have eternal life (Jn 3:16).

As my life in Christ unfolded through the years, I have been blessed richly to devote so much of it to the academic study and teaching of the Bible. Of special interest is how the New Testament writers so tightly wove the teachings and verses of the Old Testament into the New. As the series preface says, "The New Testament writers were Old Testament people." It is a joy to return to John's gospel once again these many years after my conversion to read this gospel through Old Testament eyes with a focus on the Old Testament images, motifs, metaphors, symbols, and literary patterns that give the fourth gospel such depth.

Not only my personal favorite, the gospel of John is often the first book of the New Testament to be translated into a language of a society that does not yet have Scripture. Because its profound theology is expressed in simple Greek syntax, it is a favorite for Greek professors when introducing their students to reading the Greek New Testament. Its hope of eternal life makes it a pastoral favorite to be read graveside. When human beings first arrived on the surface of the moon on July 20, 1969, John 15:5 was the first verse to be read extraterrestrially on the lunar surface when astronaut and Presbyterian elder Buzz Aldrin took Holy Communion inside the Lunar Excursion Module, making the bread and wine of Communion "the very first liquid ever poured on the moon, and the first food eaten there."[1]

As has often been said, John's gospel is shallow enough for a baby to wade in yet deep enough for an elephant to swim in.[2] When I first read John's gospel I had little to no knowledge of the Old Testament. Yet I could see the great power and authority—what John calls the "glory"—of Jesus. While I didn't know the richness of what wine symbolized in John 2:1–11, I did know enough to realize that changing water into wine involved the introduction of carbon to H_2O, making the miracle a creation event. But to read that miracle now with appreciation for the Old Testament allusions that underlie it adds a depth to the gospel message, a depth I'm still fathoming. And so whether this is your first or ninety-ninth reading of John's gospel, there is still much to see and delight in.

This series is focused on reading the New Testament books through Old Testament eyes, and that goal shapes the content of this commentary. There are a vast number of excellent commentaries on John's gospel, but this one takes a deeper dive into the Old Testament backgrounds, traditions, and texts that underlie and inform John's story of Jesus.

In the fourth gospel, Jesus does much of his teaching in the synagogue or in the temple (6:59; 7:14, 28; 8:2, 20; 18:20). As one interpreter notes, "It then becomes reasonable to imagine that much of Jesus' teaching is pictured against the background of the teaching which was performed at these institutions."[3] The Old Testament is the primary source text for the teaching of the synagogue and temple, even while recognizing the many intervening centuries of time during which the Old Testament was interpreted and the traditions of Judaism developed. The gospel of John is rich in references and allusions to, and quotations of, the Hebrew Scriptures. It mentions many of the people, practices, and festivals of ancient Israel such as Abraham (8:39, 40, 52, 53, 56, 57, 58), Jacob (4:6, 12), Moses (1:17, 45; 3:14; 5:45, 46; 6:32; 7:19, 22, 23; 8:5; 9:28, 29), Sabbath (5:9, 10, 16, 18; 7:22, 23; 9:14, 16; 19:31), Passover (2:13, 23; 6:4; 11:55; 12:1; 13:1; 18:28, 39; 19:14), Feast of Tabernacles (7:2), Feast of Dedication (10:22), and the Day of Preparation (19:14, 31, 42). The narrative structure of John's story of Jesus in chapters 5–10 is based on the four important feasts of Sabbath, Passover, Tabernacles, and Dedication. And the explanation of Jesus' identity involves an understanding of the rituals, history, and connotations of the various Jewish festivals.[4]

Accordingly, this commentary will focus on the fourth gospel as it relates to the Old Testament and Second Temple Judaism and will only briefly address many topics typically discussed in exegetical commentaries on John and will omit many others. For instance, it will not compare the Johannine tradition to the Synoptic, or engage in literary analysis of the fourth gospel, or discuss the history of Johannine scholarship. For the same reason, not every verse of the fourth gospel will receive comment.

Structure in John's Gospel

The gospel of John presents a very clear structure of four parts at the "top" level, though the exact boundary between the Books of Signs and Glory is sometimes debated.[5]

> *The Prologue* (1:1–18) privileges the reader with truths initially unknown to the people who encountered Jesus, and so provides a perspective for the reader from which to understand the story of Jesus and what happened to him. In the custom of Greek drama, the dramatist would introduce the theme of his play in a "prologue," which provided the vital information that would enable the audience "to comprehend the plot and understand unseen forces."[6] The Prologue gives readers privileged information that Jesus is the Word who came to reveal God and his redemptive plan for humankind.

> *The Book of Signs* (1:19–12:50) presents a selection of the teachings and symbolic deeds of Jesus meant to reveal his power and authority and the nature of God the Father.

> *The Book of Glory* (13:1–20:31) is the lengthy story of the last few days of Jesus' life, his execution, and his resurrection. Ironically in John's gospel, what we might consider to be the darkest days of Jesus' life are presented as most clearly revealing Jesus' power and authority, or to use one of John's favorite words, his *glory* (see commentary on Jn 17:1).

> *The Epilogue* (21:1–25) presents the encounter of the risen Jesus with his disciples that launches them into their ministry as shepherds of the embryonic Christian church.

The Book of Signs and the Book of Glory present further structure that will be discussed within the commentary.

What the Structure Means

The structure of John's presentation of Jesus supports the stated purpose for his gospel in John 20:30–31: "Jesus performed many other signs in the presence of his disciples, which are not recorded in this book. But these are written that you may believe that Jesus is the Messiah, the Son of God, and that by believing you may have life in his name." John's gospel is a call to faith intended not merely to inform but also to convict and convince its readers of Jesus' identity and the truth of his mission and message. John makes two crucial points as he tells the story of Jesus: that Jesus is the long-awaited

Messiah and that Jesus the Messiah is, against all expectations, God himself. By the time the fourth gospel was written the defense of Jesus' identity had moved beyond his credentials as the Messiah—such as the genealogies that Matthew presents—to the level of his unique relationship with God the Father. One way John accomplishes this is by highlighting Jesus' self-designation as Son of Man, an eschatological figure in the Old Testament (see Da 7:13–14).[7] See the commentary at 1:51 for more on this.

John presents evidence that Jesus is indeed the long-awaited Jewish Messiah, and so must convince his readers of Jesus' relationship to the Old Testament with its prophecies and expectations. Modern readers may think of the Messiah as a religious figure, but in the first century there were various expectations, such as the Prophet to come or a priestly figure, but in Judea it was primarily a political title, as the king who would deliver Israel from geopolitical oppression and occupation.[8] The temple in Jerusalem with its rituals was the focus of this nationalistic hope. John refocuses that hope, showing that all the expectation of national restoration "finds its ultimate realization in the work of Jesus."[9] And so to fully understand Jesus' identity and message, readers must recognize and appreciate the many ways John ties the story of Jesus to the images, motifs, metaphors, and symbols of the Old Testament. Helping readers to that fuller understanding is the whole purpose of this commentary.

John furthermore wants to convince readers that the man Jesus is the embodied eternal Son of God who shares the same nature as God, but without introducing any claim that there are *two* Gods. The claim of monotheism is perhaps the most fundamental teaching of the Old Testament as, for instance, Isaiah expresses it:

> For this is what the LORD says—
> he who created the heavens,
>   he is God;
> he who fashioned and made the earth,
>   he founded it;
> he did not create it to be empty,
>   but formed it to be inhabited—
> he says:
> "I am the LORD,
> and there is no other." (Isa 45:18)

However, "Judaism of the Second Temple period was not a single, unified Judaism. . . . We only need to point to the Dead Sea Scrolls, Jesus' disputes with the Pharisees, the wisdom traditions of Ben Sira and the Wisdom of

Solomon, and the apocalypses of 1 Enoch and 4 Ezra to indicate that there were different perspectives and interests in early Judaism."[10]

Despite the varieties of beliefs within Judaism at the time of Jesus, monotheism was arguably the essential hallmark of Judaism, and Jesus' claim to be deity (see Jn 8:12–59) challenged all understanding of the God of Israel. The ancient Shema of Deuteronomy 6:4, "Hear, O Israel: The LORD our God, the LORD is one," proclaimed the distinctive nature of Israel's God. Scholars continue to debate the origin and definition of monotheism as a historical phenomenon, and particularly "christological monotheism" as introduced by the New Testament writers. Some, such as Larry Hurtado and Richard Bauckham, claim that there was no precedent in pre-Christian Judaism that would have led to an expectation of a divine Messiah, and so Jesus' divine identity was a completely new and unique idea.[11] Others, such as Crispin Fletcher-Louis, point to the Son of Man figure in Daniel 7:13, also found in other noncanonical apocalyptic Jewish writings that might predate Christ, to argue that at least some strains of Judaism had room for the idea of a Messiah with divine qualities even before Jesus came.[12] And so it is particularly interesting to observe how the gospel of John—the fullest articulation of the deity of Christ in the New Testament—presents the identity of Jesus Christ in relation to God the Father while upholding monotheism.

Jewish monotheism at the time of Jesus claimed that the oneness of God concerned his *uniqueness* in relation to everything and everyone else rather than his unity, which became an issue only after the advent of Christ.[13] As Richard Bauckham explains, "God is the *only* Creator of all things (heavens, the earth, the sea, and all that is in them) and God is the *only* sovereign Ruler of all things (all nature and history)."[14]

There are at least five ways John presents the deity of Jesus Christ while defending monotheism. First, John prefaces his story of Jesus with a prologue that clearly intends to show the preexistence of Christ as the Son of God who was with God and who was God before the universe began. The Son of God incarnate in the person of Jesus did not come into being at Jesus' birth, but existed eternally outside of space and time and before the history of Israel began.

Second, to describe this transcendent being who became flesh and dwelt among us, John turns to metaphor, imagery, and symbolism. Although within John's gospel there are metaphors and images that refer to God the Father alone (e.g., Father, vinedresser), and others that refer to Jesus alone (e.g., lamb, bread), there are several that were used primarily for God in the Old Testament but are applied exclusively or primarily to Jesus in John's gospel (e.g., judge, king, shepherd), making an implicit claim to Jesus' deity.[15] Furthermore, there are roles played by both God the Father and the Son, with explicit declarations that "the Father has appointed or granted such roles to the Son."[16] This comes to the fore in John 5, where Jesus is charged with violating the Sabbath and responds that, like God the Father, he is the giver of life and the judge of who will receive it. John presents Jesus as claiming deity, not as another god, but with oneness with the Father in terms of purpose and actions (see commentary on Jn 5). Imagery in the gospel of John implicitly presents Jesus' divinity. For instance, God was the source of the water in the imagery of Ezekiel 47:1–12, Zechariah 14:8, and Joel 3:18. Jesus' claim to be the source of living water (Jn 7:38–39) is another claim of his divinity.

Third, John includes direct statements in his narrative of Jesus claiming to be God by claiming qualities that properly belong to God alone and yet distinguish his identity from that of God the Father. For instance, Jesus claims divine origin (3:13); claims to speak God's words (3:34); says knowledge of him is knowledge of God (8:19); claims to exist before Abraham (8:58); and declares unity with the Father (10:30; 14:10). John "gives to the words of Jesus a divine authority similar to that of the Old Testament Scripture in general (2:22) and the writings of Moses in particular (5:47)."[17]

Fourth, John repeatedly says that God "sent" Jesus, suggesting the ancient practice of the *sheliach* (שָׁלִיחַ), who was a delegate not only sent, but sent with the full power and authority of the sender to accomplish the mission for which he was sent (see further discussion in commentary on 3:17).

Fifth, Jesus explicitly redefines the oneness of God to be a unity of two divine persons. His request to be glorified (17:1, 5) by God is a request that his divine honor and splendor be reinstated as they were prior to his incarnation. Since the Old Testament states that God will share his glory with no other, there is a premise of monotheism in binitarian form. In 17:11, Jesus announces he shares God's name ("the power of *your* name, the name you gave *me*") and modifies the Jewish concept of monotheism as uniqueness to monotheism as unity of Father and Son ("so that they may be one as *we are one*").

John's presentation of Jesus' teachings and actions, and his relationship to the unique God, strongly draws the reader to infer that Jesus and the Father are one God yet two distinct persons. Only later, and probably in response to Christian Trinitarian theology, was the oneness of God interpreted to focus on his indivisible oneness as an argument against the deity of Christ. The way John writes to uphold monotheism while yet showing the divine nature of Jesus and the role of the Holy Spirit is interesting and instructive. This triune mystery is still today an obstacle keeping some people from the Christian faith, so it is important to understand how John defends monotheism within his Christ-centered faith.

John intends that at least some of his readers believe the claims about Jesus based on the evidence presented in the fourth gospel, and such faith results in life that John describes as the fullness of all that human life was created to be (Jn 10:10) as well as an eternal life that survives physical death (Jn 3:15–16; 11:25–26). John structures and builds his gospel to lead readers to faith in Christ as the intended result of God's work throughout human history. God created people for relationship with himself, and because humankind's fall into sin was caused by the rejection of God's word, the acceptance (faith) of God's revelation in Christ is the basis for the relationship God intends to have with his people.

Who Was John?

The majesty of the fourth gospel's theology and the genius of its presentation naturally make one wonder about the man who wrote such words of timeless significance. John's gospel does not specify that anyone named John wrote it. Like the other three Gospels, this one is also anonymous. When the Gospels were bound together the early church supplied a name to each based on knowledge they had, knowledge that may survive only in the traditional titles. In the case of John's gospel, the testimony of two early leaders of the church, Polycarp and Irenaeus, is especially relevant. The young Polycarp (AD 69–155) is said to have been a disciple of the elderly apostle John and apparently knew the Johannine writings, for in AD 120 he loosely quotes from 1 John.[18] Irenaeus (AD 130–202) personally knew Polycarp and writes, "John, the disciple of the Lord, who also had leaned upon his breast, did himself publish a Gospel during his residence at Ephesus in Asia" (*Haer.* 3.1.1).[19] Irenaeus also quotes the gospel of John authoritatively against Gnostic doctrine, and attributes it to "John, the disciple of the Lord," the aforesaid disciple who was at the Last Supper, making it clear that early in the second century John son of Zebedee was widely understood to be the author of this gospel just decades after it was produced. Moreover, the ancient sources present no other claims for a competing author. But because the name John was quite common there could have been two (or more) Christian men named John who could be distinguished from John the son of Zebedee, for example, John the elder. This possibility probably originated in the fourth century with Eusebius, who believed that the man John who authored the book of Revelation (Rev 1:1) was not the same man who authored the fourth gospel. Nevertheless, he affirmed that the *apostle* John was both the "disciple whom Jesus loved" and the author of the gospel, but that the man John who wrote Revelation "remained alive in Asia and administered the churches there, for after the death of Domitian, he had returned from his banishment on the island" of Patmos (*Hist. eccl.* 3.23). Johannine scholarship has made much of the possibility that there were two men named John involved in writing New Testament books. But Eusebius may have misread the writings of Papias, who "inquired into the words of the presbyters [*presbuteros*; πρεσβύτερος], what Andrew or Peter or Philip or Thomas or James or John or Matthew, or any other of the Lord's disciples [*mathētēs*; μαθητής] *had said*, and what Aristion and the presbyter [*presbuteros*; πρεσβύτερος] John, the Lord's disciples, *were saying*" (*Hist. eccl.* 30.39 [emphasis added]). Because of his convictions about the book of Revelation, Eusebius probably misread the two occurrences of the name John as referring to two different men, although it is more plausible based on the verb tenses to understand the first reference to John as among those names of the apostles (who were also called "elders" in the early church, cf. 1 Pe 5:1) who "said"[20] things of interest but by the time of Papias were deceased, and the second reference to the same man John who was still living and speaking ("were saying"). So does Papias mention the apostle John twice, once among the Twelve and then along with Aristion as still living?[21] Or were there two men named John, the apostle and the elder (despite apostles also being called elders)? This ambiguity is the origin of the debate about who wrote the gospel of John. According to Richard Bauckham, the lesser-known John the elder was replaced in the later tradition by the better-known and more prestigious John the apostle.[22] And Martin Hengel argued that John the son of Zebedee, in Jesus' inner circle, did not write *any* New Testament books and that John the elder, who may have been an eyewitness to the crucifixion, wrote all the books that bear the name.[23] Craig Keener argues that Eusebius misunderstood Papias, taking two references to John erroneously to refer to two different men, and concludes that Papias supports authorship by the apostle John, son of Zebedee.[24]

Despite the strongest of external evidence of authorship of any New Testament book, most scholars doubt the fourth gospel was in fact written by John son of Zebedee, one of Jesus' earliest disciples (Mt 4:21; Mk 1:16–19). The debate started by Eusebius is further complicated because the source of John's gospel is attributed to "the disciple whom Jesus loved" (*ton mathētēn hon ēgapa ho Iēsous* [τὸν μαθητὴν ὃν ἠγάπα ὁ Ἰησοῦς]; Jn 21:20), and that disciple is never explicitly identified as John son of Zebedee (see commentary on Jn 21:24). Furthermore, scholars argue that it would be strange and inappropriate for John to refer to himself as the "disciple whom Jesus loved."

The evidence marshaled against authorship by John son of Zebedee is based on inferences, which apparently strike some scholars as substantial and others as not compelling. James Charlesworth finds the cumulative thrust of a list of twenty-one observations compiled by Pierson Parker to be "devastating to the hypothesis that the Disciple is both the author of the GosJn and also the apostle John,"[25] but the writer of this commentary and other writers do not.[26] Parker's twenty-one points—such as John's being a Galilean and the fourth gospel's showing little interest in Galilee, or John's being called a "son of thunder" in the Synoptics and yet the fourth gospel is "the most tranquil of the four Gospels"—are weak in light of the strong external evidence attesting to the apostle John's authorship and yet are nevertheless embraced by modern scholars. Charlesworth's argument that the beloved disciple was Thomas has not received wide support,[27] and Craig Blomberg observes that the reasons Charlesworth marshals in support of Thomas argue strongly instead for John the son of Zebedee as author![28]

The "disciple whom Jesus loved," who testifies to these things and wrote them down (Jn 21:24), is mentioned in six passages (Jn 13:23; 19:26; 20:2; 21:7; 21:20, 24; see commentary in those places, esp. Jn 21:24). He had been present at the Last Supper (Jn 21:20) and was the disciple who reclined closest to Jesus and asked who it was who would betray Jesus (Jn 13:23, 25). Some have suggested that "the beloved disciple" is a purely literary figure with no historical identity, meant to portray idealized characteristics of Christian discipleship, though that seems unlikely given the weight placed on his testimony.

The writings of the disciple Jesus loved may have later become the source of material for the gospel of John as we have it today, and so the author's original self-references could have later been revised, perhaps after his death (see Jn 21:23), with some form of the honorific title "the disciple Jesus loved" by the final editor of the beloved disciple's writings.

The identity of the beloved disciple will probably never be known with certainty, but those of the Twelve explicitly named in John's gospel can probably be eliminated from contention: Simon Peter, Andrew, Philip, Thomas, Judas son of James, Nathanael, and Judas Iscariot (obviously) (see Mt 10:2–4 and Lk 6:12–16 for lists of the names of the Twelve). Interestingly, John son of Zebedee is among the Twelve who are strangely *not* explicitly named in the fourth gospel, yet he was almost certainly present (though in Jn 21:2 the "the sons of Zebedee" are listed as present at the postresurrection encounter on the beach). Peter, James, and John were Jesus' closest disciples. Peter is mentioned often in the fourth gospel. John's brother James, also unnamed in the fourth gospel, was martyred in AD 44, and so died much too early to be the author of this gospel. He is perhaps not mentioned by name because he would not have been familiar to the original readers, having lived and died in Palestine decades before. Therefore, of the three closest disciples of Jesus, John remains. Perhaps the designation of John as the disciple Jesus loved was intended, after the deaths of both James and Peter, to remind readers of John's close association with Jesus as the only surviving of the three. If John is not the beloved disciple, it is inexplicable that such a major player in the gospel story would be left out of the fourth gospel.

The identity of the beloved disciple was almost certainly known to the original readers, though it has been obscured to subsequent generations and may be preserved only in the traditional title of the book. While there was perhaps no need to make the identity of the disciple whom Jesus loved explicit because of common knowledge at the time, perhaps his anonymity serves another purpose as well. As Bauckham points out, "Anonymity is a literary device that serves to mark out the beloved disciple, who is also the author, from the other disciples in the narrative in which he appears with them. His anonymity makes him not just one named disciple among others or even the disciples closest to Jesus but, so to speak, different in kind"[29] (see commentary on Jn 21:24).

To summarize, "some of the major trends in Johannine scholarship, the dating of the fourth gospel has moved from the 90s, to the mid-to-late second century, to the mid 60s, and back to the 90s again. Views of authorship have similarly shifted from the apostle, to the Elder, to a disciple of a church leader, to a collaborative and complex community, and back to an individual author who may or may not be John the apostle."[30]

More than a hundred years ago B. F. Westcott presented substantial internal evidence that, while largely ignored by scholars today, has not been refuted. He argued "that the fourth Gospel was written by a Palestinian Jew, by an eye-witness, by *the disciple whom Jesus loved*, by John the son of Zebedee."[31] Despite the uncertainty of the identity of the disciple Jesus loved as John, son of Zebedee, or John the elder, both external and internal evidence strongly suggest the fourth gospel preserves the eyewitness testimony of one of the Twelve, even if he permitted his scribe(s) to develop the material into the form in which we have it today.[32] We will call him John, as the church has for two millennia.

Regardless of who wrote the fourth gospel, careful readers should distinguish between the *author* of the text and the *narrator* of the story of Jesus' life (see commentary on Jn 21:25). Within the gospel of John we find words of Jesus (printed in red letters in some Bibles), words of a number of other people (e.g., the Samaritan woman, Mary and Martha, Jesus' disciples, Nicodemus), and then words of the person telling the story, the narrator (e.g., "In the beginning was the Word . . ."). The author wrote *all* of the words in these various voices, but to be a careful reader of Scripture it is important to keep in mind who is saying what in the text and, by implication, who in the story knows what compared to the readers. For instance, readers of John's gospel are privileged throughout to have a great deal more knowledge than do any of the characters who encountered Jesus in the story. We know, for example, that the Word became flesh because the *narrator* tells us that before he introduces any of the characters in the story. And note that being a "character" in the story does not threaten the historical reality of that person; it just recognizes a distinction between the historical person and the way he or she is presented in the text. In another example from 12:4, 6, and 13:2, the narrator lets the reader in on two things that the disciples of Jesus did not know at the time: that Judas is the one who will betray Jesus, and that Jesus knew who would betray him before it happened. In John 13:18 and 15:25, the Scripture quoted is put on the lips of Jesus, unlike most of the quotations that are quoted by the narrator. This kind of close reading is the subject of literary analyses of the Gospels, and can reveal interesting insights. In the case of John's gospel, the reader is invited to reflect on their privileged position living *after* the crucifixion and the giving of the Spirit, which allows them to know and understand so much more than Jesus' disciples did during the time they walked with Jesus. In fact, much of what Jesus says in John's gospel *could not be understood* until after his departure and the coming of the Spirit (see Jn 2:22; 13:7; 14:26b). And so by referring to the role of the narrator rather than calling him "John" or "the author" in no way diminishes the author's role or importance but makes an important distinction that respects the way the author has written the text.

Going Deeper

The world in which John wrote his gospel was not unlike our own in the sense that it was already filled with voices advocating religions and philosophies. The fourth gospel not only presents Jesus as a historical person who lived in first-century Roman Palestine, but interprets the significance of Jesus for readers both ancient and modern. History says, "Jesus of Nazareth died on a cross in Jerusalem." If you had been there you could have videotaped that horrible execution. But the significance of historical fact requires it to be interpreted. Interpretation of that event such as we have in the New Testament says, "Jesus *Christ, Son of God*, died on a cross in Jerusalem *for our sins*." The truth represented by the words in italics would not have been visibly evident as Jesus hung on the cross. In fact, we need interpretation to make sense of the life, teachings, death, and resurrection of Jesus. God has provided just that true and inerrant interpretation for us in the books of the New Testament. To be Christian is to believe not only the historical facts about Jesus but also God's interpretation of the significance of Jesus as revealed in the New Testament.

There are many modern, and often conflicting, opinions about who Jesus was. Muslims consider him a prophet. Other religious non-Christians may believe him to have been a great moral teacher and founder of a religious movement. Most people would probably think of him at least as a good man who became a victim of a ruthless regime. But John's gospel does not permit such interpretations. All of the Gospels present Jesus' deity, his redeeming death, and his victorious resurrection (albeit only implied in Mark). But none so boldly proclaims Jesus to be the Son of God, agent of creation, eternally preexistent with the Father who took on the flesh of a human being to dwell among us. That understanding of Jesus would have been no more religiously and politically acceptable to most people when John wrote than it is today. It is truth comprehended through faith that trusts what God says. John's gospel is God's word to us, *God's* interpretation of who Jesus is.

All of the very first believers in Jesus as Christ and Son of God were *Jewish* believers. For them the problem of monotheism must have been acute. After two thousand years of Christian theology, most people today have heard of the triune God the Father, God the Son, and God the Holy Spirit, even if they reject his existence. But Jesus was a Jew, and his twelve disciples whom he designated as apostles to bear witness to him after his death were Jews. How could they possibly accept the deity of Jesus when their ancestors had resisted polytheism even to the point of death to defend monotheism? What must it have taken for them to see the truth about Jesus as God incarnate? The gospel of John presents the teaching of one who had pondered and preached the challenge of Jesus for decades. In this gospel we find the earliest apologetic for a triune monotheism. Not a theology or a philosophy book, John's gospel presents the story of Jesus in a way that leads the reader to either accept or reject the truth as God has revealed it.

John's Use of the Old Testament: Verbal Artistry

All of the four Gospels are divinely inspired interpretations of the significance of Jesus, and each of them draws on the Old Testament in various ways to tie the mission and message of Jesus to God's previous redemptive work in and through the ancient nation of Israel. Consequently, the Old Testament and the development of its messianic expectations are central to the gospel of Jesus Christ.

It is well recognized that Matthew, Mark, and Luke—the Synoptic Gospels—tell of the events of Jesus' life and his teaching in remarkably similar ways, even down to extensive verbal agreement. The similarities have led scholars to observe that Mark's gospel was probably the first to be written, with Matthew and Luke using its words in the production of their own Gospels. But John's gospel is significantly different in its content, chronology, and style. These differences were observed in the early church and led Clement of Alexandria (ca. AD 155–ca. 220) to remark, as preserved by Eusebius, "John, last of all, conscious that the outward facts [*sōmatika*; σωματικά] had been set forth in the Gospels, was urged on by his disciples, and, divinely moved by the Spirit, composed a spiritual [*pneumatikon*; πνευματικὸν] Gospel" (*Hist. eccl.* 6.14.7). While it is not explicitly clear what Clement meant by a "spiritual" gospel, I understand it to refer to the highly interpretive nature of John's gospel presented with a verbal artistry that exceeds that of the other gospel writers. John was not aiming to establish the facts of Jesus' life but to interpret the significance of that life. The sequence of historical events referred to by Clement as the "outward facts" were clear. For instance, it is a statement of fact that Jesus of Nazareth died on a Roman cross. John's gospel supports the truth of the fact, but he is interested in explaining the unseen significance of the outward facts, the "spiritual" element of the gospel. And so, for instance, he joins the other gospel writers to explain that Jesus *Christ* died at the hands of the Romans on a cross *for our sins*, an interpretation of the unseen significance of Jesus' death, identifying him as the Christ and the purpose of his death for our sins.

The interpretive elements of John's gospel are necessary because of John's perception that an eternal, spiritual reality is invisible to the human senses. The incarnation announced by John's Prologue (Jn 1:1–18) introduces the reader to two levels of reality: "In the beginning was the Word, and the Word was with God, and the Word was God. . . . The Word became flesh and made his dwelling among us" (Jn 1:1, 14). There is the commonplace reality of everyday life in first-century Palestine where "we" dwell but also the transcendent reality of the Word in his eternal glory. The incarnation of the Word as the man Jesus is conceptualized as a "descent" in John's gospel and the death on the cross as his return ascent to the realm of unseen reality with the Father, which is his glorification. The two spheres of reality implied by the incarnation present John with the opportunity to use appropriate literary devices to communicate the existence of the two levels and their relationship to one another. Because of the nature of the relationship of the unseen spiritual realities to the visible world, poetry, metaphor, symbolism, and other such literary devices lend themselves to John's purpose of interpreting the significance of Jesus' life and death. For instance, John employs the spatial metaphors of *above* and *below* to refer to the two spheres of reality that the incarnation bridges.

Throughout the fourth gospel John proclaims the significance of selected episodes from Jesus' life. In fact, the gospel of John can be thought of as a verbal painting that presents both the "outward facts" of Jesus' life and their significance. Most of the differences between John's gospel and the Synoptic Gospels are due to the rhetorical techniques John employs to present his interpretation of Jesus, such as a different (dischronologized) sequence of events and more poetic devices than is usually found in "history," such as metaphor, wordplay, double meanings, irony, and symbolism.

As Clement claims, John was likely aware of one or more of the Synoptic Gospels, but it is clear that John did not base his story of Jesus directly on them. Where Matthew, Mark, and Luke are greatly similar in sequence and content, even to the level of verbal agreement, John is distinctly different. John includes only seven miracle stories, which he calls "signs," though nowhere does he enumerate them as being seven (*hepta* [ἑπτά]). Of those, only the feeding of the five thousand is in common with the Synoptics. Like the Synoptics, John tells of the anointing of Jesus and has an extensive passion narrative, but with differences that cohere with John's purposes. John does not tell the same stories about Jesus as the Synoptics tell. John contains no birth narrative, no Sermon on the Mount (or Plain), no Lord's Prayer, no parables, no exorcisms, no story of the transfiguration. Instead of describing the Last Supper on the evening before Jesus' death, John writes about the footwashing, a metaphor for the extent of Jesus' service to cleanse his disciples by the cross (see commentary on Jn 13). As Andreas Köstenberger observes, "John frequently transposes elements of the Gospel tradition into a different key."[33] The teaching of the kingdom of God in the Synoptic Gospels correlates to the theme of eternal life in John; the miracles of Jesus in the Synoptics are replaced by selected miracles, which John calls "signs" (see commentary).

Jesus' teaching by parables in the Synoptics is replaced by long discourses in John that explain the signs. Scholars disagree whether the inclusion of long discourses arises from the conventions of Jewish Wisdom Literature or from Hellenistic consolation literature. In defense of the former, Jesus is presented in terms similar to the way wisdom (*sophia* [σοφία]) is personified in the Jewish texts, and some argue that Jesus is indeed God's wisdom incarnate. In those texts, Lady Wisdom speaks in long discourses that some relate to Jesus' teaching in the fourth gospel.[34] If, however, John wished to emphasize the motif of wisdom in his telling of Jesus' story, it is rather strange that the word *sophia* (σοφία, "wisdom") does not occur even once within the fourth gospel. On the other hand, it could be argued that Jesus is preparing his disciples for his violent departure, and life without his physical presence. The Upper Room Discourse is primarily intended to comfort the disciples and strengthen them for the road ahead. That being the case, some argue that John's presentation has been influenced by the genre of Hellenistic consolation literature.[35] Given that authors are products of their culture, the pervasive Wisdom tradition within Judaism no doubt influenced to some extent the expressions of the Jewish New Testament writers. But it is overreaching to identify Sophia and Christ, as some do, for instance in using the fourth gospel in the development of Sophia Christology.[36] It would be a similar overreach to claim that the literary genres of the Hellenistic world could explain a New Testament book without taking into account the Jewishness of its author.

In another ancient source, the writings of Plutarch, which were approximately contemporaneous with the gospel of John, we may find a clue about how to understand the highly selective nature of what John includes and his exclusion of much of the material found in the Synoptic Gospels. Plutarch is known for a series of books about major historical figures of his day. He refers to the genre he writes as "Lives" (*bios* [βίος]; pl. *bioi* [βίοι]). While similar in some ways to modern biographies, Plutarch explains his intent in his introduction to the *Life of Alexander the Great*:

> It being my purpose to write the lives of Alexander the king and of Caesar . . . *the multitude of their great actions* affords so large a field

that I were to blame if I should not by way of apology forewarn my reader that I have chosen rather to epitomize the most celebrated parts of their, story than to insist at large *on every particular circumstance of it*. It must be borne in mind that *my design is not to write histories, but lives*. And the most glorious exploits do not always furnish us with the *clearest discoveries of virtue or vice* in men; sometimes a matter of less moment, an expression or a jest, informs us better of their characters and inclinations than the most famous sieges, the greatest armaments, or the bloodiest battles whatsoever. Therefore *as portrait-painters* are more exact in the lines and features of the face, *in which the character is seen*, than in other parts of the body, so I must be allowed to give my more particular attention to the marks and indications of the souls of men, and while I endeavor by these to portray their lives, may be free to leave more weighty matters and great battles to be treated of by others. (*Alex.* 1 [emphasis added])

When John sat down to write the story of Jesus, he, like Plutarch, had "an abundance of materials," for as John mentions in John 21:25, "Jesus did many other things as well. If every one of them were written down, I suppose that even the whole world would not have room for the books that would be written." If John were aware of the other three Gospels, as Clement suggests, it makes sense that he would not repeat all of those things, but may include other memories of Jesus, particularly those that evoke ties to the Old Testament images, motifs, and symbols, such as the signs. Furthermore, Plutarch draws the analogy with portrait painters, who seek to capture not only the physical appearance but a glimpse into the soul of the subject as well. Similarly John seems to be seeking not just a telling of Jesus' life, but includes long conversations between Jesus and those he encounters, and long discourses organized around the signs. As Richard Hays observes, "John's narrative technique is analogous to the visual artistry of Rembrandt's portraits."[37]

John apparently views the Old Testament "as a vast matrix of symbols prefiguring Jesus."[38] Through verbal artistry John is revealing the divine nature of Jesus, how Jesus relates to the Old Testament prophecies, the true messianic expectation, and God's redemptive plan for humanity.

So, for instance, when John tells the story of Jesus changing water into wine (Jn 2:1–11), the symbolic value of wine in the Old Testament as a symbol of the messianic age and of blood gives depth to the significance of the act. Furthermore, John makes a point that there were six stone jars, each holding between twenty to thirty gallons (Jn 2:6). This detail may seem of questionable relevance to modern readers, but it actually may tie this miracle to imagery of the messianic age found in 2 Baruch (see commentary on Jn 2:6). The simple fact of turning water into wine is miracle enough to show Jesus' authority and power, but the artistic details included point to a deeper richness for those who have eyes to see, much as an art historian can infer more from a painting than the average viewer.

We must note here that there were many books known to the New Testament writers that were not Scripture but had been written to develop ideas found in the Old Testament. Most of the New Testament writers refer to the Old Testament people and practices as mediated through the centuries of tradition that had developed within Judaism. And so when we seek to read "through Old Testament eyes," our field of vision is centered on the Hebrew Scriptures, but we must peripherally consider as well other ancient books that would have likely been known to the New Testament writers. For instance, the books that Protestants refer to as the Apocrypha, and even some of the books we call the pseudepigrapha (such as 2 Baruch and 1 Enoch), while not Scripture, were nevertheless likely known to and valued by those who became the earliest Christians and writers of the New Testament. Just as most believers today have favorite and revered Christian authors who are often quoted and referred to, but not as Scripture, these books formed part of the conceptual religious world of the New Testament authors. We understand the New Testament writers better when we pay attention to how these noncanonical materials interpret the canonical Old Testament books and characters.

COMMENTARY

JOHN 1

1:1 *In the beginning.* The fourth gospel begins with a direct allusion to Genesis 1:1, "In the beginning God created the heavens and the earth." This allusion would have been immediately apparent to anyone even somewhat familiar with the Hebrew Scriptures, and it would have been a striking parallel, drawing the reader's mind back to creation. This flashback to primeval time sets the story of the significance of Jesus within the realm of the divine, and is John's first statement of the divinity of the Word become flesh. Furthermore, the evangelist here introduces a major theme of his gospel, "the re-creation of the cosmos that is inaugurated in Jesus the Messiah."[1]

The Word. John declares that an entity he refers to as "the Word" was "in the beginning." Scholars debate whether "the Word" (*logos* [λόγος] in Greek; *dabar* [דָּבָר] in Hebrew; *memra* in Aramaic) should be understood in terms of a Greek or Hebrew background. In Greek philosophy the *logos* (λόγος) was understood as the divine rationale that ordered the universe. "The Word" in Hebrew thought referred to the Lord's revelation of himself through the prophets (cf. "The word of the LORD came to . . ." that introduces prophetic statements). The allusions and references throughout the Prologue to Old Testament concepts and people, such as the covenant (1:17), the Lamb of God (1:29, 36), the Messiah (1:25, 41), Elijah (1:24), the tabernacle (1:14), the law and Moses (1:17), root John's presentation of Jesus squarely in Jewish history, not in Greek philosophy.[2] However, by the time John wrote these words, the Jewish people had long been living in Hellenistic culture, which had its influence on Judaism. As the writings of the Jewish philosopher Philo show, attempts to integrate Greek and Hebrew ideas were commonplace, primarily as an apologetic for the wisdom of the Jewish tradition. Philo's writings, which date from about the same time as John's gospel, also show that the *logos* (λόγος) was sometimes presented as an independent entity and sometimes included in the Godhead, but as a manifestation of the presence of God that did not threaten the Jewish doctrine of monotheism.[3]

Augustine later reported that an unnamed "Platonic philosopher had called for the first five verses of the Gospel [of John] to be written in golden letters and hung up in the most visible place in all the churches," so appealing was it to Neoplatonic thought.[4] But as Martin Hengel notes, the Word in John 1:1 is not a philosophical first principle; rather, it "expresses *the eternal being of the Word right from eternity* in inseparable communion with God."[5]

The Word was with God, and the Word was God. The Greek word *theos* (θεός) found here was used to speak of any god, such as Zeus and others in the Greco-Roman pantheon. It was also used to refer to the Lord, the God of Israel, in the ancient Greek translation of the Hebrew Scriptures known as the Septuagint. The direct allusion to the opening words of Genesis 1:1, "in the beginning," would have defined the God to whom John refers and which ideological background should be assumed. The God of ancient Israel made the heavens and the earth and the revelation of the Hebrew Bible containing Genesis (see John 10:30).

The thought that the Logos was with God in the beginning would probably not have been a completely new idea to Jewish readers, for already in Proverbs 8:22–23 the Hebrew Scriptures tell of wisdom personified and present at creation. The Aramaic targums, which are ancient commentaries on the biblical books, use the word *memra* (word) to refer to the Lord God in its discussions of Genesis. This was probably a circumlocution to avoid referring to God directly, for a person's word is the ultimate personal expression of that person. But the statement that the Logos was not only *with* God at the beginning but *was* God no doubt drew a more mystified interest. Here John begins to reveal Jesus' divine nature, though without yet using his name. And here John begins to defend monotheism, by both identifying the Word *with* God and yet distinguishing the Word *from* God.

1:3 *Through him all things were made.* The phrase "in the beginning" is here confirmed to be an allusion to Genesis 1:1 by the explicit reference to the divine act of creation. The claim that the Lord God was the creator of the universe and everything in it, including humankind, was as ancient as the book of Genesis itself. Recall that unlike the creation stories of other ancient cultures, God *spoke* the universe into existence by his *word*: "Let there be. . . ." John's identification of the Logos as the divine agent of creation could have been understood as a reference to the verbal nature of God's creative power. Therefore, God's Word is both word of creation and word of revelation. Other readers familiar with Philo's writings might have understood this statement to support the Logos as the divine reason that brought order to the universe. The bombshell of John 1:14 awaits the reader of either understanding.

1:4 *In him was life, and that life was the light of all.* As Genesis tells, God's first creative act was to create light *by his word* (Ge 1:3). God's Word brought all of reality, both physical and spiritual, into existence. "And God said . . . and it was so." John's allusion to the Genesis creation account in the Prologue reminds readers that God himself is the ground of all reality. In the account of the fall into sin, Adam and Eve chose to act on a "virtual reality" described by the word of the serpent when they ate from the forbidden tree of the knowledge of good and evil (Ge 3), rejecting the word of God and plunging the human race into darkness and death. Ever after it has been difficult for people to discern the truth of the spiritual reality God creates in a world when competing voices have grown so loud. The Genesis creation story reveals that God alone is the source of all life, and that it is the responsibility of human beings to live in the world *as God has defined it*. Therefore, genuine revelation from God (a word) is needed that deals with the darkness of sin. The Word who became flesh is that light, that needed revelation shining in the darkness.

In the Jewish tradition, light (sometimes expressed as a lamp by metonymy) was used as a symbol for God or of God's presence (Ps 4:6; 104:2; Isa 60:19–20; Da 2:22; Hab 3:4), with life closely associated to the light of God's word (Dt 8:1; 11:9; Ps 119:105; 2 Sa 21:17; 22:29; Isa 42:6; 49:6; Mic 7:8). This symbolic use of light and darkness found in John's gospel is not unique, as the Dead Sea Scrolls also divide the moral world into "sons of light" and "sons of darkness." Here John makes the point that the life and light he has in mind is not just for the Jewish people but is the light of *all* humankind. (See Isa 9:1–2, where God's light to all, including Gentiles, is tied to Galilee, which is mentioned soon in Jn 1:43.) The universal reach of the gospel is one of John's major points. John's message is unique, even though the symbolic language he uses may be the same as or similar to other ancient sectarian texts.

1:5 *The light shines in the darkness.* The fall of humankind into the darkness of sin and death (Ge 3), though unspecified, is presupposed between verses 3 and 5. As a symbol, light has many associations in the Old Testament. Light brings order out of chaos (Ge 1:2, 16), and when light is absent the result can be emptiness or terror (Dt 28:29; Job 12:25; Ps 82:5; Isa 5:30). God defeats darkness with light (Isa 9:2), and light is a symbol of truth (Ps 43:3; 119:130) and darkness of ignorance (Ps 82:5). Perhaps of particular importance for John, light is associated with God welcoming Gentiles (Isa 42:6; 49:6).

1:6 *A man sent from God whose name was John.* The first time I read the fourth gospel many years ago I mistakenly thought that the man named John referred to here was the same man to whom the gospel of John is ascribed. Not so! To distinguish the two when necessary, we'll refer to John the Baptist and John the Evangelist. John 1:6 refers to John the Baptist, the last of the prophetic figures of the Old Testament era who recognized and pointed out the Word that had become flesh. He stands at the turning point of the ages. See John 1:14–15 (see also commentary on 3:22–36).

1:9 *The true light . . . coming into the world.* John the Evangelist most likely realized how prevalent the symbol of light was in the religious and philosophical writings of his day. He has already said in 1:4 that the life that was in the Word is the light of all humankind. As Britt Leslie explains, "There are three major aspects of light to be explored: light in relation to *life* [Job 33:30; Ps 49:19], light in relation to *insight, wisdom, and/or knowledge* [Ps 119:105, 130; Da 5:14]; and light in relation to the *presence of God* or the divine [Isa 60:19–20]. In asserting that Jesus is the light, the Gospel asserts that Jesus is the one who brings life, who brings insight/wisdom, and knowledge, and who is the presence of the divine among people."[6]

With the incarnation of the Word who was with God and was God, divine life, revelation, and presence enters the world. There may be many religions, philosophies, and spiritual systems, but the Word incarnate is the only true, genuine, authentic revelation of God.

The claim that this light "gives light to everyone" is not a statement of universalism, as if every human being will internalize the light and receive salvation regardless of their beliefs and life habits. The light is external, objective, and available to everyone, but as John's gospel shows, not everyone did in fact receive the light. In fact, some hate the light because their deeds are evil (Jn 3:19). The entrance of the true light functions as moral judgment that divides the human race between those who see the light and bring their lives into it and those who flee from it. However, because the Word brings the only true light, there is no place to flee to that is not darkness. The entrance of the true light is also a claim to the uniqueness of salvation through the Word.

1:10-11 *The world did not recognize him . . . did not receive him.* It is a great irony of history that the nation of ancient Israel suffered through long centuries of unrest and persecution waiting for the Messiah and, when he came, failed to recognize him. Jesus was not the kind of Messiah expected, and I suspect many of us today would have failed as well. But there is a deeper problem with the way the human heart responds to God's presence that goes all the way back to Eden. God graciously began to redeem his fallen creation by choosing Abraham and his descendants to be the recipients of his revelations at Sinai, through the Davidic kings, through the prophets, and through the many interventions God made throughout the history of ancient Israel. And yet something in the human heart rejects God's presence and promise. Even Moses, the greatest of God's prophets, was met with all-out idolatry when he brought God's covenant to the people and found them worshiping the golden calf (Ex 32; Dt 9:7–29). But God's redemptive plan persisted alongside the rebellion and rejection of the people through the centuries. The arc of this trajectory culminates when God himself, the Word become flesh, appears at the temple in Jerusalem. Not only is he not recognized and received, he is unjustly executed. In these opening verses John foreshadows Jesus' destiny, hinting at the rejection that would lead to Jesus' execution.

1:12 *Believed in his name.* In contrast to the people of the world, John describes some who did receive the true light and who believed in his name. The Prologue introduces faith as a major theme of the gospel of John. Although the evangelist does not use the noun form *pistis* (πίστις, "faith"), he uses the verb *pisteuō* (πιστεύω, "believe") by far more often than any New Testament writer. However, the concept of faith in response to God is foundational in the Old Testament at least as far back as Abram's covenant with God (Ge 15:6). In modern thought the word *believe* might connote a system of doctrine or articles of faith that are to be cognitively accepted, based in Christian thought on perhaps the Nicene Creed or Westminster Confession or another great theological document. But in Greek, the sense of the word leaned more toward what in English we would call *trust.* John the Evangelist calls his readers to *trust* God as he is revealed by Jesus Christ.

Trust in the name of the true light who came into the world qualifies one to become a child of God. One's "name" in Jewish tradition was an important characterization of one's identity and character and could function as a metonymy for the person himself. God was in heaven, but he chose a place on earth for his "name" to dwell (Dt 12:11; 14:23; 2 Sa 7:13; 1 Ki 3:2; 8:17) such that his name became a way to refer to the divine presence. For John, the "name" of the true light coming into the world constitutes the fullness of the revelation he brings. And so belief in the name means to trust in Jesus' messianic mission (Jn 3:18), a trust that is in fact commanded by God (1 Jn 3:23; 5:13) (see further discussion at 2:11). Evoking trust in Jesus' messianic mission is also the purpose for which John writes, creating a conceptual *inclusio* with John 20:31.

1:13 *Children born . . . of God.* In contrast to the people of the world, unredeemed and apart from God because of their rejection of the true light, John describes some who encounter the true light and believe. To those God gives the right to become his children. This is the first statement of the essential importance of faith/belief in the gospel of John. Trusting in Jesus, the true light, makes all the difference between having life as a child of God or continuing in the darkness of death of the world. Although it is common to think of God as the Father of all people because he is our creator, children of God as John teaches are born only by trusting in Jesus by which they partake of God's life ("like father, like son"). This denies that simply being born to Jewish parents and belonging to ethnic Israel constitutes the relationship with God that John has in mind, even though the Old Testament refers to Israel as God's son or children (see Dt 32:20; Ps 82:6; Isa 1:2–4; 30:1, 9; 63:8; Jer 3:19; Hos 11:1). God's intent to claim people as his children even as revealed in the Old Testament extends beyond ethnic Israel as, for instance, he says in Isaiah 49:6:

> It is too small a thing for you to be my servant
> > to restore the tribes of Jacob
> > and bring back those of Israel I have kept.
> I will also make you a light for the Gentiles,
> > that my salvation may reach to the ends of the earth.

Jesus teaches the necessity of an inner rebirth, whether they be a son of Israel, such as Nicodemus, or a Gentile (see commentary on Jn 3:3, 5).

1:14 *The Word became flesh.* While most of the claims in verses 1–13 would have been somewhat familiar to Jewish readers, this statement of the Word become flesh would have exploded on the page for both Jews and pagan Greeks, for it implies the paradox of the divine, preexistent Word taking on perishable, human form. The Old Testament both states and implies that God is not physical and certainly not human (Ge 1:1; Nu 23:19; Job 9:32; 33:12; Ecc 5:2; Isa 31:3). Yet here is the statement of the Incarnation of One who, though God (1:1), became a human man. And even after the incarnation, the New Testament writers uphold the concept of God as "eternal, immortal, invisible" (Jn 4:24; Ro 1:23; 1 Ti 1:16–17; 6:16).

The verb translated *"made his dwelling"* is in the Greek the word *skēnoō* (σκηνόω), related to the word used more than a hundred times in the Greek Old Testament to refer to the tabernacle (Gk. *skēnē* [σκηνή]), the place where God dwelt with his people during their exodus wanderings. This allusion to the tabernacle presents the Word become flesh as the presence of God dwelling among us.

We have seen his glory. The prophet Isaiah associated glory with the coming of God's rule and the restoration of Israel (Isa 40:5; 60:1–2). He promised that the glory of the LORD would one day be revealed and all people would see it together (Isa 40:5); John implies a fulfillment of the promise in reference to Jesus, whose glory "we" have seen. The book of Isaiah "has had a profound influence on the content and even the structure of the Johannine narrative, particularly in its presentation of Jesus."[7] The fulfillment of God's promises to his people through the prophet Isaiah is found in Jesus.

Here we encounter the first occurrence of the word *glory* (Gk. *doxa* [δόξα]; see commentary at 17:1), a word that is not commonly used today. In biblical terms, "Glory is the visible manifestation of God."[8] The word was well known from the Greek Old Testament (*doxa* [δόξα]; Heb. *kābôd* [כָּבוֹד]), where it occurs more than four hundred times in reference to a display of God's splendor, power, and honor. For instance, the exodus of God's people from Egypt (Ex 14) displayed God's glory, and God's glory was so intense when the ark of the covenant was first brought into Solomon's temple that the priests could not perform their service (1 Ki 8:11). Here John extends that usage familiar to the Hebrew Scriptures to the Word who became flesh and was glorified with the glory of the Son of God. In Jesus, God's splendor, power, and honor are most focused and the manifestation of God's presence is most clear (cf. "Immanuel," meaning "God with us," in Mt 1:23). Ironically, according to the gospel of John the glory of the Son comes to its fullest expression on the cross of Jesus. The ability to perceive that manifestation of glory in the Word who became flesh is a major theme of John's gospel and the basis of authentic Christian faith.

The major theme of testimony is also introduced here, "in such a way that empirical observation and theological perception are inextricable. John presents the testimony of those who saw the glory of God in the flesh of Jesus Christ, as *neither* Jesus' unbelieving contemporaries *nor* later Christian believers did."[9]

One and only Son. The Word become flesh displays the glory of *the one and only* (Gk. *monogenēs* [μονογενής]) Son who came from the Father. The Son is in a unique relationship with the Father that is shared by no other. In the Old Testament the idiom "son of . . ." is used to describe a close association, and "sons of God" is used to refer to angelic beings who share God's nature as spiritual beings (Ge 6:2–4; Job 1:6; 2:1; 38:7; Ps 82:6). The phrase was used to indicate the special relationship a human being had with God, such as the Davidic Messiah-King, who derived his authority and mission from God (2 Sa 7:14; 23:5; Ps 2:7; 89:27–28). Ancient Israel collectively as one people is called God's son, a remembrance of Israel's godly heritage and of the nation's calling to bear the image of God (e.g., Ex 4:22–23 and Hos 1:10; 11:1). The title is later applied to Jesus in Matthew 2:15, revealing Jesus' close association with God as the true Israel. The gospels of Matthew and Luke make it clear that Jesus was conceived by the Holy Spirit, and has a nature uniquely and intimately shared with God—"like father, like son," as the English idiom says. John highlights this nature by describing Jesus as the Word become flesh who is God's "one and only" (Gk. *monogenēs* [μονογενής]) Son. John's emphasis on believers as being born of God (1:13) distinguishes them as "children of God" and reserves the title "Son of God" for Christ alone. A concept central to this relationship is that the Father and the Son share the same nature, perhaps the strongest claim of a differentiated monotheism where the Father and Son share the same nature but are distinguishable persons. The glory of the Word become flesh is the glory of the Son who shares the nature of Israel's God. Here is one of the strongest statements of Jesus' deity, yet preserving monotheism when it is understood as the fact that there is only one divine nature (see commentary on 1:49).

Grace and truth. The glory of the one and only Son (see commentary on 17:1) is full of grace and truth, a phrase that evokes God's Old Testament covenant character (*ḥesed we ʾĕmet* [חֶסֶד וֶאֱמֶת]) as revealed in Exodus 34. This episode in the history of ancient Israel enlightens John's presentation of Jesus as the one who reveals God's glory full of grace and truth. When God was giving the covenant to Israel through Moses at Mount Sinai, forming them as his people, amazingly they quickly turned to the idolatry of the golden calf (Ex 32). Despite this, God promised his presence would remain with his people (Ex 33:14). Moses wanted to know how he would recognize God's presence and asked to see God's glory, a visible manifestation of that presence (Ex 33:18). The Lord conceded to show Moses only a glimpse of his glory when he gave, for the second time, the covenant through Moses (Ex 34:1–7). As the glory of the Lord passes by Moses, God announces, "The LORD, the LORD, the compassionate and gracious God, slow to anger, abounding in *love and faithfulness*, maintaining love to thousands, and forgiving wickedness, rebellion and sin" (Ex 34:6–7). The phrase translated *grace and truth* in John 1:14 is a Greek equivalent of *ḥesed we ʾĕmet* (חֶסֶד וֶאֱמֶת).[10] God's covenant character revealed by word to Moses has become fully visible in the Word who became a human person.

1:16 *Grace in place of grace already given.* The work of God through Moses and the law is presented as a work of grace contrasted with God's full and final work of grace through Jesus Christ. As Gerry Wheaton observes, "The Johannine formulation [v. 16, *charin anti charitos* (χάριν ἀντὶ χάριτος), "grace in place of grace"] conveys in compact form the idea that the Law given through Moses was a glorious yet provisional revelation of the grace of God but that the incarnation and death of the Son of God was a full revelation of divine grace that brought about salvation for the world."[11] And so this phrase should probably be understood as God's grace in Christ replacing the grace God provided in previous revelation.

1:17 *The law was given through Moses; grace and truth came through Jesus Christ.* This is the first mention of both Jesus by name and Moses in John's gospel. The identity of the human being who is the Word incarnate is here revealed. In ancient Jewish literary convention what is said of a person when first mentioned is key to understanding. In this first of seven references, Moses is introduced as the lawgiver, the human authority behind the normative religious texts of Judaism (see also 1:45; 3:14; 5:45–46; 6:32; 7:19–23; 9:28–29). To present the significance of Jesus, John must explain the relationship between Moses and Jesus. Moses, the founder and leader of the ancient nation of Israel, was also its greatest prophet. Yet Jesus surpasses Moses in all regards. Moses saw only a glimpse of God's presence on Sinai (Ex 33:17–23; 34:5–7), but John will show the presence of God is fully revealed in Jesus.

If the phrase *grace and truth* is a metonymy for God's covenantal presence, as seems likely, John is not presenting the law as antithetical to grace; rather, the law of God given through Moses is being contrasted to the presence of God himself in the incarnate Son, implying the subordination of Moses to Jesus Christ. By invoking the proclamation of God's self at Mount Sinai with the phrase *grace and truth*, John is showing that the law of Moses and the words of Israel's Scriptures are essential for understanding the significance of Jesus.[12] The enfleshed Word embodied the fullness of God's love and favor, for Jesus Christ is the complete revelation of God, God in the flesh.

1:18 *No one has ever seen God . . . has made him known.* The revelation God bestowed through Moses has come to its fullest end in the one and only Son, who is himself of the same nature as God the Father. Moses was allowed to see God's glory, but not his face (Ex 33:18–20). Moses' limited revelation of God pales in light of the revelation of God that Jesus brings.

The Greek idiom translated literally "in the bosom of the Father" (NKJV) refers to the greatest possible intimacy with and knowledge of the Father and can be accurately translated with such phrases as "at the Father's side" (NIV 1984; ESV), "near to the Father's heart" (NLT), or "in closest relationship with the Father" (NIV 2011). Hengel notes it is an image "from the Jewish wisdom tradition that expresses the unity of the Father with the Son stamped by love."[13] Furthermore, the image of the Son and the Father sharing a throne, based on Psalm 110:1 and often quoted in the New Testament, is apparently insufficient in John's thought for expressing the unity of the Father with the Son. John's introduction to the mission of the incarnate Word explains that

Jesus came into human history to make God known. To see and know Jesus is to see and know God. Even in the opening to this gospel the deity of Christ is presented in the strongest terms of monotheism.

What the Structure Means:
The Prologue of the Fourth Gospel (Jn 1:1–18)

These opening verses of the fourth gospel, the Prologue (1:1–18), give readers information that the people who encounter Jesus within the story do not have, at least upon their initial encounter with Jesus. Consider how the director of a movie must decide from what perspective to film, especially an action thriller like *Jurassic Park*. For a viewer who knows that a T-Rex dinosaur is hiding just around the curve being approached by a jeep filled with people, the tension is high. The director has chosen to let viewers in on that perspective, so they know something the people in the jeep don't know. As an alternative, viewers can discover what lies ahead only when the characters do, resulting in heart-stopping surprise. Either perspective is legitimate, but the director must decide and film it accordingly. The viewers' sense of perspective informs their understanding of the story and makes for much of the emotional impact of a film.

Authors make similar choices when writing. We've all read books that keep us in the dark along with a confused character who is trying to figure out what's happening (e.g., *Dark Matter*, a sci-fi thriller by Blake Crouch). And we've all no doubt read books in which the narrator provides flashbacks or substantial information that the character(s) aren't (yet) aware of. John has chosen to provide an extensive prologue to his story of Jesus that situates the reader in a transcendent place of the Word's preexistence before time as we know it began. We are privy to knowledge that no one who first encountered Jesus would have had. With this knowledge in mind we proceed to read the awesome mystery of the Word becoming flesh (1:14), and the irony of Jesus' rejection by those who were waiting for him (1:10–11).

Although modern scholars have suggested that the Prologue was written later and subsequently added to John's gospel, it so adeptly introduces the themes and motifs that will be developed within John's story of Jesus that it is more likely the very creative work of its author. As Richard Bauckham explains, "One of the functions of the prologue to John's Gospel is to indicate to readers how, starting with the Old Testament, they should read the story of Jesus."[14] John invites the obvious tie to the Old Testament with the very first opening phrase "in the beginning." Furthermore, the last five verses of the Prologue connect John's story of Jesus with the exodus, and specifically with the covenant God made with ancient Israel through Moses at Sinai, anchoring this presentation of Jesus firmly in Jewish history. Bauckham writes, "John presents the incarnation of the Word, Jesus Christ, as the eschatological fulfillment of the Sinai covenant, a revelation of glory that fulfills the Sinai covenant by qualitatively surpassing it."[15]

As you read through this gospel what effect does the Prologue contribute to your thoughts and feelings? Are you more empathetic toward Jesus as the story develops or less? Does his story seem more ironic to you because of the Prologue? More mysterious? The knowledge conveyed in the Prologue positions the reader to have a deep sense of awe for the story that follows.

1:19 *John's testimony.* John the Baptist is consistently presented in John's gospel as a "witness" to the identity and significance of Jesus (cf. 1:7). The Baptist drew large enough crowds to attract the attention of the Jewish leaders in Jerusalem, though John baptized many miles distant.

Jewish leaders in Jerusalem. From ancient times Jewish people considered Jerusalem to be the center of the world, the place where God chose his Name to dwell (Dt 12:5) and where eventually his temple was built (1 Ki 3:1–2; 5:3, 5). At the time of Jesus, Jerusalem was occupied by the military forces of the Roman Empire but remained the religious center of Judaism. References to the Jewish leaders of Jerusalem at the time of Jesus (Gk. *oi Ioudaioi* [οἱ Ἰουδαῖοι]) were translated in the KJV and by subsequent English Bible translations as "the Jews," and has often been read as expressing an anti-Semitic bias. But this is an anachronistic judgment, as John was himself Jewish, as well as Jesus and many of the people in the story John tells, as were the majority of Christian believers in the earliest days of the church. John uses the term not to refer to the Jewish people as an ethnic group but in a more limited sense to refer to those Judean leaders in Jerusalem who opposed Jesus and eventually orchestrated his execution. John is not making a general indictment of all Jewish people for all time but of the particular players in Jerusalem who should have recognized the Messiah but didn't. The misplaced animosity toward the Jewish people that grew throughout centuries of the church has been an especially egregious misunderstanding of the biblical text. The gospel of John does not support or justify anti-Semitic accusations that have led to such horrors as history has witnessed. Jesus himself spoke words of forgiveness about those who executed him, and in reality, *all* human beings are responsible for the execution of Jesus, for he came to die for the sin of the world.

Priests and Levites. The priests and Levites oversaw the religious practices of Judaism in the Jerusalem temple, such as sacrifices and ritual purification. John's work of baptizing had apparently caught the attention of the Jewish leaders, who sent the experts in such practice to interrogate John to determine by what authority he was baptizing and whether he was violating Jewish law.

1:20 *Messiah.* This is the first mention in the gospel of John of the word *Messiah* (Gk. *messias* [μεσσίας]), a title transliterating the Hebrew word that means "anointed" (Gk. *christos* [χριστός]). In the Old Testament, kings (2 Sa 1:14), priests (Lev 4:3; Ex 29:7), and prophets (Ps 105:15; 1 Ki 19:16) were consecrated to their office by being anointed with oil. The Messiah as Israel's final king, priest, and prophet was a long-awaited expectation in Judaism that persists among conservative Jews even today. The New Testament describes Jesus as the anointed Son of God who functions as the ultimate and final King of God's kingdom who exercises all authority (Mt 28:18), the final High Priest who offers the ultimate atonement and makes intercession (Heb 10), and the promised Prophet who not only brings God's word but is God's Word incarnate (Jn 1:1–14). The priests and Levites were apparently interested in the implications of John's baptism in reference to the Messiah, a reference that would have had political as well as religious implications.

1:21 *Are you Elijah?* Elijah was an Old Testament prophet who went up to heaven in a whirlwind (2 Ki 2:11) and was expected to reappear as a herald of the Messiah (Mal 4:5–6). Even today a seat for Elijah is set at annual Passover tables in Jewish homes in expectation of the future fulfillment of the messianic hope. The Jerusalem priests and Levites in this verse question if perhaps John is Elijah returned.

Are you the Prophet? Another great expectation of Judaism was based on the promise Moses gave, that the Lord would raise up another prophet like Moses, whom the Lord knew face-to-face (Dt 18:15–18). John the Baptist denies being the Prophet, and "In this way, the evangelist introduces the category and invites the reader to consider who (besides John the Baptist) might fill this role in his narrative."[16] That expectation went unrealized (Dt 34:10) until Jesus appeared, and John 1:1 introduces Jesus the incarnate Son of God as the Word who faced God (Gk. *pros ton theon* [πρὸς τὸν θεόν]). In John 14:8–14 Jesus confers on his apostles, who saw him face-to-face and knew him personally, the status as having seen God face-to-face and declared that those who saw him have seen the Father (Jn 14:9) (see commentary on Jn 1:45).

1:23 *The words of Isaiah the prophet.* Isaiah's prophecies have had significant influence on John's gospel[17] (see commentary on Jn 12:38, 41). A reader in John's time would have recognized a conflation of the two cola of Isaiah 40:3: "prepare the way for the LORD . . . make straight . . . a highway for our God" into "make straight the way for the LORD." Clearly this is an implicit statement of the deity of Jesus, who assumes the role of "the LORD" and "our God." The "way of the LORD" is the coming of Jesus into the world. Using this quotation, the Baptist identified his own role ("I am the voice . . .") as the first person on earth to recognize the incarnate Son of God, "proclaiming God's message of imminent salvation and the universal disclosure of his glory (Isa 40:3–5)."[18] The coming of Jesus is the realization of that salvation and the revelation of God's power and authority—that is, his glory. John the Baptist is applying Isaiah's quotation to himself to call for preparation that involves repentance, as the time of deliverance through the Messiah was at hand. John the Baptist had been chosen by God to be the first to recognize and point out the man in whom the Word became flesh, thus "making straight" Jesus' way by his own testimony, and witnessing to Jesus' superiority (Jn 1:29–34).

The prophetic words of Isaiah are important for John's presentation of the story of Jesus. See also the commentary on 3:22–36. Not only is Isaiah 40:3–5 the first biblical quotation in the fourth gospel, but Isaiah's words are also quoted at the end of Jesus' public ministry in 12:38, 40, 41, framing the ministry of Jesus with the prophecies of Isaiah.

1:24 *The Pharisees.* Judaism was not a single, monolithic religion at the time of Jesus, for during the intertestamental period subgroups emerged based on differing theology and practices. At the time of Jesus the Pharisees were a strong presence in Judea, and were considered to be among the most devout keepers of the law. Along with the Sadducees, who are not mentioned in John's gospel, they constituted the Sanhedrin, which was the ruling council in Jerusalem (Jn 11:47). The Pharisees believed in a resurrection of the dead at the end of the age (Ac 23:6), while the Sadducees did not. The Pharisees accepted the authority of the oral law alongside the Torah and had strong political expectations of the Messiah. They were quite critical of Jesus because from their perspective he routinely violated their understanding of the law. And the criticism went both ways. Although strongly denounced by Jesus, they probably represented the best of Jewish pietism and devotion to the law. If they were the best representatives of religious effort to please God, Jesus targeted them, teaching that even the best human effort is insufficient to please God when it is apart from Christ's atoning sacrifice.

1:26 *I baptize with water.* Water was used in various Jewish purification rituals that prepared people to worship the Lord (Ex 19:10; Lev 14:8; Eze 36:25). In the Synoptic Gospels, John the Baptist adapts the practice to be a symbol of repentance and moral cleansing, inviting those he preached to into the waters of baptism. But in the fourth gospel, it "is neither a 'baptism of repentance' nor 'for the forgiveness of sins,' nor a call to repentance and reform, but serves entirely to 'reveal Jesus to Israel'"[19] as the one who is coming (cf. 1:27).

Water is a major symbol in the fourth gospel, but it does not always represent the same referent. For instance, it can refer to cleansing purification (Jn 13:5) or to the Holy Spirit (Jn 4:14) (see commentary on Jn 2:1–11). In the fourth gospel Jesus is presented as both the One who cleanses sin and the source of the Holy Spirit.

1:28 *Bethany.* Many biblical place names begin with *beth-*, the construct form of the Hebrew noun *bayit* (בַּיִת), which means "house" but was generalized to mean "place." The name Bethany may have derived from the Hebrew, "house of the poor" or "house of Ananiah."[20] John was baptizing at a town called Bethany that was east of the Jordan River, not to be confused with the village of Bethany near Jerusalem, which John's gospel later mentions as the home of Mary, Martha, and Lazarus (Jn 11:1, 18; 12:1).

What the Structure Means: The Descent and Ascent of the Word Who Became Flesh (Jn 1:1–29)

If a videographer were filming John 1:1–29, we could imagine an opening image of the deep space cosmos as 1:1–18 is narrated, placing the viewer in a primordial perspective in which the preexistent Word who was with God and was God operated as the agent of creation. Following the incredible statement that the Word became flesh and dwelt among us (1:14), the immediate questions would be, When? Where? Where is he? At this point a filmmaker might have the camera perspective "descend" from the reaches of deep space, enter our solar system, focus on a view of planet Earth, and then descend further through the atmosphere to the region of the Middle East, and finally to the environs of first-century Jerusalem. John accomplishes this verbally by mentioning Jerusalem for the first time, the "where" of the incarnate Word, and by referring to priests and Levites who identify for the reader the cultural and religious location of the Jewish people among whom the incarnate Word dwelled. This "descent" of perspective signals to the reader/viewer that the earthly story of the Word become flesh is about to begin, and it begins with the prophetic voice of John the Baptist catching the attention of the Jewish leaders of first-century Jerusalem.

This idea of the descent (and subsequent ascent) of the incarnate Word from God seems to be part of the deep structure of John's gospel that is subsequently developed (Jn 1:51; 3:13, 31; 6:50; 7:33; 8:23; 10:36; 13:1; 14:12; 16:28; 20:17). The Word enters history as a living human being, completes the mission for which God sent him, and then ascends back to the Father through the gateway of human death, leaving the promise that those who believe in him will also one day pass through death to be with him there.

1:29 *Look, the Lamb of God.* John the Baptist points out Jesus, calling him the Lamb of God, a title that was not known as messianic prior to Jesus. This is John's second interpretive statement about the identity of Jesus expressed in a metaphor familiar to the Old Testament sacrificial system (see Jn 1:36). (The first is found at 1:18, where the incarnate Word came to reveal the unseen Father.) This metaphor, found only in John's gospel to refer to Jesus, refers to a sacrificial animal familiar in ancient ritual practice, whether it be the Passover lamb (Ex 12), the Suffering Servant who was led like a lamb to slaughter (Isa 53), or the apocalyptic sacrificed lamb of Revelation 4[21] (see commentary on Jn 6). Jewish tradition overlaid different interpretations of the lamb, and so other understandings of the "lamb of God" are not necessarily arguments against a Passover lamb connotation here.[22] Furthermore, John frames his story of Jesus with episodes that happen on or near three annual celebrations of Passover. The "shadow of the passion week and its Johannine association with Passover" falls over the whole story of Jesus' ministry from its beginning.[23]

This introduction of Jesus as a lamb connotes substitutionary sacrifice as in Isaiah 53:7, and also invokes the Passover motif of the lamb's death as deliverance from death because the Lord passed over those homes in Egypt that had the blood of a lamb splashed on its doorposts (Ex 12:7, 12–13; cf. 1 Co 5:7).[24] Therefore, two concepts are here blended: Jesus delivers from death that threatens us, and he atones for the sin that causes it. Jesus came from God to be a sacrifice for sin. This introduction of Jesus as Lamb forms an *inclusio*[25] with John 19, with its many allusions to the Passover sacrifice, and is reinforced throughout the gospel by Passover language and symbolism (see commentary on Jn 19).

Who takes away the sin of the world. Note the singular *sin* as a condition of the world rather than the myriad of sins (pl.) committed by individuals (cf. 1 Jn 1:9; 2:2, 12; 3:5; 4:10). Repeated atonement for individual sins is no longer needed for "the power of the totality of sin is broken once and for all."[26] Jesus' mission will be completed only at the end of history, when Christ returns, but having an intention to live without sin is nevertheless the motivation for Christian life now (1 Jn 3:5).

1:31 *That he might be revealed to Israel.* Here we have the first mention of Israel, the ancient nation that God had chosen to be the agency of his revelation in the world (Ge 12:1–3; Isa 2:3; 55:5). John the Baptist explains the reason for his activity of baptizing as a revelatory act that would reveal Jesus to Israel. Through the ritual of water baptism God revealed Jesus as his Son, first to John the Baptist and then to the world (see commentary on Jn 3:22–36).

1:32 *I saw the Spirit come down.* John first mentions the Holy Spirit as the agency who pointed out the Word made flesh by descending on Jesus at his baptism. The Spirit was familiar to Old Testament readers, for he was present at creation (Ge 1:2), empowered the elders (Nu 11:25), Israel's judges (Jdg passim), and the kings (Ps 51:11), who inspired the prophets (1 Sa 10:10), and would rest powerfully on the expected Messiah (Isa 11:1–2). The Spirit is the empowering presence of God in the Old Testament who enabled people chosen by God for special acts of service.

Come down . . . as a dove. The Greek here could mean that the Spirit had the visual form of a dove (adjectival) or that the motion of the Spirit was like that of a dove (adverbial). Used symbolically, the dove's association with creation (Ge 1:2), the restoration of life on dry land after the flood (Ge 8:8–12), and the image found in other Jewish writings of a dove hovering over God's people in the last days suggest that John's use of the image indicates a new creation or era that dawned with the revealing of Jesus as God's Son.[27]

1:33–34 *God's Chosen One.*[28] John the Baptist was told by the One who sent him (i.e., God; see Jn 1:6) that the Spirit would come down and remain on one of the men John would baptize in water. In this way John the Baptist would know, and then testify, that Jesus was God's chosen, or God's Son, who would baptize people with the Holy Spirit.

What the Structure Means: Who Is the Word Become Flesh? Why Did He Come? (Jn 1:29–34)

This section of John's first chapter continues to answer the questions, Which human being is the Word who became flesh, and why did he come? John the Baptist is the witness who would tell which man was the Word incarnate when he saw the descent of the Spirit on him (Jn 1:33–34). Once John the Baptist recognized which man was God's Son, he could point him out to others, which he does using the metaphor Lamb of God (Jn 1:29, 36). And so Jesus, the Word, God's Son, the sacrificial Lamb of God, is introduced to the human race, one person at a time. The news spreads person to person in John 1:35–51, establishing a model for evangelizing. John the Baptist's mission is fulfilled, and he subordinates himself to the One who came after him, whose sandal straps he felt not worthy to untie (1:27). With this pericope, John launches his presentation of Jesus' earthly mission.

1:37 *They followed Jesus.* Two of John the Baptist's disciples were among the first disciples of Jesus, which is another way by which the Baptist prepared the way for Jesus' ministry. The Baptist is not again mentioned until 3:23, where his disciples fear the competition that they perceive Jesus and his disciples present (see commentary on Jn 3:22–36).

1:38 *"Rabbi" (which means "Teacher").* A term in both Hebrew and Aramaic meaning "my master," *rabbi* was used by students to refer to or to address their religious teachers. Eventually it became a term of respect used to address any Jewish religious leader, and a title that denoted a Torah scholar. Note that John translates it for his readers, suggesting he is writing for people who do not speak Hebrew or Aramaic or who may have never heard the term.

1:40 *Simon Peter's brother.* Peter is first mentioned without introduction, suggesting that the original readers of this gospel would have been familiar with his name as the man who later became a great apostle of Jesus. And notice that Andrew is identified in relation to Simon Peter, not vice versa, reinforcing the assumption that the original readers would have known of Simon Peter. More importantly to the story, this suggests that Peter knew Jesus from the very beginning of the Lord's ministry, and therefore would have been a reliable witness. Peter is also the last disciple named in this gospel (Jn 21:21), forming an *inclusio* that indicates Peter's presence throughout the entire ministry of Jesus from its inception to the postresurrection time. Because John could assume readers at the time he wrote knew of Simon Peter, apparently he was renowned in the early years of the Christian church.

1:41 *"We have found the Messiah" (that is, the Christ).* Andrew was a disciple of John the Baptist and one of the two men who heard John the Baptist point out Jesus. This excited Andrew, who went to find his brother, Simon, whom Jesus renamed Peter (1:42). Andrew describes Jesus as the Messiah ("anointed one"; see comment at Jn 1:20), which in the Greek is transliterated from the Aramaic as *messias* (μεσσίας). Here again John feels it necessary to translate *messias* (μεσσίας) into the corresponding Greek word for "anointed," *christos* (χριστός), which comes into English as *Christ*. In John's gospel the titles *Messiah* and *Christ* are lexically equivalent; however, how the identity of

Jesus that John presents relates to previous messianic expectations is highly debated.[29] In the Old Testament the term referred to a divinely appointed and anointed king (e.g., 1 Sa 24:6; 2 Sa 2:4), and in postbiblical times the term was closely associated with kingship, giving it a politically charged connotation during times of the Greek and then Roman occupation of the Holy Land. But as John J. Collins observes, "Christian claims for the divinity of Jesus eventually went beyond anything we find in the Jewish texts."[30] The reference to the preexistent Word who was God in the opening of the Prologue goes far beyond the various expectations of who and what the Messiah would be.

1:42 *Cephas.* Simon and Andrew's father's name was John, a very common Jewish name in the first century. It was common in ancient Jewish culture to designate a man by specifying his father's name. Jesus immediately gives Simon son of John an Aramaic nickname, *Cephas* (pronounced *kay-fas*), which means "rock." And again John translates this name for his readers with the Greek word for "rock," *petros* ($\pi\acute{\epsilon}\tau\rho\text{o}\varsigma$), which comes into English as *Peter*. The renaming of Simon by Jesus follows an Old Testament pattern of God giving new names— Abram to Abraham, Sarai to Sarah, Jacob to Israel—and signals to the reader that "the Rock" will have a significance in the story that surpasses that of other followers of Jesus (see commentary on chapters 13, 21).

1:43 *Galilee.* The region called Galilee forms the northernmost area of Israel. When Israel first inhabited the promised land at the time of the conquest, this was where the tribes of Zebulun and Naphtali settled (Isa 9:1–2; cf. Mt 4:13–16). Because Gentile peoples dominated the demographics of the region throughout its history, it was known as Galilee of the Gentiles.

Galilee was Jesus' home turf, and John's gospel speaks of Jesus often traveling between it and Jerusalem in Judea. Born in one of its villages, Nazareth, Jesus made Capernaum, on the northern shore of the Sea of Galilee, the home base for his public ministry. He apparently spent most of his earthly life in Galilee. After his execution and resurrection in Jerusalem he appeared to his disciples in Galilee before ascending (Mt 26:32; 28:7, 10, 16–20; Jn 21:1).[31] Traveling on foot, it would have taken about twenty-two hours to walk the ninety miles from Bethany on the other side of the Jordan to the Sea of Galilee, and so a two- or three-day journey.

Going Deeper into Following Jesus: John 1:29–51

In John 1:29–51 we see the newly identified Messiah (Jn 1:29, 36) handpicking his disciples. One point stands out: the presence of Jesus, the long-awaited Messiah, spread by word of mouth as John the Baptist told his disciples and then those men "found" others they knew to tell about Jesus (1:41, 45). In this day of social media, television, radio, and other means of mass communication, we need to be reminded of the power of one person simply telling another about who Jesus is. So many times I've read a post on Facebook about an exciting book a friend has read or a new TV program. We seem eager to share something good with our friends. And yet it's not unusual for us to grow tongue-tied when it comes to sharing the good news about Jesus.

It is astounding that the religion that came to be called Christianity spread only through the willingness and zeal of a small number of individuals who were excited enough about the presence of Jesus to deliberately seek out others to tell. In fact, the survival and existence of the church around the world is a remarkable historical phenomenon. The origins of such a geographically vast and long-lasting religion has historians debating how one man born in a backwater village of Galilee, away from the center of wealth and power, could have so influenced a small group of followers that the momentum of their witness propelled the gospel as far as the twenty-first century and around the world. There is probably no better evidence that the formation and preservation of Christianity is an ongoing work of the Holy Spirit (Ac 1:8; 2:38–39). So while we can be grateful for the means to broadcast the gospel through all the avenues that modern technology offers, this introduction to Jesus' disciples should also motivate us to continue the pattern of one person simply telling another about Jesus.

A second point that we encounter in this section of John's gospel is that people weren't just told that Jesus existed; they were invited to *follow Jesus*. John the Baptist's two disciples quite literally followed Jesus to see where he was staying, presumably so they would know where to go to talk with him (1:35–39). He welcomed that interest and invited them to follow him home. When Jesus began to handpick disciples who would become witnesses to his life, death, and resurrection, he asked and expected them to *follow* him (1:43). For those chosen to accompany Jesus on his ministry travels, the command was quite literal. Jesus' teaching and miracles and the way he lived and interacted with others were constantly observed by his entourage of disciples, a group that apparently grew at times to include many more than the Twelve (Lk 8:1–3). During his public ministry Jesus extended the call to follow him to all who would be his disciples (Mt 8:22; 10:38; 16:24; 19:21; Mk 8:34; 10:21; Lk 9:23, 59; 14:27; 18:22; Jn 10:27; 12:26).

Jesus' command to "follow me" is clearly a command to start walking. From the Old Testament we know that walking was a metaphor for living, for how one conducts one's life. Adam and Eve *walked* with the Lord in Eden (Ge 3:8), implying they enjoyed fellowship with God. Both Noah and Enoch were said to have *walked* with God (Ge 5:22, 24; 6:9). God commanded Abraham to *walk* blamelessly before him (Ge 17:1). Psalm 1:1 blesses "the one who does not *walk* in the counsel of the wicked."

Jesus' invitation to "come and see" in John 1:39 functions also as an invitation to the seekers reading this gospel. If our walk is a metaphor for how we live in our relationship to God, then following after Jesus requires intention and effort. To follow we must keep our focus on Jesus and put our feet on the path he defines. The call to follow him entails a growing awareness of the God Jesus came to reveal and a growing willingness to conform our lives to that revelation.

Have you been found by someone who has told you about Jesus? Have you begun to follow Jesus? How are you feeling about following Jesus these days? Is it attractive to you? Or perhaps you've been following him for many, many years—are you tired? Is it frightening to follow him in these times in our society? Are you hesitating to follow him at this point? Whatever your answers, keep reading the gospel of John for new insight and renewed motivation.

1:44 *Bethsaida.* Andrew and his brother Simon Peter were from Bethsaida, a fishing village on the northern shore of the Sea of Galilee. Jesus also called another man from Bethsaida, Philip, to be his disciple. Philip shared the news of Jesus with Nathanael, a man from nearby Cana (Jn 21:2), repeating the pattern of Andrew telling his brother Simon. In the area around Bethsaida Jesus healed a blind man (Mk 8:22) and fed five thousand (Lk 9:10–17). Nevertheless, Jesus condemned the towns of Galilee for failing to believe in him (Mt 11:21; Lk 10:13).[32]

1:45 *The one Moses wrote about in the Law.* This is the second of seven references to Moses in the gospel of John (see also 1:17; 3:14; 5:45–46; 6:32; 7:19–23; 9:28–29). In 1:17 Moses was introduced as the giver of the Law of the covenant on which the nation of ancient Israel was founded. Here John develops his thoughts about the important relationship between Moses and Jesus. Moses is a witness who accredits Jesus because he wrote about him in "the Law," probably meaning the Pentateuch more broadly. John shows that

Jesus is *not* antithetical to the Law, but that the Law itself pointed to Jesus. This is perhaps an oblique allusion to the great prophet predicted by Deuteronomy 18:15–19 (cf. Jn 14:8–14).

As Stan Harstine summarizes, "the appearance of Moses in 1:45 performs three discernable roles in the narrative. First, Moses' relationship with the law is emphasized. Second, Moses should be understood as one of the witnesses who provide testimony to Jesus' identity in this passage. Finally, Moses functions to root the story of Jesus in a Jewish context."[33]

And about whom the prophets also wrote. Moses wrote of the Messiah, but so did "the prophets." By the time of the New Testament the reference to "the Law and the Prophets" and certain variants of the phrase designated the entire canon of the Hebrew Bible.[34] A significant point of John's presentation of Jesus is that he fulfills all of what God had predicted and promised in the Messianic hope of the Old Testament.

1:46 *Nazareth.* This village in Galilee was Jesus' childhood home with his parents Mary and Joseph. It was an unremarkable place, judging by Nathanael's remark questioning what good could possibly come from there. Jesus' preaching was not well received in Nazareth, as familiarity with Jesus seemed to have bred contempt for his message (Mt 13:57, 58; Mk 6:3–4; Lk 4:16–24).

1:47 *An Israelite in whom there is no deceit.* John reports the calling of Nathanael in terms laden with Old Testament tradition. Jesus identifies him as an "Israelite," a term highlighting the ancient nationalistic identity of God's people as a whole. In contrast to the more contemporary term "Judean," which derives from the name of only one of Israel's twelve tribes (Judah), Jesus' reference to a true "Israelite" to designate one of his disciples may hearken back to the covenant promises made to the whole nation of Israel—that is, all twelve tribes. This accords with the belief that the Messiah would reunify all Israel.

1:48 *Fig tree.* The fig tree is a meaningful symbol in the Bible, as it is the first plant named in Genesis 3:7, with its leaves used to cover Adam and Eve's shameful nakedness of sin. The fig was a prevalent plant in Galilee in Jesus' time, valued for its sweetly delicious fruit as well as for the thick shade provided by its leaves. Throughout Old Testament history, the fig tree and the grapevine were adopted as symbols for the promise God saw in Israel (Hos 9:10). The expression to "sit under one's own vine and fig tree" (from Mic 4:4) became the slogan of the good life settled in the land God had given. In times of Israel's covenant unfaithfulness, a curse on the fig tree symbolized the failure of God's people to produce the spiritual fruit that God expected (Isa 34:4; Jer 5:17; Hos 2:12; Joel 1:7, 12; Am 4:9; Hab 3:17). The flourishing vine and fig tree became a symbol of God's full blessing that would come to fruition in the messianic age, as it represented a time without war and famine and symbolized the shalom of God's restoration (Mic 4:4; Zec 3:10). Nathanael apparently had just been enjoying shady solitude under a fig tree, and found Jesus' awareness of that moment to be a striking revelation. However, the double meaning is that Nathanael, truly an Israelite, is being gathered to Jesus for a future of new covenant blessing "under the vine and fig tree" of the gospel of Jesus Christ.

1:49 *Son of God . . . King of Israel.* "Son of God" is not an exclusively Christian title, for it was used in texts prior to the New Testament to refer to the Davidic king (Pss 2; 45; 89; 110; 2 Sa 7). Here Nathanael acknowledges Jesus as the Messiah in the language of Psalm 2:6–7, which declares Israel's king to be God's S/son. Jesus is the king of God's kingdom, but John will explain as the story unfolds how Jesus, Son of God, far surpasses any messianic expectation the phrase "son of God" previously connoted (see commentary on "One and only Son" at John 1:14).

1:51 *Very truly.* The gospel of John reports Jesus using this phrase twenty-five times. The Greek transliteration (*amēn* [ἀμήν]) of this Hebrew adverb is usually translated "truly," which was derived from a verb meaning "it is firm." Although the word is found in the Synoptic Gospels too, in the New Testament only in John does Jesus consistently repeat it twice, apparently to underscore both the truth and authority with which Jesus speaks (cf. Nu 5:22). The expression is often translated "truly, truly" or "very truly."

Going Deeper into "Amen" as the Ending for Our Prayers: John 1:51

The convention of ending Christian prayers and prayerful hymns with "amen" was established in the earliest days of the church. This ancient convention extends back to the time of Moses (e.g., Dt 27:15–26; Nu 5:22), and is not simply a way to end a prayer or hymn but connotes one's support and approval of the words spoken or sung. In itself it forms a petition to God to "let this be, may it happen." In the Gospels, the word occurs only on the lips of Jesus, but throughout the epistles it is found at the end of prayers and doxologies, setting the precedent for its continued use in Christian liturgy. Though simple in form and use, "amen" is a very meaningful connection to God's people, having been uttered throughout the centuries and around the world wherever prayers to God are offered in Christ.

Heaven open. Access to heaven and its mysteries was the major focus of much of the Jewish writings in the Second Temple period just before and during Jesus' lifetime. Apocalyptic writings were produced describing visits to heaven by familiar Old Testament figures such as Enoch and Ezra. Although these writings were apparently popular and widely known, Jesus states that no human being has ever gone into heaven except the Son of Man, who came down from heaven (Jn 3:13). In his own person Jesus fulfills apocalyptic longings by opening heaven to humankind. This is among the "greater things" that Nathanael and others would see (the Greek verb is plural, *opsesthe* [ὄψεσθε]).

Angels . . . ascending and descending. In further explanation of the "greater things" Jesus speaks of angelic traffic ascending and descending on himself. Commentators have been quick to see here an allusion to "Jacob's ladder" in Genesis 28:11–17, but a few recent interpreters are stepping back from the inferences made from that reading. Edward Klink observes several differences between Jacob's vision and Jesus' statement, concluding that if it is an allusion, it *"is meant to be radically redefined."* Klink notes that Jacob saw a vision; the disciples of Christ see God in human form.[35] Similarly, William Loader objects to interpretations that identify Jesus as the ladder between heaven and earth or to a typological identification of Jesus and Jacob. The ascending and descending angels (note the seemingly reversed direction of travel from what might normally be expected) is the specific point of contact between Genesis 28:11–17 and John 1:51. Loader argues this intertextual link associates by contrast Nathanael, the true Israelite in whom there is no deceit with Jacob, ironically also known as Israel, whose life was characterized by deceit.[36] In other words, Jesus' disciples are those who constitute true Israel and who will see heaven opened.

Angels as God's agents became increasingly important in Jewish thought as the idea of monotheism developed. Jan Van der Watt is probably right to see in the reference here not angels ministering to Jesus but angels as a metonymy for God's presence. He writes, "The angels of God mark the location of the divine presence of God, with Jesus. The Son of Man is the *locus* where the divine may be expected on earth."[37] Nathanael and the other disciples of Jesus will indeed see something greater than Jacob and Israel ever could have seen.

Son of Man. This is the first of eleven times Jesus refers to himself in the gospel of John as the Son of Man, his favorite self-designation as reported by all four Gospels.[38] This self-designation is one defense of monotheism that apparently originated with Jesus himself, for Jewish tradition already saw in the "one like a son of man" someone to whom God, the Ancient of Days, gave "authority, glory and sovereign power" (Da 7:13–14). In God's presence the Son of Man was given worship as "all nations and peoples of every language worshiped him. His dominion is an everlasting dominion that will not pass away, and his kingdom is one that will never be destroyed" (Da 7:14). Dating at least from the time of Daniel, the title Son of Man referred to a "cosmic messianic figure associated strongly with apocalyptic eschatology."[39] As this was Jesus' most often-used title when referring to himself, he here makes a strong claim to be not only the Messiah but also a cosmic figure who has an eternal dominion. Such a description elevates him to the same category as God himself (also see commentary at Jn 13:31).

What the Structure Means:
John's Introduction of Jesus (Jn 1)

John 1:1–18 presents the transcendent Word of God, who was with God and is God, entering the human race so he could reveal the invisible God. John 1:19–51 introduces the man who embodied the Word incarnate, Jesus of Nazareth. How in the world did anyone recognize Jesus as the Messiah and Son of God? He was not born into the palace of any king with obvious royal lineage. There was apparently nothing in his appearance that shouted "Messiah!" The author of the fourth gospel answers that question by explaining that God sent a prophet, John the Baptist, who preached a baptism of repentance to Israel. God told John that while baptizing with water a man would come for baptism on whom the Holy Spirit would descend as a dove and remain. That one, that man, is God's Chosen One, the Messiah, the Son of God.

When that incredible event happened, John the Baptist was quick to point out Jesus to his own disciples, men who were apparently spiritually seeking the cleansing that the Baptist's preaching and baptism offered. But they knew John's baptism was only provisional and preparatory for the One who would come baptizing with the Holy Spirit. Andrew and another of the Baptist's disciples sought out Jesus for conversation, and apparently followed Jesus back to Galilee, along with Simon Peter, Philip, and Nathanael. John does not include the calling of any other of the Twelve, but he does later mention Thomas (11:16), Judas son of James (14:22), and Judas Iscariot (6:71) by name. As "disciples" are mentioned throughout the fourth gospel, we can presume a similar pattern of direct engagement with Jesus and word-of-mouth testimony adding untold others to the growing group of disciples.

With this description of both the transcendent Word and the man Jesus, John ends his introduction to the gospel he is about to present to move on to the Book of Signs (chaps. 2–11), signs that reveal Jesus' glory and inspire greater faith in his disciples.

John 1 Through Old Testament Eyes

After reading only the first chapter of John's gospel there can be no doubt that its author is fully steeped in the language, images, stories, and theology of Israel's Scriptures. There are at least twenty-five direct connections to the Old Testament in these opening verses of the fourth gospel. And while John's words are completely understandable even to one who doesn't recognize those twenty-five connections, the revelation Jesus brought in his incarnation is enriched with depth and irony. John alludes to two passages from Genesis, the creation account (Ge 1:1 in Jn 1:1) and Jacob's discovery of the gateway to heaven (Ge 28:12 in 1:51). These two allusions form something of an *inclusio* that embeds John's story of Jesus squarely in the most ancient history of God's people.

John the Evangelist mentions and quotes from the prophet Isaiah (Isa 40:3 in 1:23) to herald the coming of the Lord in the person of Jesus of Nazareth. This is but one of four explicit quotations from Isaiah (Jn 1:23; 6:45; 12:38; 12:40), three of which frame the public ministry of Jesus (Isa 40:3 in Jn 1:23; Isa 53:1 and 6:10 in Jn 12:38).

The themes of the creation, the tabernacle (God's dwelling with his people), the law, and the messianic hope are foundational to John's introduction of Jesus. The motif of light and the image of the fig tree are present in John's introductory statements. Aramaic terms significant to first-century Jewish culture are translated into Greek for John's Greek-speaking audience (1:38, 41, 42). The Jewish practice of baptism—ritual water cleansing as preparation for worship—is transposed to a new spiritual plane with the call to repentance. The Pharisees, a prominent group of leaders in first-century Judaism, play a major role in John's introduction to Jesus, foreshadowing darkly the major role they will play in Jesus' execution. And no less than nine people or institutions from the Old Testament are mentioned in these fifty-one opening verses: Moses (1:17, 45), priests and Levites (1:19), prophets (1:45), Elijah (1:21, 25), the Prophet (1:21, 25), Isaiah (1:23), Israel/Israelite (1:31, 47, 49), God's Chosen One (1:34), Son of Man (1:51, cf. Da 7:13).

The gospel of John is a thoroughly Jewish story that anchors the significance of Jesus deeply in the Old Testament. To appreciate the depth of John's message we must become better readers, better acquainted with the Old Testament context of our Christian beliefs.

JOHN 2

2:1–11 Here John begins his creative work to interpret the significance of the life of Jesus by telling of episodes from his life in terms that relate the story both back to the Old Testament and forward to the cross. John presents the miracle of changing water into wine as something that happened, and he presents it in terms that connect the identity of Jesus to the Old Testament symbol of wine as an indicator of the messianic age. With Jesus' appearance in Israel, the former age was passing away and the messianic age was dawning.

2:1 *On the third day.* It is problematic to take 2:1 as merely a chronological reference, because then one must ask, On the third day after what? The narrative began with John the Baptist's conversation with the representatives from Jerusalem about who he was (Jn 1:19); then, "the next day" John the Baptist saw Jesus (1:29); and then, "the next day" John pointed Jesus out to two of his disciples (1:35); again, "the next day" Jesus left for Galilee (1:43), finding both Philip and Nathanael. Following this narrative sequence as strictly chronological would mean the wedding would have taken place on the fifth day, not the third. But perhaps "on the third day" was meant to indicate the day of the week of the wedding, perhaps on the third day of the week, on a Tuesday to our reckoning. As Richard Hays observes, "John's Gospel manifests an unsettling indifference to ordinary perceptions of linear time."[1]

The phrase "the third day," however, is probably not to be taken as a temporal reference at all, but rather a *symbolic* reference meant to suggest a day of God's deliverance, as the phrase is often used in the Old Testament. It was "on the third day" after Esther's decision to identify herself with the people of God that she appeared in her royal glory before the king, a confrontation that led to the deliverance of the Jewish people from genocide (Est 5:1). Jewish Midrash on this scene points out, "Israel are never left in dire distress more than three days."[2] In the Midrash, this "miracle" of deliverance through Esther is compared to events in the lives of Abraham, Jacob, and Jonah that also involved three days. The Midrash on this passage links it to the Jewish tradition that the dead will "come to life only after three days" from the start of the final judgment. This idea is based on Hosea 6:2: "After two days he will revive us; *on the third day* he will restore us, that we may live in his presence." Of course, the fact that Jesus rose from the dead on the third day is quite consistent with the previous Jewish tradition that God delivers from death on the third day. The man Jesus is not only delivered from death but in that event simultaneously secures life for all those who would believe in him. Therefore, John recognized a new "day" dawning in Israel with the advent of Jesus, the messianic day of God's ultimate deliverance of his people, and prefaces this first of Jesus' signs with the clue "on the third day."

2:3 *They have no more wine.* Modern readers probably find it difficult to feel the impending crisis of this situation. Weddings in first-century Palestine typically lasted several days and involved the entire village. The groom's family provided the wedding feast, and to run out of food or beverage was considered shameful, calling into question the groom's ability to provide for a wife, and even exposing the groom to a potential lawsuit if the provisions were sufficiently inadequate. In the honor-shame culture of that time, this problem would not have been easily remediated. Jesus' mother's concern about this may suggest the wedding involved one of her relatives, especially since Cana is believed to have been only about nine miles north of Nazareth, Mary's hometown.

2:4 *"Woman . . ."* It is unclear what Mary was hoping Jesus would do about the wine shortage, but his reply sounds like a rebuke. It may be debated whether Jesus' address to his mother as "woman" was rude or merely formal, but in either case it was a highly unusual way for a son to address his mother in that time and culture. It would have been particularly startling given the high respect for parents in ancient culture, including the respect of adult children for their parents, as highlighted in the Ten Commandments (Ex 20:12; Dt 5:16). Jesus' words all the more emphasize his primary relationship to his heavenly Father rather than his earthly mother (Pr 1:8–9; 4.10–12; 6:20–22). This brief interchange has been understood to reveal that Jesus needed to distance himself from his human mother as he began his public ministry of doing his Father's work. He wanted his mother to realize that his power and authority were not at her disposal. However, John later presents Jesus addressing his mother as "woman" one more time in this gospel, and that is while he is hanging on the cross (Jn 19:26). This distinctive lexical clue connects the wedding at Cana to the significance of the death of Jesus (see more on this at 2:6).

2:6 *Six stone water jars . . . each holding from twenty to thirty gallons.* Jewish cleansing rituals often involved large amounts of water. Because of a belief in constant defilement by contact with the world, worshipers poured water over their hands and the utensils they used to make themselves ritually clean for religious services. Stone pots (as opposed to clay) were often used to protect against ritual contamination (see Lev 6:28; 11:33; 15:12). John specifies not only that the pots were stone but also their number and their capacity. While these details may seem of questionable relevance to modern readers, they suggest an important part of John's interpretation of this miraculous event. The unearthing of stone vessels in the likely locations of Cana is but one of the archaeological confirmations of details in the fourth gospel.[3]

Each stone pot held twenty to thirty gallons (Gk. *metrētas* [μετρητὰς]; "two or three measures," a "measure" being a liquid unit of about ten gallons). In total the six pots therefore held about 120–180 gallons of water. As a familiar point of comparison, the average modern bathtub holds about thirty gallons of water, and so Jesus produced an enormous amount of wine, even if the whole village was feasting at the wedding, as was the custom.

In the Old Testament the abundance of wine—and specifically *new* wine—was a sign of God's blessing and a symbol of the promise of the messianic age (Isa 55:1–5; Jer 31:12; Joel 2:19, 24; 3:18; Am 9:13). Abundant, new wine would flow in the messianic age, implying the shalom and well-being, the *joie de vivre*, of God's people in the messianic age. But the wine at Cana wasn't the fulfillment of those prophetic promises of the Old Testament; it was only a small tasting, a sign pointing to Jesus' messianic significance. We find an interesting and enlightening comparison in the ancient book of 2 Baruch, which although not Scripture was probably known to many in New Testament times. Second Baruch 29:5 describes the abundance of the messianic age as a grapevine that will bear a thousand branches with each branch producing a thousand clusters of grapes; each cluster will produce a thousand grapes, and *each grape* will produce a *cor* of wine (about sixty gallons or 230 liters)![4] It's not necessary that John was directly referencing 2 Baruch, which probably preserved messianic beliefs more widely common to that culture (though see commentary on Jn 6:31 for another possible allusion to 2 Baruch). But it's nevertheless remarkable that the six stone pots of wine, as abundant as it was, amounted to that produced by only two or three grapes in the imagery of the messianic age. And so this shows that Jesus did miraculous signs inaugurating the messianic age, but the ultimate fullness of the messianic age awaits his return.

At about the same time John was writing his gospel, the first-century Jewish philosopher Philo interpreted Melchizedek, the king who offered Abraham wine and bread (Ge 14:18), as a type of the coming Messiah who would give God's people wine instead of water (*Allegorical Interpretation* 3.82). Jesus enacted that replacement of beverage at Cana as a sign that points forward to the significance of Jesus' subsequent death. When Jesus died on the cross he replaced the ceremonial waters of ritual Judaism with the wine of Holy Communion. This makes Mary's comment at Cana, "They have no wine," very poignant. Before Jesus came God's people could only look forward to the wine of the new covenant (Mt 26:28; Mk 14:24). So Mary spoke better than she knew. Nevertheless, the fact that Jesus used the water pots in this miracle, as opposed for instance to getting water directly from a well, "suggests that Jesus will (somehow) work within and utilize the Jewish religion for the accomplishment of his work—as it were, 'filling' its institutions 'to overflowing.'"[5] The intimate relationship between Jesus and the Jewish institutions in the gospel of John is complex, and cannot be fully represented by words such as "replaced" and "superseded."

Marriage was instituted by God at creation, and here Jesus affirms and honors the institution of marriage by performing this wonderful sign at a wedding. The setting of this miracle of changing water into wine at a wedding also connects with the Old Testament metaphor of marriage used to describe the relationship between God and his people. The Creator God is called the maker and husband of Israel (Isa 54:4–5). Isaiah also writes of a great banquet featuring the finest of wines (cf. Jn 2:10) that will inaugurate the messianic age and swallow up death forever (Isa 25:6–8). And so in Jewish religious imagery a wedding banquet also came to symbolize the beginning of the messianic age (cf. Rev 19:9, 17).

John reveals that the messianic age was dawning with the appearance of Jesus, but it still awaits consummation when the Lord returns. Accordingly, the miraculous signs Jesus does in John's gospel point to and accredit Jesus' identity, but in themselves they do not fulfill the Old Testament prophecies. The signs actually embody what they symbolize, but they aren't the final fulfillment of the Old Testament promises. Jesus healed many as a sign that all will be healed at the consummation. Jesus raised Lazarus from the tomb (Jn 11) to reveal his power to overcome death, but Lazarus died again, and awaits the final resurrection as the fulfillment of promise to which the sign of his first death only pointed.

John uses such traditions to reveal the significance of who Jesus is. And so Jesus' miracle at the wedding in Cana of Galilee is a sign that the Messiah has come. Jesus the Messiah provides wine instead of water—abundant *new* wine. John includes this story and describes it as he does to announce that, yes, Jesus was the Messiah, but much more than the expected Messiah.

The signs in John point us backward to promises from the Old Testament, but they also point readers forward in the gospel story to anticipate and explain the cross. Jesus' unusual way of addressing his mother as "woman" occurs just one more time in the fourth gospel, linking the miracle of water into wine with Jesus' crucifixion. When we hear Jesus address his mother as "woman" again in John 19:26 it should call to our minds the last time he had addressed her in that distinctive way—the day he changed water into wine. And so that miraculous sign becomes a context in which to understand his death. For in the Old Testament wine also symbolizes eschatological judgment (e.g., Jer 25:15; Isa 63:6), and that judgment was occurring when Jesus hung on the cross. God's wrath poured out on Jesus for all the sin of the world. John wants us to understand Jesus' death in light of the wedding miracle at Cana, where the wine symbolizes the blood of Jesus on the cross—the bridegroom providing the wine for the marriage supper of the Lamb; wine, not water, which will cleanse the bride of sin and make her pure and spotless before God.[6] Jesus reveals himself to be the true bridegroom of Israel, pouring out the wine of the new covenant messianic banquet, enacted by the church in Holy Communion. When Jesus died on the cross he replaced the ceremonial cleansing waters of Judaism with the wine of the new covenant shed for sin (see Mt 26:28; Mk 14:24). And so John explains how the messianic age was inaugurated with the life, death, and resurrection of Jesus Christ.

2:11 *The first of the signs.* The Synoptic Gospels refer to the supernatural things Jesus did as "miracles" (Gk. *dynamis* [δύναμις]) but John chooses the word "sign" (Gk. *sēmeion* [σημεῖον]), suggesting the miracles of Jesus had a significance that should be recognized to rightly understand who Jesus is.

The word *sign* is used in the Old Testament to refer to events, both supernatural and natural, which authenticated the ministry and message of a prophet. And so, for instance, God enabled Moses to perform various signs to persuade the Israelites that Moses had indeed been sent from the Lord to lead them (Ex 4:1–8). John perceives the things Jesus did as signs that were intended to persuade the people that Jesus also had been sent from God as the Messiah. John depicts Jesus as revealing his messianic glory through the particular signs he includes in his gospel. John is announcing that Jesus is the new and greater Moses, the Messiah who has begun a new exodus into the true promised land. But even so, many of the people who saw Jesus' miracles nevertheless missed the sign and rejected him (Jn 1:11).

John identifies the changing of water into wine as the first of the signs Jesus did (2:11), and in the narrative presents it as the first of several miracles. However, this sign is first not just first in the sequence; it also forms the opening act of John's story of *how Jesus reveals his glory*, and as such is the foundational pattern for everything else that follows.

Through which he revealed his glory. The revelation of Jesus' glory recalls John 1:14: "The Word became flesh and made his dwelling among us. We have seen his *glory*, the *glory* of the One and Only, who came from the Father, full of grace and truth." When read in the context of the signs that follow in the gospel's story, it seems likely that the verb *ephanerōsen* (ἐφανέρωσεν) should be read as an ingressive aorist: "He began to reveal his glory" (see also commentary at 17:1).

The word *glory* (Gk. *doxa* [δόξα]; Heb. *kābôd* [כָּבוֹד]) occurs frequently in Scripture, referring to a visible manifestation of God's honor, majesty, and power. John tells us that the Son came to make God known and did that through his teaching and miracles, but ultimately on the cross. Richard Bauckham makes the interesting observation that these signs were important because apparently "Jesus was not self-evidently the revelation of the glory of God."[7] There was nothing about his appearance that made people instantly recognize him as a visible manifestation of God's honor, majesty, and power in the flesh. There needed to be a process of perception and discernment that understood his words and actions as revelation, and then a proper response of faith to that revelation.

Although the Johannine signs are deeply connected to the promises of the Old Testament, they also involve universal human experience, and so they speak across time and cultures even to those without a deep knowledge of Scripture. The first time I read John 2 back in my college days, I had no idea of the richness of John's signs, but even I could see that such a great miracle was a sign that Jesus commanded divine power. I had just taken a course in organic chemistry and knew that the conversion of water (H_2O) into wine (CH_3CH_2OH) involved at least the introduction of the element carbon and a rearrangement of molecules. Jesus' power as creator is displayed in this miracle. Because one of the features of the divine identity in monotheism was the uniqueness of God as creator, this miracle suggests Jesus' identity with the God of Israel.

To a first-century polytheistic pagan reader, this miracle would function apologetically showing Jesus to be at least equal in power to Bacchus/Dionysius, the mythological Roman/Greek god of wine and the grape harvest. Saint Augustine notes that the Lord changes water into wine quite routinely in the annual cycle of rainfall and grape harvest, the miraculous quality of which is often overlooked because of its routine frequency.[8]

His disciples believed in him. John tells us why he wrote down the signs that Jesus did: "these are written that you may believe that Jesus is the Messiah, the Son of God, and that by believing you may have life in his name" (Jn 20:31). With the first of the signs that Jesus did, John tells us that faith resulted in the people who saw the miracle. John refers to those who came to have faith in Jesus as disciples. These are people who watched and listened to Jesus and concluded that he was, in fact, the long-awaited Messiah, and they eventually came to know him as the Son of God.

Going Deeper into Believing in Jesus: John 2

Faith is a major theme in the gospel of John, and its various degrees and forms of faith will be discussed as we encounter them throughout the book. While faith is the key that opens us to eternal life, John also presents deficient forms of faith, such as "I'll-believe-it-when-I-see-it" faith (Jn 20:24–29), a "what's-in-it-for-me" kind of faith (Jn 6:26), or faith that evaporates when its demands become difficult (Jn 6:66–69). The signs are meant to reveal not only the nature of the Father and the Son but what must be trusted as a truth to be lived. Each encounter Jesus has in this gospel helps us to understand what it means to truly be his disciple.

John's call to believe in Jesus for eternal life is a call not simply to agree with the facts of Jesus' life, but to agree with God's interpretation of the significance of those facts as inscripturated in the New Testament. Many people believe that the man Jesus lived and died in first-century Palestine. In fact, the Roman historian Tacitus mentions the execution of Jesus at the hands of Pontius Pilate (*Annals* 15.44.3, written ca. AD 116).[9] But according to John it is not enough to simply believe that Jesus lived and died, or even to consider him a great religious teacher on par, say, with Confucius, Buddha, Mohammed, Moses, or such others. Jesus may have spoken as a prophet, but he was more than a prophet. John calls for his readers to think of Jesus in the terms presented, as the Creator Word, the incarnate Son, the fulfillment of God's redemptive plan who died for sin and was raised into a life of eternal glory. The deity of Christ, his death for our sin, and his bodily resurrection are at the heart of Christian orthodoxy. John's presentation of Jesus supports these great doctrines of the church, and belief in Jesus in this sense defines what it means to be a Christian disciple. Combined with John's call to follow Jesus, the Christian life is then to be lived in response to what Jesus Christ has revealed. We must live as if we trust God's promises, for belief that is not lived out is arguably not faith at all.

What the Structure Means:
Reading the Signs of the Fourth Gospel (Jn 2–12)

The more we understand about the imagery and traditions of ancient Israel, the richer the significance of the signs in the gospel of John and their interrelationships become. As Richard Bauckham notes, this sign illustrates "John's frequently rich pattern of allusion to Scripture. . . . The quantity and the quality of the wine that he provides are far in excess of need. . . . The miracle points to the greater enhancement of life to which Jesus refers" in John 10:10.[10] The wedding feast at Cana anticipates the eschatological banquet, when the Lord will provide "a feast of rich food for all peoples, a banquet of aged wines" (Isa 25:6). With Isaiah as a context, the miracle links the banquet to the universal abolition of death (Isa 25:7–8), connecting the first sign to the seventh, the raising of Lazarus and subsequently to Jesus' own resurrection.

And so the first sign teaches us that the signs in John's gospel can be read on three levels:

1. the surface reading of the unknowledgeable reader who may be reading the fourth gospel for the first time;

2. a biblical-theological reading, recognizing and appreciating the significance of the symbolism of the signs with respect to the Old Testament and the first-century Jewish traditions that developed from it; and

3. an eschatological-soteriological reading of the sign as explaining the significance of Jesus' death and resurrection.

Following the introduction of Jesus and a few of his disciples, John structures the telling of Jesus' life around several signs, traditionally numbered as seven, though the number seven is not found in the text. Only four of Jesus' miraculous actions are designated as "signs" (Gk. sēmeia [σημεῖα]) in the text: changing water to wine (2:1–11); healing of the official's son (4:46–54); feeding the five thousand (6:1–15); and the raising of Lazarus (11:38–44; 12:18). Two other miracles, the healing of the invalid (5:1–9) and the healing of the man born blind (9:1–7) are referred to as signs by those who witnessed them (7:31 and 9:16 respectively). Since only the first and second are numbered (2:11; 4:54), interpreters disagree about how to count them. Some include the cleansing of the temple (2:13–22), though the incident does not involve a miracle. Others combine the feeding of the five thousand (6:1–15) and Jesus walking on water (6:16–24). A further question is whether Jesus' resurrection should be counted as the seventh sign. Because the signs are only pointers and not the reality to which they point, it seems best to count the bringing of Lazarus back to mortal life as the final sign in John's gospel, pointing to the resurrection of Jesus himself into an immortal life, the first moment of new creation on the eighth day.[11]

John admits of knowing many more signs that Jesus did (Jn 20:30), but he chooses to include only seven miracles in his gospel. This number may symbolize the full, complete, and perfect revelation of the significance of Jesus' life, as the numeral seven bore that special significance in the ancient world.

First sign:	The changing of water into wine (Jn 2:1–11)
Second sign:	Jesus heals the official's son from a distance (Jn 4:43–54)
Third sign:	The healing at the pool of Bethesda (Jn 5:1–15)
Fourth sign:	Feeding of the five thousand (Jn 6:1–15)
Fifth sign:	Jesus walks on the stormy sea (Jn 6:16–24)
Sixth sign:	Healing of the man born blind (Jn 9:1–41)
Seventh sign:	The raising of Lazarus (Jn 11:1–44)

The changing of water into wine at Cana is the first of these seven, with the seventh being the raising of Lazarus from the dead in John 11. This section of the gospel from chapter 2 through 12 is often referred to as the Signs Source, or Book of Signs, explaining how God the Son revealed God the Father in his words and deeds.

The nature of the "outward fact" of the sign is used to reveal something of the nature of the Word who became flesh and revealed his messianic glory to the world. Each sign that John has chosen to include is significant because of its nature, even though Jesus apparently did many others (Jn 20:30).

The signs are not direct fulfillments of Old Testament promises, but point to Jesus as the One who does fulfill the promises ultimately and fully. Nevertheless, the sign actually does embody what it symbolizes. We can consider a kiss a sign of love because it actually embodies or realizes the emotion it symbolizes. But a kiss is not to be identified with love. In the case of John's gospel, when Jesus raises Lazarus from the dead, it is a sign of his power to give life. The sign points to Jesus' ability to give life after death and embodies that point because Jesus actually does raise Lazarus from death to life. (The fact that this led to the Jewish plot to kill the one who can raise the dead is one of John's profound ironies [Jn 12:10].) The signs embody and actualize what they symbolize. However, Lazarus died again. He did not remain alive forever. And so, the eternal life that

Jesus Christ gives was merely symbolized, albeit spectacularly, in the sign of the raising of Lazarus. Even though this was the most spectacular of signs in John's gospel, it was not the ultimate and final giving of life. Jesus came not simply to resuscitate us from death and restore us to this life, but to give us eternal life after death.

The Book of Signs builds the case for Jesus' identity and is the preface to the passion narrative in chapters 13–20. Each of the signs (1) reveals the presence of God in Jesus, (2) accredits Jesus as having been sent by God, and (3) explains the crucifixion by connecting it to the Old Testament promises. By the time the reader encounters the death and resurrection of Jesus, the signs have prepared for an understanding of why Jesus had to go to the cross, and that the cross is the way the Son ascends back to the Father and is, therefore, the ultimate glorification ("lifting up") of Jesus Christ. The Book of Signs makes the cross more poignant and the rejection of Jesus more ironically tragic. This structure to the gospel leads readers to either believe or to reject by the end of the story, with a powerful nudge to believe because of the inner coherence and revelation of God's love in sending Jesus (Jn 3:16).

Cana was the location of the first sign Jesus performed, as well as of the second sign (Jn 4:46–54). Jesus performed a miraculous healing in Cana that John labels as the second sign, inviting the reader to consider these miracles as a sequence of signs even though only the first two are numbered in the text. The material from John 2:1–4:54 is therefore often referred to as the Cana cycle (see table 2.1).

Table 2.1. The Cana Cycle
> Cana—First Sign: Changing Water to Wine (2:1–12)
>> Jerusalem/Judea (2:13–3:36)
>>> Cleansing of Temple at Passover (2:13–25)
>>> First Discourse: The New Birth (3:1–21)
>>> John the Baptist's Final Testimony (3:22–36)
>> Samaria (4:1–42)
>>> Second Discourse: Living Water and True Worship (4:1–26)
> Cana—Second Sign: Healing of Official's Son (4:46–54)

Within the Book of Signs there are also several extended discourses and "I am" statements that work with the signs to reveal the identity and nature of God in Christ. These will be discussed further as we encounter them.

Going Deeper into Filling Our Water Pots: John 2:7

Although the gospel of John refers to her only as "the mother of Jesus," Mary's example at the wedding at Cana suggests how we can understand this first of Jesus' signs as applicable to our own lives as Christians. Mary has only two brief lines in this story as she states the need to Jesus: "They have no more wine" and then, instructing the servants, "Do whatever he tells you."

Although Jesus' unusual reply to his mother gets much discussion among scholars, there is a consensus that it functions to distance Mary from her mother-son relationship with Jesus as he begins to fulfill his Father's purpose for sending him as Son of God into the world. While we can only imagine how Mary felt when she heard Jesus' reply, the next thing she said is quite revealing, and provides a model for our relationship to Jesus. As Francis Moloney notes, "The mother's instruction that the attendants do whatever Jesus tells them indicates that she accepts her new role. It is *openness to the word of Jesus* that will bear fruit, because he is ultimately responding to God's designs, and not the concerns, however caring, of his mother."[12] We, too, must be open to the word of Jesus in the situations of our lives.

Mary saw a need and brought that need to Jesus. She did not specify how she wanted him to meet the need, as we so often do in our prayers and petitions. The ambiguity in what Mary expected is instructive to us as Christian disciples. We might not know specifically what to pray for when we see a need in our lives, in the lives of others, or in our world. But if we follow the example of Mary, we are simply to bring that need to the Lord in prayer and leave it with him, knowing that he has both the power and the wisdom to act. Mary was no doubt delightfully surprised when she saw the abundant, new wine that Jesus had quietly produced without fanfare. It must have gone a long way toward soothing whatever rebuke she may have felt at Jesus' verbal reply. Let's let the Lord surprise us in the way he meets the needs we lay before him. We must give up control of the situation, let go of our plans, and leave it in his hands. He is God and we are not.

Without knowing what Jesus was about to do, or even whether he would do anything, Mary expressed her trust in Jesus by instructing the servants to do whatever he told them to do (Jn 2:5). And what Jesus told the servants to do was to fill the water pots with water right up to the brim. There was no room for anything to be added to the water pots. Jesus could have produced the wine *ex nihilo*, filling even empty water pots with wine, and with no help needed from the servants. But Jesus chose, as he normally does, to involve people in his work. As servants of the Lord we, too, must do just as he instructs us. As J. C. Ryle notes, "Duties are ours. Events are God's. It is ours to fill the water-pots. It is Christ's to make the water wine."[13] This understanding of the relationship between what we do and what the Lord does is very helpful and encouraging. We may have to wait for the moment when God chooses to act, but that should not lull us into inactivity. And when we are busy filling our pots in obedience to Jesus Christ, we can be assured that his purposes will be accomplished, even when our work seems inadequate, pointless, or even impossible. I once had a friend who was a former nun. She often would say, "Pray as if it all depends on God and work as if it all depends on you." Mary the mother of Jesus might likely agree.

2:13 *Time for the Jewish Passover.* Passover was one of the three great festivals for which all Jewish men were expected to appear at the temple in Jerusalem. It was a weeklong festival at the end of March or beginning of April that originally was associated with the barley harvest and came to commemorate the deliverance from Egypt. Exodus 12 describes the origins of the festival as a day of remembrance of when God brought his people out of slavery in Egypt by preserving them through the plague of the death of the firstborn. The blood of the Passover lamb painted on the doorframes of the Hebrews' homes in Egypt to prevent death from entering became an annual ritual of animal sacrifice that was the heart of the Passover celebration centuries later at the Jerusalem temple.

The gospel of John mentions Passover eleven times, significantly more often than the other Gospels and books of the New Testament.[14] Similarly Moses, the patriarch most closely associated with the exodus and Passover, is mentioned more often in John's gospel (thirteen times) than in any other. Recall that John introduces Jesus through the lips of John the Baptist declaring Jesus to be the "Lamb of God" (Jn 1:29, 36). Even though it's uncertain whether John had in mind the Passover lamb, it seems the most plausible understanding, for Jesus had previously been referred to as the Passover lamb in Christian tradition (see 1 Co 5:7).[15] Even though the slaughter of the Passover lamb was not specifically a sin offering, it did commemorate a deliverance from death. That traditional understanding coheres well with John's focus on eternal life through Christ, suggesting that Jesus' death is the redemptive sacrifice for a new kind of exodus. Richard Hays concludes, "For John the Evangelist, Jesus 'the Lamb of God who takes away the sin of the world,' embodies in his death the true signification of the Passover and Exodus events"[16] (see commentary on Jn 1:29).

2:14 *In the temple courts.* Here John first mentions the great Jerusalem temple, the heart of Judaism, where God had promised his presence, accepted sacrifice for sin, and where his people offered confession, praise, and thanksgiving. The Holy of Holies was thought to be where God's feet touched earth as he sat on his throne in heaven (Eze 43:7). The temple was essential for worship during the era of Second Temple Judaism, for it was where the priesthood performed the mandated animal sacrifices on behalf of the people. Passover was a pilgrim festival with people traveling distances from all over Palestine and the Diaspora to participate in this sacrificial worship. It was therefore convenient for worshipers to purchase their sacrificial animals at the temple, rather than to bring animals with them. Similarly, money conversion was necessary for those required to pay the temple tax in the prescribed currency.

It is in this public, crowded space that John presents Jesus doing his first act for all to see, and it was an act that condemned the temple system. Jesus perceived a problem with the practices he saw in the temple courts. The exact nature of the problem is debated. Some point out that the sale of animals and money changing was being conducted in the temple courts, most likely the Court of the Gentiles, and therefore would have disrupted the Gentiles' access to worship. Earlier in Israel's history animal merchants had been located nearby across the Kidron Valley, and so a move to the Court of the Gentiles may have indicated a shift of priorities that diminished Gentiles' participation.[17] The offense, as Jesus' remarks suggest, is a defilement of the temple as the Father's house, but John does not suggest unethical practices in the temple, as the Synoptic Gospels do, which refer to "a den of robbers" (Mt 21:12–13; Mk 11:15–17; Lk 19:45–46). Rather, in John's presentation, Jesus seems to be attacking the entire sacrificial system as practiced in the Jerusalem temple, as he is about to announce his own body as a new temple and will die on the cross to end animal sacrifice. As Bauckham explains, Jesus' zealous outburst was "an attack on the whole of the financial arrangements for the sacrificial system," and as such, an attack on the sacrificial system itself.[18] Accordingly, the animals were to be released because the true Lamb of God was standing in the temple. The tax to support the temple was no longer needed, because the true temple was Jesus himself (see commentary on Jn 2:18–19). And indeed the Jerusalem temple was permanently destroyed just a few decades after this event in AD 70.

2:17 *Zeal for your house will consume me.* There are seven quotations of the Psalms in John's gospel, and they are especially important as part of John's explanation of the life of Jesus.[19] As Margaret Daly-Denton explains, Israel believed King David to be in some sense the author of the Psalms.[20] David's words and the events of his life were considered to point prophetically to the great Son of David whose dynasty would be eternal, as promised in 2 Samuel 7. The early Christians understood Jesus to be the long-awaited Davidic King and, therefore, interpreted his life in light of the Psalms (on Jesus as king see commentary on Jn 1:20, 41, 49; 3:3; 6:15; 7:42; 12:13–15). Because the Psalms foreshadow Christ, early in Christian tradition they came to be read as the words of Christ himself (see 1 Pe 1:10–11).[21]

John never refers to Jesus explicitly as the Son of David, perhaps because of the prominence of Moses in Jesus' words. But Moses wasn't God's last word, and the significant Davidic institutions that pointed to an eschatological hope—the temple and monarchy—also had to be taken into account.[22] The fourth gospel integrates Jesus' identity with both Moses and David, but the setting of this incident in the temple would have provided a rich context of Davidic overtones. After all, "the Temple is David's project. It is the sign of God's goodness to David (1 Kgs 8:66). Zeal for the Temple and for the cult which it housed is the outstanding characteristic of David."[23]

Here in John 2:17 the disciples remember Psalm 69:9 as if on the lips of Jesus, taking "your house" in the original psalm as "my Father's house" and "me" as a reference, not to David, but now to Jesus. It is unclear if John means to say the disciples remembered the psalm as Jesus was clearing the temple or only quite some time later upon further reflection. But the memory of the disciples is a major point in John, and apparently remembrance is closely associated with faith (see Jn 2:22).

The word translated *consume* (Heb. *'kl* [אָכַל]; Gk. *katesthiō* [κατεσθίω]) means to eat up, to devour, and by figurative extension, to destroy. The Synoptic Gospels place this event in the last week of Jesus' life, as if it were the final precipitating event that directly led to Jesus' arrest and the destruction of his earthly life on the cross. John places it early in his gospel, probably not to disagree with the chronology of the Synoptic writers but to show early on in the story a harbinger of what is to come.[24] W. D. Davies argues that the theme of a new Passover accounts for placement of this episode in John early, "to signify that a New Order had arrived. The 'Holy Place' is to be displaced by a new reality, a rebuilt 'temple (*naos*),' which John refers to as 'the temple of his [Jesus'] body'"[25] (see further discussion in "What the Structure Means: When Did Jesus Clear the Temple? (Jn 2:13–22)"). This incident of the clearing of the temple, which incited the wrath of the Jewish authorities, is placed at the beginning of John's narrative of Jesus' life to introduce the theme of persecution of the righteous, which was the theme of the psalm in David's life and which had characterized Jesus' earthly experience.

Although John quotes here only one colon of Psalm 69:9a (68:10 LXX), there are several echoes of other, unquoted parts of Psalm 69 found in John's story of Jesus that connect this quotation, and therefore the clearing of the temple, to the death of Jesus. As Daly-Denton has found, "the Evangelist's usage of the psalms is not confined to isolated phrases which seem pertinent to Jesus, but extends, at least in some cases, to the psalm as a whole."[26] Although a full examination of the echoes of Psalm 69 (Ps 68 LXX) in John's gospel is well outside the scope of this commentary, we note here a couple distinctive echoes. The very next colon, Psalm 69:9b, though unquoted, may also have been a meaningful memory to the Johannine disciples: "and the insults of those who insult you fall on me." Originally, as king of Israel, David bore the opposition of those who opposed God; John then presents the hostility that greeted Jesus when he came to his own in the temple (Jn 1:11), and then further shows that the hostility toward Jesus would overflow on his disciples (Jn 15:20). For John 15:25 puts another verse from Psalm 69 on Jesus' lips: "They hated me without reason" (see Ps 69:4).

Finally, that hatred and rejection led to Jesus' execution, where ironically the One who offers living water (Jn 4:10) is thirsty. John echoes Psalm 69:20–21 in John 19:29 when he describes how Jesus was offered vinegar on the cross:

> Scorn has broken my heart
>   and has left me helpless;
> I looked for sympathy, but there was none,
>   for comforters, but I found none.
> They put gall in my food
>   and gave me *vinegar* for my thirst.

This use of Psalm 69:20 (68 LXX) conforms with both of the two forms of usage Matthew Scott found of the same psalm in Romans 15: "1) details from the psalm are woven without notice into the narrative of Jesus' passion" (in this case vinegar); and "2) words from the psalm (John 2:17) . . . are placed in the mouth of Jesus."[27]

And so the quotation of Psalm 69:9 in John 2:17, the chapter in which John *begins* to describe hostility toward Jesus, forms an *inclusio* with an allusion to the same psalm in John 19:29, the climax of hostility that ended Jesus' life. This signals that John, like the other gospel writers, remembered this episode in Jesus' life as the major event that led to his death even though John places it in a different place in his gospel.

With this John teaches us how he relates the psalms to Jesus. As Daly-Denton explains, "We might think in terms of three levels of interpretation—the

Jewish reading where David speaks the psalms, the Christian reading where Jesus is the prophetically foretold prayer [pray-er] of the psalms, the Christological reading in which Jesus is the Lord described or addressed in the psalms."[28]

2:18–19 *"What sign can you show us?"* . . . *"Destroy this temple."* The Jewish rulers of the temple understandably ask Jesus what *sign* he can give them to authorize his stunning actions. Jesus replies by hinting at the resurrection of his body from the grave: "Destroy this temple, and I will raise it again in three days." The conversation John records here is the first of many characterized by misunderstanding and irony. Understandably the Jewish leaders take Jesus to be referring to the temple building, and they find his boast ludicrous to raise it from destruction in three days. Jesus, however, has switched references from the physical building to his physical body, an explanation offered here much later to John's readers but not to the Jewish leaders in the moment.

One of the distinctive characteristics of John's gospel is that Jesus is almost always ironically misunderstood when he's having a conversation. First, John reports Jesus making a statement that is ambiguous, metaphorical, or a double entendre. Second, the person listening to Jesus responds in terms of the literal meaning, showing that he or she has missed the true sense of Jesus' statement. Then, Jesus or the narrator offers the explanation to the reader, so the reader is let in on what the "victim" of the irony misses. In this case, by explaining that Jesus was talking about his body, the reader is invited to ponder the intriguing analogy between the temple building and Jesus' body. In what way is Jesus' body a temple?

The Jerusalem temple was the place where heaven touched earth (1 Ch 28:2; Ps 99:5; 132:7–8; Isa 66:1; La 2:1), the place where God dwelled in the midst of his people (2 Sa 7:1–5, 12–13). It was the place where sacrifice for sin was offered, and where the people praised and worshiped God (1 Ki 8:62–63; 12:27). Jesus himself fulfills every function of the temple, the priesthood, the sacrifices, because in his body, God the Son came to earth. Heaven meets earth in the person of Jesus Christ (cf. Jn 1:51). Jesus himself is where God dwells with his people. Jesus himself is the once-for-all, ultimate sacrifice for sin. And it is in Christ, and in him alone, that we are to worship God (see Jn 4:21). John's Prologue hinted at this in John 1:14, with the verb *eskēnōsen* (ἐσκήνωσεν), *dwelt* among us. This verb is etymologically related to the Greek noun for "tent" (*skēnē* [σκηνή]), an allusion to the tent of meeting where God met with Moses during Israel's wilderness journey (Ex 25:8–9). The idea that Jesus is the final and ultimate temple of humankind is also reflected in Revelation 21:1–5, 22, where John, whether or not the same author as the gospel, did *not* see a temple in the city, because the Lord God Almighty and the Lamb *are* its temple.

2:22 *After he was raised . . . they believed the scripture and the words that Jesus had spoken.* John is very clear that at the time Jesus spoke he was more often than not misunderstood. Only after the resurrection, when the disciples reflected on the Scriptures and on Jesus' words, did they begin to understand the true significance of Jesus' life and death. In other words, the cross of Christ was not just a historical event; it was also a *hermeneutical* event. As Hays explains, "Jesus' life and death and resurrection were in fact *revelatory*: they held the key to understanding all that had gone before."[29] Hays refers to this as "a Gospel-shaped hermeneutic" that "necessarily entails reading backwards, reinterpreting Israel's Scripture in light of the story of Jesus."[30] This passage of the clearing of the temple is "one of the clearest expressions of this hermeneutical device,"[31] though here it is the earlier story of Jesus that is reread in light of the cross (see commentary on Jn 19:28).

But for this hermeneutic to function, the memory of Jesus after he was gone had to come into full play, even as Jesus promised it would (Jn 16:13). Under the inspiration of the Spirit the apostles Jesus had chosen remembered what he said and did that helped them to understand Jesus' identity in light of the Scriptures of Israel, and that shaped the gospel presentations. The Scriptures John had in mind are likely those he quotes, such as Exodus (12:46; 16:4), Numbers (9:12), Nehemiah (9:15), Isaiah (6:10; 40:3; 53:1; 54:13), the Psalms (22:18; 34:20; 35:19; 41:9; 69:4, 9; 78:24, 25; 82:6; 118:25, 26), and the Minor Prophets (Zec 9:9; 12:10). Because these citations span the three-part Hebrew canon, from which New Testament writers cite in explaining the significance of Jesus, John's point might refer more broadly to the entire Hebrew Bible. Certainly the more we understand of the Old Testament, the better we will understand the New.

The role of memory is emphasized with John 2:22a repeating verbatim "his disciples recalled" (*emnēsthēsan* [ἐμνήσθησαν]). In the first case they remembered Scripture; in the second, they remembered Jesus' words. And so the essential ingredients of John's hermeneutic are revealed. To be a disciple of Jesus Christ is to believe both the words of Scripture and the revelation Jesus brought.

2:23 *Many people saw the signs . . . and believed in his name.* John here develops the theme of authentic faith in Christ. As J. B. Lightfoot observes,

> The verb "to believe," as used in 2:22, does not necessarily imply more than to give credence to a passage of scripture, or a statement, or a person; but "to believe on the name of the Lord" [2:23], an expression which has already occurred in the prologue [1:12] and will recur at 3:18, is equivalent to the strong expression "to believe on" Him (cf. 2:11), the only

difference being that "to believe on His name" expresses more precisely a recognition of the significance of His Person, e.g., that He is "the only begotten Son of God" [3:18].[32]

It is those who "believe in his name"—that is, his divine identity as Son of God—who are given the right to become children of God (Jn 1:12).

What the Structure Means: When Did Jesus Clear the Temple? (Jn 2:13–22)

There are many differences between John's gospel and the three Synoptic Gospels, but one of the most debated is when the clearing of the temple occurred. As we've seen, John places his telling of the incident early in his gospel, as Jesus' first public act in Jerusalem. Matthew, Mark, and Luke place the incident in the final week of Jesus' life, showing it to be the last straw in the tension between Jesus and the Jewish authorities, the incident that directly led to his arrest. In their concern for historical accuracy among all four Gospels, scholars have made various arguments, including the rather desperate conclusion that Jesus must have cleared the temple twice, once near the beginning of his public ministry and again the final week of his life. This and similar attempts to reconcile John and the Synoptics fail to recognize what John is doing.

It is consistent with the character of the fourth gospel that readers recognize dischronologized events as part of the verbal artistry by which John interprets the significance of Jesus' life and death. As Clement stated, John is not interested in presenting "the outward facts" once again, but rather in presenting the spiritual significance of those facts (*Eccl. Hist.* 6.14.7). J. B. Lightfoot explains, "The setting of the event in the first three Gospels, very soon after the Lord's arrival at the capital towards the end of His ministry, is more likely to be historically correct than that in John. One reason for the position assigned to it in John may be that it is part of his purpose to represent the judgement or discrimination effected by the presence and work of the Lord among men as in operation from the outset of His activity."[33]

Further examination of how John tells the story of the water into wine and the temple that is Jesus' body suggests that even the placement of these events in the telling of his gospel is to help the reader understand the interpretive themes, Old Testament connections, and to explain the meaning of the cross rather than to document a strict chronology of

Jesus' ministry. Recognizing this as John's intent does not threaten the historical accuracy of the fourth gospel; rather it underscores that the structures of John's gospel are purposeful, and when examined offer profound truth and beauty.

John 2 Through Old Testament Eyes

John makes two major points relating to the Old Testament in John 2: (1) the miracle of changing water to wine announced the dawning of the long-awaited messianic age, ironically pointing to the death of its Messiah; and (2) to quote Richard Hays, "*Jesus now takes over the temple's function as a place of mediation between God and human beings.*"[34] It is probably difficult for modern readers benefiting from two thousand years of Christian theology to appreciate the radical, revolutionary effect of these points on those who knew God only through Israel's Scriptures.

The resurrection of Jesus was an unprecedented and unique event in the history of humankind, far exceeding any prior expectations Second Temple Judaism may have held. The Messiah turns out to be none other than God himself! All that God had begun to do in centuries of past redemptive history was being caught up and embodied in the crucified and risen Jesus: the festivals, the temple, the priesthood, the sacrifices, the prophetic images of promise for the messianic age. For those who have eyes to see, John announces a new age where Jesus the Creator provides a new Passover where Jesus was the perfect sacrifice; a new temple where God meets us and we meet God in the person of Jesus Christ; a new location where we worship in spirit and truth.

Again we see a triple depth of meaning: "First the Lord performs an act by which he condemns the methods and manner of the existing Jewish worship [i.e., water purification rites and the sacrificial system of the Jerusalem temple]. Secondly, this act, as set forth by St. John, is a sign of the destruction of the old order of worship . . . and its replacement by a new order. . . . And thirdly, intermediate between the old order and the new order is the 'work'—the ministry, death, and resurrection—of the Lord which alone makes possible the inauguration and life of the new temple."[35]

Additionally in this second chapter John teaches us to read his gospel through Old Testament eyes by learning to read how he uses quotations, allusions, and echoes of the Old Testament and its themes and images.

JOHN 3

3:1–21 Here we find Jesus' first extensive conversation with an individual, an example of one of the hallmarks of the gospel of John. Whereas in the Synoptic Gospels Jesus more frequently teaches and preaches to crowds, in the fourth gospel he speaks long discourses presented within conversation with an individual. So far in John's story, Jesus has gathered around himself a few disciples (chap. 1), has announced the arrival of the messianic age by changing water into wine (2:1–11), and has revealed himself as the new temple for the new age by clearing the temple in Jerusalem (2:13–25). Now John presents Jesus' first encounter with an individual, Nicodemus, in which he will begin to explain how one is born again into the dawning kingdom of God's Messiah.

3:1 *A Pharisee . . . named Nicodemus.* Because Nicodemus was a Pharisee (see commentary on Jn 1:24), we can infer he probably was a very devout Jew, devoted to obeying the Law of Moses and perhaps had strong nationalistic hopes that the coming Messiah would liberate the Jewish people from Roman occupation.

3:2 *He came to Jesus at night.* The Prologue declares that life was in the Word and that the Life "was the light of all mankind" (1:4). The metaphor of light is multifaceted, but in this gospel it represents the ideal human condition of having a life-giving relationship with this Life who had come from God and was God (1:1). This fundamental statement in the Prologue sets up a light-darkness dualism in which the negative opposite of life in relationship with God is represented by darkness and death.[1] This dualism permeates John's gospel and is found elsewhere in John's story of Jesus in the motifs of night and blindness, which by their nature are equivalent to the absence of light and, hence, darkness.[2] Nicodemus most likely really did come to Jesus during the nighttime hours, but John chooses to tell the reader that detail not simply because it was true, for there are myriad details that an author could choose to include or not. In the context of the light-darkness dualism, the detail suggests that this Pharisee, though a teacher of the law, nevertheless was in the dark because he did not have a life-giving relationship with the God he worshiped.

Rabbi. Nicodemus respectfully acknowledges Jesus as a religious teacher (see commentary on Jn 1:38).

No one could perform the signs you are doing if God were not with him. Nicodemus realized that God enabled those he sent to perform miraculous signs to accredit the message of their teaching (see commentary on Jn 2:6, 11, 18–19, 23). The signs he had heard Jesus had performed no doubt had attracted his attention to Jesus.

3:3 *Kingdom of God.* The rule and reign of God in an age to come was one of the hallmarks of first-century Jewish eschatology. God is the king whose subjects, beginning with Adam and Eve, rebelled and opposed him. The coming of the kingdom was associated with the appearance of the expected Messiah and an accompanying central belief that the Jewish people would be liberated from all oppressors. When Jesus first began his ministry he announced, "The time has come. . . . The kingdom of God has come near. Repent and believe the good news!" (Mk 1:15). Repentance from sin defined as rebellion and opposition to God and trust in the good news Jesus taught was the proper response to the coming of the kingdom. In the Synoptic Gospels, the phrase "kingdom of God" occurs frequently to refer to the state of being in right relationship with God through Christ, but John mentions the kingdom only twice in his gospel, here in 3:3 and in 3:5. Instead, he speaks of having abundant and eternal life as equivalent to being in the kingdom of God.[3] And just as one enters physical life by being born into a tribe or nation, Jesus speaks of new birth as the way to enter the kingdom of God (on Jesus as king see commentary on Jn 1:20, 41, 49; 2:17; 6:15; 7:42; 12:13–15).

Born again. When evangelicals speak of being born again as the essential personal experience of an individual's Christian faith, they are alluding to this passage in John 3. There is probably no more sweeping metaphor for a transformation of one's identity than the concept of a new birth. Although John mentions rebirth only here, the concept was apparently more broadly embraced among the apostles, for it is also found in 1 Peter 1:23. Birth imagery is used in both Old and New Testaments to describe the relationship between God and his people. Moses sings to the gathered people of Israel, "You forgot the God who gave you birth" (Dt 32:18) (see commentary on Jn 1:12, 13).

A person is born into a life largely defined by the genetics, nationality, ethnicity, character, socioeconomic status, and so on of his or her parents. Jesus emphasizes that the abundant, eternal life he offers cannot be entered through any of these ways gained by natural birth (see Jn 1:13). In other words, simply being born Jewish does not bestow the life that makes one a child of God. Salvation is not limited to national or ethnic Israel, human character falls short of God's standard of righteousness, and wealth or status does not impress God. The reader has already been introduced to this concept in John 1:12, where John explains that it is only by receiving Jesus through faith that one is reborn as a child of God (Jn 1:12). But Nicodemus does not yet know this.

3:4 *How can someone be born . . . a second time?* Nicodemus, knowing only of physical birth, points out how ludicrous Jesus sounds. This is the second ironic misunderstanding of Jesus so far in John's story. The first occurred in John 2:19–20, where the Jewish leaders objected to Jesus' statement that he would raise the temple in three days. The phrase translated "born again" is somewhat ambiguous in the Greek (*gennēthēnai anōthen* [γεννηθῆναι ἄνωθεν]), as the preposition *anōthen* (ἄνωθεν) could refer either to the origin of the birth (born from above) or indicate a repetition (born again). In fact, the Greek allows a nice wordplay that unfortunately cannot be captured in translation, for Jesus speaks of both—a second birth that is from God above.

3:5 *Born of water and the Spirit.* Water as a physical substance has been twice previously mentioned: in reference to John's baptism (1:26, 31, 33) and in the sign at Cana of changing water into wine (2:7, 9). However, water, associated with the metaphor of thirst as need for God, is also an important symbol of the Holy Spirit in John's gospel (4:10–15; 7:37–39). Therefore, interpreters raise the question here whether water indicates a physical substance or symbolizes a spiritual reality. If water is to be understood as a physical substance, it would likely refer to baptism, either a baptism of repentance as John the Baptist was practicing in that moment or to Christian baptism, which was practiced only after Jesus' lifetime[4] (see "What the Structure Means: Reading the Gospels Today (Jn 3:1–21)"). If symbolic, the metaphor of water elsewhere in the fourth gospel symbolizes the Spirit, but that would be redundant here, where the Spirit is explicitly mentioned in the second half of the phrase "water and the Spirit." So if symbolic what would water represent?

Let's look at the phrase "water and the Spirit" through Old Testament eyes, especially since Jesus rebukes Nicodemus, a teacher of the Hebrew Scriptures, for not understanding. In the narrative moment Nicodemus could not have recognized water as the sacrament of Christian baptism as that came much later. But being a teacher of Israel, he could have, and apparently should have, understood it as an allusion to the use of those words in the Hebrew Bible. The phrase "water and the Spirit" does not occur in the Old Testament, but Ezekiel 36:25–27 is a plausible allusion:[5]

> I will sprinkle clean *water* on you, and you will be clean; I will cleanse you from all your impurities and from all your idols. I will give you a new heart and put a new spirit in you; I will remove from you your heart of stone and give you a heart of flesh. And I will put my *Spirit* in you and move you to follow my decrees and be careful to keep my laws.

This promise is given as an assurance of Israel's restoration to a covenant relationship with God despite their great idolatry and rebellion. Their genealogy as descendants of Abraham neither prevented them from sin nor secured their destiny with God. An act of God was needed to purify and regenerate them, an act promised using the words "water" and "Spirit."

Because the phrase "water and the Spirit" in John 3:5 is (in the Greek) governed by one preposition (*ek*; ἐκ) denoting the source of the new birth, "water and the Spirit" should be read as denoting one concept, not two. For instance, the syntax does not support the interpretation of two baptisms such as water baptism and Spirit baptism. The one concept in view here would be God's promise of restoration to right relationship with him that he made through Ezekiel and other prophets (see Jer 31:31–34). As D. A. Carson explains, "'Water' refers to the eschatological cleanings accomplished through God's Spirit, and 'spirit' to the imparting of God's nature (i.e., what is born of the Spirit is spirit). Water and spirit together define the nature of the second birth that characterizes the promised new covenant; and this, Jesus tells Nicodemus in 3:10, his interlocutor should have known."[6]

What the Structure Means:
Reading the Gospels Today (Jn 3:1–21)

The issue of what Nicodemus could have been expected to know during his encounter with Jesus is a good example of a complexity we face when reading and interpreting the gospel accounts. All four of the Gospels were written decades after Jesus' earthly life, and were written for specific audiences with purposes relevant to those audiences in mind. The gospel of John was apparently the last to be written, after as much as six decades had passed. And so while all the ospels document the events and activities of Jesus' life lived in the first half of the first century, there is a second plane of history that forms a historical context for interpreters—the context of the Christian church for whom each of the gospels were written in the second half of the first century.

As demonstrated above, this distinction may limit the interpretive options. If we read Jesus' encounter with Nicodemus in the context of the time of the encounter during Jesus' life, Nicodemus and other people in the story could not have known about the still-future crucifixion and resurrection, or the establishment of the early Christian church and its practices. But John was writing several decades after Jesus' life, when the church and its sacraments of the Eucharist and baptism had been long practiced. It was written after Christianity was no longer thought of as a sect of Judaism but as a new religion rejected by the Jews but embraced by the Gentiles, who at that time formed the majority of Christian believers. And so, Does John write the story of Jesus to be read in its historical moment or in the later historical moment of his original readers, making allusions to baptism and the Eucharist plausible interpretations? Scholars debate this question, but the average reader should at least recognize the distinction as we interpret and discuss the gospel's story. John himself reflects this temporal distinction in his several references to the disciples not understanding in the moment but only later after Jesus' resurrection and the giving of the Spirit (e.g., 2:22; 16:4). The people who encountered Jesus during his earthly life were unable to fully comprehend his message in the moment; only by remembering Jesus' life after the resurrection did his meaning become clear. And so we learn that the resurrection of Jesus was not only a historical event, it was a *hermeneutical* event as well. Without his resurrection and the coming of the Spirit Jesus' life probably would have made little sense.

3:8 *The wind.* The word translated *wind* (Gk. *pneuma* [πνεῦμα]) can also mean "spirit" and "breath" in other contexts (which is also true of Heb. *rûaḥ* [רוּחַ]). It is probably one of the many wordplays in John's gospel. Jesus makes the point that while the wind is invisible it is nevertheless real and powerful, despite being discernible only by its effects, and it is not under the control of human beings. Wind is symbolic of the mystery of God's work in the Old Testament (e.g., Ecc 11:5). Just as Jesus may have alluded to Ezekiel 36:25–27 when mentioning "water and the Spirit," the play on the word *wind/breath/spirit* is plausibly an allusion to a few verses later in Ezekiel 37:1–14. There Ezekiel sees a vision of a valley full of bones when the Lord summons the "wind" (v. 9) to enter them as "breath" (v. 10) and they came to life again (v.

10)—a second birth—to fulfill a promise that the Lord would put his "Spirit" in them (v. 14). This is a prophetic vision of a second birth with which Nicodemus would likely have been well acquainted. And so when Jesus concludes, "So it is with everyone born of the Spirit," he is pointing Nicodemus to the fulfillment of a long-standing promise of a second, new life for God's people.

3:10 *Do you not understand these things?* Jesus apparently views his message of the new birth of God's people to stand in the same tradition of the prophecies of a future outpouring of the Spirit (Isa 32:15; Eze 36:27; Hos 1:10; Joel 2:28–29 and the apocryphal book Jub 1:23–28).[7]

3:13 *Son of Man.* This is now the second occurrence of Jesus' self-designation as Son of Man (see the commentary on 1:51 and 13:31).

3:14 *Just as Moses lifted up the snake.* This reference to Numbers 21:4–9 is the third time Moses is mentioned in the fourth gospel. During the exodus journey the Hebrews lost faith, complained bitterly, and spoke against Moses and against God. Then the Lord sent venomous snakes among the people, snakes who bit many and caused their deaths. When the people recognized their sin, Moses intervened. Then, "The LORD said to Moses, 'Make a snake and put it up on a pole; anyone who is bitten can look at it and live'" (Nu 21:8). The representation of what was causing their deaths became, by faith, the means of saving their life. Similarly, when the Son of Man was lifted up on the cross, "everyone who believes may have eternal life in him" (Jn 3:15). As Stan Harstine observes, "The introduction of Moses by name reinforces the veracity of Jesus' statements about rebirth: the law is not sufficient to save them from death," for Moses, the giver of the law himself, was unable to prevent their deaths.[8]

Although the snake imagery may be an affront to modern sensibilities, especially as a comparison to Jesus, at the time this gospel was written the symbol of the serpent, or snake, was associated with Asclepius, the Roman god of medicine and healing. That association is preserved even in our time by the logo of the American Medical Association, which portrays a snake coiled around a staff. In John 3:14 the primary intertextual reference to Numbers 21:8 happens to have been reinforced in Greco-Roman times by the imagery of the snake symbolizing healing and renewed life.[9]

The verb translated "lifted up" (Gk. *hupsoō* [ὑψόω]) in John 3:14 is significant. Another play on words, it has two senses: to physically lift something up and to exalt or glorify. John says Moses "lifted up" physically the snake in the wilderness, and the "lifting up" of the Son of Man refers to the cross. But John consistently speaks of Jesus' "lifting up" on the cross as one and the same as his exaltation and the way he returns to the Father (Jn 3:14; 8:28; 12:32, 34).

By doing this John alludes to the prophecy of God's Suffering Servant in Isaiah 52:13–53:12, especially 52:13 LXX: "Behold, my servant will be lifted up and highly exalted." Richard Bauckham comments on the glorification of Jesus in such a violent death: "John is not . . . suppressing the horror and shame in order to turn the death of Jesus into a glorious act of divine heroism. This would negate the whole purpose of John's use of the language of glorification, which is that the horror and shame of the event constitute the extraordinary lengths to which God's love for the world went."[10] This theological interpretation of Jesus' crucifixion as the clearest revelation of God's love and Christ's glory is unique to John's gospel. The Word became flesh through physical birth to a human mother, and he returns to the Father through physical death, thus sharing in the origin and destiny of all human beings.

To the Old Testament apocalyptic image of the Son of Man in Daniel 7 as "coming on the clouds," Jesus here reveals that the Son of Man has descended from heaven (Jn 3:13) and will return there via execution by crucifixion. To explain the significance of Jesus, John has overlaid three Old Testament texts without quoting any of them: Daniel 7:13–14, Numbers 21:8–9, and Isaiah 52:13. The fusion of these texts occurs solely through allusion and echo. Yet, as Richard Hays points out, "The theological result of this fusion is explosive: it generates an interpretation of Jesus' death on a cross as the triumphant exaltation of the Son of Man."[11]

3:15 *May have eternal life.* This is the first mention of eternal life, a major theological theme in the gospel of John. Where the Synoptic Gospels use the phrase "kingdom of God" to refer to the sphere of life under the reign of God, we find that phrase only twice in John, in 3:3 and 3:5. Here John makes the phrase "eternal life" equivalent to "kingdom of God," for as Bauckham observes, "The only two occurrences of 'kingdom of God' in this Gospel are early in the narrative, associated with 'birth from above,' and are followed by a transition to talk of 'eternal life' (3:3–16), which then becomes a frequent usage."[12]

3:16 *God so loved the world.* This is perhaps the most well-known verse of the New Testament, even among those who are not Bible readers. It is the gospel of Jesus Christ in a nutshell, a succinct statement of Jesus' mission in the world. God the Father sent God the Son into human history because God loves us. "For God so loved the world" is usually understood as a statement of the extent of God's love—that God loved the world very much. But the word translated "so" (Gk. *houtōs* [οὕτως]) is in the Greek an adverb meaning "in this manner" and referring back to the preceding thought. It can also indicate degree or extent.[13] In what may be another wordplay, John is saying that the *way* God loved us was by the lifting up of the Son of Man (v. 14) on the cross.

This certainly is also an indication of the *extent* of God's love for us. A father's sacrifice of his son is pictured in the story of Abraham and Isaac in Genesis 22, where the substitutionary nature of sacrifice is highlighted when God provides the ram. In the fourth gospel Jesus *is* the lamb that God provides.

May have eternal life. The Jewish expectation of the age to come was of a period of time in history when God would relieve his people of foreign oppression through the Messiah and prosper them beyond even the prosperity of King Solomon's time (1 Ch 22:10; Mic 4:4; Zec 3:10), for the Messiah's reign would last forever (2 Sa 7:13; Ps 89:36–37). But God had planned something much greater than even an everlasting geopolitical dynasty. All of the Gospels speak of eternal life after physical death: the Synoptics together total nine references (Mt 19:16, 29; 25:46; Mk 10:17, 30; Lk 10:25; 18:18, 30); the gospel of John almost twice as many, seventeen references (Jn 3:15, 16, 36; 4:14, 36; 5:24, 39; 6:27, 40, 47, 54, 68; 10:28; 12:25, 50; 17:2, 3). Jesus very clearly explains in this chapter that one is born again into eternal life through belief in him (Jn 3:12, 15, 16, 18) (see "Going Deeper into Believing in Jesus: John 2"). As Jan Van der Watt explains, "The fact that all believers are born of the Spirit, directly implies that they have eternal life. In other words, they share the qualitative life Jesus brought from God. . . . This type of life qualitatively corresponds to that which God possesses. . . . Eternal basically marks life as being of the quality or nature of above."[14] In John 3:16 the remedy for perishing after death is shown to be accepting God's gift of love through belief in the one and only Son (see 3:17–18).

What the Structure Means: The Role of Nicodemus (Jn 3:1–21)

Given the opening statement in 3:1, "Now there was a Pharisee, a man named Nicodemus who was a member of the Jewish ruling council," a reader might think that this narrative will be about Nicodemus. He was a member of the Jewish sect that was devoted to the obedience of God's law, the study of Torah, and he was a member of the council who ruled the Jews, albeit under the thumb of the Roman officials. We're told Nicodemus came to Jesus "at night," almost certainly a signal that despite being a Pharisee and a religious leader, Nicodemus was truly in the dark about the kingdom of God. Nicodemus greets Jesus respectfully, acknowledging Jesus as a teacher come from God by pointing to the signs for which Jesus is becoming famous.

Jesus replies with a very blunt statement that rejects the identity of mere teacher, even if one from God, and immediately challenges the Pharisee on a matter of central importance to Jesus: "No one can see the kingdom of God unless they are born again" (3:3). The rest of the narrative, through verse 21, continues the dialogue of misunderstanding between Nicodemus and Jesus about the nature of new birth into the kingdom of God. Although the discourse extends to verse 21, the last we hear from Nicodemus is his final question in verse 9: "How can this [Spirit birth] be?" The reader is left wondering whether Nicodemus ever did understand Jesus, and we hear nothing more of him until John 7:50, where in a meeting of Pharisees, he speaks up for Jesus.

Jesus replies with a rebuking question, pointing up the ignorance of "Israel's teacher" and his failure to receive testimony from the One God has sent (3:11). While the start of Jesus' reply to Nicodemus is clear and marked by an opening quotation mark, "You [sg.] are Israel's teacher . . .", Bible translators have a difficult time knowing where to end the quotation. Where does Jesus' direct address to Nicodemus end?[15] The second-person pronoun switches from the singular "you" to the plural in the Greek in verse 12. And from verse 13 through 21, only the third person is used and the tense switches to past tense, as if Jesus has stopped talking and the narrator is further unpacking the meaning of conversation. J. B. Lightfoot is among those interpreters who see 3:16–21 probably "as an elaboration, by the evangelist, of the import of that conversation."[16] See "What the Structure Means: The Ambiguity of Who Is Speaking (Jn 3:13–36)."

If this is the case, then Jesus' last word to Nicodemus in this conversation is a veiled reference to his crucifixion (3:14). Jesus rejects Nicodemus' identification of him as merely a teacher sent from God, and instead identifies himself as the Son of Man who has come down from heaven. Furthermore he states the necessity that he be "lifted up" just as Moses lifted the bronze snake in the wilderness. In keeping with John's habit of telling the readers more than is known by the characters in the story, that final enigmatic statement needs explanation, and so John continues for the benefit of his readers, "For God so loved the world. . . ."

Jesus clearly claims to be more than a teacher of Israel, but we don't know for sure that Nicodemus ever reached that understanding, even though he later helped prepare Jesus' body for burial (19:39).[17] And so Nicodemus stands as a very religious, well-educated person—the best religion could produce—attracted to Jesus but who never clearly came to faith. How many readers of John's gospel today can identify with him, those who admire Jesus but have not come to belief in God's one and only Son?

3:17 *God did not send his Son . . . to condemn . . . but to save.* Nicodemus recognized Jesus as a teacher who had "come from God" (Gk. *elēluthas* [ἐλήλυθας]; see 3:2). While that statement is true as far as it goes, Nicodemus did not realize that God had *sent* (Gk. *apesteilen* [ἀπέστειλεν]) Jesus for the mission of saving the world. Ancient Middle East culture, including Judaism at the time of Christ, knew the practice of the *sheliach* (שָׁלִיחַ), a word from the Hebrew verb *to send*. A *sheliach* (שָׁלִיחַ) was a person who had been designated as an agent and sent with full "power of attorney" for a given mission on behalf of the sender. The English word *plenipotentiary*, from the Latin *plenus* (full) and *potens* (powerful), refers to the modern form of this practice. When government leaders dispatch their designated "plenipotentiary, they are not just sending an agent to deal with foreign affairs but one having full power to act on the behalf of his or her country and government."[18] In the cultures of the ancient world, the *sheliach* (שָׁלִיחַ) was to be treated just as one would treat the sender himself.[19]

The *sheliach* (שָׁלִיחַ) sent by a king was to be received and treated as the king himself would have been treated. Inadequate treatment or mistreatment of the *sheliach* (שָׁלִיחַ) was cause for broken diplomatic relations between nations. In the ancient Greek translation of the Hebrew Old Testament, both the noun and verb forms of *sheliach* (שָׁלִיחַ) were consistently translated by the Greek words *apostellō* (ἀποστέλλω) and its cognates. John uses that same Greek verb *apostellein* (ἀποστέλλειν; to send) more than twenty-five times, most often to describe the Son's incarnation in human history. (Interestingly, the noun form of *apostellō* (ἀποστέλλω), from which derives the English *apostle*, is used only once in John's gospel [Jn 13:16], though it is used copiously in the Synoptic Gospels and Acts.) God sent Jesus with the full power and authority of the Godhead; to receive Jesus is to receive God. As Larry Hurtado observes, "Jesus' ministry provoked a crisis that had to do with his validity as one sent by God. Indeed given the apparent significance he attached to his mission, we could restate this crisis as precisely the question of whether he was the one now sent by God, for Jesus seems to have made response to his ministry the key factor in preparing for eschatological judgment."[20] How much more tragic the rejection of Jesus by the people he came to save becomes in light of this cultural background!

Going Deeper into No Other *Sheliach* (שָׁלִיחַ): John 3:16–17

Many people today describe themselves as "spiritual but not religious," usually in rejection of Christianity and other organized, historical religions. They seem to think that God is unconcerned with what they believe, perhaps as long as they have a sincerely held belief about the spiritual world. John 3:16 states that God sent his Son because of his love for the world and that trusting in Jesus, the incarnate Son, results in eternal life. "For God did not send his Son into the world to condemn the world"—even though the deeds of people are evil—"but to save the world through him." Jesus is God's *sheliach* (שָׁלִיחַ), his plenipotentiary, the fully authorized and empowered emissary to accomplish salvation. Jesus is not just a prophet bringing another message from God to the people, as Moses, Isaiah, Ezekiel, and the other prophets were. Jesus is the one, and the only one, who can close the deal that releases people from the sin and darkness separating them from God.

It is certainly common today, and perhaps it always has been, for someone who encounters the gospel of Jesus Christ to think that their response to Jesus is a neutral matter. But against the cultural background of the *sheliach* (שָׁלִיחַ), an encounter with Jesus is anything but neutral! To reject Jesus is to reject the God whose plenipotentiary he is; to accept Jesus and embrace his message is to reconcile one's relationship with the creator God of the universe. Whether one is aware of it or not, after an encounter with Jesus through the gospel no one leaves unchanged. One leaves either continuing under the condemnation of darkness or brought into the light by the truth (3:36). And so one must consider carefully one's response to Jesus Christ. There is no other *sheliach* (שָׁלִיחַ) of God.

3:22–4:3 *After this . . . Jesus and his disciples . . . baptized.* In this second half of chapter 3, John the Evangelist clarifies the relationship between John the Baptist and Jesus. John the Baptist was a religious leader with apparently great influence, even after his death. In fact, the Jewish historian Josephus records the belief that Herod's army was destroyed as God's judgment for Herod's execution of John the Baptist (*Antiquities* 18.5.2). John the Evangelist is believed to have written this gospel in or near Ephesus in the province of Asia where, decades after John the Baptist's death, there were still groups of the Baptist's disciples who had been baptized by him, presumably in Palestine (Ac 19:1–7). Furthermore, the apostles marked the time of Jesus' ministry from his baptism by John to his ascension, when they needed to replace Judas with someone who had been with them for that whole time (Ac 1:21–22).

John the Baptist was introduced in John 1:6 as a witness to the man who was the Word that became flesh, so that all might believe that Jesus is the light of the world (1:6, 8, 23). He administered a baptism of repentance in preparation of Jesus' announcement of the kingdom of God (Jn 1:23, 33). It is notable that the

Baptist had continued his own preaching and baptism for repentance even after Jesus had begun his public ministry. This suggests that the people who heard and responded to the Baptist were being prepared for reception of the gospel of Jesus Christ (see Ac 19:3–4). The primary purpose of the Baptist's ministry was revelatory—to identify Jesus from among all the Jewish men of that day when Jesus came to him to be baptized (see commentary on Jn 1:29–34). Apparently there was nothing visibly different about Jesus, the Word enfleshed—a mystifying idea, though consistent with Isaiah's prophecy of the Suffering Servant: "He had no beauty or majesty to attract us to him" (Isa 53:2).

In these verses (Jn 3:22–4:3) John the Baptist apparently recognizes the completion of his ministry of revealing the identity of the Messiah. He does not appear again as a character in the fourth gospel (though he is mentioned in 5:33 and 10:40). Therefore, what he has to say at the conclusion of his work is significant for understanding the identity of Jesus. As Lightfoot observes, "In 3:22–30 . . . the Baptist is the representative of the old order, as Nicodemus was in 3:1–15."[21] Therefore, chapter 3 marks the end of the Old Testament order, first, through Jesus' conversation with a prominent Pharisee about authentic spiritual rebirth and then with a clarification of Jesus' relationship with the last of the Old Testament prophets, John the Baptist. Just as the word of the Lord came to the prophets of old—to Samuel (1 Sa 15:10), Isaiah (Isa 38:4), Jeremiah (Jer 1:2), Ezekiel (Eze 1:3), Hosea (Hos 1:1), Joel (Joel 1:1), Jonah (Jnh 1:1), Micah (Mic 1:1), Zephaniah (Zep 1:1), Haggai (Hag 1:1), Zechariah (Zec 1:1), and Malachi (Mal 1:1)—the full and final Word of the Lord incarnate came to John the Baptist (Jn 1:29) so that John might reveal him to Israel (Jn 1:31). Thus the Old Testament age of the prophets came to a close when John the Baptist completed his prophetic mission of revealing the incarnate Word of the Lord to Israel. See "What the Structure Means: The End of the Old Testament Era (Jn 3)."

3:24 *This was before John was put in prison.* The last Old Testament prophet was imprisoned and executed by beheading (Mt 14:3–12; Mk 6:17–29; Lk 3:19–20). John's gospel doesn't record John's imprisonment and death but assumes its readers have heard about it. It is nevertheless an odd comment for those who already knew that John was never released from prison but died a prisoner, for of course these things *had* to have happened before his imprisonment. Could this remark have been somehow directed to contemporary disciples of John the Baptist who lived in Ephesus to teach that the Baptist submitted himself to Jesus, and so should they (Ac 19:3–4)?

3:26 *Everyone is going to him.* The jealousy and competitive spirit of the Baptist's disciples highlights the success of Jesus. John the Baptist knew that it was right for "everyone" to go to Jesus, for that is exactly why the Baptist was called to his prophetic ministry—to reveal Jesus, the incarnate Son of God to Israel, that all might accept his gospel. This implies that John's disciples and those like them viewed Jesus as merely another preacher like the Baptist. John does not tolerate that thought but in his final testimony in the fourth gospel explains once again Jesus' superior status in God's plan.

3:28 *I am not the Messiah but am sent ahead of him.* John the Baptist understood his role to be a precursor of the Messiah, as predicted in Malachi 3:1. The Baptist is the messenger sent ahead, and then suddenly the Lord will come to his temple, the messenger of the covenant.

3:29 *The bride belongs to the bridegroom.* Most likely, Jesus was never married during his earthly life (despite some recent arguments otherwise), but John the Baptist uses the metaphor of a bridegroom and his bride to explain why Jesus was gaining disciples while John apparently was not. This metaphor implies the role of Jesus as bridegroom to his disciples (see Mt 9:15; 25:1–13; Mk 2:19), a spiritual role that was later embraced by the church, which perceived itself as the bride of Christ (2 Co 11:2; Eph 5:21–31; Rev 19:7; 21:2, 9; 22:17). Given that John the Evangelist knows Jesus to be the Son of God incarnate, this metaphor is an extension of the Old Testament metaphor of God as the husband of Israel (Isa 54:5; 61:10; Jer 2:2; Hos 2:16–20).[22]

John the Baptist identifies himself as the "friend who attends the bridegroom" or what today we would call the best man at a wedding.[23] But in first-century Judean culture, the "best man" had a much greater role that began even before the couple's official engagement by conducting negotiations between the two families over the bride price. After a successful negotiation, the "friend of the bridegroom" escorted the bride to the groom's home, and organized and presided over the logistics of the wedding celebration (see Jn 2:8–9). So involved was the "friend of the bridegroom" that by law he could not enter into a marriage with the bride should the wedding under his oversight fail or not take place, to avoid suspicion of sabotaging the couple's relationship. His greatest joy was to see the bride and bridegroom be united with great rejoicing.

The Baptist explains his relationship to Jesus' disciples and the later church as analogous to that of the "friend of the bridegroom," a familiar term to the betrothal and marriage customs of that day that his disciples would comprehend. As Herman Ridderbos notes, "It is not merely with resignation therefore that John witnesses Jesus' success among the people; it is rather a sense of full and unmixed joy that fills him when he sees that his work of preparation has reached its intended goal. All that is now left for him to do is to withdraw like the friend of the bridegroom."[24] And this the Baptist does with his final statement: "He must become greater; I must become less" (Jn 3:30).

3:31–36 With verses 3:31–36 the same narrative uncertainty arises as at 3:16–21: Who is speaking? Some interpreters think these verses to be a continuation of the Baptist's words to his disciples, but more likely they are John the Evangelist's reflections on the Baptist's relationship with Jesus because they pick up some of the same themes and language used in previous chapters.

What the Structure Means: The Ambiguity of Who Is Speaking (Jn 3:13–36)

One of the notable features of the gospel of John is that it is sometimes difficult to tell where the words of Jesus end and those of the narrator begin—for instance, in 3:13–21 and 3:31–36. The ambiguity is worsened when Jesus speaks of himself using the third person, as he often does when referring to himself as the Son of Man. For instance, who spoke what is perhaps the most famous verse of the New Testament, John 3:16? Did Jesus himself say this, or do Jesus' words end in 3:15 and the narrator's begin in 3:16 to explain the significance of Jesus' words in 3:3–15? This ambiguous blend of direct speech and narration is found outside the New Testament—for instance, in Thucydides' *History* and in Plato's *Theaetetus*.[25] Both cases result in dramatic immediacy, producing the effect of the author as an observer of the dialogue, increasing historical reliability and erasing the narrator's voice "in order to allow later generations to hear the dialogue of Socrates [in the case of Plato's writings] as though it is taking place in their own presence, and as though they are participating in that dialogue."[26] Like Thucydides and Plato, John wishes to make Jesus more accessible to readers and to pull them into the presence of Jesus, as if we were ourselves listening to Jesus' conversations. This is no doubt part of what makes the gospel of John such an effective evangelistic tract, "that you may believe that Jesus is the Messiah, the Son of God, and that by believing you may have life in his name" (Jn 20:31).

3:31 *The one who comes from above . . . the one who comes from heaven.* Echoing John 1:14, John reminds his readers that Jesus is the one who has come down from above, from heaven where he was with God (1:1). This contrasts with the prophetic calling of John the Baptist and all the prophets before him, who were merely humans speaking a message God had given them. Jesus is therefore "above all" others and all earthly circumstances. Jesus too, like the Baptist, is a witness and testifies to the knowledge of heaven that can be revealed only by one who has come from there (cf. 1:18). Tragically, "no one accepts his testimony" (3:32), repeating Jesus' pessimistic view in 3:11. Jesus was not surprised at the rejection of his message by those to whom he was sent.

3:34 *The one whom God has sent.* Again Jesus is identified as a *sheliach* (שָׁלִיחַ; see commentary on Jn 3:17), sent by God and speaking the words of God. What God says Jesus says. What Jesus says God says. Within ancient Jewish tradition it was understood that God gave the Spirit to the prophets of the Old Testament in accordance with their mission and task (e.g., Nu 11:25–29; Jdg 3:10; 1 Ch 12:18). But Jesus, the Son of God, has been given the Spirit "without limit." Here again the evangelist presents a reason Jesus is superior to any of the Old Testament prophets, even the final of them, John the Baptist. This statement must figure into the doctrine of the Trinity, for if the Spirit is God's to give, and is given without limit to Jesus the Son of God, then there is a correspondence of limitlessness between Father, Son, and Spirit. John will develop the role of the Holy Spirit and his relationship to Jesus in subsequent chapters (see commentary on Jn 7:39; 15:26–16:15; 19:30, 34; 20:21–22).

3:36 *Whoever believes in the Son has eternal life.* John returns to belief in the Son as the basis for eternal life, first mentioned in 3:15–16. To believe the testimony and witness of the Son is to believe God, whose life is eternal. John develops the dualism of light and darkness by equating belief in the Son as coming to the light and rejection of the Son as remaining in darkness, which is here equated with the state of God's wrath. John mentions God's love often in his writings, but only once, here in this verse, does he bring up God's wrath. From here on, in the fourth gospel to be in darkness is to be in the place of God's wrath.

What the Structure Means:
The End of the Old Testament Era (Jn 3)

John's presentation of Jesus in chapter 3 announces the end of the Old Testament era. After Jesus revealed the dawn of the messianic age by changing water into wine (2:1–12) and announcing his own body to be the true temple and place of worship (2:13–25), John presents the ending of the Old Testament era in chapter 3. The sunrise of the New means the sunset of the Old. In the first half of chapter 3 Jesus' conversation with Nicodemus, the Pharisee and teacher of Israel, reveals that even the most devout and respected Pharisees did not understand the kingdom of God and Israel's need for rebirth, even to the extent it had already been revealed in the Old Testament (3:10).

In the second half of chapter 3, John reveals the last of Israel's long prophetic tradition, when the Word of the Lord came finally and fully to John the Baptist to be revealed to Israel as their Messiah and Savior. In first-century Judea, the beliefs and practices of the Pharisees and the word of the prophets were pillars of the Jewish religion. John shows the cataclysmic change brought by Jesus' appearance, not merely tweaking the theology and practices of Judaism, but fulfilling them such that the old ways could no longer stand. Jesus stood in continuity with what God had revealed in the Old Testament but was not just another prophet or rabbi expounding the Scriptures of Israel. He embodied God's Word within himself. Jesus taught an obedience to the Law of Moses that demanded an internal transformation that he described in the sweeping terms of a new birth. He observed the festivals of Israel but used them to explain the significance of his own life and ministry. He respected the temple and sacrificial system but rendered it defunct by the sacrifice of his own life. After thousands of years of Jerusalem's primacy for God's people, and within just a few decades of the end of Jesus' life, its temple was gone, destroyed by the Romans, and the followers of Jesus were drawn increasingly from the Gentile world, which had more tenuous connections to Jerusalem and Judaism. By the late first century, Christianity had largely lost whatever protections it enjoyed in its earliest days when the Romans considered it a sect of Judaism. This widening divide eventually made Christianity a religion distinct from Judaism, a religion that sometimes forgets its heritage in the Old Testament.

John 3 Through Old Testament Eyes

This chapter presents a number of Old Testament terms, concepts, and traditions that were transformed by the coming of Jesus Christ. One of the most important is the transformation of the Old Testament concept of the kingdom of the Lord into the transcendent realm of eternal life after death. Israel's concept of the kingdom developed from the monarchy of David and his son Solomon, with an expectation that one day the land of Israel would regain and exceed its former geopolitical prominence under the rule of the Messiah. This expectation was in the mind of Jesus' disciples when they asked him after his resurrection, "Lord, are you at this time going to restore the kingdom to Israel?" (Ac 1:6). An indestructible king raised from the grave would indeed make an invincible ruler of an earthly nation, and they can be forgiven for their misunderstanding. No one could have expected God to step into human history! And so even Jesus' handpicked apostles needed a transformation in their thinking, such as John presents in chapter 3. Jesus begins with a reference to seeing "the kingdom of God" (3:3) but defines entry into that kingdom only through spiritual rebirth (3:5). The kingdom of God is a place that one must be born into, and Jesus makes the point here that physical birth into the nation of Israel is *not* that birth. This is the last we hear of the "kingdom of God" in John's gospel, where it has been replaced in chapter 3 onward by eternal life based on belief in Jesus, the Son of God.

Similarly, the wrath of God, mentioned so frequently in the Old Testament as the consequence of Israel's sin, is mentioned only once in the gospel of John (3:36). The context shows that John considered everyone to have been living in the darkness with the wrath of God already on them (3:36). All are under God's wrath, but God nevertheless loves all (3:16). To save them from perishing God sent his Son so that all who believe in him will be delivered from God's wrath and have eternal life (3:15–16).

The concept of God sending his Son into the world as his *sheliach* (שָׁלִיחַ), or plenipotentiary, is one of John's major defenses of monotheism. This ancient Middle Eastern practice identified the sender with the one sent for all intents and purposes. By use of this familiar custom, Jesus could be identified with, yet remain distinct from, God the Father. An implication for Johannine soteriology is that the treatment of the *sheliach* (שָׁלִיחַ) was taken to be the treatment of the sender, and so the rejection of Jesus was in reality the rejection of God. Therefore, to accept Jesus was to accept God's gift of eternal life and to be reborn by water and Spirit (3:5).

The Old Testament background of the second birth that Jesus apparently expected Nicodemus to recognize is likely Ezekiel 36:25–27, triggered by the echo of water and Spirit in 3:5. This phrase alludes to that Old Testament passage with its promise that God needed to purify and regenerate a spiritually dead Israel. This was an act that only God could do, and no amount of Torah obedience or geopolitical national power could realize the second birth of God's people.

Chapter 3 also sees the development of the Son of Man title, Jesus' preferred self-designation, as John looks back on the crucifixion and ascension, superimposing echoes of Daniel 7:13–14, Numbers 21:8–9, and Isaiah 52:13. The Son of Man in the apocalyptic vision of Daniel 7:14 "was given authority, glory and sovereign power; all nations and peoples of every language worshiped him. His dominion is an everlasting dominion that will not pass away, and his kingdom is one that will never be destroyed." According to John, this Son of Man comes into his Danielic glory as the LORD's servant who suffered, was raised and lifted up and highly exalted (Isa 52:13), hinting early within John's narrative sequence at the crucifixion that would end Jesus' life. Of course, the original readers of this gospel most likely already knew that the story ended with Jesus' crucifixion, and John writes to explain the significance of that violent end. John understood the efficacy of belief in Jesus despite his violent end to have been prefigured in Numbers 21:8–9, when Israel was saved through faith by looking on the bronze snake that Moses raised up on a pole.

Without even one explicit quotation of the Old Testament in chapter 3, we can see nevertheless how thoroughly the Old Testament formed John's understanding of who Jesus is and the significance of his incarnation, death, and ascension.

JOHN 4

With the clearing of the temple (Jn 2:13–25) Jesus announced himself to be the true temple where efficacious sacrifice for sin was truly located. Here in the story of Jesus' encounter with the Samaritan woman at the well Jesus announces a closely related truth: that worship is no longer tied to a geographical location—Jerusalem or Samaria—but that worship is to be in him wherever his followers happen to be.

This epoch-changing announcement that the true worship of God is no longer linked to one physical location is accompanied by an invitation for people everywhere, from whatever religious or ethnic background, to worship God in Jesus Christ. Jesus demonstrates that invitation by opening his gospel to the Samaritans, who from that day forward could be among those saved by faith in Christ.

4:1–3 *Gaining and baptizing more disciples.* John reminds us that the Pharisees kept a watchful eye on anyone who was attracting a following. The crowds that Jesus began to draw caught their attention, as had the crowds following John the Baptist (Jn 1:19, 24). This is an ominous harbinger of the future indictment of Jesus by the Sanhedrin (Jn 11:45–54). To avoid prematurely encountering the Pharisees in Judea, Jesus returns to Galilee.

4:4 *He had to go through Samaria.* Samaria was the region of land situated between Judea to the south and Galilee to the north. It lay on the most direct route between Jerusalem and Galilee, but many Jews apparently avoided travel in that "unclean" region by taking a long detour around it to the east of the Jordan (cf. 4:9). Although in our English idiom "a good Samaritan" refers to an admirable person who has taken the trouble to stop and help someone in need (see Lk 10:30–37), this sense developed only after the gospel of Luke became influential in Western culture. To the contrary, at the time of Jesus there was great animosity between the Samaritans and Jews, and travel through Samaria would have been risky. The Samaritans were a people of mixed Israelite-pagan blood whose ancestry originated with pagan peoples brought into the kingdom of Israel after the Assyrian deportation of the ten northern tribes (see 2 Ki 17:24–40). The few Israelites left in the region were assimilated into pagan ways and, even centuries later at the time of Jesus, the Samaritan culture and religious practices were at odds with the worship of Israel's God. Nevertheless, according to John, Jesus "had to go" through Samaria—a divine providence no doubt that offered eternal life even to the Samaritans, the people the Jews at that time most loved to hate.

4:5 *Sychar, near the plot of ground Jacob had given to his son Joseph.* Memory of the ancient possession of this land by the ten tribes persisted (Ge 33:18–19; Jos 24:32), as this reference to the patriarch Jacob recalls the inheritance the Lord had promised in his covenant with Abraham (Ge 17:8–9; 48:22). Jesus walks on ground that had been given by his Father to ancient Israel's ten tribes. As Marianne Meye Thompson observes, "The Samaritans viewed themselves as descendants of Ephraim and Manasseh, the sons of Joseph, the beloved son of Jacob [Ge 48:5–7]. . . . The references to Jacob and his well, and to the land he gave to Joseph, remind the reader that this conversation takes place in territory once inhabited by the patriarchs—and that Samaritans and Jews share a common ancestry."[1] Has he come to claim his rightful inheritance?

4:6 *Jacob's well was there.* In the Old Testament the meeting of a man and a woman at a well was often the prelude to marriage (Ge 29:10–20; Ex 2:16–21). In John 3:29, John the Baptist had just referred to Jesus as the bridegroom.[2] Was this meeting at a well the prelude to Christ's encounter with his bride in Samaria?[3]

It was about noon. Scholars debate whether the several references to time in the fourth gospel are according to Jewish time, making "the sixth hour" about noon, or according to Roman time, making it about six in the evening, which would have been a more typical time for drawing water. Although many interpreters see the Samaritan woman's noontime appearance at the well as an avoidance of other women and an indication of guilt, that may be reading more than is intended. The Jewish historian Josephus speaks of noon encounters between Moses and the daughters of Jethro (Ex 2:15–21) and Jacob's midday meeting with Rachel (Ge 29:6–7). Neither of these encounters are understood to reflect on the women's character.[4] Instead, John may have reported the time of day of various events in his gospel to connote light and darkness, a major dualism throughout his gospel. In John 3:2, Nicodemus comes to Jesus at night in the dark, and in John 13:30, Judas goes out to betray Jesus at night, again in the dark. Assuming the Jewish reckoning of time from sunrise this woman encounters Jesus at noon ("the sixth hour"), the time of maximum light.[5] John may be inviting readers to contrast the *Jewish* Pharisee Nicodemus, a *man* who comes to Jesus in the dark and never makes a clear statement of faith, with a *Samaritan woman*, who not only opens her heart to Jesus but evangelizes her village as well (4:39).

4:7 *A Samaritan woman came to draw water.* In Jewish culture of that time a holy man would not allow himself to be alone with a woman to whom he was not related. Worse yet, she was a Samaritan woman, whom the rabbis considered perpetually impure.[6] And finally, she was a woman whose personal history suggested a questionable moral character[7] (see commentary on 4:15–18).

4:10–15 *Living water.* Just as in English idiom we speak of "running water," the idiom of that time, "living water," referred to fresh, flowing water, such as a spring, river, waterfall, or fountain (in contrast to water contained in a cistern or a dug well). Water is, of course, essential for life, and is used ubiquitously in religious ritual and metaphor, both ancient and modern. God's provision of water during ancient Israel's exodus journey expresses the omnipotent goodness of the Father's provision of life for his people (Nu 20:8–11).

Water has already figured prominently in the fourth gospel (Jn 1:26, 31, 33; 2:6, 7, 9; 3:5, 23). Here, Jesus asks the woman for a drink, the first clue that he transcends the schism between Jews and Samaritans. He then offers her living water, in contrast to the still water that fills the well shaft. She is amused at his offer, and observes that he has nothing with which to draw water from the well.

The reader is also invited to puzzle over the phrase "living water," which is not further explained until John 7:37–39, where Jesus identifies living water as a metaphor for the Holy Spirit (see also Isa 44:3; Joel 2:28–29; 3:18). Abundant, running water—often in the image of a river—is a biblical symbol of the fulfillment of all things, the restoration of Israel, and the presence of God (Ge 2:10; Ps 36:8; 46:4; Isa 32:1–2; 35:1–6; Eze 47; Joel 3:18; Zec 14:8; Rev 22:1–2).

On the contrast between Jacob's well and living water, Gerry Wheaton comments, "With the arrival of the Messiah, who brings the 'gift of God,' the former provision of the patriarch finds its 'telos' [or endpoint] in the lifegiving Spirit of God, a provision of a *different order of being*"[8] (see commentary on Jn 7:37–39).

4:12 *Are you greater than our father Jacob?* For readers who have been informed by the prologue of John's gospel, this is a deeply ironic question. The Word who became flesh is standing at the well dug by the patriarch Jacob.

Again by this we are reminded that there was nothing about Jesus' physical appearance that revealed his glory.

4:14–15 *A spring of water welling up to eternal life.* Here Jesus uses metaphor to speak in spiritual terms, referring to a thirst caused by humanity's separation from God (cf. Isa 12:3; Jer 2:13). Only eternal life can quench that thirst, and Jesus refers to the spring (*pēgē* [πηγή]) that never runs dry—that is, the indwelling Holy Spirit who secures those who come to faith in Christ. But the woman continues to think in physical terms of water to quench merely physical thirst.

4:15–18 *You have had five husbands.* Given that Jesus has broken a taboo about being alone with a woman, it would not be surprising that he summon her husband before continuing the conversation. Of course, by his divine insight he is also aware of this woman's past, and uses this to show her his supernatural nature. Jesus calls her out on the technical truth of her reply, "I have no husband," by which she hopes to evade his summons of the man she is living with. Notably he doesn't rebuke her sexual history (see Jn 4:17). There is nothing in the text that indicates the five men had divorced her, but even if they were all legitimate husbands who had died, more than three marriages for any reason was viewed as morally questionable in Jewish culture,[9] and presumably Samaritan culture did not look favorably on such a situation either. The past five husbands and her current situation of living with a man who is not her husband raises the question of her morality. Interpreters since the Reformation have not hesitated to label her "wanton,"[10] "mincing and coy,"[11] and immoral, labels that persist when this story is preached or taught today. But certainly this encounter is an example of 3:17, that Jesus did not come into the world to condemn but to save. As Janeth Norfleete Day reads it, Jesus may have referred to her relationships with men "because it most truly represents her life situation as the victim of a system that depersonalized her," and he is "expressing his compassion and concern for the suffering she has endured."[12] And as Robert Kysar points out, "Her sin (if it is such, and that is not entirely clear) is not the central feature of the conversation."[13] Jesus does not condemn her, and even allows her to continue the conversation in 4:19–26. While Jesus does confront her with her morally questionable situation, it is his supernatural knowledge of her situation that reveals his own abilities, a point not lost on the woman (4:19).[14] It is that revelation of Jesus' identity that leads to the central point of the entire chapter, the definition of true worship (4:21–24) (see "The Meaning of the Structure: True Worship (Jn 4:5–42)"). Notably, neither the woman's gender, nor her ethnicity as a

Samaritan, nor her unusual, if not promiscuous, sexual history disqualified her from receiving the gift of living water, and from becoming the first gospel fruit among the Samaritans (see "Going Deeper into Promiscuity and the Gospel: John 4:1–42").

4:21 *Neither on this mountain nor in Jerusalem.* Mount Gerizim was a place of early Israelite worship (Dt 11:29; 27:12; Jos 8:33). Later the Samaritans conducted animal sacrifice in a temple that had stood on Mount Gerizim until the Hasmoneans destroyed it around 110 BC.[15] The temple in Jerusalem was destroyed by the Romans in AD 70. Jesus dismisses worship in either place or any physical temple as a passing practice, for he himself is the new temple where the true worship of God must be practiced (see commentary on Jn 2:18–19). In Jesus' own body God dwelled on earth; Jesus Christ is the great priest who mediates between human beings and God; and Jesus is the full and final sacrifice for sin. All the functions of the ancient temple have been replaced by Christ himself.[16]

4:22 *Salvation is from the Jews.* Despite the failure of Pharisees, the most learned of religious Jews, to comprehend truly the revelation God had given them, Jesus nevertheless affirms that salvation is from the Jews, not the Samaritans. All the work that God had done and all the truth revealed in the Old Testament reached its redemptive culmination in Jesus Christ. Jesus did not reject the truths of Judaism, even though he was largely rejected by the Jewish people of his time. Throughout the fourth gospel Jesus is presented as utilizing the practices and institutions of Judaism to accomplish his mission, showing the intimate relationship between himself and God's redemptive work through Israel's history that culminates in his death and resurrection. This statement that "salvation is from the Jews" is the strongest affirmation of the value and importance of ancient Judaism in God's redemptive plan for humankind (Ge 12:3; Isa 2:3).

4:23 *Will worship the Father in the Spirit and in truth.* Using language reminiscent of Israel's prophets (e.g., 1 Sa 2:31; 2 Ki 20:17; Jer 31:31)—namely, "a time is coming"—Jesus adds, "and now is." Jesus solemnly announces that authentic worship is to be done "in Spirit and truth." Jesus indicates more than a merely temporal succession. Christ is opening a new way to the Father (cf. 14:6) apart from the temple sacrifices. The phrase "Spirit and truth" (both terms governed by one preposition *en* [ἐν] in the Greek) should not be understood as *two* modes of authentic worship, but as the one way of worshiping the Father that is mediated by the Spirit and practiced in the truth of Christ's redemptive work.

4:25 *"Messiah" (called Christ) is coming.* This nameless Samaritan woman apparently had some extent of religious knowledge, knowing the difference between the Jewish and Samaritan place of worship and here expressing belief in the coming Messiah. Note that John translates the term *Messiah* into Greek for his original readers, *called Christ.* By the time John wrote this gospel, Jesus was recognized as the long-awaited Messiah, yes, but as the Christ his divine identity was in view.

4:26 *I am he.* This is the first time in the gospel that Jesus uses the phrase "I am" (Gk. *egō eimi* [ἐγώ εἰμι]), a phrase for which John's gospel is known. An allusion to God's initial self-revelation to Moses in Exodus 3:14, the phrase "I am he" occurs in Isaiah 41:4; 43:10; 46:4; 48:12; 45:18; 51:12; Deuteronomy 32:39, translated in the Septuagint as *egō eimi* (ἐγώ εἰμι). The phrase is both a divine self-reference and simply an ordinary form of self-identification. As Catrin Williams observes, the phrase is "invariably, and progressively, accompanied by thematic and structural parallels to several Isaianic passages; this strongly suggests that John has consciously reflected on both the setting and significance of 'I am' as God's self-declaration, primarily in the Septuagint version of Isaiah. Consequently, the Johannine Jesus used the phrase as a succinct expression of his identity as the revelatory and salvific presence of God."[17]

Jesus came as the revealer of God (see Jn 1:18). Here, Jesus reveals himself only as the expected Messiah, with the full meaning and significance of that title to be developed later in the gospel. Although the Jews and Samaritans expected the Messiah, the revelation that the Messiah would be God himself in the flesh was totally unexpected (see commentary on Jn 6:35).

What the Structure Means: True Worship (Jn 4:5–42)

Although it may seem easy to make this story a morality tale, either condemning the assumed promiscuity of the Samaritan woman or exonerating her, her character is not the major point of the story. John includes this conversation to redefine what it means to truly worship God. He has shown that Jesus announced the messianic age and proclaimed himself the true temple in chapter 2. In chapter 3 John shows Jesus' ministry ends the old age of the Pharisees (Nicodemus) and the prophets (John the Baptist) while announcing the free gift of eternal life from God. In chapter 4 Jesus frees worship from a temple building in a specific location and from animal sacrifice, for his death on the cross will once and for all time secure redemption from sin. From the advent of Jesus Christ onward, true worship of the Father will be done in the Holy Spirit, the living water that bubbles up in believers unto eternal life (4:14) found only in the truth of the gospel of Jesus Christ.

Joseph Cahill presents a chiastic structure of chapter 4 that shows the central and major point to be the dialogue on true worship, as seen in table 4.1.[18]

Table 4.1. True Worship in John 4:5–42
    A. Meeting of Jesus and the Samaritan woman (4:5–9)
        B. Dialogue on living water (4:10–15)
            C. Dialogue on true worship (4:16–26)
        B'. Dialogue on true food (4:27–38)
    A'. Meeting of Samaritans and Jesus (4:39–42)

Although the morality of the Samaritan woman is not the central point of the passage, her encounter with Jesus is exemplary because it makes the important point that (1) women can directly receive living water from the Lord, a point that would have been controversial in the ancient world; (2) Samaritans are not excluded from receiving living water; and (3) even people with morally questionable personal histories are not disqualified from becoming a true worshiper of God.

4:28 *Leaving her water jar.* The return of Jesus' disciples interrupts the conversation, and their surprise at Jesus' violation of a social taboo probably prompted the woman to leave the scene. But the woman was apparently excited by her conversation with Jesus to the point that she abandoned a necessary tool for the essential chore of drawing water to run back into the village. This is reminiscent of the disciples leaving everything to follow Jesus (Mt 4:22; Mk 1:18, 20; Lk 5:11, 28), suggesting that the woman is on the way to becoming a disciple.

4:29 *Could this be the Messiah?* The townspeople apparently do not shun or dismiss the woman's testimony, indicating perhaps that she was not an outcast in spite of her apparent morally compromised life. Elisabeth Schüssler Fiorenza "draws an analogy between the woman's testimony as motivation for the Samaritans coming to Jesus and Andrew's drawing of Peter to Jesus by his confession that 'we have found the Messiah' (1:40–42)."[19] Her willingness to tell of her encounter with Jesus is another indication she is on the path to discipleship.

4:31 *Rabbi, eat something.* The disciples had returned from their food shopping, and naturally encourage Jesus to eat. Verses 31–38 form the second of the three major segments of this episode (first: vv. 1–30; second: vv. 31–38; third: vv. 39–42). The metaphors of eating and drinking are a sign of the messianic kingdom in the Old Testament (e.g., Isa 25:6; 55:1–3) and, not surprisingly, are prominent in the gospel of John. This is their first occurrence, where Jesus defines drinking and eating as denoting spiritual truth necessary for eternal life (see commentary on Jn 6).

4:34 *My food . . . is to do . . . and to finish. . . .* The odd thought that Jesus' food is *to do* God's will, especially following his offer of *living* water to drink, alerts the astute reader that drinking and eating are being used metaphorically to reveal a spiritual reality. In Jesus' statement something to eat is something *to do*, and for Jesus it is to do the will of the one who sent him—Jesus' frequent circumlocution for God—and to finish the work. This statement is likely an echo of Deuteronomy 8:3: "He humbled you, causing you to hunger and then feeding you with manna, which neither you nor your ancestors had known, to teach you that *man does not live on bread alone but on every word that comes from the mouth of the* Lord," a verse in Matthew 4:4 and Luke 4:4 that comprises Jesus' response to Satan's testing. Jesus is not diminishing the need for physical food to sustain physical life but points his disciples to that which nourishes a greater, eternal life—the very words of God.

He hints here that finishing God's redemptive mission is of greater priority to him than sustaining his own physical life, as he will later demonstrate on the cross.

4:35 *Four months until harvest.* The story of the Samaritan woman seems interrupted by this conversation with the disciples about harvest, but it is in this conversation that Jesus further defines the mission on which he has been sent and his disciples' role in it. The metaphors of harvest, sowing, and reaping are defined by the context of evangelism and conversion. The imminence of the harvest of which Jesus speaks may be another announcement of the eschatological age prophesied by Amos 9:13 (see also Joel 2:24; 3:18):

> "The days are coming," declares the Lord,
> > "when the reaper will be overtaken by the plowman
> > and the planter by the one treading grapes."

As D. A. Carson observes, "The colourful image betokens the blessing of miraculous and unceasing fertility and prosperity. Jesus may therefore be saying that the eschatological age has dawned in his ministry, in which sowing and reaping are coming together in the harvest of the crop, the messianic community."[20] Just as Jesus turns fishermen into fishers of people in the Synoptic Gospels (Mt 4:19; Mk 1:17; Lk 5:10), here he turns the sowing and reaping of the harvest into evangelism. As Gerry Wheaton notes, "The most striking feature of this metaphor is that it makes Jesus and his disciples part of the *same enterprise* as the 'others' who came before."[21] Jesus came *to finish* the work that God had been doing all throughout redemptive history (Jn 4:34), linking Jesus and his disciples to the promises and prophecies of the Old Testament regarding the restoration of Israel, the gathering of the nations, and the eschatological peaceable kingdom (e.g., Isa 11:6; 43:6; 65:25; Jer 21:10; 24:6, 7; Eze 34:23; 37:15–17; Hos 1:11; Am 9:11–15; Mic 2:12).

4:39 *Many of the Samaritans . . . believed in him because of the woman's testimony.* Jesus asked the woman to return with her husband (4:16), but instead she returns with the whole village (4:30), many of whom end up believing in him (4:39).[22] In this encounter Jesus shows his disciples what he means by sowing and reaping the harvest—evangelizing even people who are not Jews, even people who are not male. Now that he declared true worship of God to be independent of any one temple or location (4:21), people everywhere, even in Samaria, could be invited into true worship. Concurrently with that declaration Jesus shows the Samaritan woman her thirsty need for that true worship. "For those 'born of the Spirit' (3.8), who live in intimacy of relationship with God, true worship is found no longer in a specific sacred place, but rather through the believing community in whom the Spirit of Jesus abides (14.16–17; 15.26; 16.7, 14–15)."[23] And it appears no one is to be excluded from that community on the basis of race, gender, or past personal history.

While Jesus' own disciples are getting schooled, the Samaritan woman has actualized the work of evangelism, inviting her neighbors to hear her testimony and to accompany her back to the well to consider Jesus for themselves (4:29–30, 39).[24] While it would be overstating the case to call this unnamed woman an apostle, it is certainly an example for the male disciples that women should not be overlooked in their work, for women, even those with compromised morals, can respond in faith to the message of Jesus and become sowers and reapers themselves. The Old Testament preserves the stories of Tamar (Ge 38), Rahab (Jos 2), and Esther (Esther), all women steeped in scandal and yet used mightily by God.

4:42 *This man really is the Savior of the world.* Ironically, the first declaration within the gospel of John that recognizes Jesus as Savior comes not from his own disciples, nor from the learned Pharisee Nicodemus, and not even from the Jews, but from the half-breed Samaritans, the people the Jews of that time loved to hate. As Thompson points out, "*Savior* reflects an Old Testament designation for God that figures especially prominently in the second part of Isaiah (e.g., 43:3, 11; 45:15, 21–22; 49:26; 60:16; 63:8–9; cf. 2 Sam 22:3; Pss 17:7; 106:21; Jer 14:8; Hos 13:4). . . . There are also promises of the universal scope of God's salvation (e.g., Isa 45:21–22)."[25] The beginnings of the realization of the universal scope of God's salvation are seen here in John's gospel. Dorothy Lee explains, "The breaking down of sexual and racial barriers has disclosed a new and universal vision of Jesus."[26] He not only is the Messiah and Savior of Israel but invites the entire world into the community of those who believe in him.

Going Deeper into Promiscuity and the Gospel: John 4:1–42

The story of Jesus' encounter with the Samaritan woman, and through her, a Samaritan town presents the epoch-changing message that true worship of God is not confined to a particular people, nation, or sacred location. The coming of Christ to finish God's work on behalf of the human race opened up a universal invitation to all people. It is not insignificant that Jesus chose this particular Samaritan woman for his first contact with the Samaritans, and it is not insignificant that John chose to include this story in his gospel.

The Samaritan woman had three strikes against her according to the cultural norms of that day: she was female in a patriarchal society; she was a Samaritan, an unclean outcast in a Jewish world; and she was morally compromised by religious standards.

The text does not tell us whether the Samaritan woman was to blame for having had six men (Jn 4:17–18). By that count, Jesus was the seventh man to encounter her, and he will offer her perfect and complete acceptance that no other man could offer.[27] In a culture where women had little control over their own lives, she may have been a victim of coercion or exploitation. Regardless of how it happened, she had been a partner of several men and would have been viewed as a promiscuous woman. It is interesting that in our modern society it is not uncommon for a person to have several sexual partners throughout their life. A casual browse of statistics on the web indicates that in the United States the average is about seven, while in other parts of the world it is over ten. Some people are sexually abused as children. Some have one after another marriage sour and divorce. Some are unwillingly exploited by people in power over them. Everyone is constantly bombarded by messages and images of the oversexualized society in which we live. It appears almost impossible to reach midlife without being morally compromised.

The story of the Samaritan woman speaks a strong message of encouragement to people bearing the shame and guilt of moral compromise, whether it be as victims of exploitation or by their own doing. The gospel of John also includes the story of the woman caught in adultery (Jn 7:53–8:11) which, while not part of the original gospel, is probably an authentic story that found its home within the pages of John's gospel. Neither of these stories are found elsewhere in the New Testament, though Matthew's genealogy makes a point of including five woman who were also viewed as morally compromised and yet became part of Jesus' family tree (Mt 1:1–16). The story of each of these women indicts a man as well, for by its nature a man was involved in each case. Jesus did not condemn the Samaritan woman or the woman caught in adultery but received and forgave them, encouraging them on their way to a more healthy and righteous future. Even in light of these situations John tells us, "God did not send his Son into the world to condemn the world, but to save the world through him" (Jn 3:17). Moral compromise and sexual immorality do not disqualify one from becoming a disciple of Jesus, anymore than does one's gender, race, or nationality. Jesus came to save us from such sin and free us from its consequences. Jesus "had to go through Samaria" (4:4) to show us that his grace and mercy extend to all.

4:46 *Once more he visited Cana.* On Jesus' return from celebrating the Passover in Judea, where he cleared the temple (2:13–25) and conversed with Nicodemus (3:1–21), he stopped for a couple days in Samaria (4:1–42) before returning to Cana in Galilee. Cana was where he first revealed his power and glory and hinted at his identity by changing water into wine (2:11). Clearly John intends readers to understand the material between the first sign performed in Cana and the second sign as a unit.

In the second sign Jesus heals the son of a royal official who lay dying in Capernaum, a distance of about forty kilometers from Cana,. The power and glory that Jesus had revealed in the first sign is not limited to his physical presence, as the second sign proves.

In the unit of narrative that is framed by the first and second signs, Jesus has announced the true temple, the true birth, and the true place of worship, bringing the beginning of the end to the sacrificial system, the rituals of

Judaism, the prophetic age, and the constraints of one physical sacred space. But more must change now that Jesus, the Savior of the world, has come.

4:48 *Unless you people see signs and wonders.* God performed signs and wonders to display his power as he freed his people from Egypt (e.g., Ex 7:9; Dt 6:22; 34:11). Signs had been part of God's redemptive work in the Old Testament, and yet Jesus seems to rebuke the people of Galilee (the "you" is plural in Gk.) for their interest in signs and wonders. Moses also warned that signs and wonders could be used by false prophets (Dt 13:1–3; 18:20–22), so Jesus wants people who will not seek signs and wonders but trust in his word, as the royal official does (Jn 4:50). Christianity is based on the sign and wonder of Jesus' resurrection, but his disciples are called to take him at his word that trust in him is the way to eternal life. This second sign of a near-death healing signals a transition from belief in miraculous signs to a trust in the word of Jesus required for true faith. In this round trip from Cana to Jerusalem and back to Cana Jesus has revealed the true temple, the true birth, the true place of worship, and now the nature of true faith.

4:50 *Your son will live.* This first healing in the gospel of John is the second sign (4:54), reminiscent of similar healings performed by Elijah (1 Ki 17:19–22) and Elisha (2 Ki 4:27–37), but done at a distance and without touch. The encounter of Jesus with the royal official, likely an official of Herod Antipas, provides an example of taking Jesus at his word, just as the Samaritans had done (4:41). Almost paradoxically, in John's gospel faith based on seeing miraculous signs is inadequate faith, but it may be a first step toward believing without seeing (Jn 20:29). The signs are meant to lead to an accurate perception of Jesus' divine identity and authority, not simply a belief in his power to work wonders (see Jn 6:26–27) (see "What the Structure Means: Reading the Signs of the Fourth Gospel (Jn 2–12)").

Jesus' word alone should be enough to evoke saving faith, for Jesus holds all authority to do exactly what he says. He need perform no rituals, say no magic words, nor stir the emotions of a crowd to produce "faith." He need only say the word, "Your son will live," and a boy near death many miles away in Capernaum is healed. The first and second signs have in common the efficacy of Jesus' word. As Thompson notes, "In both accounts of signs done at Cana, Jesus' word brings about the desired result: he commands the servants to draw the water, and they discover it has turned to wine; he tells the official that his son will live, and the father discovers his son has been cured."[28]

The man took Jesus at his word. What was it about Jesus that the royal official should be convinced to take him at his word? Although the crowds may have sought signs, this father saw something in Jesus that allowed him to leave

Jesus' presence with no more than a simple statement. The man took Jesus at his word even before the healing was later verified. Recognizing the power and authority of Jesus' word is the basis of true faith in the gospel of John (see Jn 20:29). Ironically, the hated Samaritans and this royal official took Jesus at his word while the Pharisee Nicodemus failed to understand, and Jesus' own disciples were slow to learn.

What the Structure Means:
A Janus Passage (Jn 4:43–54)

In Greco-Roman mythology the god Janus was thought to be the god of beginnings and endings, transitions and doorways. He was sculpted to have two faces, looking both to the past and to the future. Biblical scholars recognize passages in Scripture that seem to have the purpose of bridging the thoughts of the previous material to what lies ahead, and refer to such a passage as a Janus passage. Such is John 4:43–54. It ends a section of material that began in 2:1, introducing the early days of Jesus' public ministry. The revelation of Jesus' identity is introduced with stories that show his authority over nature by changing water to wine; his authority over the religious establishment by clearing the temple; his authority to extend the gospel to those outside of ethnic Israel by evangelizing the Samaritans; and his authority to sustain life by healing the son of the official. With this introduction to Jesus, the story moves forward to develop these themes, documenting Jesus' teaching and miracles, and showing the varied responses Jesus evoked. Those who responded with faith are called his disciples; other responses eventually led to his execution on the cross.

Going Deeper into Taking Jesus at His Word:
John 4:43–54

Many years ago I worked with a man who was a devout atheist. Foolishly perhaps, I tried to tell him about God's love extended to us in Christ. I still vividly remember his forceful words: "If God exists, I demand he do a miracle right here and right now! And then I'll believe in him!" It is that attitude of making demands of God that is the opposite of faith. What kind of god would such a god be who meekly submits to the demands of mere creatures? Why worship a god we have control of? Seeking signs and wonders, and with the wrong attitude at that, is an attitude that prevents saving faith in Christ. For true faith is simply taking Jesus at his word, trusting him to do exactly what he says he will. He told the royal official that his son would live, and the son lived. Jesus promises any and all eternal life, an undeserved gift based only on trusting that Jesus can and will bring us through the experience of physical death and into an eternal existence with him and the Father. During his public ministry he did and taught many things intended to accredit his power and authority. And then he embraced a physical death of the most horrendous kind, coming out of the grave three days later to show he is capable of doing everything he says he will do.

It is right to pray in moments of great need, even as the royal official came to Jesus in desperation for his son's life. It is right to ask the Lord to heal and to save and to provide. But it is not right to base one's faith on whether God answers those prayers as we define, and even demand, our expectations to be met. Genuine faith is trust in God through Jesus Christ regardless of what God does or doesn't do for us.

JOHN 5

5:1 *For one of the Jewish Festivals.* Jesus habitually traveled to Jerusalem to attend the festivals as was expected of all devout Jewish men. Throughout his gospel John routinely uses the association of symbols and concepts of the Jewish festivals (or feasts) as the background for understanding the significance of Jesus' words and actions.[1] John does not mention for which of the Jewish festivals Jesus was in Jerusalem, but he does say that this episode occurred on the Sabbath, which is mentioned four times in the chapter. Sabbath was a weekly festival when all were commanded to cease work and celebrate Israel's covenant with God (Ex 20:8–11; Dt 5:12–15).

Table 5.1. Jewish Festivals in the Gospel of John

Festival	Old Testament References	References in John	Season
Passover	Ex 12:48; 34:25; Eze 45:21	2:13, 23; 6:4; 11:55; 12:1; 13:1; 18:28, 39; 19:14	Spring, possibly April
Tabernacles (or Booths; also known as Sukkot)	Lev 23:34; Dt 16:13, 16; 2 Ch 8:13; Ezr 3:4	7:2	Fall, possibly September
Dedication (also known as Hanukkah)	1 Mc 4:52–59; 2 Mc 10:5–7 (apocrypha)	10:22	Winter, possibly December
"one of the Jewish festivals"		5:1	
Sabbath	Ex 20:8–11; Dt 5:12–15	5:9, 10, 16, 18; 7:22, 23; 9:14, 16; 20:1, 19	Weekly celebration of the covenant

5:2 *Near the Sheep Gate.* This was an ancient gate into the temple precinct of the city. It was in the northern wall (cf. Ne 3:1, 32; 12:39). The pool of Bethesda may have been used for ritual cleansing before entering the sacred grounds, either for people or for sacrificial animals.

Surrounded by five covered colonnades. The accuracy of John's description has been verified by modern archaeology. Excavation located exactly where the fourth gospel indicated exposed four covered colonnades enclosing two pools separated by a fifth colonnade. During the reign of the Roman emperor Hadrian (AD 117–38) it was rededicated to Asclepius, the Roman god of healing, as an *Asclepeion*, or a healing sanctuary, verifying an enduring belief in its healing powers.[3]

5:7 *When the water is stirred.* A natural geological phenomenon may have caused water to bubble up from time to time from springs that fed the pool (as suggested by the name Bethesda, which may mean "house of the two springs").[4] The exceptional nature of the bubbling water, and perhaps the odor of the minerals they brought to the surface, may have led to the belief that the waters had special healing properties. In some manuscripts an explanatory note was later added attributing the stirring of the waters to an angel of the Lord. The note has been preserved in some older English translations as verse 5:4.

5:9 *At once the man was healed.* This is the third of the seven signs in John's gospel (see "What the Structure Means: Reading the Signs of the Fourth Gospel (Jn 2–12)").

The day on which this took place was a Sabbath. This is the first occurrence of the word *Sabbath* in John's gospel, and it introduces a major motif: Jesus' actions on the Sabbath provoke the Jewish leaders who view him only as a Sabbath-breaker despite the spectacular nature of what he does. This motif will play a major role in how John reveals the divine identity of Jesus, how he defends monotheism, and his narrative of what transpired that led to Jesus' execution.

5:10 *The law forbids you to carry your mat.* It is interesting that the Jewish leaders completely overlook the fact that a man who has been unable to walk for thirty-eight years is now *able* to stand, pick up his mat, and walk! Seemingly blind to that miracle, they are more concerned with what they perceive to be a violation of Sabbath rules. While the general command regarding the Sabbath is found in Exodus 20:10, the "law" mentioned may be a reference to Jeremiah 17:21–22: "This is what the Lord says: Be careful not to carry a load on the Sabbath day or bring it through the gates of Jerusalem. Do not bring a load out of your houses or do any work on the Sabbath, but keep the Sabbath day holy, as I commanded your ancestors."

Later rabbinic law actually mandated that life-threatening conditions should be treated on the Sabbath, but this man had been chronically ill for thirty-eight years; surely Jesus could have waited one more day! This may have been one reason John tells his readers of the thirty-eight years. Another may be that Jesus, with simply a word, is able to cure even hard and permanent medical conditions. Jesus seeks out those who apart from him have no hope for wholeness. The healing miracles of Jesus are a sign not just of Jesus' compassion and his divine abilities but also of the coming of the messianic kingdom (e.g., Isa 35:5–6). Ironically it is by obeying Jesus that the man is healed, yet in apparent violation of the old covenant.

5:12 *Who is this fellow?* The Jewish leaders confront the healed man, who defends himself by appealing to the authority of the one who told him to pick up his mat and walk. They want to know who it is who thinks he has the right to command a violation of the Sabbath. Was this "fellow" claiming an authority greater than Moses who gave the Law (see Jn 1:17)? But the question posed at a deeper level is exactly the question that John wishes to answer through telling his story of Jesus. Who *is* this who has power to heal and has an authority greater than that of Sabbath law?

5:14 *Stop sinning or something worse may happen.* Jesus associates sin with this man's illness, a commonly held presumption in the ancient world and sometimes in our own today. It must be admitted that one's personal sin can lead to various forms of suffering, but, as Jesus says elsewhere, not all suffering is the result of sin. The Old Testament also cautions against drawing lines too directly between personal sin and suffering and death (e.g. Ge 5; 11:28, 32; 25:8; 48:1; 49:33; 1 Ki 14:1, 4). At another healing of the man born blind (Jn 9), the question of sin is also brought up. There Jesus says, "neither this man nor his parents sinned . . . ," correcting the disciples' presumption of the involvement of sin (see commentary on Jn 9:2–3). Here in 5:14 it would appear that Jesus is warning the man that there is something even worse than being an invalid for thirty-eight years, probably a veiled reference to the eventual judgment of those who do not honor Jesus, as that topic follows in the immediate context (5:22–23). There is no hint that the healed man was awed by or even grateful to Jesus for his healing. Instead he throws Jesus under the bus, so to speak, by going to the Jewish leaders and reporting Jesus as the man who had commanded him to violate the Sabbath. By doing this he aligns himself with those who oppose and will eventually kill Jesus.

Going Deeper into Christians and the Sabbath: John 5:1–17

"Observe the Sabbath [i.e., seventh] day by keeping it holy," says the Lord (Ex 20:8; Dt 5:12). Right there, among the commands about not coveting, not killing, not stealing, not committing adultery, we find a command about how to observe every seventh day, based on the pattern set by God's own rest from creation (Ge 2:1–2). Why? Why does Sabbath keeping rank with killing, stealing, and adultery? Why is this one of the Ten Commandments? And how should Christians today obey it? Or should they decide not to?

Debate continues about not only whether and how Christians should observe the Sabbath but also about which day is to be considered the Sabbath (i.e., the seventh day). Is it the "day" from Friday sunset to Saturday sunset, as Judaism and Seventh-Day Adventists define it? Or is it the Lord's Day, Sunday, the first day of the week on which Jesus left the grave and had his first postresurrection meeting with his disciples (Jn 20:19, 26)?

And what should be done or not done on that day to keep it "holy," which means set apart for God? In ancient Israelite times when the commandment was first given, the day was to be set apart for God by ceasing from one's usual work. The cessation of work on the Sabbath, even during planting and harvest seasons, was the way one expressed trust in God for provision. It was a way of saying that we are God's people, supplied by his provision. It was a feast day celebrating the covenant God had made with his people, based both in creation (Ex 20:11) and in deliverance from slavery in Egypt (Dt 5:15).

Because Jesus Christ has fulfilled the covenant made at Sinai, some Christians feel no obligation to treat any day differently from others. The apostle Paul may be called to support that view in Colossians 2:16. Yet the concept of routinely ceasing work to express trust and gratitude for all God has done, most supremely on the cross of Christ, is not obsolete. While it would be wrong for a Christian to adopt the 613 Jewish *mitzvot* (commandments), the Sabbath *principle* seems to reflect something profound and permanent about our relationship with the Lord. The willingness to stop working for a day not only expresses trust that God will provide but also reflects concern about his creatures' health and well-being, for even the foreigner, the slaves, and the draft animals were to enjoy the rest God commanded. And although Christians met for worship in the ancient world long before the modern concept of the weekend was adopted, in cultures under Judeo-Christian influence, it became a practical convenience that Sunday was available for Christians to meet unencumbered by other responsibilities. In our modern 24/7 society that custom has all but disappeared.

And so while Christians are not required to observe a Sabbath with specific regulations, the place of Sabbath in the Ten Commandments and Jesus Christ's fulfillment of what Sabbath pointed to provide ample reasons to live thoughtfully in ways that reflect our relationship with God every seventh day.

5:16–17 *Because Jesus was doing these things on the Sabbath, the Jewish leaders began to persecute him.* In verses 5:16–30 John defines Jesus as God while simultaneously upholding the monotheism that was at the heart of Judaism. John approaches this topic by recalling Jesus' provocative "work" done on the Sabbath and his claim that his relationship with God entitled him—in fact *required* him—to do the things he did on the Sabbath. Judaism of that day understood that God worked on the Sabbath to sustain an orderly creation (cf. Dt 12:10). Therefore, as Dorothy Lee observes, "Jesus' breach of the Sabbath reveals not that he has broken the Law, but that he is engaged in carrying out the Sabbath work of God." His action "in some way transcends the normal Sabbath regulations. John's claim here is that Jesus shares the same divine exemption."[5] (Regarding Old Testament monotheism, the Father, and Jesus, see "What the Structure Means" in the introduction.)

5:18 *They tried all the more to kill him.* Jesus' defense for healing the man on a Sabbath was that he was doing the work of God, his own Father. This opened him to the charge of blasphemy, one of the most serious sins in the Old Testament and punishable by death (Ex 22:28; Lev 24:16). Blasphemy is speech that denies and mocks God's sovereignty as Creator, violating the creature-Creator distinction (note 1 Ti 1:13, where the apostle Paul describes himself as a former blasphemer). Jesus' reference to the Creator God being his own Father would be the supreme blasphemy were it not true. This episode begins a new segment of John's gospel by showing the Jewish leaders' hostility to Jesus' claims, a subject that will run throughout Jesus' public ministry until the raising of Lazarus in chapter 11, when their hostility gels into a plot to kill him. See commentary there.

5:19 *Whatever the Father does the Son also does.* The concurrence of Jesus' actions with the Father's goes beyond his model of filial loyalty and piety as portrayed in the ideal son of Proverbs (1:8; 2:1; 3:1; 4:1; 5:1; 7:1; 10:1; 15:20).

Having made himself equal to God in the eyes of the Jewish leaders, Jesus begins in verses 5:18–30 to explain that he is not another, independent god, but is one with God the Father. His explanation here is the foundation of John's defense of monotheism. As Marianne Meye Thompson writes, "The rest of chapter 5 contains this Gospel's most theologically packed account of Jesus' identity with respect to God."[6]

5:21 *Just as the Father raises the dead.* Although the Old Testament does not present a clear doctrine of the resurrection of the dead, passages such as the promise that the dead will live in Isaiah 26:19, Ezekiel's vision of the dry bones (Eze 37), Job's belief in a coming redeemer (Job 19:25–27), and Daniel's vision of multitudes rising from their graves (Da 12:2) have been interpreted to suggest some form of an afterlife. During the intertestamental period the belief in an afterlife for individuals developed during the time of great persecution of the Jews by the Hellenistic king Antiochus (e.g., 2 Mc 7, esp. vv. 9, 14, 23). By the time of Jesus, belief in a general resurrection "at the last day" in which individuals would participate was current (see Jn 11:24). It was understood that it was God himself who would raise the dead.

The Son gives life. Jesus' claim to be the Son of God is accompanied by his claim that he gives life to whomever he pleases and will raise them at the last day (5:25, 28–29). And so the Word who became flesh reveals his own role in the resurrection of the dead, further developing the belief in the afterlife to require also a belief in the Son of God. What Jesus declares here in chapter 5 he will demonstrate by the sign in chapter 11 of raising Lazarus to life after four days in the tomb, proving that he is capable of doing just as he says he will do. Thompson draws an interesting and important distinction:

> To raise the dead means to bring dead bodies to life; to "give life" [in John] means to grant knowledge of God so that one may participate, forever, in God's own life (17:3). Not all the dead who are raised finally receive eternal life (5:29). Eternal life properly belongs to the time following the resurrection, but it is experienced in the present as fellowship with the life-giving God (17:3). Jesus has the twin powers to give eternal life (5:24–25) and to call the dead out of the tombs (v. 28); the latter power will be demonstrated in Jesus' raising of Lazarus, which in turn foreshadows and guarantees Jesus' power to grant eternal life.[7]

5:22 *The Father . . . has entrusted all judgment to the Son.* God's role as the ultimate Judge of all human beings is agreed by both the Old Testament and the New (Ge 18:25; Ps 96:10; Isa 33:22; Heb 12:23; Jas 4:12; 1 Pe 1:17). His role as Judge emerges from his role as Creator, who possesses the authority, omniscience, omnipotence, righteousness, and, most thankfully, love to judge rightly. The *telos* of God's judgment is justice as only God can know and execute it. It is astonishing that "the Father has entrusted all judgment to the Son" (Jn 5:22), as that divine prerogative puts Jesus Christ in a unique intermediating role between God and humankind.

Judgment by God was understood to decide one's fate either for resurrection to life or resurrection to condemnation, and so judgment and the afterlife have been closely associated in the Judeo-Christian tradition. John explains that Jesus claims not only the life-giving power of God but also the authority to judge between those who will rise to live with God and those who will rise to condemnation (5:28–29). While Judaism considered the basis of this judgment to be compliance with the Law of Moses, Jesus reveals the basis of his judgment: belief in his word, the revelation he came to bring (5:24). In fact, those who believe him are said to have already crossed over into life after death (5:24).

5:23 *Whoever does not honor the Son.* This belief in Jesus' word is described here as honoring the Son just as one honors the Father. This is the basis of the earliest worship of Jesus, "not because early Christians felt at liberty to do so, but because they felt required to do so by God. They reverenced Jesus in observance of God's exaltation of him and in obedience to God's revealed will."[8]

The Father, who sent him. The oneness of the mission of the incarnate Son and God the Father is expressed through the ancient cultural concept of the *sheliach* (שָׁלִיחַ; one who is sent). In later rabbinic texts the *sheliach* (שָׁלִיחַ) "represents 'the one who sent him' in a legally binding relationship, authorized to carry out a specific commission on behalf of the sender, so that 'a *saliah* [שָׁלִיחַ] is as the one who sent him.'"[9] The one who is sent is to be regarded just as the one who has sent. In this context, Jesus was sent by God, so the Son of God should have been received and honored as God the Father himself. For John, "Jesus' actions embody or incarnate the work of the Father. They are the means through which God's life giving work is realized in this world. . . . God is presented to the world by the one whom he has sent. . . . (5:19–21, 36; 10:25, 32, 37–38)"[10] (see commentary on Jn 3:17).

Jesus explains to the Jewish leaders, and indirectly to John's readers, that the work he has been sent to do is "the eschatological work of God—judging and giving life—which is radically present in the Sabbath activities of Jesus (Jn 5:24–27)."[11] Therefore, when Jesus acts on the Sabbath he is not guilty of violating the Sabbath but, to the contrary, is *fulfilling* all that the Sabbath pointed to under the old covenant.

5:24 *Hears . . . and believes . . . has eternal life.* Authentic faith according to the gospel of John is not based in witnessing the miracles Jesus did, but in believing Jesus' word that he is who he says he is, and trusting that he will do just as he says he will. This continues the concept of faith as trust in God that is the basis of humankind's relationship to God as described in the Old Testament. Abram *believed* God and it was credited to him as righteousness (Ge 15:6; Ro 4:3; Gal 3:6; Jas 2:23). Even the whole system of animal sacrifice in the temple was based on the belief that God would indeed accept the sacrifices he had commanded; that his word and character are trustworthy. The New Testament continues that idea of trusting God but with a specific focus on trusting in the atoning sacrifice of Jesus on the cross.

Jesus here explains that whoever hears his words and believes God the Father who sent Jesus has eternal life. Notably Jesus did no spectacular miracle among the Samaritans beyond demonstrating an unusual knowledge of the Samaritan woman's past personal history. Yet "because of his words" (4:41) they became believers who recognized him as "Savior of the world" (4:42). Their openness to believing Jesus stands in contrast to even his own disciples who, like Thomas, refused to believe without seeing (Jn 20:24–29). But Jesus pronounced a blessing on those who have *not* seen and yet have believed. We, too, are called to believe the message of the Word who became flesh and are blessed with eternal life when we do.

Has crossed over from death to life. The life one receives from Jesus is continuous with this earthly life, but qualitatively different as well. Jan Van der Watt explains, "Passing from death to life in 5:24 implies moving to another state of being where existence and relations within the divine sphere become a reality." [12] Human beings received life from God's breath at creation; they receive life from God's Spirit upon being born from above (see commentary on Jn 3:4, 5, 8). "The nature of the birth and consequent existence depend on the source (*ek*) from which the birth is initiated. The fact that all believers are born of the Spirit, directly implies that they have eternal life. In other words, they share the qualitative life Jesus brought from God." [13]

5:27 *Because he is the Son of Man.* This is a clear allusion to Daniel 7:13–14: "In my vision at night I looked, and there before me was one like a son of man. . . . He was given authority, glory and sovereign power; all nations and peoples of every language worshiped him. His dominion is an everlasting dominion that will not pass away, and his kingdom is one that will never be destroyed" (also see commentary at Jn 1:51 and 13:31).

5:28 *All who are in their graves will hear his voice.* Compare Daniel 12:2: "Multitudes who sleep in the dust of the earth will awake: some to everlasting life, others to shame and everlasting contempt."

5:30 *My judgment is just.* Jesus aligns himself as judge with the Father's role as Judge (e.g., Ge 18:25; Dt 32:4; 2 Ch 19:7; Job 8:3; Ps 58:11; Da 7:9, 10, 13–14) (see commentary on 5:22).

5:31 *If I testify about myself.* Verse 31 begins the third segment of this chapter by introducing testimonies about Jesus to verify his identity (see "What the Structure Means: Jesus Heals on the Sabbath (Jn 5)"). This segment introduces an almost courtlike scene suggesting a trial with witnesses brought forth to establish the truth. The Old Testament law calls for at least two or three witnesses to testify regarding any crime (Dt 19:15; also Dt 4:26; 17:6–7; 30:19). The crime in question here is blasphemy. Jesus did not come in a vacuum, so to speak, but points the Jewish leaders to four witnesses that should have prepared them for the claims he makes here: John the Baptist, the nature of the works Jesus does, the Father himself, and the Scriptures, especially Moses.

5:33 *John . . . has testified to the truth.* When John the Baptist was baptizing people in the Jordan River, the Jewish leaders had inquired of him whether he was the Messiah (Jn 1:19–28). The fact that John could have been mistaken to be the Messiah shows his unusual quality and credibility. John denied being the Messiah but pointed the Jewish leaders to Jesus, whom God had identified to John as his "Chosen One" (Jn 1:29–34). Why, Jesus asks, do they not believe the answer John the Baptist gave them?

5:36 *The works . . . testify.* The nature of the works Jesus did were not only great miracles but also signs that resonated with characterizations of the Messianic age found in Old Testament promises for peace, health, and abundance (Isa 35:5–6; 55:1–3). As the debates about who Jesus is develops in John's gospel, some are convinced by these signs to believe in Jesus, at least as the Messiah if not as Son of God (cf. Jn 7:31).

5:37 *The Father . . . has himself testified concerning me.* God himself is a witness corroborating Jesus' claims, though when and how is not made explicit here. John's gospel does not include the baptism of Jesus as do the Synoptic Gospels, where God speaks from heaven during Jesus' baptism: "This is my Son, whom I love. Listen to him" (Mk 9:7; also Mt 17:5; Lk 9:35). But this gospel does include John the Baptist's testimony that he saw the Spirit come down from heaven as a dove and remain on Jesus, identifying the one who would baptize with the Holy Spirit (Jn 1:32–34). Furthermore, Jesus' authority to judge and his power to give life were God-given, and Jesus would demonstrate them throughout his public ministry as claims of God's own testimony about him.

5:39 *The very Scriptures . . . testify about me.* The Jewish leaders were Hebrew Bible readers (Jn 5:39) and no doubt could have quoted much of it from memory. In their search for eternal life within its pages, however, they misread its revelation. To be fair, though, reading Israel's messianic hope for life and prosperity as a geopolitical, this-worldly expectation is understandable, for how could anyone have imagined the resurrection? Jesus is the fulfillment of all the old covenant promises for forgiveness for sin and life in a new age (Dt 32:39; 1 Sa 2:6; Hos 13:14; Isa 25:8; 26:19; Eze 37:1–10; Da 12:2). Though he offered so much more than what they sought, they refused to come to him to have life (for further discussion of the Messiah in John see commentary on Jn 1:20, 41, 49; 2:17; 3:3; 6:15; 7:42; 12:13–15).

5:45 *Your accuser is Moses, on whom you set your hopes.* Precedent for Moses and his Law being a source of indictment against Israel is found, for example, in Deuteronomy 31:19, 26–27.

5:46 *If you believe Moses, you would believe me.* This is the fourth of twelve times Moses is mentioned in the gospel of John. In Judaism there was, and is, no greater prophet than Moses, who enjoyed a close, unprecedented fellowship with God. Moreover, it was Moses who had given the fourth commandment, about the Sabbath day, and therefore it was Moses' authority the Jewish leaders implicitly invoked when they accused Jesus of violating Sabbath. But Jesus turns the tables on them. As D. A. Carson so aptly explains, "[The Jewish leaders] take [the Law] as an end in itself, the final epitome of right religion, and not, as Jesus insists it was, as witness to Christ himself. If scrupulous adherence to the law brings people to hope for salvation in the law itself, and to reject the Messiah to whom the law pointed, then the law itself, and its human author, Moses, must stand up in outraged accusation."[14]

Both deep irony and deep theological truth are in Jesus' accusations against the Jewish leaders. They, in truth, did not keep the law and sought ways around it, especially the Sabbath laws. They were themselves guilty of the very charge they brought against Jesus. But more importantly, because they did not truly understand God's purposes for giving the law and the sacrifices, they missed the redemptive nature of the covenant and ironically failed to recognize the Messiah they had been expecting.[15]

The chapter ends with Jesus turning the charge of violating the law against his accusers and presenting the witnesses they should have listened to. The confrontation precipitates increasing hostility toward Jesus that will ultimately lead to his execution not in spite of but because he was the Messiah, the Son of God.

What the Structure Means:
Jesus Heals on the Sabbath (Jn 5)

Chapter 5 is foundational for understanding the following chapters in the story of Jesus. It is composed of three segments:

Segment 1: 5:1–15, the healing of a man on the Sabbath

Segment 2: 5:16–30, the response of wishing to kill Jesus because he claims the authority and power of God, even to raise the dead

Segment 3: 5:31–47, testimonies about Jesus

The works Jesus did on the Sabbath were not violations of but fulfillments of all that Sabbath promised. Ancient Israel's cessation from work on every seventh day was an acknowledgment of dependence on the Creator for well-being (Ex 20:11) and redemption (Dt 5:15). Sabbath-keeping was a sign of allegiance to God's covenant (Ex 31:13; Isa 56:4; Eze 20:12, 20) that became symbolic of well-being and rest from enemies (Dt 12:10; Ps 95:11). Sabbath rest took on eschatological aspects beyond the weekly ritual (Isa 56:4–8; 58:13–14) and in the New Testament came to represent the state of salvation (Heb 4:1–11), in which there was healing, peace, and freedom from death. Jesus' healing acts on the Sabbath point to his fulfillment of covenant promises. The reaction of the Jewish leaders that sees only a technical violation of Sabbath ritual shows their deep misunderstanding of God's purposes for the outworking of the covenant.

When confronted, Jesus claims God as his Father, and claims that his work and God's work are the same. "Like father, like son," as the saying goes. This was understood to be a direct claim of deity that deeply offended the Jewish leaders. Their (self-)righteous response to what they believed to be blasphemy was a desire to kill Jesus. What is first stated in 5:18 is successfully carried out in chapter 19. Everything in between is presented to the reader as evidence that one must either accept that Jesus is who he claims to be, resulting in faith, or reject his claims, resulting in agreement with the Jewish leaders. In the end, Jesus was executed for being exactly who he said he was.

The third segment, 5:31–47, evokes the image of a court of law where testimony is heard and weighed to establish innocence or guilt. Jesus raises the topic of testimony, in effect putting the Jewish leaders on trial. Have they not believed the testimony of John the Baptist? Or that of the spectacular works that Jesus did? Of Moses and their own Scriptures? If they have not believed these testimonies, then whence comes their authority to be religious leaders in Jerusalem? Clearly they have not believed rightly, or they would have accepted Jesus' claims and recognized who he was (5:45–47).

There is genius in the movement of 5:19–47. "In the first part Jesus is revealed as judge of the world (vv. 19–30); in the second he becomes the one who is on trial (vv. 31–32); in the third he turns the tables on his opponents and pronounces judgment against them (vv. 45–47). The role reversal from judge to accused to judge again acts with the realism of drama."[16]

As Dorothy Lee points out, "John 5 therefore demonstrates a completely different narrative response to Jesus. While the narrative of John 3 is about the indecision of Nicodemus contrasted with the faith of John the Baptist, and the story of the Samaritan woman demonstrates the development of mature faith, the healing in John 5 is primarily about unbelief and rejection."[17]

The tragic irony of Jesus' execution is revealed early in John's telling of the gospel story. As readers continue through chapters 6–18 they must consider the evidence John presents about Jesus. By the story's end, will readers believe the claims of Jesus, or reject him?

JOHN 6

6:1 *Jesus crossed to the far shore of the Sea of Galilee (that is, the Sea of Tiberias).* Jesus grew up in Galilee and spent much of his public ministry there, especially around the Sea of Galilee. John includes its newer, alternate name, the Sea of Tiberias, named for a Roman city built on its western shore by Herod Antipas in honor of the Roman emperor Caesar Tiberias (see v. 23). The "far shore" was considered to be the eastern shore.

6:4 *The Jewish Passover Festival was near.* Passover (Ex 12) was arguably the most important feast at the time of Jesus. It was one of three feasts when all adult men were expected to travel to Jerusalem, swelling the population of the city and causing the Romans to be especially wary of possible revolts. During Roman occupation, Passover took on nationalistic overtones, since it celebrated the release of the Israelites from Egyptian slavery and the establishment of ancient Israel as a nation. It is notable both that Jesus is not heading to Jerusalem, and that five thousand men traveled to him (6:5) rather than to the temple in Jerusalem (see commentary on 6:15). This scene pictures the fulfillment of the prediction Jesus had recently made to the Samaritan woman in 4:21 about the place of worship.

6:5 *Bread for these people to eat.* Jesus asks Philip, who was from nearby Bethsaida (Jn 1:44), where they might get food for the crowd.

6:7 *More than half a year's wages.* This phrase translates a reference to two hundred denarii. A denarius was the going rate for a day's wages, so the magnitude of the need is huge.

6:9 *Five small barley loaves and two small fish.* Barley bread rather than wheat bread was the staple of the poor. In contrast to the magnitude of the need in 6:7 the available resources were ridiculously inadequate.

6:10 *There was plenty of grass.* This is the only miracle reported in all four Gospels. The scene may echo Psalm 23 (v. 2, "He makes me lie down in green pastures"). The shepherd/sheep metaphor will become prominent later in John's gospel (see commentary on Jn 10). The major point of Psalm 23 is that the Lord supplies all the needs of those who are his. Jesus is about to teach the people their greatest need.

About five thousand men were there. Why were these five thousand men, as well as women and children, seeking Jesus rather than heading to Jerusalem? See 6:15.

6:11 *Jesus took the loaves, gave thanks, and distributed. . . .* The conventional Jewish prayer of thanksgiving was "Blessed are you, O Lord, our God, King of the universe, who brings forth bread from the earth" (Mishnah Berakot 6:1).[1] The words of the later Christian Eucharist, or Holy Communion, echo this miracle of Jesus.

6:13 *Gathered and filled twelve baskets.* This is the fourth of the signs of John's gospel (see "What the Structure Means: Reading the Signs of the Fourth Gospel (Jn 2–12)"). The amount of leftovers after thousands of people had eaten their fill attests to the magnitude of the miracle. Superabundant provision is characteristic of Jesus, as in the abundant wine he provided at Cana (Jn 2), and of the messianic banquet (Ps 23:5; Isa 25:6; Eze 34:14). The *twelve* baskets is likely a subtle pointer to the twelve tribes of Israel that are being reconstituted through the mission of the twelve apostles bringing those who would follow Jesus into the church. The gathering of the leftover miraculous bread, apparently for a later distribution, may suggest that the bread of life is distributed through the apostolic ministry that establishes the Christian church. This is possibly an allusion to the Eucharist or Holy Communion, when those who believe in Christ feed from his body and blood.

6:14 *Surely this is the Prophet.* The people clearly have in mind how Moses provided manna for their ancestors in the wilderness, and remember his promise of Deuteronomy 18:15–18, that God would raise up another prophet like him. Jesus fulfills this prophecy, but is more than any prophet.

6:15 *Jesus, knowing that they intended to . . . make him king by force.* It was near Passover, the festival that commemorated victory over the oppression of

Egypt. Because of that, the festival had accrued nationalistic overtones during times of occupation by both the Greeks and later the Romans. It was a small step from seeing Jesus as a second Moses to seeing him as a rising leader of Israel who might fulfill messianic expectations of another liberator. The presence of five thousand men would make a great military force had Jesus chosen to lead them into Jerusalem under the cover of Passover. If Jesus wanted to be an earthly leader against Rome's rule, here was his big opportunity. But the people's intent to rally around Jesus for political purposes was not an act of faith but a failure to see who Jesus truly was. Jesus knew that his kingdom was not of this world (Jn 18:36). Anyone acclaimed as a king would draw the attention of the Roman authorities and be in jeopardy of treason. To avoid a confrontation with the crowd, Jesus withdraws alone to a mountain. Mountains are common sites of divine activity in the Old Testament (e.g., Ge 22:1–2; Ex 3:1; 19:17–23; 1 Ki 19:8). This may imply that to find fortitude for his continuing journey to the cross, Jesus sought to meet with God the Father (see commentary on Jn 1:20, 41, 49; 2:17; 3:3; 7:42; 12:13–15).

Going Deeper into the Problem of Our Inadequacy: John 6:5–15

Have you ever been in over your head? Perhaps at work or school, in a community project, or in relationships with family or friends? Life often seems to demand more of us than we feel up to. And not to mention the great needs of the world around us that press on us day by day. In the face of life's challenges our own resources often seem completely inadequate, much as the five barley loaves and two fishes seemed in the face of the hunger of thousands of people. But when we give what we *do* have to Jesus, this miracle shows he can meet the need.

The miracle of the feeding of the five thousand has at times been explained in purely humanistic terms: the little boy's willingness to share his food evoked a similar selflessness in the hearts of others in the crowd who then pulled out their lunches to share as well.[2] The collective resources of the crowd were able to meet the need. According to this interpretation, the point of the story is that those who follow Jesus should be willing to share their resources with their community, and if they do, no one will go hungry. That may be a good application, well within Jesus' teaching of loving one's neighbor as oneself. But it misses the deeper point.

The miracle reveals the power and authority of Jesus to create. Jesus already knew how he would provide for the people's hunger even before he asked Philip what should be done (6:6). Just as God, not Moses, provided the manna in the wilderness, the disciples needed to see Jesus as more than another Moses. Here was God in the flesh providing material resources needed to sustain physical life. Just as the servants at the wedding in Cana filled the water pots but Jesus turned it into wine (Jn 2), here the disciples participate in the miracle by providing the bread and fish offered by the boy. But it is Jesus, not the crowd's sudden willingness to share, who creates the miracle. It is certainly appropriate when faced with overwhelming need to offer up our loaves and fishes in faith to Jesus. He is fully adequate when we are not. At those times when we feel inadequate to the need, offering what we have to the Lord—not what we do not have—is the obedience of faith.

The provision of food, even as spectacular as the miracle was, is not the main point of the story. Jesus will go on to explain what will satisfy the even greater need for eternal life (6:25–59, esp. vv. 53–55; see commentary there). The feeding of the five thousand teaches our complete and ridiculous inadequacy to save ourselves. Just as we cannot keep ourselves alive without taking in food from outside of our own bodies, we cannot sustain ourselves spiritually without taking in the spiritual food that only Jesus provides.

6:17 *Across the lake for Capernaum.* The scene shifts. When Jesus was not out in the countryside teaching and preaching, he made his home in Capernaum, an important crossroads town located at the northern end of the Sea of Galilee. The crowds would follow Jesus there later in the story (6:22–24).

By now it was dark. John includes such details as clues for the significance of his stories. Because Jesus is the light (Jn 1:4–5, 9), where Jesus is absent there is spiritual darkness. It was already dark when the disciples got into the boat—they had waited a long time for Jesus—and John includes that detail in anticipation of the storm that would overtake them in the night. They apparently needed to row the six or seven miles back to Capernaum. They still had about halfway to go when they found themselves facing a dire threat, and Jesus was absent.

6:19 *Walking on the water.* This fifth sign reveals the violence of nature is no match for the One who can tread on the sea ("You rule over the surging sea," Ps 89:9) (see "What the Structure Means: Reading the Signs of the Fourth Gospel (Jn 2–12)"). In the psalm, "you" refers to the Creator God. As Francis

Moloney observes, "Jesus' coming to his disciples across the waters repeats an Old Testament literary form for a theophany (see, for example, Ge 15:1; 26:24; 46:3; Isa 41:13–14; 43:1, 3)."[3] Significantly, this echo of the psalm applied to Jesus implicitly identifies him as God.

This is the first story in the gospel of John in which the disciples are in personal, life-threatening jeopardy. But it won't be the last as the gospel story unfolds around the Roman world. This episode reveals Jesus' power and authority to protect his disciples, a protection they will later need when Jesus has returned to the Father and persecution comes against his followers. Even though absent from his disciples in the boat, he apparently knew of their situation and came to deliver them in an unforgettable way, walking on the churning sea.

6:20 *It is I.* The Greek *ego eimi* (ἐγώ εἰμι) here translated "It is I" can also be translated "I am" (cf. 8:58). The gospel of John is known for its seven "I am" statements (see table 6.1), the first of which occurs in this chapter. But the phrase also represents the name of God revealed to Moses when he asks God what he should say if questioned about the authenticity of his mission. "Moses said to God, 'Suppose I go to the Israelites and say to them, "The God of your fathers has sent me to you," and they ask me, "What is his name?" Then what shall I tell them?' God said to Moses, 'I AM WHO I AM. This is what you are to say to the Israelites: "I AM has sent me to you"'" (Ex 3:13–14). Here Jesus is identified as the Creator God who controls the sea and announces himself to his disciples as "I am." Just as Moses was given signs to perform to accredit his authenticity (Ex 4:8), Jesus performs signs throughout this gospel to accredit his ministry as the One God has sent, who is no less than God himself.

This tale of Jesus walking on water follows the feeding of the five thousand also in Matthew (14:22–33) and Mark (6:47–51), and so the two events were evidently understood as related beyond simple chronology. John must have thought it an apt prelude to the first of his seven "I am" statements that follows in 6:35 (see commentary there).

What the Structure Means:
Walking on Water after Feeding the Five Thousand (Jn 6)

This long pericope (Jn 6:1–71) marks a transition to a new section of the gospel. John has presented Jesus as announcing the dawn of the messianic age and his body as the new temple in chapter 2. Chapter 3 shows Jesus' first engagement with Judaism in his conversation with Nicodemus, a Pharisee, while chapter 4 extends the mission of Jesus to the Samaritans through his conversation with the woman at the well. Chapter 5 stressed the point that belief in what Jesus said is the necessary condition of authentic faith. Now in chapter 6 John reveals Jesus as the "I Am" who will proceed in chapters 6–15 to reveal what the great "I Am" is like through a series of seven statements accompanied by miraculous signs. Chapter 6 describes the one miracle performed by Jesus that is included in all four Gospels, the feeding of the five thousand. For John, this miracle presents the opportunity for Jesus to instruct the people about eternal life and how that life is sustained, with his statement "I am the bread of life" (6:35).

In three of the Gospels (here, as well as in Mt 14:22–33 and Mk 6:47–51), the feeding of the five thousand is immediately followed by Jesus walking through darkness on a stormy sea to rescue his disciples, and in doing so revealing his divine powers of omniscience and mastery over the forces of nature. Given the context of Passover, it is inviting to think of this water event alongside Exodus 14, when during the exodus God delivered his threatened people through a watery passage of the Red Sea.[4] Three similarities evoke the exodus story: a strong wind blowing, the fact that both are a sea crossing, and the demonstration of God's power over the sea.[5] Jesus is here suggested to be the God of the exodus. While there are no convincing verbal parallels, the effect of the experience on the Israelites was that they "put their trust in him [the Lord] and in Moses his servant." Perhaps those who would become apostles experienced the same effect, as Jesus' role parallels God's in the exodus. The three New Testament Gospels that present this story in close association with the feeding of the five thousand may be showing Jesus' episode of walking on a stormy sea to be formative in the development of the authentic faith of the original disciples, for only God "treads on the waves of the sea" (Job 9:8).

In all three accounts as Jesus strides across the waves he proclaims, *egō eimi: mē phobeisthe* ([ἐγώ εἰμι· μὴ φοβεῖσθε] "I am;[6] do not be afraid"). But only John uses this phrase to such literary effect through the next several chapters of his gospel by combining it with a predicate nominative to reveal something about Jesus who has come to reveal God—for example, "I am the bread of life"; "I am the good shepherd"; "I am the way, the truth, and the life." Readers of John's gospel must be prepared to believe what Jesus says in the context of the messianic age calling forth a new birth into a kingdom of God that reaches beyond the Jews.

6:26 *Because you ate the loaves and had your fill.* The crowds sought Jesus not because they understood who he was and what he came to accomplish, but for the pragmatic reason that he had the ability to provide food, and without work at that. This self-centered, earthly approach was a completely inadequate reason given the larger mission of Jesus. The crowd misunderstands Jesus' purposes, perhaps reminiscent of the cry of Isaiah 55:1–3:

> Come, all you who are thirsty,
> > come to the waters;
> and you who have no money,
> > come, buy and eat!
> Come, buy wine and milk
> > without money and without cost.
> Why spend money on what is not bread,
> > and your labor on what does not satisfy?
> Listen, listen to me, and eat what is good,
> > and you will delight in the richest of fare.
> Give ear and come to me;
> > listen, that you may live.
> I will make an everlasting covenant with you,
> > my faithful love promised to David.[7]

Going Deeper into Reasons to Seek Jesus: John 6:24–27

"God loves you and has a wonderful plan for your life." Anyone who remembers evangelism in the 1960s and '70s might recognize that slogan. And it is certainly a true statement. However, many people, both those who have heard that statement and those who haven't, have a certain expectation of what a "wonderful" life looks like. For the people Jesus preached to in Galilee, a wonderful life involved an abundant supply of food that appeared without labor. Nearly 80 percent of people in the ancient Mediterranean world lived in subsistence poverty. Their daily task was to look for bread every day.[8]

Many in our own times are susceptible to a gospel that offers health and wealth as the primary blessings of God. Scripture does promise that those who are God's will not lack what is needed. For instance, Psalm 23, which is evoked by the grassy location of the feeding of the five thousand, says that because the Lord is my shepherd, "I have all that I need" (NLT). Whether we see our need as modest or extravagant, Jesus speaks against those who seek him for material gain, even as in John 6 for the necessity of food. For to do so is to miss the point that this world and *all* that is in it is passing away, but whoever does the will of God lives forever (1 Jn 2:17). Jesus taught that to do the will of God is to believe in his Son (Jn 6:29). Eternal life is the only gift that makes death a moot point, and the only way to survive the passing away that characterizes human life. God is generous toward his children, so that those who believe in Christ may indeed have what they need in the here and now. But seeking Jesus for what he might provide cannot be the basis of authentic Christian faith.

6:27 *Food that endures to eternal life.* Although almost always translated as "food" in this verse, the noun *brōsis* (βρῶσις; cf. *brōma* [βρῶμα]) here is likely not a reference to the material substance of food itself but to the act of eating.[9] Those interpreters who see a eucharistic allusion here lean toward understanding the referent as food. But 6:51 guides the understanding of the metaphor of eating and drinking: "whoever *eats* this bread will live forever." The verbal act of eating metaphorically stands for the verbal act of believing the teaching of Jesus. Jesus declares that there is such a thing as eternal life and that one must eat/believe in order to live forever. "In other words, in the thought world of the gospel of John, whoever receives the incarnated word and believes in it will live forever"[10] (on "Son of Man" see commentary at 1:51 and 13:31).

6:29 *The work of God is this: to believe in the one he has sent.* Despite their stomach-centered quest, the people have enough spiritual sensitivity to ask Jesus what kind of "works" God requires of them. But their overconfidence is astonishing. Jesus' reply is stunning; the "work" is to believe in the one God sent. Sheer faith in Christ is the way to eternal life. The similarity between working and believing is that faith-motivated action is required from a person who believes.[11] Moreover, that act of faith is itself something that God gives (6:37).[12]

6:31 *He gave them bread from heaven.* Oddly, the feeding of five thousand from five loaves and two fish is seemingly overlooked when they request some other "sign" that would accredit Jesus as believable. It was near Passover, and they remembered their ancestors ate bread (manna) that God had sent them from heaven (Ex 16:4; Ps 78:23–25).[13] By quoting this biblical verse they implicitly request more bread to prove that Jesus is as great as Moses and sent by God.

Manna became a symbol of the messianic age when "they will eat of it in those years because these are they who will have arrived at the consummation of time" (2 Baruch 29:8). This expectation is also reflected in Revelation 2:17, where "someone like a son of man" (Rev 1:13) will offer the hidden manna. Jesus takes the opportunity afforded by the feeding of the five thousand to show himself as the source of that promised manna.

6:33 *The bread that comes down from heaven and gives life to the world.* The bread that God provides originates in heaven and sustains life not just for Israel, as it did in the wilderness, but for the world. Passover recalled not only the gift of manna but also the giving of the law during the exodus at Sinai, so it is understandable why manna later came to represent the gift of the law. As Andreas Köstenberger observes, "The giving of the law at Mount Sinai was described in similar terms: 'the earth trembled when he gave life to the world' (*Exod. Rab.* 29.9). In the present passage, the same function is said to be fulfilled by Jesus (cf. 5:39)."[14] As the law was the word of God present with his people, the Lord's presence was perfected in his Word become flesh in Jesus. As Moloney explains, "Jesus promises eternal life to those who would perfect their adherence to the Law by believing in the Son sent by the Father. . . . This 'living presence,' the visible assurance that God cares for and guides his people, is no longer found in a written law. It is to be seen and believed in the presence of the Son."[15]

6:35 *I am the bread of life.* Upon their request (6:34), Jesus reveals *himself* to be the expected manna of the messianic age. Neither of the two elements that sustain life, food and water, can be self-produced but must be sought after and ingested from outside oneself, and preferably on a daily basis at that. R. A. Culpepper has characterized these symbols of water and bread in the fourth gospel, writing, "Water, which is more closely tied to the Spirit, purification, and entrance into eternal life, is never used in an 'I am' pronouncement, and never identified with Jesus beyond the affirmations that he is its source and giver. Bread, on the other hand, whether because it was already identified with the Passover, wisdom, and the Torah in Jewish thought, or because it had Eucharistic overtones, or because its function is the sustenance of life, has a great attributive and interpretive role in symbolically defining Jesus' identity."[16] Jesus declares himself to be the sustenance of life for those who come to him. It is interesting that Philo understood the messianic manna as referring to the Word of God, or the divine Logos. John seems to be thinking along similar lines (cf. Jn 1:1, 14), but recognizes the messianic manna to be the man Jesus Christ.

This is the first of seven formal "I am" statements in the gospel of John, composed of "I am" (*egō eimi* [ἐγώ εἰμι]) plus a predicate and rooted in the Old Testament (see table 6.1).

Table 6.1. The Seven "I Am" Statements

References in John	"I Am" Statement
6:35	I am the bread of life.
8:12; 9:5	I am the light of the world.
10:7, 9	I am the door for the sheep.
10:11, 14	I am the good shepherd.
11:25	I am the resurrection and the life.
14:6	I am the way, the truth, and the life.
15:1	I am the vine.

These statements with a predicate are not defining Jesus' ontological nature, but how he functions in his role in God's redemptive plan.[18]

This first of the seven statements communicates the absolute necessity of Jesus Christ, who offers "an eternal sufficiency in which there is no want."[19] This statement also shows something of how John relates his gospel story to the Old Testament. The physical event of manna points typologically to a supra-physical reality in Jesus Christ. Belief in the testimony about Jesus is the way the bread of life is taken into oneself.

6:37 *All those the Father gives me will come to me.* One of the strong theological points of the gospel of John is that the faith of those who come to Jesus Christ is an outworking of having already been chosen by the Father. Jesus speaks of a category of people, those given to him by the Father, as certain to come to him in faith and to remain with him ("I will never drive away"). See "Going Deeper into Divine Election: John 6:37–65."

6:41 *The Jews there began to grumble about him.* Previously Jesus' audience was referred to as "the crowd" (6:2, 5, 22, 24), but here "the Jews" emerge from the crowd. Earlier in the gospel the Jewish leaders of Jerusalem were offended by Jesus; here, the Jews, who may have been the leaders of the synagogue at Capernaum in Galilee (see 6:59), are offended at his claim to have come down from heaven. Readers know something the people who first encountered Jesus did not know, that the Word became flesh in the man Jesus (Jn 1:14). How difficult it would be to stand in their shoes, to see Jesus as a man, a neighbor, and to hear him claim to have come down from heaven. John tells us they grumbled about him, using a form of the same word (Gk. *gogguzō* [γογγύζω]) as found in Exodus 16:7 and Numbers 14:27. Ironically, both the Jews of Jesus' generation and their ancestors grumbled against what God was doing in their times. The negative response of "the Jews" across Palestine from Jerusalem to Galilee suggests that their opposition to Jesus will play an increasing role in his story (regarding "the Jews," see commentary on "Jewish leaders in Jerusalem" at 1:19).

6:45 *They will all be taught by God.* Jesus quotes, or paraphrases "the prophets" (see Isa 54:13; Jer 31:34) claiming that if someone learns from God they will come to Jesus. This implies that these prophecies are fulfilled by an understanding of Jesus that leads to salvation. Implicitly, Jesus claims that those Jews who rejected him had *not* learned from God, though they claimed him as their Father (cf. Jn 8:41).

6:51 *Whoever eats this bread will live forever.* Jesus reminds his audience that a repeat of manna is insufficient, as their ancestors ate miraculous bread from heaven and yet they nevertheless died (6:49). This provides a clue as to why the miracles Jesus performed were in and of themselves insufficient to produce saving faith: because they operate in the plane of the here and now. It is insufficient to believe in Jesus as a wonder-worker whose powers operated only within the physical world of his time (see Jn 6:26). Rather, saving faith understands Jesus as the incarnate Word and Son of God who entered this physical world from eternity beyond it to raise us up from the here and now of our graves. Jesus clearly could have showered manna down on first-century Galilee as easily as he turned water into wine. But that might have been misunderstood to be the complete fulfillment of that messianic expectation. Jesus has something much greater to reveal: eternal life, a forever life that death in the here and now cannot end and that ordinary food in the here and now cannot nourish.

This bread is my flesh. This discourse has moved from the provision of material bread in 6:1–14 to remembrance of the manna in the wilderness, to discussion of some kind of mysterious spiritual bread that Jesus offers to sustain one for eternal life. Throughout Jewish interpretation in both the Wisdom tradition and the Midrash, the manna provided by God through Moses to keep his people alive during the exodus was understood by the subsequent generations of Israel to be the Sinai Law. The understanding of manna as a typology pointing to a spiritual reality should have been familiar.[20] But then Jesus made a statement that challenges us yet today: "This bread I've been talking about is my flesh." It is likely that his audience was still thinking in material terms of the here and now, in terms of bread multiplied and manna. The hint of a transition to metaphor came in 6:35, where hunger was said to be satisfied by coming to Jesus and thirst by believing in what he said. The graphic and gruesome image of physically eating Jesus' flesh forced their minds to metaphor, else they would conclude he was insane (cf. 6:52, 60–70). He offers the interpretive clue by adding that his flesh will be given for the life of the world, suggesting a sacrificial act. Those who have read the Prologue remember that the Word became flesh (1:14), and so here the purpose of the incarnation begins to be revealed—not so Jesus could teach and heal and do miracles, but so he could offer his flesh as a sacrifice.

6:54 *Whoever eats my flesh and drinks my blood has eternal life.* The verb here shifts to the more graphic *trōgein* [τρώγειν], not simply to eat but to chew Jesus' flesh. The gruesome image is then heightened when he further speaks of drinking his blood. The colocation of *flesh* and *blood* reinforces the sacrificial imagery, but also brings to mind the Torah prohibition:

> For the life of a creature is in the blood, and I have given it to you to make atonement for yourselves on the altar; it is the blood that makes atonement for one's life. (Lev 17:11)

> But be sure you do not eat the blood, because the blood is the life, and you must not eat the life with the meat. (Dt 12:23)

It is no wonder Jesus' Jewish audience was horrified and repulsed. And yet, Jesus claims that this is the food of eternal life!

Although the metaphor may be gruesome, and certainly was in no way to be taken literally, it points to the purpose of the incarnation, which John has already referred to in 1:14 as the Word become flesh (and blood) when he became a human being. As Moloney explains, "Flesh and blood emphasize that it is the incarnate life of the Son which is life-giving food."[21]

Furthermore, because this discourse on the bread of heaven was given near the time of Passover, which recapitulates the exodus from Egypt, it also brings to mind the blood on the doorposts that protected occupants of the house from the angel of death. This is the first clear hint that Jesus will die a sacrificial death, especially in light of the Baptist's "Lamb of God" proclamation (Jn 1:29, 36). Notably, the sacrificial Passover lamb was *eaten*, its flesh chewed.

Moreover, Jesus has already provided the clue of what it means to eat his flesh and drink his blood in 6:35: "Whoever *comes to me* will never go hungry, and whoever *believes in me* will never be thirsty." Eating Jesus' flesh and drinking his blood means to come to and believe in him, to believe the spiritual truths he reveals.

6:57 *The one who feeds on me will live.* Jesus clarifies by replacing "my flesh" and "my blood" in verse 56 with "me." The whole person of Christ imparts life, not simply what some interpreters have identified as the eucharistic elements.

6:58 *This is the bread that came down from heaven.* Jesus again identifies himself as the bread that sustains eternal life (see commentary on Jn 6:31, 33, 35).

Going Deeper into the Sacrament: John 6:25–59

A Christian cannot read John 6 without recognizing that its language of eating and drinking may evoke the sacrament of the Eucharist, or Holy Communion. And while the crowds who originally heard Jesus could not have made that association because the Christian sacrament had not yet been established by Jesus and practiced by the church, John's original readers certainly could have, because John wrote these words decades after the sacrament was established. But in fact the Bread of Life Discourse does *not* use the liturgical language of the Eucharist, "this is my *body*; this is my blood," though "eating flesh" and "drinking blood" is perhaps close enough to suggest the sacrament, surely to those who are familiar with it. Nevertheless, "a sacramental interpretation misleads unless it is allowed only a secondary place."[22] For it would be an overly literal interpretation of the Bread of Heaven Discourse to conclude that without partaking of the sacrament of Holy Communion a person cannot have eternal life.

Jesus does not teach that the literal act of eating and drinking imparts eternal life. He uses these verbs as metaphors for faith, for "the commitment of the believer to the revelation that Jesus brings."[23] Or, as Jan Heilmann puts it, "the complex metaphorical network in the Bread of Life discourse rests on conceptual imagery that we might refer to as EATING/DRINKING IS ADOPTING TEACHING" that Jesus himself embodies (see Isa 55:1–3, 10–11; Jer 15:16; Eze 2:7–3:3)[24] (see "Going Deeper into Eating and Drinking as Apt Metaphors for Faith: John 7:37–39"). And so John 6 does not refer directly to the sacrament, but *both* John 6 and the sacrament that had been established point to the revelation that Jesus' life and death make eternal life for the believer possible. As Bauckham explains, "John used Eucharistic language to speak, not of the Eucharist, but of faith in the crucified Jesus and participation in his life. . . . The primary meaning is both more basic and more extensive than the sacramental overtone."[25]

John 6:1–59 Through Old Testament Eyes

The exodus of the Israelites from Egypt was the seminal event of Israel's history still commemorated today in the feast of Passover. That experience of exodus and travel from Egypt to the Promised Land was marked especially by the deliverance from the angel of death, by crossing the Red Sea, by God's provision of manna in the wilderness, and by the giving of the Law of God at Sinai. John 6 significantly engages each of these four Old Testament concepts to present the significance of the incarnation of the Son of God in the man Jesus. In these early chapters of John's gospel we find hints of the violence that will end Jesus' life (3:14; 6:51). Because Jesus is "the Lamb of God" (1:29, 36) and the events of John 6 occur near Passover, readers cannot help but infer that Jesus' death will be a sacrifice similar to those offered at Passover and with an efficacious protection from death to those who partake of the sacrifice as suggested by the death-defying blood of the first Passover lamb.

Crossing the Red Sea was God's quintessential act of deliverance for Israel. When Jesus walks on the water we are reminded of God's control over the seas. And by announcing that "It is I" or "I am" he identifies himself with the God of Exodus who met Moses on the mountain and brought them out of Egypt (Ex 3:14).

The crowds whom Jesus miraculously fed asked him for a further sign that would accredit his authority as equal to that of Moses (Jn 6:30–31). They pointed out that Moses provided manna in the wilderness, a veiled request that Jesus continually provide miraculous bread for them for which they need not work. Jesus makes the point that all those who ate that miraculous bread in the wilderness nevertheless died, but God has sent him, the true bread of life, to be eaten as the food of eternal life (6:58). Readers of the gospel of John recognize that God is not ultimately interested in providing material blessings for this life alone, but in the eternal destiny of his people. The purpose of the incarnation of Jesus Christ was to be the sacrifice that cleared the way to eternal life; eating his flesh and drinking his blood are metaphors of acceptance of and belief in Christ's sacrifice that is the means of appropriating that gift of life. We eat and drink our way to eternal life, so to speak. As Gerry Wheaton explains, "Jesus' language of eating and drinking, particularly in verses 52–56, refers to a pattern of ongoing belief and fellowship with Jesus. As the annual observance of Passover was requisite for the continued membership among the people of God, so one must go on 'eating and drinking' the flesh and blood of Jesus to continue among his restored people. The call of Jesus is not merely to *enter into* his fellowship, but to *abide in* his fellowship."[26]

John's presentation of Jesus in chapter 6 also shows him to be of *greater* authority than Moses. Moses was the mediator of God's law, known as the "Ten Words" in Hebrew (the Ten Commandments in English). But Jesus is greater than Moses and has greater authority because he *is* the Word of God incarnate (1:14). Jesus is the new Torah, as well as the new place of worship (2:21), and the new and final sacrifice. The origin of the ingestion of the word of God in Old Testament tradition may have begun when Ezekiel ate the scroll containing God's words (Eze 2:7–3:3). In later Jewish tradition manna from heaven came to symbolize the Torah and Wisdom tradition that God's people were to ingest and make part of themselves, fueling their lives.[27] And so what appears as perhaps a bizarre metaphor to English readers, to eat Jesus' flesh and drink his blood, did have antecedent concepts in Judaism. The strange twist is that here it is being applied to a person, a person who *is* the Word of God. The revelation Jesus brought was not presented on stone tablets but was embodied in his own person.

Passover also held future-looking hopes of national restoration. Just as God had brought the Israelites out of Egypt and constituted them as a nation, first-century Jews celebrated the hope that one day they would again be an independent nation free from the occupation of Rome. In the first century this hope interpreted prophecies found in Isaiah 53 (the Suffering Servant), Isaiah 54 (the rebuilding of Jerusalem), and Isaiah 55 (the eschatological messianic banquet). With this nationalistic hope as the background, "John, then, has drawn upon key images from the first exodus and wilderness wandering (filtered through Ps 78) and interpreted them within the framework of the new exodus hope of Isaiah 55. By this means, he represents Jesus as the provider of the food and drink that lead to life.

Moreover, when we recall that John 6:26–27 opens the discourse by referring to the paschal meal symbolically provided by Jesus in 6:5–11, the introduction of Isaiah 55 into the very heart of the discourse effectively *conflates the paschal meal with the eschatological meal of Israel's restoration.* In this way John signals that the true paschal meal Jesus would provide was nothing short of *the means by which one might participate in the eschatological new exodus of Isaiah.*"[28]

John 6 provides an excellent example of how the apostles read the Old Testament in light of Christ.

6:60 *Who can accept it?* The Christian doctrine of salvation from sin and new birth into eternal life through faith in Jesus Christ is fantastic, both in the sense that it is strange and that it is excellent. The great religions of the world focus on the felt need that human beings have for justice, including punishment for one's own sin. Consequently, in most religions people must work in one way or another to pay for their sin. The gospel of Jesus Christ is strange in that it eliminates the requirement for penitential works and replaces it with faith in Jesus' atoning death alone. All the penitential works of all the human beings who will ever live is replaced by the singular sacrifice of the eternally perfect Son of God. This gospel is excellent, for otherwise no one could pay the debt their sin incurs. Just as Jesus' disciples found the metaphor of eating flesh and drinking blood difficult to understand, many today who are willing to accept Jesus as a great religious teacher find the heart of his gospel of grace too difficult to accept.

6:61 *His disciples were grumbling.* Here is likely another allusion to the exodus, for the verb is *gogguzō* (γογγύζω), the same verb found in the Septuagint to describe Israel's reaction to their circumstances during the exodus journey (Ex 17:3; Nu 11:1; 14:27, 29; 16:41; 17:5). The verb is used to express complaints and disagreement with God as in, "How long will this wicked community *grumble* against me? I have heard the complaints of these grumbling Israelites" (Nu 14:27). The faithless response of the Israelites brought them under God's judgment (Nu 14:29). Jesus gently warns his disciples, even though they don't understand the ways of God, not to grumble against the means of salvation by faith that the Lord has provided. They think they know Jesus fully, and are offended by his teaching that he came down from heaven (Jn 6:41–42, 61). The incarnation of Christ continues to be a difficult teaching today. Only the enabling of the Father makes faith in the incarnate Christ possible (6:65).

6:62 *The Son of Man ascend to where he was before.* Jesus refers to a time and place other than that of his earthly life (see Jn 1:14), showing an awareness of his divine origin and mission. In the gospel of John the verb *to descend* (*katabainō* [καταβαίνω]) describes the appearance of the Spirit (1:32–33), the transit of angels (1:51), the descent from heaven of the Son of Man (3:13; 6:38), and the origin of the bread of heaven (6:41; 50–51, 58) (on "Son of Man" also see commentary at 1:51 and 13:31). In 6:62 Jesus refers to an ascent back to heaven, and implies that his disciples will witness it.

6:64 *Jesus had known from the beginning.* Most likely a reference to the beginning of his ministry, when he personally handpicked his twelve disciples, even Judas Iscariot, who would ultimately betray him (cf. 6:70). Jesus drew many people who followed him for what they could get from it (Jn 6:26) or to be titillated by his miracles. Unbelief was beginning to manifest itself among the many who followed him as he revealed more of himself and his mission, showing "fundamentally, the inability and refusal to accept Jesus for who he is."[29]

6:65 *No one can come to me unless the Father has enabled them.* Jesus teaches the sovereignty of God the Father over those who will believe unto eternal life. Anyone could traipse around behind Jesus as he traveled throughout Galilee, but to overcome disbelief and accept Jesus' true identity as the Son of God incarnate, sent by the Father to atone for sin, requires a spiritual enabling of God.

6:66 *Many of his disciples turned back and no longer followed him.* Many could follow Jesus to some extent and for a time, but when he began to teach his true identity and mission, many of those following him ("his disciples") turned away. It is a process and a journey for someone to move from an initial interest in Jesus to a lifetime of saving faith in him.

6:68 *Lord, to whom shall we go?* Although many turned away from Jesus, there were some who truly understood that there was no other way to eternal life. Peter confesses this truth that every Christian must come to: that to turn away from Jesus is to turn away from life because there is no other way to God the Father.

The Holy One of God. This exact phrase is found only in Mark 1:24 and Luke 4:34 in the mouth of the demons who address Jesus. In the Old Testament, "the Holy One of Israel" occurs frequently as a reference to God (Ps 71:22; Isa 40:25; Hab 1:12) and in Isaiah as Israel's creator (e.g., Isa 41:20; 43:15; 45:11) and redeemer (e.g. Isa 43:3, 14; 48:17; 49:7). Based on this Old Testament usage, "the Holy One of God" was probably a messianic title. Applied to Jesus it closely associates him with the person and work of the Father, and implies that Jesus is the creator and redeemer of God's people.

Going Deeper into Divine Election: John 6:37–65

The gospel of John is known for its strong message that only those whom God has enabled will find the message of Jesus compelling and come to faith in Christ. In John 6:37 Jesus confidently proclaims that "*all* those the Father gives me will come to me." This is the most encouraging foundation for evangelism, for it assures success by revealing that those God the Father has chosen *will come* to Christ. So it is simply our job to present the gospel message to all, being confident that some will indeed find faith through the message.

But Jesus also knew that not everyone would come to faith, and because "some of you do not believe" (6:64), he says in 6:65, "This is why I told you that no one *can* come to me unless the Father has enabled them." This is the other side of the coin of God's enabling choice of people who will believe— apart from his enabling grace no one is able to come to faith in Christ (see

6:44). When the promise of 6:37 (all who are chosen will come to faith) and the restriction of 6:44, 65 (no can come unless enabled by God), are combined, one inference is that the number of those who will come to saving faith in Christ is fixed by God's intent and known only to him. It is certain that many will come to Christ and that many will not.

This theological point is often construed as harsh, and is rejected even by many believing Christians. But rather than rejecting Jesus' teaching here, believers should appreciate the grace that has been extended to them, should take no credit for their own salvation, and should gratefully praise God for his merciful and gracious choice. Those who hear this teaching of Jesus and are not believers should not despair, for all Christians were at some point unbelievers. The unbeliever should turn to God and ask for his mercy and grace, repenting of sin.

They say there will be two surprising things about heaven: those who are there and those who aren't. So just because Jesus has told us that God has a chosen people, we can never presume in this life to know who is "in" and who is "out." We should preach and share the gospel with every unbeliever while his or her life persists, for Jesus does not say when faith will emerge in the life of a person chosen by God and that one may indeed respond in faith at some point.

We find in John 6 also a wonderful promise of reassurance for Christians who doubt that Jesus will accept their faith. Jesus promises he will *never* drive away anyone who comes to him (6:37) and he *will* raise up to eternal life the one who comes to him (6:44) because this is the Father's will in drawing a person to faith in Christ (6:39). Jesus promises to lose no one who has come to him but to bring each one to their eternal destiny. This is also a message that must be preached and shared with those who believe, that we may all live in the peace and confidence of salvation through the days of our lives.

The doctrine of divine election is often misunderstood as harsh or arbitrary, and either rejected or ignored. But it is neither harsh nor arbitrary. God has not left the fallen human race to perish, but has chosen a people for himself. God knows who are his (6:64). Divine election is the very great and precious promise of God's irresistible grace.[30]

JOHN 7

7:2 *The Jewish Festival of Tabernacles was near.* John consistently makes use of the traditions and symbols of the Jewish feasts as background for explaining the significance of Jesus. Nowhere is that more important for interpretation than John 7, which assumes the reader is familiar with the light and water liturgies that were performed at the Festival of Tabernacles. Tabernacles, or Sukkot, was an autumn festival that commemorated God's presence and provision during the exodus journey when Israel lived in temporary shelters along the way and when Moses met with God in the tabernacle, or Tent of Meeting.

God's presence was symbolized at the Jerusalem temple during the seven-day Festival of Tabernacles by large bonfires within the temple precincts that could be seen for miles. In the Old Testament, fire symbolized God's presence in his first appearance to Moses (see Ex 3:1–6) and in the shekinah glory that had descended on the first temple (2 Ch 7:1–2) indicating God's divine presence. The fiery presence of God is found also in the pillar of fire that accompanied Israel during the exodus (Ex 13:21; 14:24) and provides the symbolic meaning of the tongues of fire that rested on the first disciples of Jesus on the day of Pentecost (Ac 2:3). It is in the context of the fiery temple illuminations of Tabernacles that Jesus declares himself to be the "light of the world" (Jn 8:12; see commentary there).

A second meaningful ritual was the drawing of water by the priests, who then walked in procession back to the temple where the libation was poured out on the altar. This symbolic enactment commemorated the Lord's provision of water from the rock during the exodus (Ps 78:16, 20; Isa 48:21; Ne 9:15; behind all of which stood Ex 17:1–6 and Nu 20:2–13) and reminded of the eschatological promise of water running from the temple (Eze 47:1–10; Joel 3:18) or Jerusalem (Zec 14:8) during the messianic age. The exodus was the story of Israel's national origins, and the prophets envisioned a renewed theocracy ushered in by the Messiah, so Tabernacles, like Passover, had taken on both nationalistic and eschatological connotations, especially during Jerusalem's occupation first by the Hellenistic kings and then by the Romans. Only with that assumed background do Jesus' statements make profound sense, as "the festival's key symbols of water and light then provide central metaphors in the ensuing discourses, especially in John 7:37–39."[1]

7:8 *I am not going up to this festival.* Although all men in Israel were expected to make the pilgrimage to Jerusalem for the three major feasts (Passover, Pentecost, and Tabernacles), Jesus knew that the Jewish leaders of Jerusalem were scheming against him (Jn 7:1). Jesus was living under a death threat. His unbelieving brothers egged him on to go and display his "works," though they apparently did not have his best interests at heart. Their words seem to be a dare.

Because my time has not yet fully come. Jesus declines their dare, suggesting that to go to Judea and Jerusalem to publicly display his works there would somehow violate an implicit plan. As Francis Moloney explains, "Violence is in the air, and is yet to be played out, but only at the 'time/hour' appointed by God. Jesus' words to his brothers encourage them to go up to the feast, but he tells them that he will not go up to *this* feast. As the story unfolds, Jesus does 'secretly' go up to the feast (v. 10), but the 'hour' of Jesus will not take place at *this* feast. The strong demonstrative adjective ('this') clearly hints to the reader/listener that the 'hour' will come at *another* feast."[2]

7:14 *Go up to the temple courts.* However, about halfway through the festival, Jesus *does* go secretly to Jerusalem, not to do works but to teach.[3] He had declined to travel in the pilgrim caravan with his extended family, which was customary, but chose to separate himself from them.[4] While some interpreters debate the ethics of what appears to be Jesus' duplicity, a nobler motive may have been to protect his brothers and family from any violence that might have broken out around him, given that he had become a target of the Jewish leaders.

7:19 *Has not Moses given you the law?* This is the seventh time Moses has been mentioned in the gospel of John, and again Jesus is turning the tables on the Jewish leaders who challenge his teaching presuming to have the law on their side. They don't recognize that Moses "is no longer the impartial mediator of the law but an individual who stands ready to bring charges against those who do not believe in Jesus."[5] Jesus claims that his teaching is consistent with the law, and brings the countercharge that "not one of you keeps the law," a claim that no doubt surprised the Pharisees among them. John presents Jesus as one who stood in continuity with Moses, yet surpassed the authority of Moses. Ironically, the Jewish leaders of Jerusalem fail to recognize the law's true meaning and miss the truth that Jesus reveals.[6] Their failure will prove fatal to Jesus, and yet it is that very catastrophe by which God's redemptive plan is fully and finally achieved.

7:20 *You are demon-possessed.* In response to Jesus' question of why the Jewish leaders wish to kill him, the crowd, possibly unaware of their leaders' schemes, accuses Jesus of being demon-possessed. This shows the crowd siding with the leaders and interpreting Jesus as paranoid. But Jesus had good reason to suspect the Jewish leaders who, during his last visit in Jerusalem, had begun to persecute him (Jn 5:16) and wished to kill him (5:18). The "crowd" whispered their debate about Jesus (7:12), for even they feared the Jewish leaders of Jerusalem.

7:22 *You circumcise a boy on the Sabbath.* The origins of circumcision are found in Genesis 17:10-13 and Leviticus 12:3. When Jesus answers the question, "Who is trying to kill you?" (Jn 7:20), he reminds the crowd of the consequence of his last temple visit when he performed one miracle, healing a man on the Sabbath (Jn 5:8-9). He defended his authority to do so by claiming God's authority (5:16-47), which made the Jewish leaders only the more determined to kill him. Here Jesus resumes his defense of healing on the Sabbath by pointing out that some activities, such as circumcision, are performed even on the Sabbath.

7:23 *So that the law of Moses may not be broken.* Jesus' logic seems to be that circumcision, a sign of the covenant, is lawful even when performed on the Sabbath. Circumcision, though given by Moses (Lev 12:3), was originally the sign of God's covenant with Israel through the patriarch Abraham (Ge 17), and as Sabbath commemorates the covenant it is especially apt to perform circumcision on the Sabbath. This invites the crowd to consider that Jesus' healing on the Sabbath may similarly be a sign of the covenant, and therefore not a violation of the law. And indeed, the signs Jesus performs on the Sabbath are fulfillments of the covenant promises that point to the dawn of the messianic age. Jesus faults them for not judging his signs correctly. Far from being unlawful, it was uniquely appropriate for Jesus to heal on the Sabbath.

7:24 *Stop judging by mere appearances, but instead judge correctly.* Jesus echoes the tradition throughout the Old Testament of doing justice impartially and not showing favoritism in the courts and in life (Lev 19:15; Dt 1:17; 16:19; 2 Ch 19:7; Pr 18:5; 24:23; Mal 2:9).

7:27 *When the Messiah comes, no one will know where he is from.* In the first century one strand of messianism held to an idea that the Messiah was a preexistent but hidden figure who would eventually be revealed having no known origin.[7] The crowd believes that they know where Jesus is from—Nazareth, or perhaps Capernaum—and therefore he is ineligible to be the Messiah. But ultimately Jesus claims to have been from God, sent by him on a mission.

7:30 *His hour had not yet come.* References to an "hour" (Gk. *hora* [ὥρα]) as an appointed time of a significant event in redemptive history characterize the gospel of John. Here the author speaks of Jesus' "hour" yet to come, alerting the reader that his life is moving toward an appointed time. While attempts to seize Jesus during his public ministry are thwarted, the reader senses that will not always be the case.

7:32 *The chief priests and the Pharisees.* The Pharisees and chief priests were among the Jewish leadership of Jerusalem. When they heard the crowds murmuring whispers of belief in Jesus, they ordered that he be arrested.

Temple guards to arrest him. The temple had its own police responsible for keeping the peace especially during peak times of large crowds, such as would have been present for the Festival of Tabernacles. These were presumably Jewish men who could move freely in the temple precincts. The concern of the Jewish leaders was not to allow nationalistic and messianic feelings to incite the crowds to riot, which would bring Roman soldiers into the festival.

7:35 *Our people live scattered among the Greeks.* Jesus had stated that his ministry among the people was short-lived (7:33), a shadowy alert of the trouble that lay ahead. Because he was marked as a troublemaker in Judea, the crowd speculated that Jesus might remove himself to live in the Jewish Diaspora among the Gentiles. But John's readers know that Jesus here alludes to his death and departure back to the Father.

7:37 *On the last and greatest day of the festival.* The festival's "key symbols of water and light provide the central metaphors in the ensuing discourses, especially in John 7:37–39."[8] The Festival of Tabernacles was celebrated with large bonfires symbolizing God's presence in the shekinah glory that came down on the dedication of the first temple and in water-pouring rituals that symbolized God's blessing of the land with rain, which pointed to the giving of the Spirit as a river running from the temple in Jerusalem in the last days (see commentary on 7:2). On each of the seven days of the festival the priests and people would form a procession bearing water in a golden pitcher from the Pool of Siloam to the temple.[9] Three blasts of the shofar sounded, the temple choir sang the Hallel, and at the sound of Psalm 118 the men shook willow and myrtle branches (the *lulab*) with citrus and with shouts of thanksgiving. While all watched, the golden pitcher of water would be poured out with great ceremony on the altar.

Water was an important religious symbol in the temple rituals based largely on images from Ezekiel. Gary Manning explains,

> For Ezekiel, water used in the Temple cult came to symbolize moral and spiritual cleansing, and thus God's promise to give his Spirit. Water was also a symbol of God's abundant provision, and especially of his ability to re-create and heal, as in the river from the Temple [Eze 47:1–12]. The image of the river from the Temple appears to combine these ideas: water comes from God's presence, purifying, healing, and bringing life to the land and its people. Like Ezekiel's other symbols, water communicates both outward physical restoration of the land as well as a spiritual transformation of the people.[10]

It is against this symbolic background that Jesus chooses to speak of the fulfillment of these symbols in himself. The noun *tabernacle* means a dwelling, and God *is* present with the crowds at the temple in the presence of the incarnate Son. Furthermore, Jesus promises that the Spirit symbolized by the promised rivers of water would flow when he is "glorified," indicating the arrival of the messianic age. Ezekiel 47 is a likely Old Testament background, connecting Jesus as the source of living water with God's promise of living water from the temple (cf. Jn 2:21 and 4:10–26, which is also concerned with proper places for worship).

The festival lasted seven days, from the fifteenth to the twenty-first of the lunar month of Tishri, corresponding to September-October. It is debated whether the "last" day of the feast refers to the seventh day or the eighth, which was itself a special day of rejoicing as the pilgrims prepared to return to their homes. D. A. Carson observes that in favor of the eighth day, Jesus' words would have had special force if he spoke them immediately after the light and water rituals had ceased for another year. For Jesus claims to provide a light and water that is continuously available[11] (cf. Isa 44:1–5; Eze 36:24–27).

Come to me and drink. Echoing Isaiah 55:1, Jesus extends this invitation to all who were within hearing. This invitation parallels that of John 6:35–58, where the metaphor of eating the bread of life for eternal life refers to believing in Jesus and what he accomplishes. Here, the metaphor of drinking water is used to refer to faith in Christ, which quenches spiritual thirst. As drinking water is a daily necessity, the presence of Jesus is offered as a well to be drawn from routinely.[12] As Craig Koester explains, "This thirst rises from the lack of the eternal life that Jesus offers; and since eternal life comes through knowing

God (17:3), Jesus speaks about a thirst for God (4:13–15). . . . Therefore, in a theological sense the thirsty are those who desire a relationship with God."[13] The opposite of thirsting is believing in Christ. Together with the feeding of the five thousand in John 6, bread and water echo Deuteronomy 8, where God provided water out of hard rock and manna in the wilderness. The water and bread ingested to sustain life are reminders of dependence on God without which the people perish.

7:38 *Rivers of living water.* Jesus explicitly links faith in him to the Spirit here, for it is "the one who believes" in Jesus who receives the water, which is the Spirit. Jesus does not appear to be citing any exact quotation of any one verse of Scripture, but rather refers to scriptural promises within the context of the symbolism of Tabernacles, such as promises of God's presence and provision (cf. Nu 20:11; Ne 9:19–20; Ps 77:16, 20; Isa 58:11; Zec 14:8). As Gerry Wheaton explains, "Jesus does not set aside the various ceremonies associated with the feast. Rather, he evokes prominent Old Testament and contemporary Jewish traditions connected with these ceremonies in such a way as to reveal their eschatological enactment in his very person and work. By entering into the symbolic customs of Tabernacles and 'filling them up to the top,' Jesus brings to full realization the eschatological, salvific aspiration of those who celebrate the festival."[14]

There is some ambiguity in the syntax of 7:38 whether the rivers of living water are to flow from Jesus or from the ones who believe in him. While the perhaps intentional ambiguity can stand in Greek, English translators must make a choice between "out of him" or "out of them." Obviously, Jesus is the source of the living water first (see Jn 20:22) and the Spirit flows from believers only if they have first been filled with the waters that Jesus gives.

Going Deeper into Eating and Drinking as Apt Metaphors for Faith: John 7:37–39

The metaphors of eating Jesus' flesh and of drinking his blood and water that flows from him may seem confusing and even macabre. In English idiom we can speak of swallowing our pride, eating crow, chewing it over, food for thought, and hard to swallow, among other phrases of ingestion as metaphor. Because eating and drinking are universal and necessary acts of the human body, almost every language uses ingestion metaphorically.[15] Reflection on what such metaphors imply helps us to understand the rather startling statements of Jesus as bread and water and what eating his flesh and drinking of him might mean.

Both eating and drinking involve taking something *outside* of ourselves, something that we cannot produce, *into* ourselves. Food and water are necessary for life, and no one can generate the substances that sustain life within themselves. We are helplessly dependent creatures. If for any reason we are unable to take in the needed nutrition, we die. Through the metaphors of ingestion, Jesus reveals himself to be essential to spiritual life. We cannot nourish our spiritual lives without him.

Furthermore, ingestion means taking an external substance and making it a part of ourselves, taking it into our innermost parts through swallowing it. This aspect of ingestion means that Christians must internalize Jesus, making his embodied teaching a part of ourselves. Just as the English metaphor of swallowing something means to believe it and accept it, eating and drinking Jesus means to believe him and accept the truths he reveals as part of our own internal belief system.

Moreover, eating and drinking are not one-time events. They are repeated, continual, and daily events. The biblical metaphor suggests that believing Jesus and accepting his truth only once are insufficient if that belief and acceptance do not persist daily throughout life. Salvation is not a ticket to heaven that, once acquired, can be tucked away for the future day of death; rather, it is following Jesus daily by internalizing his truth and letting that truth fuel our daily lives. Just as food and drink convert to energy within our bodies that animate us and fuel our daily activities, belief in Jesus Christ and the truths he revealed should be the spiritual fuel by which Christians live. The Johannine metaphor of eating and drinking of Jesus means nothing other than to believe and accept him as the incarnate Son of God and Savior of the world.

7:40 *Surely this man is the Prophet.* Based on the promise of Deuteronomy 18:15 for a future prophet like Moses, some viewed Jesus as that expected one who would have God's words in his mouth and tell the people everything God commands him (Dt 18:18; cf. Jn 5:37–38; 7:16; 8:28). At the time of Jesus, the Prophet and the Messiah were thought to be two different men. But the people were not completely wrong, for Jesus is indeed the Prophet who speaks the very words of God. Within himself the Son of God is both the Prophet and the Messiah.

7:42 *The Messiah will come from David's descendants and from Bethlehem.* Based on 2 Samuel 7:12–16, Psalm 89:3–4, and Isaiah 9:7 and 55:3, the people expected a Messiah to be in the lineage of King David. Furthermore, from messianic tradition based on Micah 5:2, which John does not quote or loudly echo, they expected the Messiah to be born in Bethlehem, the city of David. The crowds in Jerusalem knew Jesus was from Galilee and, therefore, they thought him ineligible to be the Messiah. But they didn't know the story of his birth in Bethlehem, and they also didn't share the readers' knowledge of his existence with God before the earth began (Jn 1:1–3) (see commentary on Jn 1:20, 41, 49; 2:17; 3:3; 6:15; 12:13–15).

7:49 *There is a curse on them.* The elite Pharisees and educated Jews looked down on "the people of the land" who without benefit of rabbinic education were believed to be incapable of knowing the law and living pious lives and were, therefore, cursed. Ironically, they would have considered Jesus to be among those who didn't know or keep the law. Nevertheless, the crowds and the temple guards heard something in Jesus' words that gave them pause. They sensed there was something more to him, while the prejudice of the Jewish leaders blinded them to the truth Jesus revealed.

7:53 *They all went home.* See "What the Structure Means: The Adulterous Woman (Jn 8:1–11)."

John 7 Through Old Testament Eyes

John is a master of using the symbolic traditions of Judaism to interpret the identity and significance of Jesus. The event at the heart of Israel's origins, the exodus, had by the time of Jesus become symbolic of deliverance from death and of the promise of national independence. The water imagery in John 7 "draws on two dominant uses of water symbolism found in the OT: the water from the rock in the exodus; and the water that would come from the Temple. . . . (Ezek 47:1–12; Zech 14:8; Joel 3:18)."[16] As God was the source of the water in these images, Jesus' claim to be the source of living water is another claim to stand in place of the temple as well as of his divinity. Ironically, at the time of Jesus, the temple and its rituals witnessed the very presence of the Son of God and yet failed to perceive his fulfillment of their promise of hope. As Ruben Zimmermann writes, "In many cases, symbolic traditions have been renewed and revised by being applied to Jesus. This 'Christologizing of symbols' takes place when, for example, the deeper meaning of Jewish temple celebrations is transferred to Jesus or is surpassed by him, as in the promise water at the Sukkot celebration (John 7:37). . . . Of special importance is the manner in which symbols that were traditionally reserved for God are employed for Jesus, for example, 'walking on water' (John 6:16–21) or the claim to be 'owner of the flock' (John 10:1–18)."[17]

John used the echoes of Scripture evoked by a quotation to shape his thoughts and memories of Jesus. Using this evocative and allusive technique, he shows who Jesus is and how he fulfills the deepest hopes and expectations of Israel's religion. "The signs and shadows of the celebration of Tabernacles in the Temple have become flesh in the person of Jesus, the Sent One of the Father."[18] No other gospel writer creates such a finely textured story of Jesus woven from threads of Old Testament Scripture that intimately bind the new covenant to the old.

JOHN 8

What the Structure Means: The Adulterous Woman (Jn 8:1–11)

Scholars who study the handwritten manuscripts that have preserved the text of the gospel of John almost unanimously agree that this passage, which actually includes 7:53, was not written by the author of the fourth gospel but added at some later time by an unknown scribe. This is because the passage is absent from virtually all extant Greek, Syriac, Coptic, and Old Latin manuscripts of John from the premedieval period, and appears only in later medieval manuscripts. It makes its first appearance in the fifth-century Codex Bezae (D). The early church fathers prior to the late fourth century apparently did not know of this passage as they pass from what we refer to as 7:52 directly to 8:12 in their commentaries. The passage often referred to as "the woman caught in adultery" has appeared in English Bibles because the medieval manuscript from which the earliest English translations were made happened to have included the passage.

Only through more recent scholarship when the earliest manuscripts were gathered and studied did it become evident that this passage is a later addition almost certainly not written by the same author as the gospel. Not only was the passage missing from the earliest manuscripts, but it was found inserted in various other places in manuscripts, after John 7:44, 7:36, or 12:25, and even in another book, Luke 21:38.[1] Based on similarities to ancient extrabiblical stories of Jesus, some believe it may preserve an authentic event in the Lord's ministry. But even if that is the case, the passage should not be considered part of the divinely inspired, canonical text. It would be sheer speculation to guess why this passage was inserted in the medieval manuscripts or to trace its origin. Out of respect for the English biblical tradition, our modern Bibles usually include the passage but print it in a different font, perhaps smaller or italics, than the authentic text.

8:12 *I am the light of the world.* The people were divided, and the Jewish leaders were confrontational after Jesus healed a man on the Sabbath (Jn 7:23, 43). The dispute continues in chapter 8, when Jesus speaks again to the people in the temple courts. It revolves around the validity of Jesus' testimony about himself. The fourth gospel claims that Jesus' testimony is qualitatively superior because in him the eternal Son of God entered the world (Jn 1:4, 9). John has already set this thought within the light-darkness duality, teaching that darkness is the realm of death and moral failure by evil deeds (3:19–20). But those who wish to live by God's truth come into the light—that is, enter the life that the incarnate Son of God offers (3:21) and live in the sight of God. Here Jesus tells the people what John has previously told readers, that Jesus is the light of the world. Those who follow him have the light of eternal life (see commentary on John 1:4, 5 and 6:35).

8:13 *Your testimony is not valid.* The Pharisees, a Jewish sect known for its standard of righteous living, challenge Jesus' claim. Jesus points out that the Pharisees judge by human standards, putting Jesus' words on the same level as all other human words, and if Jesus were merely human perhaps they would be right. As C. S. Lewis once argued, if Jesus is not the Son of God he is either a liar or a lunatic.[2] The option of his being merely a good man is not on the table given the claims he made. As Lewis' argument goes, if Jesus wasn't the Son of God but thought he was, he was a lunatic; if Jesus knew he wasn't the Son of God but said he was, he was a liar. But Jesus is apparently aware of his identity as the preexistent Son of God sent by God the Father. He claims that his divine origin makes his testimony about himself and any other topic trustworthy and valid beyond any human standard.

8:15–16 *You judge by human standards; I pass judgment on no one. But if I do judge, my decisions are true because I am not alone. I stand with the Father, who sent me.* Jesus did not come to be an arbitrator of human disputes, which are necessarily judged by human standards. For instance, Jesus refused to get involved in settling a dispute between brothers over an inheritance (Lk 12:13–14). And when the truth is known, even many religious judgments made in the church by godly people will likely boil down to human standards. For human beings cannot transcend their humanness and cannot help but judge by human standards—limited in knowledge, flawed by biases, blinded by cultural moment and historical location. Jesus does not stand with human beings when he judges; he stands with the Father in full divine authority, knowing everything. (Regarding *judgment* see commentary at John 5:22. Regarding *Father* see commentary at John 1:14 on "One and only Son" and at John 5:23 on "The Father, who sent him.")

8:17 *In your own law . . . the testimony of two witnesses is true.* Truth-telling was an important aspect of the covenant God made with his people at Sinai. The ninth of the Ten Commandments bound the godly person to "not give false testimony against your neighbor" (Ex 20:16; Dt 5:20). In the legal code of ancient Israel this entailed that any legal claim required the testimony of at least two witnesses before it could be accepted as truth (Dt 17:6; 19:15). In John 8:17 Jesus refers to this legal requirement with the emphatic "your own law" (*humeteros* [ὑμέτερος]), dissociating himself from the way the Pharisees used the law against him (see also commentary at 10:34 and 15:25). In a previous dispute with the Jewish leaders (Jn 5:31) Jesus himself had referred to this legal tradition, and listed four witnesses on his behalf: John the Baptist (5:33), the works Jesus did (5:36), the voice of God proclaiming Jesus his Son (5:37), and the Scriptures themselves (5:39). Here Jesus points to his divine origin and destination—that is, his identity as the eternal Son of God—to validate his words. His second witness is God the Father, who sent him. John the Baptist, the events of Jesus' life, and the Scripture may point to the divine Messiah, but it all comes down to either believing Jesus is who he says he is or not. There is no other testimony by which the claims of the Son of God can be validated.

8:19 *You do not know me or my Father.* Jesus' claim that "the Father, who sent me" is his second witness raises the issue of paternity that becomes central to the debate in the subsequent verses of chapter 8. The lack of knowledge of the Father by the highest leaders of first-century Judaism who claimed such knowledge has already been mentioned in John 7:28–29, which was also in the context of public debate about Jesus' identity and authority. If they truly knew God, Jesus' claims would not sound "strange and presumptuous in their ears . . . they would know that what he says is of God and that the Father is his witness. But by rejecting him in unbelief they show that they do not know his Father either."[3] The knowledge of God as knowledge of Jesus Christ and vice versa is "the underlying presupposition of this entire Gospel"[4] (cf. Jn 14:9).

Going Deeper into the Role of Evidence in Christian Conversion: John 8:12–20

Jesus' conversation with the Pharisees suggests an important point of later theological understanding concerning the nature of conversion. There is much historical evidence with which a person can support their belief in Christ. The very existence of the New Testament writings and the church itself, despite their incredible claims of Jesus' resurrection, are themselves historical phenomena that demand explanation. A singular event of epoch-making significance must lie behind Christianity, propelling it from generation to generation for two thousand years. While Judaism, Islam, and Eastern religions may be ancient, none of them have as their central tenant a supra-historical event the magnitude of a resurrection from the grave. And so one might ask, What evidence or testimony has led millions of people from many cultures, language groups, ethnicities, and centuries to rest their faith in the resurrected Jesus Christ? Evidence alone is insufficient. Jesus offered the Pharisees evidence—John the Baptist, the miraculous events of his life, and the Scriptures we know as the Old Testament—but here Jesus reveals an important limit to the role of evidence in conversion. Jesus says his second witness is "the Father, who sent me" (Jn 8:18).

God himself in some mysterious way validates the testimony of Jesus as preserved in the New Testament writings, opening the eyes of faith to its truth. Many can look at that same evidence but not come to faith in Christ. In fact, that is one of the major points of the gospel of John, that the response to Jesus in light of his claims was bifurcated. Some see and believe; others see and do not. The gospel of John and later Christian theology accounts for this through the doctrines of divine election and effectual calling. Jesus himself said, "No one can come to me unless the Father who sent me draws them" (Jn 6:44) (see "Going Deeper into Divine Election: John 6:37–65").

To the one whom the Father draws, the testimony and evidences of Jesus' identity are a reasonable and believable basis on which to rest one's faith. As John Murray wrote of this call, "It is an act of God, and of God alone, and does not derive its definition from any activity on our part, such as faith or repentance or conversion. Calling is not to be defined in terms of the responses which the called yield to this act of God's grace."[5] This calling is the witness of God the Father, testifying in the hearts of millions that Jesus is exactly who he says he is.

8:20 *Teaching in the temple courts near the place where the offerings were put.* The gospel writers in general, and John in particular, do not add irrelevant details, and so the location of Jesus' encounter with the Pharisees is meaningful. First, the place where the offerings were put was in the Court of the Women, to which both men and women had access. It was the place where the great illuminations took place during the Feast of Tabernacles, and poignantly, probably where Jesus declared that he is "the light of the world" (see 8:12). In other words, this confrontation had taken place in a public and probably crowded area of the temple precinct, heightening John's amazing observation, "Yet no one seized him" (see 7:30).

His hour had not yet come. John perhaps was surprised that Jesus had gotten away with this confrontation, and takes it as confirmation that "his hour had not yet come." The Father who had sent him into the world would determine, and he alone, when Jesus would leave it. This is not a claim for fatalism but attests to the involvement of God the Father with the mission of the Son in the world.

8:21 *You will die in your sin.* Jesus pronounces a judgment that widens the gulf between himself and those challenging him (cf. Eze 3:16–18). Jesus is going to the Father, a destination they cannot reach apart from him. The singular "sin" here likely refers to that state of darkness in which "sins" (8:24) are committed. Only the light of life, Jesus Christ, can dispel that darkness. These two realms—that of God, life, and light versus death, darkness, and sin—are separate and can be bridged only by crossing from death to life in Christ (Jn 5:24).

8:22 *Will he kill himself?* Rather than take Jesus' pronouncement of judgment seriously, they mock him by raising the question of his mental competence with the speculation of suicide, which was abhorrent in Judaism and considered an act of insanity. Although the Greek syntax of the question (*mēti* [μήτι]) shows they expected a negative answer, the rhetorical question itself functions to insult Jesus.

8:23 *You are from below; I am from above.* "Below" here is not a reference to the state after death but specifies the realm of the moral darkness of this world; "above" refers to the realm of light and life with God. Jesus replies to their mockery that they do not understand him because they are foreign to God's perspective, from which he speaks.

8:24 *If you do not believe that I am.* Jesus continues to act as their judge, restating that they will die in their sins unless they believe that "I am" (*egō* *eimi* [ἐγώ εἰμι]). Translators must decide whether to translate "I am" or "I am he," as the syntax permits either. Interpreters must decide whether this is an allusion to the divine name as first revealed to Moses in Exodus 3:14, which seems likely (cf. 8:58). An allusion to God's self-revelation in Isaiah, where the same phrase appears, seems especially apt in reference to Jesus. See Isaiah 41:4 (calling forth the generations), 43:10 (the unique God), 43:13 (eternally existent), 43:25 (blots out transgressions), 46:4 (sustains and carries his own), 48:12 (the first and the last) (see commentary on 6:35).

8:25 *Who are you?* The debate that began in chapter 5 concerning Jesus' authority to heal a man on the Sabbath has developed from a discussion of witnesses to the ultimate question of his identity. That is the crucial question. Who is Jesus? Destiny hangs on one's answer. Craig Koester writes, "People may ask who Jesus is, but their encounters with Jesus also disclose who they are. If he is the light, then the world lies in darkness; if he gives the living water, then people must be thirsty; if he is the bread, then people must hunger. Each of the main images for Jesus has a corresponding image for human beings, and this allows us to ask what the gospel's imagery might say about what it means to be human."[6] In this debate we learn that religious privilege does not compensate for or satisfy the spiritual need that all human beings have. For "to be human is to be created for life with God, to be separated from God, and to receive life with God by being brought to faith."[7]

8:28 *When you have lifted up the Son of Man.* They will know who Jesus is when they have killed him on the cross (see commentary on Jn 3:14). At that point it will be too late for the Jewish nation to recognize and receive their Messiah; he will have gone away to the Father, killed by their hand. This suggests that John uses the term "the Jews" in encounters with Jesus in the fourth gospel as a cipher for first-century Judaism in its rejection of the Messiah. By mentioning his execution Jesus also alludes to his resurrection, which will vindicate his claims. In the gospel of John Jesus' execution is understood to be his exaltation to glory upon the completion of his mission from the Father. His death is the doorway to the realm of life. He must die, but his resurrection will be proof of his identity for all who truly wish to know (on "Son of Man" see commentary at 1:51 and 13:31).

8:31 *If you hold to my teaching, you are really my disciples.* As Jan Van der Watt observes, "The mission from the Father guarantees the *authenticity* of Jesus' message. The message of Jesus is true, because he simply retells what he has heard from his Father who sent him and who is true (8:26). He is not on his own mission, but on a mission from above for the Father (8:42). By delivering the words of the Father his words become the revelation that can set people free (8:31–32, 55)."[8]

8:33 *We are Abraham's descendants.* John 1:12 already announced that God would make children of those who receive the true light that came into the world. The need for this new birth was established in John 3:3–5. And so the corollary question of who one's father is becomes a major motif in the Johannine writings. The Jewish nation claimed Abraham as the father of their nation based on God's covenant with the patriarch in Genesis 12 and 15 (see also Ex 2:24; 3:6, 15–16, where the link between Abraham and the nation is foundational). By their reasoning they were, therefore, children of God. Here, Jesus is debating with "the Jews who had believed in him" (8:31), but their belief is yet flawed. Jesus acknowledges that they are indeed descendants of Abraham (8:37) but denies that Abraham is their father (8:39), much less God (8:42). With this, Jesus severs the biological descent from Abraham as the defining truth about who the children born of God are (cf. Jn 1:13). This is the truth that will set them free from the penalty of the law and its sentence of death (8:32).

Have never been slaves of anyone. Jesus' claim for freedom raises its opposite, slavery, in the minds of his hearers. Strictly speaking, the descendants of Abraham through his grandson, Jacob, went into Egypt and *were* enslaved for 430 years (Ge 46:3–7; Ex 1:8–14; 12:40). God greatly multiplied their number, and they came out of Egypt as a nation called forth by God. Furthermore, as a nation they had been later ruled by Assyria, Babylon, Greece, and Rome. Surely the Jerusalem Jews at the time of Jesus had not forgotten their founding story and national history, especially as Rome occupied Jerusalem right before their eyes. Nevertheless, they did not think of themselves as slaves.

But there is a sense in which they had been free, and that is in their observance of monotheism. While politically ruled and oppressed by several world powers, they were never enslaved by idolatry to the extent that the monotheism that defined them was extinguished. They engaged in idolatry and were sent into exile for it, but spiritually monotheism remained the hallmark of Judaism through the millennia. Their statement recognizes that Jesus is speaking of spiritual, not political, matters. They are indignant that he would perceive them as spiritually enslaved and they rebuke Jesus saying, "How can you say that we will be set free?" If Jesus is still speaking to the Jews who had believed in him (8:31a), they had not heeded his teaching that to be his disciples they must hold to his teaching (8:31b). Their national pride had given them a sense of inherited religious privilege that prevented them from seeing their bondage to sin. As D. A. Carson observes, on Mark 2:17, "The Jews are convinced they are whole and therefore need no physician—just as they are here convinced they are free and therefore need no liberation."[9]

8:35 *Now a slave has no permanent place in the family, but a son belongs to it forever.* In the context of Abraham and his descendants (Jn 8:33, 39), we recall the story of Sarah's slave, Hagar, and her son by Abraham, Ishmael, who were sent away after the birth of Abraham's son Isaac by his wife Sarah (Ge 16:1–21).

Going Deeper into the Sin of Religious Pride: John 8:33–46

The first-century Jewish nation had good reason to feel religiously privileged. Theirs was the Abrahamic, Mosaic, and Davidic covenants, theirs was the promised land, the prophets, the temple, the priesthood, and the sacrifices. God had revealed himself through them, his chosen people, and had preserved them as a nation through millennia. If any group of people had reason to feel entitled, it was the Jewish nation. And yet Jesus claimed that, despite the privilege they enjoyed, they nevertheless needed new birth, as all human beings need. None of their historical and national privilege could free them from the penalty of sin that is death, as defined by their own law. None of the trappings of their God-given religion could substitute for personal faith in the Son whom God had sent at the right moment in their history.

Jesus offended them. He offended even those who had at least begun to believe in him (Jn 8:31). These first-century Jews are not unique in that respect. Throughout the ages and around the world, Jesus offends. He offends our self-sufficiency, our autonomy, our attempts to define for ourselves a belief system that we can live comfortably within. Even many who would self-identify as Christian almost inevitably encounter a teaching of Jesus that wounds and offends. How could it be otherwise when God is holy and just and we are not?

What will you do when Jesus offends you? What have you done when offended by Jesus? Jesus says, "If you hold to my teaching, you are really my disciple" (8:31). This is hard. When Jesus exposes our rationalization for our favorite sins, it's hard to deny ourselves and hold to his teaching. When Jesus says our lifelong membership in a church does not make us a child of God, it's hard to hold to his teaching. When the world in which we live sees Jesus' teaching as ridiculous, it's hard to hold to it and live it out in obedience. Willingness to be offended by Jesus and yet, nevertheless, hold to his teaching and live by it defines one as a true disciple. Are you?

8:39 *Abraham's children . . . do what Abraham did.* Jesus introduces a concept familiar from genetics, that offspring share the nature of the parent, or as the English aphorism puts it, "Like father, like son." The child's nature is expressed by what they do and say, by how they behave. This coheres with Johannine teaching that God's children must display God's character in all they do and say.

If Abraham's children do what Abraham did, what did Abraham do? What Abraham did was to *believe* God, and it was credited to him as righteousness (Ge 15:6). Abraham believed God for something that was, humanly speaking, impossible. He trusted God's power and authority for something only God could do: the birth of a son to him with Sarah when they were long past their fertile years. But instead of believing Jesus, the Son of God, these Jerusalem descendants of Abraham were plotting to kill him, showing the extent of the offense they took at his claims. No, Jesus says, denying their claimed paternity. God is *not* your Father or you would do what Abraham did. You would believe the message of the Son whom God sent.

8:44 *Your father, the devil, . . . was a murderer from the beginning.* Instead, Jesus tells them that, in spite of being Abraham's descendants, their behavior reveals that their true father is the devil! Speak of offense! If by definition, those who receive the light that came into the world become children of God (Jn 1:12), then those who do not recognize him and do not receive him (Jn 1:10–11) do not have God as their Father. This is not to say that God is not their Creator. In some contexts, the Fatherhood of God is based on his role as Creator. But in the Johannine writings the Fatherhood of God is based in the new birth of those who receive Jesus and believe the incarnate Word. In that context, those who do not receive Jesus cannot claim God as their Father.

It would have been shocking enough for Jesus to simply deny that God was the Father of those who do not believe in him. But to say that their spiritual father is the devil would be unthinkable. Jesus makes this claim for two reasons, both based on the behavior he observes: (1) they want to kill Jesus, even though he has done nothing worthy of such a sentence (8:46); (2) they reject the truth Jesus brings and prefer to believe the lie (8:44–45). As Jesus points out, these two points characterize the devil in his first encounter with Adam and Eve, and through whose lies death entered the human race (Ge 3). The Son of God was sent to undo the work of the devil by bringing truth and life into the world; whoever is a "son" of God will recognize Jesus, the Son of God, as true kin (see commentary on 13:27 for further discussion of Satan and the devil).

8:48 *You are a Samaritan and demon-possessed.* But rather than recognizing Jesus as their true kin, these Jerusalem descendants of Abraham continue their rejection of Jesus by calling him a Samaritan, whose ancestors centuries before, after the exile of the northern tribes of Israel, intermarried with pagan people brought by the Assyrians into Samaria (2 Ki 17:24). In other words, by accusing Jesus of being a Samaritan, they accused Jesus of not being a Jew. As Edward Klink explains it, "Jesus declared 'the Jews' to be outsiders to God . . . and the Jews reciprocate by declaring Jesus to be an outsider to Judaism."[10] In fact, Adele Reinhartz points out that "from a Jewish perspective, the Johannine Jesus bears a striking resemblance to the deceitful prophet as described in" Deuteronomy 13:1–5 and worthy of stoning.[11]

Furthermore, they accuse him of being demon-possessed, a way of aligning him with the devil *against* God. "By claiming Jesus is *both* a Samaritan and possessed by a demon, the Jews are effectively calling him a heretic, 'accusing him of straying from the one true God.'"[12] Jesus strongly denies this accusation, pointing out that he honors his Father. But his accusers dishonor him with their words of rejection. Given the cultural convention that one honors the one sent as one would honor the one who sent him, Jesus points out that they are, in fact, dishonoring God when they dishonor him.

8:51 *Whoever obeys my word will never see death.* The Old Testament repeatedly exhorts readers to "keep" or "obey" the laws, decrees and commands of the Lord (e.g., Ex 24:7; Lev 18:4, 5, 30; 22:31; Nu 15:40; Dt 4:40; 5:10; 6:17; 11:1; 13:4; 26:17; 27:10; 1 Sa 15:22; 1 Ki 8:61; Ne 10:29; Ps 119:44). Ancient Israel was to be that people who kept covenant and lived in obedience to what the Lord God had said, with a promise of long life (Dt 4:40; 30:16; Eze 18:19). Here Jesus extends the promise from long life to eternal life and bases it on obedience to his own word, equating his authority with that of God in the Old Testament.

If Abraham believed God for something only God could do, then Jesus clearly invites the Jews of Jerusalem to imitate Abraham by believing that eternal life, which only God can give, is offered to them through the word of Jesus. The syntax of "will never see death" (note the double negative in the Greek, *ou mē* [οὐ μὴ]) is the logical equivalent of having eternal life. To "obey" the word (sg.) of Jesus is to admit that all the inherited religious privilege on which they stand has not released them from the penalty of sin and death. They must believe Jesus is the Son sent by the Father to secure their eternal life.

8:53 *Are you greater than our father Abraham?* The "Jews" have not been convinced that Abraham is not their father, and so rightly infer that Jesus' claims about himself would make him greater than Abraham. The Greek syntax of this question (*mē* [μή] with an indicative mood verb) signals that they expect Jesus to back down and to give them the expected negative reply.

And for good measure they try to put Jesus in his place with the additional question, "Who do you think you are?" (cf. 5:18). But Jesus the Son of God knows that he is exactly who he claims to be.

8:57 *Not yet fifty years old.* Jesus was, in fact, about thirty years old when this conversation happened, and so the observation that he was not yet fifty underscores the apparent absurdity of Jesus' alleged personal knowledge about Abraham. It is unclear when Abraham rejoiced at the thought of seeing Jesus' day, or when he did see it. Either it is an oblique allusion to Abraham's faith in the efficacy of the covenant God had made with him during his lifetime, or it is a mysterious reference to Abraham's postmortem awareness of the advent of Jesus. The point Jesus makes does not depend on our understanding which of these it was, as much as our curiosity might demand an answer. He is claiming to fulfill the covenant promise God made with Abraham.

8:58 *Before Abraham was born, I am!* This is one of those statements in the fourth gospel that prompted Richard Hays to say, "John's Gospel manifests an unsettling indifference to ordinary perceptions of linear time."[13] And there is good reason for that "unsettling indifference."

The debate that began back in chapter 5 over whether Jesus had the authority to heal on the Sabbath developed through chapter 7 and reaches this crescendo at the end of chapter 8 with an unmistakable claim to deity. Using the same phrase, "I am" (*egō eimi* [ἐγώ εἰμι]), with which God revealed himself to Moses at the beginning of ancient Israel's national identity (Ex 3:14), Jesus reveals by what authority he heals on the Sabbath, the authority of Israel's God. It is probably insufficient to claim by this a simple ontological identity of Jesus Christ with Israel's God. Not only would that violate Christian Trinitarian theology—it was not Yahweh who was incarnate in Jesus—but it fails to recognize the distinctive authority of Jesus, the *Son* of God. Perhaps John Calvin makes a more nuanced point that the statement makes a pan-historical claim about Jesus' authority. He writes, "Christ's power and grace, inasmuch as He is the Redeemer of the world, *were common to all ages.*"[14] Jesus was not claiming authority for just that historical moment in first-century Jerusalem, but was claiming a continuity of authority that spanned Abraham's day as well. Calvin continues, "Yet that the grace of the Mediator flourished in all ages depended on His eternal Divinity. And this saying of Christ contains a remarkable statement of His divine essence."[15] With this statement Jesus asserts not a simple identity with Yahweh but an equality of power and authority that is in effect through all the millennia of human history (see commentary on 6:35).

8:59 *Picked up stones to stone him.* Throughout the back and forth of this extended conversation Jesus develops his claims until in 8:58 he presents an undeniable claim to divine power and authority that is equal to Yahweh's. The Jews heard this claim clearly, for they understood Jesus to be enticing them to worship another god, and they intended to execute the punishment for that sin: death by stoning (Dt 13:1–11). Ironically, the monotheism that characterized Judaism, which had been refined in the fire of exile, obscured their ability to perceive the one true God when he appeared, as the Old Testament had predicted he would.

What the Structure Means: Why Jesus Was Executed (Jn 5–8)

John 5–8 forms an important subunit of the fourth gospel. John 8 brings to its culmination the long, extended debate about Jesus' authority and identity that began in chapter 5 when he healed a lame man on the Sabbath. In 5:18 the Jewish leaders begin plotting to kill Jesus because "he was even calling God his own Father, making himself equal with God." The identity of Jesus in relation to God is, according to John, the essential question in the gospel that readers must consider.

Jesus claims that he does as God does: he raises the dead (5:21) and executes judgment (5:22), because God has granted the life that he has in himself to the Son to have life in himself as well (5:26). This is a key concept in the relationship between Jesus and God, presenting Jesus' deity while yet defending monotheism. There is only *one* divine life of God that is by definition eternal, and because it is found in both the Father and the Son, both are divine.

Within the cultural context of first-century Judaism, the debate about Jesus' identity and authority involves the question of the testimony of witnesses, as if Jesus is being put on trial—a foreshadowing of the future "trial" that will end with his execution. But throughout the debate in which the Jewish leaders are in some sense trying Jesus, Jesus is shown at the same time to be trying and judging the Jewish leaders, and his authority will ultimately exceed theirs. As his witnesses, Jesus calls to his defense John the Baptist (5:33–35), the works that he did (5:36), the Father himself (5:37–38), Scripture (5:39–40), and Moses (5:45–47).

In chapter 7 the threat against Jesus has not subsided (7:1, 19), but he nevertheless appears teaching in the temple at the Feast of Tabernacles, claiming to be the true fulfillment of that festival's eschatological promise (7:37–39). He begins to gain traction with the people, some of whom think him to be "the Prophet" (7:40), while others believe him to be the Messiah (7:41). Again the Pharisees challenge him with the accusation that his testimony "is not valid" (7:13) and some want to arrest him as a troublemaker (7:44).

In the next episode, in 8:12–59, Jesus claims his origin with the Father who sent him as his defense. His witness as Son of God plus the Father's testimony by virtue of sending him should satisfy the law's requirement of two witnesses to establish the truth (Dt 17:6). As Son of God, Jesus claims to be Judge (8:24, 26); he disenfranchises the first-century Jerusalem Jews from their perceived privilege as descendants of Abraham and children of God (8:37–43, 47); and he links their paternity with the devil (8:44). He reveals himself to be their liberator (8:36), who was sent by God (8:42), to reveal truth (8:45), promising eternal life to those who follow him (8:52), who knows the God who himself seeks Jesus' glory (8:50, 55). Finally, he uses the divine name revealed to Moses at the foundation of Israel's ancient nation to claim a power and authority equal to the Father's (8:58).

Throughout this debate Jesus is protected from the increasing threat against him (7:1, 13, 30, 44; 8:20, 59) because "his hour had not yet come." This signals the Father's providential involvement in the unfolding of Jesus' earthly life. The Father's purposes for sending the Son into the world will be accomplished in his perfect timing. These chapters prepare the reader for what is coming, revealing that Jesus' life is endangered, not in spite of who he is, but *because* of who he is. Jesus will be brought to trial and executed for being Israel's Messiah, who turned out to be no less than the Son of God incarnate.

JOHN 9

9:1 *As he went along.* This very general marker of a shift in scene does not specifically locate the episode in time or place. But because both the Pharisees and the pool of Siloam figure so prominently in this episode, it is likely Jesus was still in Jerusalem sometime between the Festival of Tabernacles (mid-fall; Jn 7) and the Festival of Dedication (early December; Jn 10:22). Moreover, there are significant links in John 9 with both John 7 and John 10. John does not enumerate all the signs, nor does he refer to all of Jesus' miracles as "signs" (see "What the Structure Means: Reading the Signs of the Fourth Gospel (Jn 2–12)"). Although this healing is not identified as a "sign" (*sēmeion* [σημεῖον]), it is the sixth symbolic miracle, exposing what it means that Jesus is the light of the world by connecting the healing of the man born blind with fulfillment of the prophecies of Isaiah (29:18; 35:5; 42:7, 16, 18; 43:8; 59:10).

A man blind from birth. While the modern world understands blindness as the body's inability to sense light coming into the eyes, many ancients thought vision to be accomplished by an inner ray that emanated outward from the heart through the eyes (see Ezr 9:8; Ps 19:8; 38:10).[1] In other words, inner light was required for healthy sight. But inner darkness could also be projected (see Mt 6:22, 23; Lk 11:33–36), as reflected in the belief in the "evil eye," the concept that darkness of the heart could project harm from a wicked person onto whomever they gazed upon. Blindness was thought to be the darkness of the heart emanating from the eyes of sightless people, and therefore had strong spiritual and moral connotations. This ancient concept helps us to understand the spiritual significance developed throughout this episode using the categories of light/darkness and sight/blindness.

9:2 *Rabbi, who sinned.* The idea that children suffer due to the sins of their parents is found in the Ten Commandments (Ex 20:5; but cf. Jer 31:29–30).

Jesus transforms this notion into a new way in which God can be glorified, not just by keeping the law but by trusting in the Son who heals (Jn 9:3–7).

In the Old Testament, blindness was used as a negative metaphor to indicate guilt, corruption, and spiritual darkness (Ex 23:8; Dt 16:19; 28:28–29; Job 9:24; Isa 29:18; 32:3; 35:5; 42:7, 18–20). In Old Testament prophecy the healing of blindness and the restoration of sight symbolized eschatological fulfillment (e.g., Isa 29:18; 35:5; 42:7, 18). In the New Testament Jesus' healing ministry was understood to be a fulfillment of these prophecies that indicated the inauguration of the eschaton in Jesus (Mt 11:5; Lk 1:79; 7:22; and especially Lk 4:16–21).

Because blindness was typically considered to indicate a darkened heart, it was believed to be a direct consequence of a person's sin. The disciples are curious whether blindness from birth should be attributed to the baby or to his or her parents. Personal responsibility seems to be the only option in the disciples' minds, a view also reflected in later rabbinic writing that attributed congenital disabilities to the sin of the unborn child in utero.[2] Certainly there are incidents in the Old Testament where illness or disability *did* result from a person's disobedience, such as Miriam in Numbers 12:9–10, and in the New Testament, for instance, Jesus' warning in John 5:14. But the belief seems to be an inference that if death is the consequence of sin, illness and disability are part of that necessary consequence. However, much biblical teaching denies that personal sin and illness or disability are necessarily linked (the book of Job, and the apostle Paul's own testimony in Gal 4:13 and 2 Co 12:7). Jesus himself corrects the disciples' assumption in his reply, "Neither this man nor his parents sinned" (Jn 9:3a). And so it is incorrect to infer that because the maladies of the human race originated with sin (Ge 3) there is a necessary and direct connection between an individual's sin and their illness or disability. Jesus suggests another way to think about it.

9:3 *The works of God.* Due to no fault of his own or of his parents, this man had suffered blindness his entire life, and almost certainly the stigma that went with it in the ancient world. He would have been pitied at best, and possibly feared as a spiritual or physical danger to the community. The disciples and others in the ancient world observed the suffering of illness and disability and supposed its purpose was to punish sins committed (Dt 28:28–29; though blindness is not always attributed to sin; 1 Ki 14:1, 4). Using the strong adversative *alla* (ἀλλά), Jesus gives a different kind of answer: not punishment but rather that the works of God might be made known in him. (The noun is plural in the Greek, *ta erga* [τὰ ἔργα]) A natural question arises from the syntax of the genitive: are these works that are done by the man in the service of God (objective genitive) or works that God himself does (subjective genitive)?[3] The ambiguity might serve the thought that such works are the concurrent action of both what the believer and God do. John uses this phrase elsewhere only in John 6:29, where the crowd asks Jesus what *they* must do to do "the works of God," clearly an objective genitive (see Jn 3:21 NRSV). Elsewhere in the fourth gospel (Jn 3:21; 8:39–47; 9:4) commendable works are attributed to both Jesus and the disciples. But 6:29 is significant for interpreting the phrase, for Jesus there answers the questions about "the works of God" by establishing a fundamental principle of John's gospel: "The work of God is this: to believe in the one he has sent." Faith in Christ is necessary for doing any works of God, and that faith is described as "coming to" Jesus in 6:37 as itself a work that *God* performs (subjective genitive).[4]

In this case of the man blind from birth, Jesus describes his blindness as the *circumstance* in which faith in Christ will be made known, showing that God wants to set life right by restoring sight and that Jesus is the one who has the power to do it. As George Beasley-Murray observes, "The works of the Father have basically one meaning: to show and to glorify him [Jesus] as Revealer and Bringer of salvation. It would therefore be a mistake to make out of the saying of Jesus a general truth."[5] Moreover, it should not be thought that God *caused* the man's blindness; rather the Lord "overruled the disaster" of blindness, showing even that particular circumstance to be not beyond the power of Jesus.[6] The disciples, as many of us, see this as a chance to moralize about the victim, but Jesus sees it as a chance to relieve someone's suffering without reflection on its cause.[7] For the man's blindness represents the blindness of the whole world, of all of us until Jesus heals our spiritual blindness.

9:5 *I am the light of the world.* The reader has already been told that Jesus is the true light of the world (Jn 1:9), but here he says it of himself. The Festival of Tabernacles had just lit up the Jerusalem darkness with its great fire bowls on the Temple Mount, which could be seen for miles around (see commentary on 7:37–39). Shortly the people to whom Jesus spoke would celebrate the Festival of Dedication (10:22; what we know as Hanukkah), which features light to commemorate the rededication of the temple when its golden lamp had miraculously burned for eight nights. But blindness is the inability to perceive light, and that lies at the heart of Jesus' message here (regarding "light," see commentary on 1:4, 5, and 9; regarding the "I am" statements see commentary on 6:35).

9:6 *Made some mud with the saliva.* This odd act is often discussed in terms of the medicinal value of saliva, or the purity laws, or recapitulating the original act of God's creation of the human being from the dust of the earth. In the culture of that day it was likely taken to indicate the power and purity of Jesus, for body fluids "that might otherwise contaminate can heal or remove impurity if drawn from a particularly pure or powerful specimen."[8] Furthermore, it was likely a prophetic reenactment of Isaiah 6:10, where the Lord tells Isaiah to "close the eyes" of the people. The Hebrew verb translated "close" (š'' [שעע]) in its *hiphil* form, as in Isaiah 6:10, means "to seal over" and may have been an idiom that meant to blind.[9] Ironically, it was this act of making and smearing mud to seal over the blind man's eyes that turns the Pharisees once again against Jesus, despite its miraculous efficacy, because he did it on the Sabbath (see commentary on 9:14). The end result of Jesus' healing miracle was the restoration of sight to the blind man and the continued blindness of the Pharisees, the first-century representatives of the people to whom Isaiah had ages before been sent, apparently in vain.

9:7 *Wash in the Pool of Siloam.* Significantly, Isaiah 6:8 is in the context of Isaiah's great commissioning scene, where God asks, "Whom shall I send?" and Isaiah replies, "Here am I. Send me!" In John's gospel Jesus is characterized as the one who was *sent*, and he sends the blind man with eyes now sealed with mud to wash in the pool of Siloam, which John tells his readers means "sent." This too has connections to the Isaiah tradition preserved in the ancient text Lives of the Prophets, a Jerusalem text that predates the Christian era and contains "a collection of extra-Biblical Jewish traditions concerning the history and the activities" of the three Major Prophets (Isaiah, Jeremiah, and Ezekiel), Daniel, and the Twelve.[10] According to the tradition associated with the prophet Isaiah, God performed a miraculous sign (*sēmeion* [σημεῖον]) in answer to Isaiah's dying prayer for water. God *sent* water that resulted in the pool called *Siloam* (sent). Moreover, John 12:40 quotes Isaiah 6:10 in summary of Jesus' public ministry, specifically the Jewish rejection of Jesus:

> Make the heart of this people calloused;
>> make their ears dull
>> and close their eyes.
> Otherwise they might see with their eyes,
>> hear with their ears,
>> understand with their hearts,
> and turn and be healed.

Isaiah's prophecy of a great light that would dawn on the people walking in darkness (Isa 9:2) is evoked by Jesus' declaration that "I am the light of the world." The Pharisees' rejection of Jesus' prophetic act of healing echoes Isaiah 8:6, the rejection of "the gently flowing waters of Siloam."[11] During the just-past Festival of Tabernacles the priests fetched water from the pool of Siloam for their liturgy in commemoration of the messianic promises. It was on that greatest day of the festival when Jesus stood and cried out, "Let anyone who is thirsty come to me and drink" (Jn 7:37 and see commentary there), deepening the irony of the Pharisees' rejection. But in obedience to the *Sent One* the blind man washes his mud smeared eyes in the waters called "*Sent*" because they had long before been *sent* by God to Isaiah. "And then I could see," said the newly sighted man (Jn 9:11).

9:14 *The day . . . was a Sabbath.* Apparently the healed man was brought to the Pharisees by those who witnessed the miracle, for it is very clear that by making mud on the Sabbath Jesus broke the law as the Pharisees understood it. Just as when Jesus healed the lame man and commanded him to pick up his mat on a Sabbath (Jn 5:8–9), the Pharisees are provoked by Jesus' actions. In the socioreligious context of their day, such violations of sacred time "jeopardize the continued presence of God with the nation and in the temple."[12] So they were understandably upset. But what the Pharisees failed to understand is that, as a sign of the covenant, Sabbath pointed to the day of the fullness of God's covenant promises, which Jesus had come to inaugurate. Given that John links this Sabbath-day miracle to Isaiah's prophecy, the Messiah has been sent, according to Isaiah 61:1, "to proclaim . . . release from darkness for the prisoners," which in the Septuagint was interpreted as the "recovery of sight to the blind." The Pharisees were offended that Jesus had the audacity to violate their laws, rather than seeing how singularly appropriate it was for Jesus, the Son of God, to do miracles of restoration and healing on the Sabbath, a day that commemorated the promises of the covenant. As Britt Leslie observes, for them "to reject the symbol of God's presence in order to preserve God's presence is a dramatic irony (they do not know but the audience does) reflected in the entire passage and ultimately in the whole Gospel as foreshadowed in the omniscient prologue (1:11)."[13]

9:17 *He is a prophet.* Rather than recognize their Messiah, the Pharisees pronounce him to be "not from God," dividing the people who reasoned that only a man from God could heal blindness. The Pharisees put the healed man on the spot by asking whom he believed Jesus to be. The man affirmed that Jesus must have been from God, calling him a prophet (cf. Jn 6:14).

Of course, if it could be shown that no miracle had in fact resulted from this violation of the Sabbath, then Jesus could be dismissed as simply a sinner. And so the Pharisees sent for the man's parents because they did not believe that he had been blind from birth and had been healed.

9:22 *Would be put out of the synagogue.* Verse 22 has been seminal in the modern history of interpretation of the gospel of John because of this phrase. Scholars, most prominently J. Louis Martyn, have argued that those who recognized Jesus as the Messiah were at risk of being put out of the synagogue only decades after his death, not during his lifetime. From that assumption Martyn developed the elaborate theory that the fourth gospel was written more to address the Johannine community's experience than to explain the historical Jesus. The theory became a dominant paradigm in Johannine studies, and scholars began to interpret all parts of the fourth gospel through that lens.[14] Martyn's hypothesis has influenced the way the gospel of John has been read ever since, although his assumptions have begun to be challenged and his influence may be waning. For instance, William Wright concludes from his analysis of John 9 that it "should be read as primarily ordered to demonstrate a claim about Jesus' identity, not to tell the story of the Johannine community."[15]

9:24 *Give glory to God.* The man's parents confirmed that this man was their son and that he had been blind from birth, reinforcing the claim that Jesus had performed a great miracle. Finding no satisfaction with the parents, the Pharisees called the man a second time, commanding him to tell the truth (cf. Jos 7:19), and to agree with them that Jesus was a sinner. But the man, to his credit, sticks to the truth that he had truly been born blind and had been healed by Jesus.

9:28 *We are disciples of Moses!* Because the man believed Jesus to be a prophet, the Pharisees accuse him of being "this fellow's" disciple. They assert their superiority as disciples of Moses, Israel's prophet par excellence. This is the seventh and final time Moses will be mentioned in the gospel of John (see Jn 1:17, 45; 3:14; 5:45–46; 6:32; 7:19–23; and 9:28–29), here raising the question of the relationship of Jesus to Moses. The Pharisees "know" that God spoke through Moses, and Jesus has tried to point out to them during the last debate over Jesus' authority that Moses spoke of him (Jn 5:46). Readers see the great irony, because they have been informed that Jesus is the Word of God become flesh, fulfiller of the covenant promises given through Moses (Jn 1:17).

9:29 *We don't even know where he comes from.* This entire episode of the healing can be understood as witnessing to who Jesus is and where he is from (9:29–33).[16] Previously, the Jews of Galilee had used their personal knowledge of Jesus' family as a reason to reject his divine origin (6:42). Here, the Pharisees of Jerusalem claim their lack of knowledge of Jesus' origin as reason to reject him as having been sent from God. The mysterious origin of the Messiah, "no one will know where he is from," was thought to argue against Jesus in John 7:27; here, they argue the opposite. The Pharisees' offended pride prevents them from seeing the true light of the world. As Craig Koester observes, "Not knowing becomes not believing, and not believing means they have become blind to the light."[17]

9:31 *God does not listen to sinners.* The Old Testament frequently asserts that God listens to the godly and not to sinners (Ps 34:15–16; 66:18; 145:19; Pr 15:29; Isa 1:15; 59:1–2). The man boldly rebukes the Pharisees, claiming that Jesus is a godly person who does God's will (cf. Jn 3:2; 4:34; 5:19) and who has performed one of the greatest of miracles. His reasoning leads him closer to the truth about Jesus, whereas the Pharisees' reasoning prevents them from seeing the truth. The effect of such dramatic irony is to bond readers with the healed man because they already know from the Prologue that the Pharisees are wrong in their judgment of who Jesus is and where he came from. "In this way the narrative itself creates insiders"[18] and leads readers to decide on which side they will take their stand.

9:34 *Steeped in sin at birth.* The Pharisees press the idea that Jesus himself had rejected when his disciples brought it up in 9:3, that the man's blindness was punishment for his and/or his parents' sin, and they use it against him. Jesus said that this man's blindness was not caused by sin but would reveal the works of God (9:3). The Pharisees may have had in mind Psalm 51:1: "Surely I was sinful at birth, sinful from the time my mother conceived me." Because of the fall of Adam and Eve, every human being is born in a state of sin that sooner rather than later expresses itself in sinful words and deeds. Jesus does not deny the sinfulness of human nature, but explains that there is no direct connection between the sinful deeds and words of either the parents or the man and his blindness in this case.

And they threw him out. Exactly what his parents feared is now realized in the life of their son (9:22). This excommunication from the synagogue would have long-reaching social and spiritual implications in the community. The verb *ekballō* (ἐκβάλλω), to be cast out, is picked up again in John 10:4: "When he [Jesus] has brought out [*ekballō*; ἐκβάλλω] all his own, he goes ahead of them, and his sheep follow him" (Jn 10:4). In other words, John interprets being cast out of the synagogue as having been brought out by Jesus, who makes this man and those like him part of Jesus' own community (see commentary on Jn 10:3). And the one who follows Jesus he will never "drive away" (Jn 6:37).

9:35 *Believe in the Son of Man?* Just as Jesus later found the lame man he had healed (5:14), Jesus here seeks out the man who had been thrown out of the synagogue. Jesus asks him a pointed question: "Do you believe in the Son of Man?" Jesus, the Son of God, has already been identified as Jesus, the Son of Man, in John 5:27 (cf. Da 7:13). As an apocalyptic end-time figure his presence functions for both judgment and rescue from the sociopolitical and spiritual oppression of the world (Da 7:23–27), and "his coming will mark the beginning of God's judgment."[19] In that context, Jesus' role as judge is in view, as it is here also in John 9:39. In the fourth gospel, seeing and believing are paired, for those who truly have the sight to see the significance of Jesus' miraculous signs are led to faith by them (Jn 2:11, 23; 4:53; 7:31; 11:42, 45; 12:37; 20:30–31). Having received his sight physically, the formerly blind man has also stood up to the Pharisees, testifying to the authority and power of Jesus as a prophet (9:30–33). Now it is time for Jesus to perfect the "sight" of the man, by revealing himself as the Son of Man.

The formerly blind man had not previously seen Jesus, for he was still blind and mud-smeared when they last parted. Jesus declares himself to the formerly blind man. As Stan Harstine observes, "The sight of the blind man continually improves until he understands and believes that Jesus is the Son of Man, not merely a prophet or one from God."[20] The man believes Jesus and worships him, bringing the manifested work of God to its goal (cf. 9:3) (on "Son of Man" also see commentary at 1:51 and 13:31).

9:39 *For judgment I have come.* The English word *judgment* may suggest punishment, but the Greek word *krima* (κρίμα) refers here more to the process or action of judging than to its outcome. Jesus has come into the world to sort things out, to be light to the blind, and to confirm those who reject his light to darkness (cf. Mt 25:32). Those like the Pharisees who think they are righteous apart from Christ claim they can see (9:41), but because they fail to see their own inner darkness, their guilt remains and confines them to darkness. Here John begins to explain the rejection of Jesus that will culminate his public ministry and lead to his execution (see commentary at Jn 5:22 on judgment and at 12:37–41 on believing).

9:41 *Your guilt remains.* Jesus confirms the Pharisees' decision to remain in the darkness. Recognized spiritual blindness can be healed, but the denial of one's blindness is itself sin. This episode is a high point in the dramatic irony that characterizes the fourth gospel. While the Pharisees exclude the man who was blind, they are ironically the ones who are in the dark, not knowing where Jesus comes from or who he is. But John's readers are enlightened because from the Prologue we do know. This skillful use of dramatic irony in the gospel of John makes it a very effective evangelistic tract, as John leads readers to recognize the truth of who Jesus is.

John 9 Through Old Testament Eyes

The gospel of John records several of the signs Jesus did "that you may believe that Jesus is the Messiah, the Son of God, and that by believing you may have life in his name" (Jn 20:31). But not everyone believed, even among those who saw the miracles with their own eyes but who failed to perceive what Jesus' miracles signified: the fulfillment of the covenantal promises God had made in the Old Testament. With the incarnation the true light of God came into the world (Jn 1:9), but many then, as now, were blind to it. As William Wright explains, "The narrative action in John presents in a symbolic manner the manifestation of God's work and the judgment and giving of life associated with Jesus as the Light. In this way, John 9 displays narratively what it is for Jesus to be the Light of the World."[21] But the light of the world often fell on blind eyes.

As John tells the story of Jesus, he does so in a way that shows Jesus as divisive. He shows that encounters with Jesus produced reactions of either some degree of belief or some degree of rejection. In the successive conversations in this chapter the Pharisees grow increasingly hostile to Jesus and the formerly blind man, while the man who was healed grows in his understanding and acceptance of Jesus until he makes a full profession of faith in 9:38: "Lord, I believe" that you are the Son of Man who has come from God to judge the nations (Da 7:13–14).

John's indictment of the Pharisees for their unwillingness to hear and believe Jesus resonates with an echo of Isaiah 6:8–10, the commissioning of the prophet Isaiah, who was sent by God to a people who would not understand, not perceive, and not be healed of their blindness. As J. Alec Motyer observes, Isaiah 6:10 presents "a rounded structure (*heart, ears, eyes, eyes, ears, heart*) thus emphasizing a total inability to comprehend."[22] Such a strange task for a prophet, "to effect heart-hardening and spiritual blindness."[23] If the message of Isaiah had such a blinding effect, how much more would the true light of the world effectively blind those who refused to see.

Those who refused to see Jesus were the religious elite of his day, the Pharisees to whom first-century Jewish society looked up as to the cream of the crop. The Pharisees who devotedly sought God failed to recognize him when he appeared, and instead criticized and condemned him. John understands the healing of the man born blind to clearly show not only that Jesus fulfills Isaiah's prophecies of messianic healing (Isa 29:18; 35:5; 42:7, 16, 18; 43:8; 59:10) but also that he himself is the ultimate division between those who are given life and those who remain in darkness and death.

JOHN 10

10:1 *Very truly I tell you Pharisees.* Jesus addresses the Pharisees, making it likely that 10:1–21 continues the encounter begun in chapter 9.[1] The double *amēn* (ἀμήν) without an introductory formula (e.g., "Jesus said . . .") follows the pattern of six other instances that continue Jesus' discourse, suggesting the Good Shepherd Discourse is to be read as a continuation of the healing of the blind man.[2] Britt Leslie explains the connection between the two chapters: "Jesus, using the extended metaphor of himself as the good shepherd, speaks of himself as 'bringing out' . . . all of his own. This reframes the 'throwing out' of the man from the synagogue by the Pharisees and the 'bringing out' of the man into the sheep fold by Jesus."[3]

Therefore, the reference in 10:21 back to the healing of chapter 9 ends the encounter and provides for the Pharisees the example of the formerly blind man as one of Jesus' new sheep. When this chapter is read against the background of the biblical shepherd theme, it is a rebuke of the Jewish authorities who had been charged with the care for God's flock, for "the main thematic link between the close of John 9 and Jesus' words in John 10 is the question of true and false leadership."[4]

The sheep pen. Sheep are especially defenseless animals, having neither claws nor fangs to fight off attacks by predators. Their only true defense is their shepherd. In the ancient world the sheep pen was an area enclosed by short walls of stone with only one entrance into which sheep would be gathered for protection. A gatekeeper often guarded the entrance (see 10:3). In small villages, several families might combine their flocks in the pen for overnight protection, hiring a gatekeeper to keep a watchful eye.[5] When human beings are metaphorically described as sheep, it is to highlight their helplessness and inability to take care of themselves. Sheep without a shepherd are in life-threatening trouble.

A thief and a robber. These near-synonyms may have been a conventional idiom (cf. Ob 5), but the former suggests stealth and the latter suggests violence. Anyone who did not openly approach the gatekeeper for access to the sheep was considered up to no good.

10:2 *The one who enters by the gate is the shepherd.* The gatekeeper would allow access to the shepherd of the sheep, and the sheep would recognize his or her voice. Jesus tells the Pharisees that he is both the gate (10:7) and the Good Shepherd (10:11, 14).

The Pharisees and John's original readers would probably not have missed Jesus' point, for shepherd imagery is significant in the Old Testament. There the shepherd metaphor refers (1) to God's relationship to his people; (2) to leaders of ancient Israel, primarily those who have failed God; (3) to a promised new leader, understood to be the Messiah.[6] Perhaps the most well-known use of the shepherd metaphor is Psalm 23:1, where the Lord is the shepherd who provides all things needed by the sheep: "The LORD is my shepherd, I lack nothing." King David, who shepherded his father's sheep as a boy, was chosen by God to shepherd the people as king (2 Sa 5:2). The prophets use the shepherd metaphor to describe leaders of God's people who destroy and scatter the Lord's sheep and consequently come under judgment (Jer 23:1–2; Eze 34:1–10; Zec 10:3). In response to the evil shepherds, God promises that he will himself shepherd his people, searching for and gathering the lost, tending the weak, and healing the injured (Ps 100:3; Jer 23:3; Eze 34:11–16). The promised ruler who would come out of Bethlehem "will stand and shepherd his flock in the strength of the LORD, in the majesty of the name of the LORD his God" (Mic 5:4), a prophecy fulfilled in the coming of Jesus the Messiah (Mt 2:4–6). When read through Old Testament eyes, Jesus both indicts the Pharisees as evil shepherds in their generation and declares himself to be the Good Shepherd who acts with the power and authority of God (cf. Jn 10:6).

10:3 *Calls his own sheep by name and leads them out.* If more than one family used the same sheep pen, each shepherd would have to gather his or her own flock to take them out to pasture. Kenneth Bailey describes the morning scene in modern-day Middle Eastern sheep pens where the flocks of several shepherds had spent the night.[7] The shepherd will stand in the street, give his own unique call, and his sheep, and only his sheep, will come out to him, ready to be led to pasture. It is the unique sound of the shepherd's voice, not the words spoken, that his sheep recognize, so someone who was merely using the same call would not be successful. So here John uses what would have been very familiar to portray the work of Jesus, the Good Shepherd, as leading those who are *uniquely* his (see Jn 6:37, 40, 44) out of the synagogue and into the Christian community that Jesus is creating. His divine voice of revelation would be recognized by those the Father had given to him (10:29) but unheeded by those who are not his sheep.

10:7 *I am the gate* (sometimes translated "door," but because the structure is a pen, "gate" seems the more apt English word). Herman Ridderbos points out that in light of 10:1–2 and 8a, the gate "gives access *to* the sheep and by which the shepherd, unlike the thieves and robbers, enters the sheepfold."[8] This would suggest that oversight of God's people is gained legitimately only through Jesus, and that all others claiming oversight are thieves and robbers. However in 10:9 he is also the gate through which the sheep enter the sheepfold. Perhaps Psalm 118:20 is significant here: "This is the gate of the LORD through which the righteous may enter." There is only one gate in Jesus' imagery, so he is claiming to be the entrance into righteousness and the only legitimate way to the flock of God's people (cf. Jn 14:6). This claim would have, of course, been highly offensive to the Pharisees, priests, and Jewish leaders, implying that they have lost their right to lead Israel and that it has now gone to Jesus (see commentary on 6:35).

10:8 *All who have come before me are thieves and robbers.* This negative indictment is directed against all who have claimed to be mediators of salvation, other gates so to speak. "As such it would embrace false messiahs within Judaism and redeemer gods of the pagan world, and in the present context, perhaps even more obviously, Pharisees who claimed to hold the keys of the kingdom."[9]

10:9 *Will be saved.* This is the third of four times John mentions salvation using the verb *sōzō* (σώζω; Jn 3:17; 5:34; 10:9; 12:47). Jesus, and Jesus alone, is the gate to salvation. The human race in general, and Israel in particular, is like lost sheep who will certainly perish without the proper care of a shepherd. In the Old Testament God rebukes the bad shepherds and promises he himself will seek and save his lost sheep (Eze 34:11–16).

Come in and go out. An echo of Numbers 27:17 (cf. Mic 5:4), when at the origin of God's covenant people Moses prays for his successor to be a leader "who will lead them out and bring them in, so the LORD's people will not be like sheep without a shepherd." The image of sheep without a shepherd recurs in the Old Testament portraying God's people in political and spiritual jeopardy as an indictment against the kings and leaders of Israel (1 Ki 22:17; 2 Ch 18:16; Isa 13:14). But none is as damning as Ezekiel 34, in which the Lord condemns "the shepherds of Israel" for taking care only of themselves (Eze 34:2, 8), profiting from the people without caring for them (Eze 34:3), and ruling them harshly and brutally (Eze 34:4). Here we see that the shepherd metaphor in the Old Testament refers not to sheep farmers but to kings and priests, making Jesus' claims here to be implicitly claims of kingship.

10:10 *Have life . . . to the full.* Ezekiel 34 speaks of the good grazing and rich pastures the Lord will provide the sheep when he is their shepherd: "I will bring them out from the nations and gather them from the countries, and I will bring them into their own land. . . . I will tend them in a good pasture, . . . they will lie down in good grazing land, and there they will feed in a rich pasture. . . . I myself will tend my sheep and have them lie down, declares the Sovereign LORD. I will search for the lost and bring back the strays" (Eze 34:13–16). He will also provide a life of peace and safety with all threats removed (Eze 34:25–31). Jesus came to bring his people into that abundant life in the present as the start of an eternal life that will one day be lived out in the ultimate fulfillment of Ezekiel's visions.

10:11 *I am the good shepherd.* Like David before him, who ruled Israel as "a man after God's own heart" (1 Sa 13:14; 17:15; Ac 13:22), Jesus here declares himself to be the Good Shepherd, the promised messianic shepherd (Eze 34:24) who fulfills God's promise to be Israel's shepherd (Eze 34:11–24). As Beth Stovell notes, "Besides asserting Jesus' authority to rule and establishing his divine and royal identity, . . . John 9–10 moves one step further to establishing Jesus' role as the God who is king of the disadvantaged. In John 9, Jesus' care for the man born blind and his miraculous healing represents the good deeds that the Father commissioned Jesus to do. . . . As in Ezek 34 where Yahweh shepherds his sheep in justice, Jesus' role as the 'good' shepherd is characterized by his 'good' deeds. This manifests itself in his desire for justice for those who have been oppressed, namely his sheep."[10]

Lays down his life for the sheep. Shepherds in the field had a hazardous job, as wild animals or sheep stealers could come upon the flock at any time (cf. 1 Sa 17:34–37). The shepherd was armed to drive away such threats, but in doing so exposed himself to injury or even death. Shockingly, Israel's princes, priests, and officials were described as lions and wolves, predators of the flock, because they failed to represent God to the people and to uphold standards of righteousness (Eze 22:23–29). In the absence of righteous leadership, the people practiced extortion and robbery, oppressed the poor, and mistreated the foreigner, denying them justice (Eze 22:29). In contrast, Jesus obliquely refers to his coming death as laying down his life for the sheep (also 10:17). Richard Bauckham notes that the fully voluntary nature of Jesus' self-giving "makes it an act of pure love."[11]

10:16 *Sheep that are not of this sheep pen.* Jesus was in Jerusalem speaking to the Pharisees, but he refers here to people outside the nation of Israel, the Gentiles, from whom he would also lead out his sheep (see "What the Structure Means: Same Question, Three Times [Jn 21:15–19]"). The early church applied the metaphor of (under-)shepherds to pastors and elders, who have responsibility for the safety and well-being of the flock (cf. 1 Pe 5:1–4).

One flock and one shepherd. Jesus implicitly claims to be the fulfillment of Ezekiel 34:23–24, where God promises, "I will place over them one shepherd, my servant David, and he will tend them; he will tend them and be their shepherd. I the LORD will be their God, and my servant David will be prince among them. I the LORD have spoken." As Ezekiel's words were written centuries after David died, they were always understood to refer to David's promised son, the Messiah.

This is one of six times John uses the word "one" to describe the people of God (10:16; 11:52; 17:11, 21, 22 twice). It was understood there was only *one* people of God. Jesus is here challenging the deeply rooted understanding of the oneness of God's people, who were, as Bauckham explains, "united in their devotion to the one God, whose one law they obey and in whose one temple they gather to worship him."[12] The "calling out" from God's people those who would follow Jesus represented a theological, political, and sociological division in the heretofore unity of the Jews. The Pharisees and temple priests would have perceived this to be a great threat to the stability of their society and establishment.

Those whom Jesus calls out to follow him are called to one community that reaches around the globe and throughout the ages. The flock that God shepherds is the flock that follows Jesus alone. But as Bauckham explains, "The people of God are to be unified not just by their allegiance to one shepherd . . . but also by the fact that the shepherd lays down his life for the flock."[13] Jesus' flock are those for whom he died. To reject the atoning death of the Good Shepherd is to remain outside the flock of Christ.

10:17 *Take it up again.* Jesus alluded to his crucifixion as laying down his life of his own accord. The death of the Lord's Messiah was not a horrible accident, not a matter of a good man being in the wrong place at the wrong time. Jesus came into this world and lived toward that moment when he would offer up his own life for the lives of his sheep. No one—not the Romans, not "the Jews"—took Jesus' life. He entered into his execution as a freewill offering to God, to fulfill the work of the covenant. Christians can blame no other group of people for the death of Jesus.

10:21 *Can a demon open the eyes of the blind?* This reference back to the healing of chapter 9 that led to this long discourse suggests the unity of John

9–10. The Greek syntax of this rhetorical question (μή plus a verb in the indicative mood) suggests a negative answer was expected (cf. 8:48). It is the Lord God, not the powers of darkness, who gives sight to the blind (Ex 4:11; Ps 146:8), and the Pharisees should have been utterly astounded at the power and authority of Jesus.

Going Deeper into Seeing the Light, Hearing the Voice of the Shepherd: John 10:1–21

In this encounter with the Pharisees, faith in Christ is expressed in the metaphors of a God-given sight that allows the blind to see the light of the world, as well as the ability to hear and follow the voice of the Good Shepherd. Out of all the peoples of the world, throughout all the ages, God has given sight to see and ears to hear the revelation of himself in Jesus Christ to those who are his. Like the amazing phenomenon of sheep separating themselves from all the sheep of the pen only at the sound of the shepherd's unique voice, people who are God's see and hear his voice of salvation in the proclamation of the gospel of Jesus Christ and follow him.

However, as Kenneth Bailey notes, there is *one* flock of Christ but not just one sheep pen, for "our differing languages, cultures, styles of worship and theological heritages all deserve to be preserved and nourished. Let the Coptic Orthodox rejoice in Athanasius, the Lutherans in Luther, the Latin Catholics in Thomas Aquinas, the Syrian Orthodox in Ephrem the Syrian, the Orthodox in Chrysostom and the Reformed tradition in Calvin and Barth. At the same time, all of these towering figures belong to all of us. This text summons 'all who call upon his name' to recognize that they are a single flock, even though they dwell in different sheepfolds."[14]

The unity of the flock despite the particular differences among its sheep is the hallmark of the Christian church based on the sheep's allegiance to Jesus Christ alone (see commentary on Jn 17).

10:22 *Festival of Dedication.* This is the Jewish holiday known today as Hanukkah, celebrated annually in December to commemorate the retaking of the Jerusalem temple by the Maccabees from the occupying Seleucids about two centuries before Jesus was born. The Seleucid ruler Antiochus Epiphanes IV had instituted oppressive laws that were intended to force the Jewish people to give up their observance of Torah, such as circumcision and the food laws. Antiochus had profaned the altar in Jerusalem by sacrificing a pig on it and dedicating it to the Greek god Zeus. In response, the Maccabees led a revolt that retook Jerusalem and rededicated the temple to the worship of Yahweh. As such, Hanukkah had connotations of national independence, being celebrated at the time of Jesus under occupation by yet another foreign power, Rome.

As Rekha Chennattu has noted, "John situates the ministry of Jesus within the literary context of the celebrations of these feasts and develops a unique Christology in each section in relationship to the rituals associated with the respective Jewish festival."[15] For chapters 5–10 John has related the story of Jesus to the Sabbath, Passover, Tabernacles, and Dedication, each with its religious and political connotations. "This complex of themes (national restoration, judgment of the Jewish leaders, and worship of Jesus) reaches its climax in the final dispute with the Jewish leaders in the Temple during Hanukkah (Jn 10:22–39)."[16]

10:23 *Solomon's Colonnade.* Solomon's Colonnade commemorated King David's son Solomon, who had brought Israel to the height of glory of its ancient monarchy. The long-awaited Messiah would be a new Son of David, and against this background the Jewish leaders would directly question Jesus' identity (see 10:24).

10:24–25 *If you are the Messiah, tell us plainly.* In his claim to be the Good Shepherd, Jesus has made a claim to be the Messiah using symbolic and figurative language familiar to the Old Testament. Those who had gathered around Jesus as he walked in Solomon's Colonnade understood Jesus' implicit claims to be the Messiah but couldn't trust their inferences and believe in him. And so they ask him directly (cf. 8:25). Jesus insists that they infer his identity from his works. As Gary Manning explains, "In the context of the allusion to Ezekiel, the 'good shepherd' is God. . . . In John's metaphor, Jesus fulfills all the tasks that God fulfills in Ezekiel 34."[17] In Ezekiel's prophecy God rebukes Israel's leaders and Jesus rebukes them in the gospel of John. Both God in Ezekiel and Jesus in John lead and save the sheep, Jesus at the cost of his own life. Both Jesus and God refer to the people as "my sheep" or "my flock." In the Old Testament God claims ownership of the sheep even when they are tended by a human shepherd (Jer 23; Eze 34). In light of this Old Testament background, Jesus' reference to "my sheep," "my flock" implies "an identity of purpose and function" that "suggests a sharing of authority that transcends most OT messianic expectations."[18] This may explain, at least in part, why Jesus resists simply saying that he is the Messiah, for their concept of the Messiah fell far short of who Jesus truly is. Jesus is God, an identity that will bring Jesus' revelation of himself to a head in 10:30, and eventually lead to his execution.

Jesus replies that he has already told them who he is, that the works he has done, especially on the Sabbath, support his claims, but they don't believe him because they are not among the sheep the Father has given to him.

10:26–27 *My sheep.* The works that Jesus has done suggest his deity, but here he begins to reveal his divine nature in his teaching. John has constructed the gospel in such a way as to present Jesus' deity while yet preserving monotheism. As Manning points out, "The phrase 'my sheep' occurs only in Jeremiah 23 and Ezekiel 34 in the OT, and in both metaphors, the speaker is God. Thus, when John's Jesus uses the phrase 'my sheep,' a reader familiar with the OT is drawn to consider the close connection between Jesus and God. That connection must at least be an identity of purpose and function; furthermore, it suggests a sharing of authority that transcends most OT messianic expectation."[19]

10:28–29 *Snatch them out of my hand . . . out of my Father's hand.* Jesus makes the claim that no one can snatch his sheep out of both *his* hand and "my Father's hand," suggesting that there is but one divine hand of protection for the sheep. As Margaret Daly-Denton observes, "Once this identity is established, the reader can hear in Jesus' claim that his sheep recognize and listen to his voice an echo" of Psalm 95:7–8, especially in its LXX form (Ps 94:7–8), "because he is our God and we are people of his pasture and *sheep of his hand*! Today *if you hear his voice*, do not harden your hearts." Daly-Denton continues, "The echoes of Ps 94 produce the effect of aligning those who refuse to listen to Jesus with 'the fathers' who tested God in the desert, in spite of having seen God's works. As in John 6, they repeat the pattern of their ancestors' unbelief."[20]

10:30 *I and the Father are one.* Jesus makes a claim here that is either mysteriously awesome or outrageously blasphemous (10:33, 36). Whichever one thinks it is becomes the criterion for bringing Jesus' sheep out from all others (10:26). The statement brings to a head the debate with the religious leaders about who Jesus is, a debate that began back in 5:12. Is Jesus worthy of worship, or is he outrageously blasphemous (cf. 5:18; 8:58–59)? Those are the two choices that remain at the end of the debate (see "Going Deeper into Liar, Lunatic, Lord: John 10:22–42").

Jesus' claim is not formally a statement of being of the same divine essence as the Father (*homoousios* [ὁμοούσιος]) that was later debated and adopted by the church councils, but neither does it contradict the metaphysical conclusion of the Nicene Creed. Jesus claims to be of one nature with God the Father but yet distinguishable from him as a person. As Larry Hurtado explains, no New Testament writer "simply collapses the distinction between Jesus and God 'the Father'" in a way that "flatly identifies Jesus as Yahweh of the Old Testament."[21] In the immediate context of Jesus' "works" (10:25, 32, 37–38), it is a statement that everything Jesus does as the Good Shepherd is done in the power and authority of the Father. Therefore in response to the challenge in 10:24, Jesus makes three points: (1) he has the authority to protect the sheep; (2) his Father has given him that authority and, therefore, his authority is equal to the Father's; (3) the Father and Jesus are concurrently doing the same work.[22]

Jesus claims the unity of purpose and intent and the equality of power and authority with the Father, which have rightly been described as functional claims, not metaphysical. But in the context of a book where Jesus has already in the first sentence been declared the incarnate Word who was with God and was God (Jn 1:1), this statement is an entailment and extension of his divine nature. D. A. Carson writes, "If . . . Jesus' will is exhaustively one with his Father's will, some kind of metaphysical unity is presupposed, even if not articulated."[23]

Of course, the Jewish leaders who questioned Jesus had not read John's Prologue! Understandably they would have heard Jesus' statement as blasphemous, especially because it almost certainly evoked the Shema in their minds. The Shema (Dt 6:4) was the hallmark statement of the uniqueness of Israel's God, the foundation of monotheism, given to them at the establishment of their nation: "Hear, O Israel, the LORD our God, the LORD is one" (LXX: Akoue, Israēl: kurios ho theos hēmōn kurios eis estin [Ἄκουε, Ισραηλ· κύριος ὁ θεὸς ἡμῶν κύριος εἷς ἐστιν]). Jesus' statement, "I and the Father are one" (egō kai ho patēr hen esmen [ἐγὼ καὶ ὁ πατὴρ ἕν ἐσμεν]) notably uses the neuter adjective for "one" (hen [ἕν]), a carefully worded statement to avoid the masculine adjective eis [εἷς], suggesting Jesus and the Father are one person. In the context of the Shema, which claims the uniqueness of Israel's God, "Jesus is claiming that the unique deity of the God of Israel consists in the communion between Father and Son"[24] (cf. 10:38). This masterful statement of the revelation of Jesus' identity avoids the suggestion that his divinity competed with the Father, as if there were now two Gods, yet preserves the distinction between the Son of God and God the Father. As Edward Klink notes, "The work of the Father and Son are so intertwined that it can only be one work. In the same way, the identity of the Father and Son are so intertwined that they must be described as one God."[25] (10:38). John presents Jesus' revelation of himself in a way that preserves monotheism.

10:31 *Picked up stones to stone him.* This is the second time a crowd has been offended by what they perceive as Jesus' blasphemy and attempt to stone him, the Old Testament punishment for that sin (Dt 13:1–11). In John 8:59 a similar attempt followed Jesus' statement in 8:58, "'Very truly I tell you,' Jesus answered, 'before Abraham was born, I am!'" (Note that claim to preexistence was also prefaced by the double *amēn* [ἀμήν] phrase.) But just as the previous attempt failed (8:59), here also Jesus escapes their grasp. His hour had not yet come.

10:33 *Blasphemy, because you . . . claim to be God.* Although Jesus' miracles, especially those performed on the Sabbath, precipitated the conflict with the Jewish leaders, Jesus' words justifying his actions brought charges of blasphemy against him (see commentary on Jn 5:18). Regardless of how modern readers understand Jesus' claim to be one with the Father in 10:30, those who heard his words clearly understood them as a claim to be God. And so the modern reader is, like Jesus' original hearers, left with the question: Is Jesus God or is he a blasphemer, either lying or crazy (see "Going Deeper into Liar, Lunatic, Lord: John 10:22–42")? This chapter forms a turning point in the gospel for Jesus' destiny and for that of readers as well.

10:34 *Written in your Law.* It is surprising to hear the Messiah, the fulfillment of the Old Testament covenant and all of its promises, refer to the Law as "your" Law, as if distancing himself from it. The Pharisees and Jewish leaders had misinterpreted the Law, including its commandment concerning the Sabbath, and were therefore not prepared to recognize the Messiah when he appeared. Jesus distances himself from their understanding of the Law, and once again uses the Law in his defense (cf. Jn 5:45, 46; 7:19; see also commentary at 8:17 and 15:25).

The quotation is of Psalm 82:6 LXX, where God says, "I have said you are 'gods'" and continues with, "you are all sons of the Most High." Perhaps employing a bit of rabbinic gamesmanship, Jesus points to a scriptural example of other humans whom God himself has addressed as gods and sons of God. Therefore, strictly speaking, his claim to be Son of God is not unprecedented. It does not necessarily violate the Shema or monotheism. As Carson explains, "In the heat of their opposition to what they hear Jesus to be saying, they are partly right (he does make himself equal with God), partly wrong (this fact does not establish a competing God), and profoundly mistaken (they have not grasped the drift of their own Scriptures to see how he fulfills them, nor have they known God well enough to perceive that the revelation he is and brings is in continuity with and the capstone of the revelation of God already provided.)"[26]

10:35 *Scripture cannot be set aside.* Jesus has pointed out an inconvenient truth from the psalm, and is now reminding them "the Scripture cannot be annulled or set aside or proved false."[27] He has removed, at least technically, the basis of their anger against him, and yet they nevertheless try to seize him (10:39). Note that in 10:34–35 Jesus uses "the Law" and "Scripture" almost interchangeably (cf. Jn 12:34).

10:38 *The Father is in me, and I in the Father.* Jesus further exposits his claim in 10:30 to be one with the Father. Bauckham explains that this language of mutual indwelling "points to a relational intimacy of Jesus and the Father within the identity of the one God" (see Jn 1:18).[28] While it is true that Jesus and the Father share a unity of mission, as well as a unity of works and words, these statements of indwelling express a oneness that exceeds mere agency or two minds working together. Nonetheless, Christianity does not prescribe worship of two Gods, although there are two figures who receive devotion. Within this "duality (God and Jesus as recipients of devotion) there is also a clearly evident commitment to an exclusivistic monotheism."[29]

10:40 *Went back across the Jordan.* Jesus leaves Jerusalem and will not return to it again until he enters it the last week of his life, on what we know as Palm Sunday. He returned to the place of his baptism, where John had been baptizing at the start of Jesus' public ministry. John the Baptist had announced Jesus as "God's Chosen One" (1:34) and as "the Lamb of God" (1:36). John the Baptist had affirmed that Jesus had been sent by God (3:31), speaking the words of God, having the Spirit without limit (3:34), the one who bestows eternal life (3:36). Many people came to Jesus and affirmed all these things John the Baptist had said (10:41). And there many believed in Jesus.

Going Deeper into Liar, Lunatic, Lord: John 10:22–42

The gospel of John leaves no doubt that Jesus claimed to be the Son of God who is one with the Father. But many through the ages have wanted to affirm Jesus as a good, moral man and wise religious teacher. Is that view really an option? In the nineteenth century a Scottish preacher, John Duncan (1796–1870), published *Colloquia Peripatetica*, in which he presented a "trilemma" having three options: "Christ either deceived mankind by conscious fraud, or he was himself deluded and self-deceived, or he was Divine. There is no getting out of this trilemma. It is inexorable."[30] In other words, Jesus was either a liar, a lunatic (cf. Jn 8:48; 10:20), or he is Lord.

In the mid-twentieth century C. S. Lewis presented the same argument, saying, "I am trying here to prevent anyone saying the really foolish thing that people often say about Him: I'm ready to accept Jesus as a great moral teacher, but I don't accept his claim to be God. That is the one thing we must not say. A man who was merely a man and said the sort of things Jesus said would not be a great moral teacher."[31] This is a convincing argument on the premise that Jesus really did say the statements about himself recorded in the Gospels. Even if Jesus' recorded statements are not verbatim quotations, the premise is that the historical man Jesus actually made such claims of divinity, especially as we read in the gospel of John.

In the twentieth and twenty-first centuries there has been great effort to demonstrate that the New Testament is historically unreliable and that Jesus never said most of what the Gospels say he said. The gospel of John has been especially susceptible to such work. For instance, the Jesus Seminar was a body of scholars who met in the late twentieth century to vote on what statements of Jesus they deemed historically true. They ruled out about 80 percent of Jesus' words in the Gospels, and virtually all of Jesus' words in the gospel of John.[32] In other words, there are actually four options about who Jesus is: liar, lunatic, legend, or Lord.

Similar opinion predated the Jesus Seminar, for Lewis also explained why the Gospels could not be legend. First, the gospel texts originated in a monotheistic Jewish milieu convinced that there was only one God. Lewis considered it highly implausible that any Jewish writer would invent a story that Israel's God became a man, for what could be gained by such a thing? Second, Lewis was a literary historian who spent a lifetime reading ancient legends, and he was "perfectly convinced that whatever else the Gospels are they are not legends"[33] because they read nothing like Greco-Roman legends. Moreover, the existence of Christianity itself after two thousand years is historical evidence for the unique life and resurrection of Jesus, for it is difficult to see why the earliest Christians would have believed in Christ's resurrection if it were not so.

If we believe that the gospel writers preserve the truth about what Jesus said and did—and there are good reasons for that belief—then we are indeed left with but three options: Jesus was a liar or a lunatic, or he is Lord.

John 10 Through Old Testament Eyes

The Good Shepherd motif of the Old Testament forms the basis of Jesus' self-revelation in John 10. Israel's king David was a shepherd boy when he was chosen to lead God's people, and in the ancient Near East the metaphor of shepherd was often used in reference to leadership, both political and spiritual. Accordingly, the people being shepherded were metaphorically referred to as sheep, especially in regard to their defenselessness. The bad, or evil, shepherd characterized condemnation of Israel's spiritual leadership, accompanied by God's promise that he himself would shepherd his people. Psalm 23 famously portrays the Lord in this role: "The LORD is my shepherd, I have everything I need." Jesus builds on this Old Testament motif to reveal that he is the fulfillment of God's promise to gather his sheep and lead them into safe, abundant pasture. But it would come only at the high personal cost of the Good Shepherd's death.

What the Structure Means: The Rising Conflict (Jn 5–10)

Chapters 5–10 of the gospel of John form a major unit in which the conflict between Jesus and the Jewish leaders of Jerusalem that would eventually lead to his death arises and grows. The conflict is precipitated when Jesus heals a lame man and orders him to carry his mat on a Sabbath (5:8–12): "So, because Jesus was doing these things on the Sabbath, the Jewish leaders began to persecute him" (5:16). Observance of the Sabbath throughout the ages was the hallmark of ancient Judaism, as documented by the fourth commandment (Ex 20:8; Dt 5:12–15). By the time of Jesus, the regulations of Sabbath observance had multiplied, but the reality to which it pointed had become obscured by Pharisaical legalism. Jesus' "work" on the Sabbath was a sign that he was fulfilling the promises of the covenant that were symbolized by the Sabbath, but those who accused him of Sabbath violation failed to see that. By using the word *persecute* clearly John interprets the opposition against Jesus to be unjust. But persecution quickly becomes murderous in 5:18, when Jesus defends his Sabbath actions by identifying his work with God's work, calling God "my Father," and therefore making himself equal with God (5:17–18). So in the eyes of the Jerusalem leaders Jesus moves from Sabbath violator to blasphemer, making himself liable to execution.

The question of Jesus' identity and authority develops throughout chapters 5–10, with Jesus healing the lame man on a Sabbath, feeding the five thousand, walking on water, teaching messianic truth at the

Feast of Tabernacles, and performing a healing of the blind man, once again on the Sabbath. The Jerusalem leaders continue to engage him about his identity and authority, and Jesus consistently defends himself by claiming God as his Father, leading to subsequent attempts to arrest and kill Jesus (7:32; 8:59; 10:31; 11:53). Therefore, "chapters 5 and 10 form an inclusio on the theme of conflict," beginning and ending with a miracle of healing on the Sabbath.[34] The arguments for and against Jesus have been fully presented through his miraculous signs and his extensive discourses about his origin and identity, and he leaves Jerusalem at the end of chapter 10 (10:40) not to return again until the last week of his life (12:12–19). There remains one great sign for Jesus to perform, the raising of Lazarus from the dead in chapter 11. This will be the last straw for the Pharisees, who ironically conclude that Jesus, the one who has power to bring the dead to life, must himself die (11:53; 12:10).

JOHN 11

11:1 *From Bethany.* This village lay on the eastern slope of the Mount of Olives, about two miles east of Jerusalem (see 11:18). It is not the village of the same name mentioned in 1:28, which was a location on the east side of the Jordan River (see 10:40).

11:2 *This Mary.* Mary was a common name at the time of Jesus, and several women with that name are mentioned in the gospel accounts. This Mary, a sister of Lazarus, was the one who became famous in the earliest Christian communities for anointing Jesus' feet (see Jn 12:1–8). This reference reveals that the audience to whom John originally wrote was probably already familiar with the traditions about Jesus, either from reading other Gospels or from oral tradition. Furthermore, because Mary's act of devotion turned out to be a proleptic (prophetic?) preparation for Jesus' burial (12:7), the shadow of Jesus' death is introduced into the Lazarus story of resurrection life from its start.

The name Lazarus is the Greek form of the Hebrew name Eleazer, which was also a quite common name. The Lazarus of Bethany in John 11 is not to be confused with the beggar named Lazarus of Luke 16:20–27.

11:3 *The one you love.* Although it is evident from the stories told that Jesus had affection for his friends Mary, Martha, and Lazarus, this description of Lazarus as one whom Jesus loved is a hint that foreshadows the cost Jesus will pay for calling Lazarus out of the tomb. For in the Johannine writings love for one's friends demands laying down one's life (see Jn 15:13; 1 Jn 3:16). In the gospel of John the raising of Lazarus was the final straw that rallied the Sanhedrin to decree Jesus' execution (see Jn 11:47–53). The act of love that restored life to Lazarus meant death for Jesus. And in that is a hint of the atoning value of Jesus' crucifixion as John's gospel story begins its turn toward the end of Jesus' life.

11:4 *It is for God's glory.* Although it is far from obvious to the first-time reader, this statement begins the story of Jesus' death, as it "foreshadows and interprets the rest of the narrative."[1] Jesus explains that Lazarus' illness "is for God's glory," a similar statement to John 9:3, that a man's blindness was so "the works of God might be displayed in him" (see commentary there; cf. Jn 2:11). There Jesus' power and authority to overrule even a lifetime disability was revealed; here his power and authority to overrule even death is displayed. The display of God's power and authority as an expression of his presence is often referred to as his "glory" throughout the Bible (e.g., Ex 14:4; 15:11; 16:10; 2 Chr 7:3; Ps 29:2; 96:3; Isa 44:23; 66:18), and especially in the fourth gospel (see Jn 1:14; 2:11; 8:54; 12:41; 15:8; 17:4, 5, 10, 22, 24). See also commentary at 17:1.

So that God's Son may be glorified. However, according to John, the crucifixion most spectacularly revealed Jesus' glory, though that thought might seem so counterintuitive (Jn 7:39; 12:16, 23; 13:31; 17:1). We do not usually associate glory by any definition with the indignities and horrors of execution, especially by crucifixion. Jesus redefines kingly glory on his cross. Beth Stovell notes, "A key component of the narrative of Lazarus' death is the glorification of the Son of God (11:4). . . . While glory can be used of other figures besides a king, it . . . is frequently used of kings in the Hebrew Bible (Esther 1:4; Isa 11:10; Ps 24:7–8) and commonly used of Yahweh as King. . . . The continuity of kingship from Father to Son stressed Jesus' similarity to the Father, moving the Gospel towards a high Christology."[2] The raising of Lazarus shows Jesus' kingship—even over death.

11:7 *Back to Judea.* Jesus suggests a return to Judea even though he knows the danger that awaits him there.

11:9 *See by this world's light.* This reference to the natural order of things—with daylight present when the sun rises and darkness when it sets—suggests that, just as no one can foreshorten the hours of daylight, Jesus' life (and the lives of his followers) cannot be foreshortened by any threat apart from the Father's plan. It is during the daylight hours that the tasks at hand must be accomplished, and a final sign of Jesus' glory must occur. Darkness is coming, when Jesus' earthly life ends in death (cf. Jn 13:30b), but not before everything he came to reveal is accomplished. In John's writings, Jesus himself is the light of the world, and those who walk in that light have safety and security (see 11:25–26). When darkness finally falls it will bring betrayal and Jesus' death (see Jn 13:30) (regarding *light* and *darkness*, see commentary at John 1:4, 5, and 9).

11:13 *Jesus had been speaking of his [Lazarus'] death.* The euphemistic metaphor of sleep to refer to death is almost universal, used today as well as in the ancient world (Job 14:10–12; Isa 57:2; Da 12:2, 14). Jesus intended his eventual presence at Bethany to be a demonstration of his power not simply over illness but even over death. The raising of Lazarus signified that Jesus was able to do all that he had said, and was a sign pointing to eternal life for all who believe. Therefore, Jesus delayed his response to the message that Lazarus was ill until the death had occurred (see 11:17). What seemed like a cruel tragedy set the stage for the greatest of Jesus' miracles.

11:19 *Many Jews had come.* The home of Mary, Martha, and Lazarus was not far from Jerusalem, and the presence of many Jewish mourners indicates that despite the family's close friendship with Jesus, their fellow Jews were not shunning them (cf. 9:22). In times of grief the custom was for the community to come together (Ge 37:35; Job 2:11; 42:11).

11:21 *If you had been here* (cf. v. 32). Martha expresses a thought that seems to be a mixture of faith in and criticism of Jesus. The reader knows that Jesus deliberately delayed going to Bethany (11:6); almost certainly Martha and Mary surmised that he could have arrived more quickly or even could have healed Lazarus from a distance. Both Martha and Mary believed Jesus could heal and forestall death, a belief that required great faith (cf. 11:37). Interpreters debate whether Martha or Mary or neither possessed full faith in Jesus based on his revelation.[3] To say the least, they are clearly disappointed that Jesus failed to arrive in time to prevent their brother's death. Martha knows that "even now" God would do whatever Jesus asks, yet neither sister makes an explicit request (11:22; cf. Jn 2:3–5). But Jesus intended something much greater than another healing, and is moving them by means of this experience of bereavement to an even greater and truer understanding of who he is.

11:22 *God will give you whatever you ask.* See commentary on John 14:13 and 15:7.

11:23–24 *"Your brother will rise again."* . . . *"In the resurrection at the last day."* The concept of resurrection developed within Judaism during the intertestamental period, during a time of great persecution that took the lives of many Jews of Jerusalem and Judea (cf. 2 Mc 7:9).[4] A resurrection of the righteous was expected at the end of the age of this world. But not all Jews at the time of Jesus embraced the belief in resurrection—the Pharisees did but the Sadducees did not (Josephus, *Ant.* 18.1.3–4; Ac 23:6–8). Here Jesus affirms belief in a future resurrection of the dead that is not only part of God's redemptive plan but also centers on Jesus the Messiah himself. His raising of Lazarus will demonstrate that the Messiah has the power and authority to raise the dead. Furthermore, it foreshadows his own resurrection as a human being into eternal life.

11:25 *I am the resurrection and the life.* Should the two terms of this famous statement be understood as "I am the resurrection that leads to life" or "I am the resurrection and I am the life"? Life follows resurrection, much as life follows birth (and as eternal life follows new birth; see Jn 3:1–15). Jesus teaches here that death is a necessary prelude to resurrection, and resurrection a necessary prelude to eternal life.

It is commonly said that there are seven signs and seven "I am" statements in the gospel of John. Although interpreters may not agree whether the raising of Lazarus is the sixth sign or the seventh, this sign points to the spiritual reality that Jesus is the agent of resurrection into eternal life (see commentary on Jn 6:35).

11:27 *You are the Messiah, the Son of God* (regarding "Messiah," see "What the Structure Means" in the introduction and commentary at Jn 1:20; regarding "Son of God," see commentary on Jn 1:49). Although Martha pronounces this belief in Jesus as Messiah and, in some sense, Son of God, it nevertheless falls short of understanding the true identity of Jesus as the *incarnation* of God. John 11:39 hints at her lack of understanding and trust in the full agency of Jesus.

11:33 *He was deeply moved . . . and troubled.* Perhaps only in the garden of Gethsemane do we see Jesus displaying such intense human emotion as he does at the tomb of Lazarus. Jesus has come to Bethany at the risk of his life, knowing that Lazarus had already passed, and is here confronted by the pain and sorrow death inevitably brings to the bereaved even as he faces into his own death. The emotion he experiences is likely indignation and perhaps anger, not against those who grieve, but anger with the vast suffering that has accompanied death throughout human history.[5] Jesus' emotion may be seen as part of the grief for his own impending death, linking Lazarus' death with his own, for to raise Lazarus from the tomb will lead to his own inevitable death.

11:35 *Jesus wept.* The shortest verse of the Bible describes Jesus expressing the universal human emotion of grief. At the tomb, he is God with us in the fullness of our human experience. As Marianne Meye Thompson explains, Jesus is overcome by emotion because of "the death-dealing ways of the world and humankind that elicit the response of anger and grief. And so, Jesus wept."[6]

11:38 *Came to the tomb.* Rock-cut tombs of the first century were either natural caves or quarried, into which a ledge was carved to lay out the corpse.

The body would lie within the tomb for about a year with the opening sealed against predators or thieves by a large, flat stone. After the remains had become skeletal, a family member would enter the tomb to collect the bones and deposit them into an ossuary, freeing the tomb for the next burial.

(An ossuary was a stone box the length of the femur bone, if for an individual, or a large box if intended to hold the bones of several family members. Archaeologists have found many around the Near East, attesting that this was a common practice at the time of Christ.) See Ezekiel 37:12.

11:39 *Been there four days.* In the ancient world, and particularly within Judaism, the belief that the soul lingered around the body for three days is probably in play here (see Hos 6:2). By the fourth day following death, decomposition would become apparent, and no natural resuscitation was possible. Jesus' delay in coming to Bethany was likely calculated to assure that Lazarus was thoroughly dead by the standards of that day. Death's finality "could hardly be expressed more graphically than in the stench of decomposition."[7] Jesus' power and authority to restore Lazarus' life from such a dire condition is a revelation of "the glory of God" (11:40). It is debatable whether Martha's remark should count against the authenticity of her faith, for as Gail O'Day notes, "Jesus' gift of life is so radical that no one, no matter how faithful, could be expected to have anticipated it."[8]

11:40 *You will see the glory of God.* As Francis Moloney observes, "There have been several uses of the expression δόξα; *doxa* [glory] throughout the ministry (see 2:11; 5:41–44; 7:18; 8:50–54) which suggest to the reader that the revelation of the δόξα τοῦ θεοῦ; *doxa tou theou* [glory of God] associated with the gift of the Law at Sinai has been perfected in the gift of Jesus Christ (see 1:17)."[9] Regarding *glory*, see commentary on John 1:14.

11:41–42 *That they may believe that you sent me.* The purpose of the signs in the gospel of John is to lead people to faith in Jesus as the incarnate Son of God sent by the Father for the purpose of going to his glorification on the cross (cf. Jn 20:30–31). Indirectly referred to as a "sign" (Gk. *sēmeion* [σημεῖον]) in 11:47, this is the seventh and greatest miracle that Jesus performs in the fourth gospel. It evokes faith but also rejection (see "What the Structure Means: Reading the Signs of the Fourth Gospel (Jn 2–12)"). The presence of "the Jews" at this miracle provides another opportunity for faith in the Messiah, but it also puts Jesus at risk of being reported and his location disclosed to the authorities (cf. 11:45–57).

11:43 *Lazarus, come out!* The efficacy of hearing the powerful voice of Jesus is dramatically narrated here. Although it is in one sense true that Christian faith saves the believer, this incident shows that it is Christ alone who saves from death. John tells us nothing about Lazarus' faith in Christ, but once in the tomb only the power of God, and nothing within Lazarus himself, could free him from death's grip. Jesus teaches, "whoever believes in me will live, even though they die," and so faith is a central and essential component of one's relationship with Christ. But it is the power of Jesus' divine love for those who are his that is the active agent of salvation.

11:44 *The dead man came out.* The English expression "dead man walking" describes in modern times someone on his way to certain execution, but on that long ago day in Bethany, a dead man walked *out* of his tomb. It is amazing that John records nothing of Lazarus' reaction to find himself back among the living and shares nothing of his experience of four days of death! John does not develop Lazarus as a character in this story, but as the object of Jesus' power who became a symbol of life after death. Yet even this spectacular miracle was only a sign, since Lazarus was raised to the same physical life he had enjoyed prior to his illness. In this experience he joins the widow's son at Zarephath (1 Ki 17:17–24), the son of the Shunammite (2 Ki 4:32–37), and the man whose corpse was thrown into Elisha's grave (2 Ki 13:21). He wasn't raised to life in the new creation (as Jesus was with a transformed body), but he was restored to life eventually to die again, as apparently were others in the Synoptics, such as the daughter of Jairus, the son of the widow of Nain, and Tabitha. And if the chief priests and Pharisees had their way, Lazarus would soon be back in a tomb (Jn 12:10). But "because the giver of eternal life is also the giver of the physical life we know . . . even temporary restoration to this life becomes cogent as a pointer to the transcendent reality of eternal life."[10] It is also a great irony that the raising of Lazarus results in a plot to kill the creator of life. Life for Lazarus means death for Jesus, and in some sense we are all Lazarus.

But Jesus' bringing Lazarus back to life after four days of death is an apt seventh and final sign before Jesus himself goes to his death on the cross. Richard Bauckham explains, "Jesus brings Lazarus back to mortal life as a sign of the eternal life that his own death will acquire for his friends. The paradox of the cross—of life through death . . . is signaled in this story by the fact that Jesus declares himself to be 'the resurrection and the life' (11:25) in the course of ensuring that he himself will die."[11]

As Ruben Zimmerman notes, "Even if John 11 does not directly refer to the Passion and Easter, the Lazarus story deals from beginning to end with the death and resurrection of Jesus."[12] This sign suggests that his disciples should understand—though they didn't in the moment—Jesus' death to be a necessary experience for him to complete his identification with the human race, but nevertheless an experience that he himself had power and authority over (10:17–18). As a human being, Jesus' death was a necessary prelude to his glorious resurrection into eternal life and implies that because we are made like him, like him we too will rise. As Thompson notes, "John 11 demonstrates in action the claims of Jesus to give life, in particular as found in John 5" (especially Jn 5:25–29).[13]

It is striking that in the fourth gospel Lazarus at no time professes faith in Jesus, either before or after his return to life, thus graphically demonstrating "the theological point that it is not faith that guarantees life, but God."[14]

His hands and feet wrapped . . . and a cloth around his face. This was the conventional way a corpse was prepared for burial, often with herbs and spices tucked within the cloth (cf. Jn 19:39–40; 20:6–7).

Going Deeper into Jesus' Grief: John 11:35

Why should we cry and mourn when a Christian dies? They have gone to be with the Lord, so isn't that a reason to rejoice and even celebrate? They have been released from the pain and suffering of this life. Even if rejoicing is beyond the emotional range of the bereaved, shouldn't we at least keep our chin up and put on a smile, lest others take our grief as a lapse of faith in the gospel message of eternal life? How should a Christian mourn when bereaved?

Jesus gives us an example. The One who said, "I am the resurrection and the life" is also the one who stood at the grave of a friend and wept. In Christ, God has entered into the human experience, an experience that universally and inevitably ends in death for each and every one of us. And so it is fitting that God incarnate as a human being should also die. And the death of the incarnate God is the means to resurrection and life. In God's wisdom, death becomes for his people not an ultimate end but a doorway into life everlasting in the green pastures and still waters of the new creation. As Ruben Zimmerman notes, "No tomb can be so tightly sealed that the voice of Jesus can not enter it and call us out to a new life that cannot be destroyed by any form of death."[15]

Yet Jesus wept. This teaches us that even resurrection does not negate or trivialize the experience of death. Even though Christ has overcome death, it is still a deeply wrenching loss to see a loved one slip away from us into that mysterious absence. We cannot psychologize Jesus' thoughts and emotions as he stood at the tomb of Lazarus, but we do see him enter into the human experience of grief, and in so doing, he sanctifies the grief of the living. Although it is right to mark the death of a Christian with a "celebration of life," it is wrong to avoid the holy experience of grieving for the loss, the suffering, and the indignities of death. It is not a lack of faith to weep, to mourn, to hurt when death invades our homes and churches and neighborhoods. We may comfort each other with the reminder that our beloved deceased is now at peace with the Lord, but that should never be an admonishment to stop crying and avoid grief. And those who mourn should certainly never be accused of a lack of faith!

Jesus, the One who is the Resurrection and the Life, wept. He entered into not only the grief of losing his friend Lazarus, but also into the vast suffering that death has brought to the human race throughout history. He felt that pain of death for which he himself would die. In so doing, Jesus introduced a dignity to death that is a comfort as our bodies age and decline toward the inevitable. And so, Jesus wept, even while knowing that death would be how he would return to the Father and the exit through which his flock would enter eternal life fully and finally.

11:47 *Called a meeting of the Sanhedrin.* The Sanhedrin was the ruling council of the Jews composed of both Pharisees and Sadducees. They enjoyed considerable power in matters of religion, but they were constrained by the Roman procurator in the affairs of state. Capital punishment, such as stipulated by the law for blasphemy, required Roman approval and execution (see 18:28–40).

Performing many signs . . . everyone will believe in him. Just as John perceived, the signs Jesus did lead many to believe in him (Jn 20:30–31). But John also tells of others who saw the signs but rejected Jesus for reasons of their own self-interest (cf. Jn 3:19). "Ironically, the lack of faith on the part of some of 'the Jews' and the leaders of 'the Jews' is matched by the fear that Jesus' miracles might arouse universal belief in him."[16] The Sanhedrin acknowledges the persuasive efficacy of the signs Jesus does, but has what they believe to be the higher concern of placating the Romans. The Romans had the power to take away the temple and the nation, and actually did so not many years later in AD 70, so this was no idle fear (11:48).

11:49 *One man die for the people.* In a mysterious and poignant mix of human motivation and divine providence (cf. Ac 4:27–28), the Sanhedrin concludes it was clearly the lesser evil to eliminate the threat Jesus had become. Speaking better than he knows in his high priestly office of representing God to the people, Caiaphas declares it better politically for the Jewish nation that one man die to keep the people safe. More than a political expedient, the high priest's pronouncement was an unwitting prophecy of the atonement for the whole world through the death of Jesus. The idea that one dies in place of the many is a Passover concept, as the Lamb of God is sacrificed to protect those under his blood (Ex 12:21–23).

11:52 *For the scattered children of God, to bring them together.* Within the context of Judaism, the scattered children would be understood to be the Jews of the Diaspora, living outside the land. Regathering the people of Israel after exile is a significant prayer and a prophetic theme (Ps 106:47; 107:3; Isa 11:12; 43:5–6; 49:6; 56:8; Jer 32:37; Eze 34:13; Zec 10:6), which is rooted in Moses' original exhortations and warnings to the nation about keeping the law (Dt 30:3–5). John suggests Jesus' death enables fulfillment of this Old Testament eschatological hope. But within the context of John's gospel, the scattered children of God are those who receive the Word who became flesh and believe in his name (Jn 1:12–13). John extends the prophecy of Caiaphas beyond the Jewish nation, for all whom the Father would give to Jesus (Jn 6:37). The promised regathering of Israel is realized as both Jews and Gentiles are gathered into one through faith in Christ. Here we see a hint of the unity of believers that will become a major theme in the following chapters.

11:53 *They plotted to take his life.* The irony of it! "Jesus just raised Lazarus from the grave! Let's kill him!" Life for Lazarus meant death for Jesus. Life for us meant death for Jesus.

11:54 *Withdrew . . . to a village called Ephraim.* Although Jesus was prepared to die, he nevertheless had a sense of timing about it. He does not stay in Bethany but relocates to Ephraim, a village believed to have been about four miles northeast of Bethel and less than twenty miles (i.e., a day's journey) north of Jerusalem.[17]

11:55 *Almost time for the Jewish Passover . . . for their ceremonial cleansing.* Jesus was in Jerusalem teaching publicly at the Festival of Tabernacles in the autumn (chap. 7), the Festival of Dedication in the winter (chap. 10), and is here facing his last Passover in Jerusalem, an early spring festival (chap. 11). The rest of John's story of Jesus focuses on Jesus' final days cloistered with his disciples, preparing them for his death, and for its immediate aftermath.

Cleansing was required before the Passover, especially when one had had recent contact with a dead body, as Jesus and his disciples may have had with Lazarus (Nu 9:6–11; 2 Ch 30:17–18).

What the Structure Means:
The Turning Point (Jn 11–12)

John 11 is a pivotal point in the story of Jesus' life and death. As Colleen Conway, among others, has observed, "Structurally, chapters 11–12 form a pivotal point in the Gospel. They both culminate the first half of the Gospel, the Book of Signs, and foreshadow the events in the second half, the Book of Glory."[18] These chapters provide "the link between the first part of the story, with its depiction of the public mission of Jesus, and the second part, with its depiction of Jesus' final visit to Jerusalem, including the farewell material, the trial, passion, and resurrection."[19] The signs of chapters 2–11 present language, images, and motifs that connect the significance of Jesus' life back to the Old Testament, while simultaneously revealing the significance of his crucifixion that will be narrated later in the gospel story.

The raising of Lazarus is a fitting pivotal point, for it shows the extent of Jesus' power to not only heal (4:46–54; 5:1–15; 9:1–41) but also to restore life from even death. It also points to the significance of Jesus' own death, for his story would be unfinished if, after raising Lazarus from the tomb, Jesus remained in the grave upon his own death. Life for Lazarus meant death for Jesus, showing that Jesus gave his own life for those he loved, to gather his one flock.

In addition, Jesus' power to raise Lazarus demonstrates that God's love for the world (Jn 3:16) means that death, although pronounced by God in the garden of Eden (Ge 2:17; 3:19) "is not God's final word over creation."[20] John has made Lazarus a symbol of life after death, a sign pointing to the new reality Jesus' resurrection would reveal (cf. 12:18). Lazarus lived again only to eventually die again (cf. 12:10), but as Andrew Lincoln observes, "Because the giver of eternal life is also the giver of physical life . . . even temporary restoration to this life becomes a cogent pointer to the transcendent reality of eternal life."[21] The purpose of the fourth gospel is to convince its readers of the transcendent reality of eternal life after death (Jn 20:30–31). This final sign of a resurrection leads the gospel story on to Jesus' final days of teaching his disciples, and to his passion on the cross.

JOHN 12

12:1 *Six days before the Passover.* This is the third Passover mentioned in the gospel of John during Jesus' public ministry (cf. Jn 2:13; 6:4), and it would be the last of his earthly life. Passover, a spring festival, was to begin on the night of the first full moon after the northern vernal equinox, which typically fell on the fifteenth of the first month of the Jewish year, Nisan (previously called Aviv; or March-April on the Gregorian calendar we use today). The paschal lamb, male and without blemish, was selected on the tenth of the month, five days before Passover, and was slaughtered on the evening of the fourteenth (Dt 16:6). John's reference here to six days before Passover was likely intended to set the scene for the sacrifice of the Lamb of God (Jn 1:29, 36) (see commentary on Jn 12:12–16).

Jesus came [back] to Bethany. John 12:1–11 continues the story of Jesus and Lazarus despite the chapter break.

12:3 *A pint of pure nard.* (Spike)nard was an aromatic oil extracted from a plant native to northern India. A pint (sixteen ounces) in modern units was an extraordinary amount of oil that would have cost nearly a year's wage for the typical worker of that time. Given its value, Judas Iscariot's complaint (12:4–6) was understandable, even though wrongly motivated.

12:7 *It was intended . . . for the day of my burial.* The Greek is difficult here: *hina . . . tērēsē auto* (ἵνα . . . τηρήσῃ αὐτό), but the sense of the statement answers Judas' question, "Why wasn't this perfume sold?" "According to Jesus, Mary had kept the perfume—unwittingly no doubt, but in the providence of God—for just this purpose."[1]

In the culture of the time aromatic oils were commonly used in much smaller amounts for cosmetic and medicinal purposes, as well as for honoring a deceased loved one with a final washing and anointing immediately prior to

burial. In the Old Testament, anointing with oil was used ritually for the instal-
lation of kings (1 Sa 10:1; 1 Ki 1:39, 45; 19:16; 2 Ki 9:6; 11:12), priests (Ex 28:41;
29:7; 30:30; 40:13–15; Lev 4:3; 8:12, 30; 16:32; 21:10), and possibly prophets (1
Ki 19:16; 1 Chr 16:22). Mary performs a burial ritual by anointing Jesus with the
oil and wiping it with her hair, a very unconventional and perhaps shocking act
(cf. Jn 13:14–15). Knowing that the authorities were looking for Jesus (11:57),
Mary surmised Jesus was approaching the end of his life, and this may well have
been the last time Mary was to see him before his arrest. John makes it clear
that Jesus' crucifixion would be his exalted return to the Father, embodying
the atoning sacrifice as he ascended to the heavenly throne, and so this burial
anointing evokes overtones of Jesus' kingship and priesthood as well.

12:8 *You will always have the poor.* Jesus rebukes the hypocrisy of Judas
Iscariot's accusation of Mary's misappropriation by alluding to Deuteronomy
15:11: "There will always be poor people in the land. Therefore I command
you to be openhanded toward your fellow Israelites who are poor and needy
in your land." Judas apparently felt no compunction about helping the poor
when he was helping himself to the moneybag (Jn 12:6). God's care for the poor
is a major theme of Scripture (e.g., Ex 23:11; Lev 19:10; 1 Sa 2:8, Job 29:12; Ps
12:5; 35:10; 68:10; 82:3), and so we should not take Jesus nor Deuteronomy to
mean that we don't have to help the poor because they will always be around.
Rather the opposite is intended—we can always help them since they are
always around. Jesus is saying do both—help the poor and honor me.

12:12 *The next day.* Based on the Johannine chronology, this was probably
the Sunday before Jesus died, hence the Christian tradition of celebrating
"Palm Sunday."

12:13 *They took palm branches.* The branches of the date palm were associated
with the Feast of Tabernacles in the Old Testament (Lev 23:40) but at the
time of Jesus were also a symbol of victory in the Greco-Roman world (e.g.,
Suetonius, *Caligula* 32), and in the context of occupied Jerusalem were
a symbol of Israel's nationalistic hopes. For palm branches were used in
the rededication of the temple in the Maccabean times (2 Mc 10:7) and to
celebrate victory over the Syrians (1 Mc 13:51). They are suggestive that the
crowd looked to Jesus for nationalistic hope.
    They . . . went out to meet him. The verb *hupantaō* (ὑπαντάω) is synony-
mous with another, *apantaō* (ἀπαντάω), which was used to refer to the cultural
practice of meeting a king or visiting dignitary before he entered a city to accompany him in a procession back through the city gates. The scene John portrays is of this crowd welcoming a dignitary whom they regarded as important.

Hosanna! The crowd shouts (Heb. or Aramaic, *hôš 'nn'*), which John transliterated (not translated) into Greek as *hōsanna* (ὡσαννά), "Save now! Blessed is he who comes in the name of the Lord!" With these shouts the crowds of Passover worshipers acknowledge that Jesus was one "who comes in the name of the LORD" (Ps 118:25a, 26a). At the time of Jesus, Psalm 118 was part of the liturgy of the Festival of Tabernacles in the autumn and of Passover in the spring, but during the preexilic time of the monarchy it would have been recited at the annual new year's reenthronement of the king as he entered the city and temple.[2] Because of the contemporary liturgical use of the psalm, this single quotation would likely have brought to mind the entire psalm, which celebrates God's deliverance of Israel's king, who was received into Jerusalem by the priests of the temple shouting,

> Blessed is he who comes in the name of the LORD.
>   From the house of the LORD we bless you.
> The LORD is God,
>   and he has *made his light shine on us*.
> *With boughs in hand*, join in the festal procession
>   up to the horns of the altar.
>   (Ps 118:26–27)

By shouting it out in this context the crowd not only acknowledged that Jesus was one "who comes in the name of the LORD," but implies also he was "the king of Israel" (cf. Jn 19:19). Their hopes were high that Jesus, who had demonstrated the power to raise the dead, was coming into Jerusalem to use his superpower against the Romans and restore Israel as an independent nation. All four Gospels include quotes of Psalm 118 in describing Jesus' final entrance into Jerusalem (Mt 21:9; Mk 11:9, 10; Lk 19:38) as an important part of defining Jesus' identity and role, as well as the serious, even if understandable, misunderstanding of his mission.

12:14 *Jesus found a young donkey.* Up to this point Jesus had apparently been on foot, but before entering the city he needed a young donkey to fulfill the messianic expectation of how a son of David would enter Jerusalem for his coronation as king (Zec 9:9). A conquering king would have gloriously ridden into a city on a warhorse such as a stallion, but the donkey suggested humility and peace rather than violence and conquest. Not simply a mode of transportation, this symbolic act would have been a statement of Jesus' claim to messianic kingship, an act that would surely inflame the Jewish leaders who would have recognized its implications. "According to the psalm [118] the priests from the temple steps should have greeted Jesus after the disciples shouted the Hosanna, but they did not; so the disciples also went on and shouted the 'Blessed be he . . .'"; otherwise the stones of the temple would have found voices at this historic moment (cf. Lk 19:40).[3] As John continues to recount Jesus' last hours, he will also show how it could be that the long-awaited Messiah came and went unrecognized by his own people (cf. Jn 1:11; 12:23, 37–41).

12:15 *Your king is coming.* By introducing this quotation of Zechariah 9:9 John identifies Jesus as the Davidic king foreseen by the prophet Zechariah. The prophetic image of a king on a donkey triggers all the prophetic promise of Zechariah 9. The reassurance "Do not be afraid" is not found in Zechariah 9, but is often the formula that introduces theophanies and announcement of salvation in the Old Testament (e.g., Ge 15:1; Ex 20:20; Jdg 6:23; Isa 43:5; Jer 46:28; Zec 8:15). "By reenacting Zechariah 9, Jesus does not offer a critique of the crowd's nationalistic expectations of a monarchy; rather, he offers the announcement of salvation which he has come to establish by 'the blood of my covenant with you' (Zech 9:11)."[4] Regarding Jesus as king and Messiah, see also commentary on John 1:20, 41, 49; 2:17; 3:3; 6:15; 7:42.

12:16 *His disciples did not understand all this.* The blindness of the people, including Jesus' own disciples, is understandable. As Herman Ridderbos explains, "No one in Jerusalem but Jesus . . . understood that he entered Jerusalem, sitting on a donkey, to receive that kingship and, as Son of man, to be lifted up on the cross. . . . the story of the entry . . . is the story of Jesus' hidden glory, the deep meaning of which only the progress of the events of salvation would disclose."[5]

12:19 *So the Pharisees said . . . "Look how the whole world has gone after him!"* Though a hyperbolic statement at that historical moment, like Caiaphas (11:49–52), the Pharisees spoke proleptically of the universal scope of the gospel.

12:21 *Sir . . . we would like to see Jesus.* As if on cue, some Greeks representing the "whole world's" interest in Jesus show up asking to meet and speak with Jesus. They approach Philip, possibly because he would have spoken Greek, being from Bethsaida in Galilee. Philip reports this to Andrew, one of Jesus' earliest disciples who had brought his brother Simon Peter to Christ (see Jn 1:40; 6:8).

12:23 *The hour has come for the Son of Man to be glorified.* Throughout the preceding chapters of the gospel of John, Jesus' hour had *not* yet come (2:4; 7:30; 8:20; possibly 4:21, 23). The interest of the Greeks who had come to

Jerusalem to worship seems to have been a signal that now, in fact, Jesus' hour *has* come. This may be tied to his statement in 12:32 that when he is lifted up from the earth (i.e., crucified, see 12:33), he would draw *all* people to himself, people like the Greeks who were seeking to know him. Jesus reveals himself not only as the Messiah of the Jews but as the Savior of all nations (regarding "Son of Man," see commentary at 1:51 and 13:31; regarding "be glorified," see commentary on 11:4).

12:24 *A kernel of wheat.* This analogy "redefines death as being a positive and fruitful event not only for Jesus but also for his followers. The death of Jesus thus becomes a pattern or example of ethics, since the followers must follow suit."[6]

12:27 *For this very reason I came to this hour.* Jesus, knowing his crucifixion is imminent, is troubled. Despite being disturbed and troubled, he acknowledges that it was for the very reason to die by crucifixion that he had come to "this hour." Lament is unfamiliar to most modern readers, but is a well-recognized form of some psalms and the Old Testament book of Lamentations (e.g., Pss 6:3; 42:5, 11) that vents grief and pain while yet looking to God in hope. Jesus more than any other deserves to lament even as he chooses to go to the cross. The Son of God came into history as a human being that he might be executed by those who had been most eagerly anticipating him. Jesus' execution was not to be a tragic accident, a case of being in the wrong place at the wrong time. It was the very reason for his existence as a human being!

12:28 *A voice came from heaven.* Jesus asks that his "hour" would glorify the Father's name—that is, that it would make the Father's character visibly evident (see commentary on Jn 17:1). As Richard Bauckham observes, "Had the cross been Jesus' end, it would not have revealed God. . . . This investment of the horror and shame of the cross with glory makes sense because glory is the manifestation of God's character. The cross as the supreme enactment of God's love is also the supreme revelation of his glory—of who he is."[7]

12:31 *Prince of this world.* This term, understood to refer to Satan, is found only in the gospel of John (here; 14:30; 16:11). The exaltation of Jesus on the cross inaugurates a new world order where God's judgment has been fully executed and where there is no place for the reign of evil. Although the new world has been inaugurated in this age, it will be fully realized only by the promised new heavens and new earth (Isa 65:17; Rev 21:1). In Revelation 12:7–9 a cosmic "war in heaven'" takes place with Satan and his angels in which they are defeated by being "cast out" (*ballō* [βάλλω]). As Edward Klink observes, "Jesus' statement depicts the cross as 'the locus of a cosmic battle, in which Jesus achieves a decisive victory over Satan.'"[8] The cross dethrones Satan and inaugurates the rule of Christ.

12:32 *When I am lifted up.* See commentary on John 3:14. Jesus' public ministry is coming to a close because his hour has come. The darkness of this world is closing in on the true light that came into the world, but it will not extinguish it (cf. Jn 1:5). Darkness will crucify Jesus, but he explains his execution as being at the same time the way the world will be drawn to him (cf. Jn 3:14–15). Evil is inexcusably evil, but there is a concurrency of evil with God's sovereign power for good.

12:34 *The Messiah will remain forever.* The people listening to Jesus clearly understood him to say that his death was imminent. In their understanding of the messianic prophecies (from "the Law") Jesus could, therefore, not be the Messiah after all, for the Messiah "will remain forever" (Ps 110:4; Isa 9:7; Eze 37:25; Da 2:44; 7:14). (John uses "the Law" and the "Scripture" almost interchangeably; cf. 10:34–35.) Another false messianic expectation is exploded by Jesus' revelation of himself. Rather than allowing their messianic expectations to be corrected, many will walk away in rejection of Jesus, who will die as a criminal on the cross. But in fact, the messianic prophecy found in the Law is transposed to its proper sphere—the eternal reign of the Messiah as Son of God, not simply as king of geopolitical Jerusalem (cf. Ac 1:6).

Who is this Son of Man? Jesus had not mentioned the "Son of Man," nearly synonymous here with "Messiah," in the immediate context. It refers the reader back to John 3:14: "Just as Moses lifted up the snake in the wilderness, so the Son of Man must be lifted up, that everyone who believes may have eternal life" (see commentary there; on "Son of Man" see commentary at 1:51 and 13:31).

12:35 *Walk while you have the light, before darkness overtakes you.* See commentary at 1:4, 5, and 9.

12:37 *They still would not believe in him.* As a summary of Jesus' public ministry at its close, this is a disheartening statement. Jesus had, in both word and deed, revealed himself as the Messiah who was sent by the Father. And yet, by some measure, Jesus' ministry among his own people was a failure (Jn 1:11–12). Or was it? We are presented with a profound mystery. Jesus' coming into this world created a divide between light and darkness, between those who would believe in him ("children of light") and those who would not (those who walk in the darkness of this world). In fact, the rejection of Jesus by many was exactly the effect his incarnation was to accomplish, and it had been prophetically foretold. And yet in God's wisdom, those who refused to believe Jesus became the agency of God's will, to crucify Jesus for the atonement of that rejection, which is the essence of all sin.

12:38 *This was to fulfill the word of Isaiah.* The words of Isaiah frame the public ministry of Jesus, forming an *inclusio* between 1:23 and 12:38 and indicating how important Isaiah was for John's understanding of Jesus (see commentary on John 1:23). John understands Jesus "to be the visible embodiment of 'the arm of the Lord'"[9] who was not visible to those whose eyes are blinded and whose hearts are hardened.

John himself had apparently pondered the rejection of Jesus by the Jews of Jerusalem, for preaching the gospel in the intervening years between the crucifixion and John's writing would no doubt have demanded an answer. For "the death of Jesus as a criminal seems to have been the one historical fact about him known to both Jew and Greek."[10] John found an explanation of the rejection of Jesus that led to his execution in the words of Isaiah written centuries before. The apostle considers the rejection of Jesus by so many and so violently to be the fulfillment of Isaiah's prophecy (*hina ho logos Ēsaiou tou prophētou plērōthē* [ἵνα ὁ λόγος Ἡσαΐου τοῦ προφήτου πληρωθῇ]). John presents two quotations in response to unbelief: Isaiah 53:1 and 6:10, which have two verbal links in their immediate contexts ("glorify," *doxazein* [δοξάζειν], and "lift up," *hupsoun* [ὑψοῦν]) that are not immediately evident from the quotations themselves.[11] Neither quotation should be understood out of the context of their Old Testament sources nor in isolation from each other. At first glance they seem to refer to opposing topics: violent humiliation on the one hand and exalted glory on the other. Isaiah 53:1 introduces the envisioned description of the Suffering Servant, and Isaiah 6:10 evokes the larger context of Isaiah's vision of the glory of the Lord. This juxtaposition of violent humiliation that is concurrently exaltation is precisely the lynchpin of Johannine Christology. The quotation of Isaiah 53:1 evokes many resonances between the extended humiliation of the Suffering Servant passage and the experience of Jesus as described by John. And so with this quotation of Isaiah 53:1, John presents Jesus as the Suffering Servant prophesied by Isaiah. The Servant was despised and rejected (Isa 53:3), led like a lamb to slaughter (Isa 53:7), but who nevertheless would "be raised and lifted up and highly exalted" (Isa 52:13), the same language that John uses later to describe Jesus' crucifixion.

Isaiah 6:10 also evokes its immediate context of the vision of the Lord's throne, "high and lifted up" in Isaiah 6:1, suggesting that John views the crucifixion as the basis of Jesus' kingship and reign. Isaiah 6:10 describes the disheartening commission of the prophet who, after seeing the Lord, volunteered to be sent as his messenger. Isaiah is given the message quoted in John 12:40, that Isaiah's prophetic ministry would make the people blind and deaf with hardened hearts; Jesus had the same effect on the Jews of Jerusalem (taking the antecedent of the pronoun "he" in John 12:40 back to "Jesus" in 12:37). John apparently adapts the quotation by omitting the references to hearing, to fit with his motif of light/darkness, i.e., faith/blindness (see commentary on Jn 9). For God's redemptive plan to move toward its fulfillment, the Messiah's revelation of himself in messianic deeds would provoke those who (wrongly) believe themselves to be already righteous to reject God's redemptive work (cf. Jn 9:39, 41). Such people are blind both to Jesus' identity and to their own sin.

John describes the incarnation of Jesus into this world as true light, and describes those who cannot receive him as being blind to the light. Jesus did not speak and act as they expected the Messiah would speak and act, and they rejected him with blind eyes and hard hearts.[12] The rejection of Jesus was part of a larger pattern of Israel's defiant relationship with the Lord that stretched back before the time of Isaiah. It is also a part of the pattern of humankind's relationship with God that goes all the way back to the garden of Eden (see "Going Deeper into God's Sovereignty in Salvation: John 12:37–50"). As George Beasley-Murray explains, "But as in Isaiah's day the hardening of the nation was qualified by the creation of an obedient remnant, so the blindness of Israel in Jesus' day was qualified by the calling of a remnant of believers, with the prospect of a redemption that includes all peoples, a day when the hidden shall be revealed (Mark 4:22) and the rule of God shall be universally manifested."[13]

12:41 *Isaiah . . . saw Jesus' glory.* This is a remarkable statement of how John understood the Old Testament's relationship to Jesus. Isaiah "saw the Lord, high and exalted, seated on a throne, and the train of his robe filled the temple" (Isa 6:1). John explains that Isaiah saw "Jesus' glory," the glory of the preincarnate Christ. The power, authority, and majesty of God's kingship is here attributed to Jesus Christ. And just as Isaiah's people rejected his message, John here explains that the people of his time also rejected the Lord, even after he "had performed so many signs in their presence" (Jn 12:37). For "even though many of the Jewish leaders believed in him they would not openly acknowledge their faith because they loved human glory [*doxa*] more than the glory of God" (Jn 12:42–43, author's translation). Greg Beale relates both instances of rejection to the blindness caused by idolatry.[14] "This preference for human glory instead of God's glory is an idolatrous concept that we have seen repeatedly already in the Old Testament."[15]

The English word *glory* and its modern connotations probably distract from understanding what it was that Isaiah saw. In the biblical sense, glory refers to the visible manifestation of God's presence, and so "Jesus is being identified as the embodiment of God's glory, the visible manifestation of his presence."[16] For John, that visible manifestation occurs most clearly at the point of Jesus' lowest humiliation at his execution and continues through his elevation to the highest place of honor in the resurrection. The absence of glory in the Suffering Servant and its presence in Isaiah's vision of Jesus' rule allows John to see both passages as explanatory for Jesus' rejection. Isaiah saw Jesus' glory and spoke the words of the quotation in John 12:40 ("Isaiah said this because he saw Jesus' glory . . .") *because* Isaiah foresaw a visible manifestation of God ("glory") in a form that sinful people are blind to, unless Jesus heals their blindness and gives them sight (Jn 9:39–41). In his prophetic ministry Isaiah experienced the division of the people that resulted from the work of God in his time, a proleptic episode that foreshadowed the ultimate rejection of the future Messiah. Moreover, John "is building on a long history of associating Isaiah 6 with Isaiah 52–53," the rejection of the suffering servant.[17] John is hinting that the prophet Isaiah saw not only the glory of Jesus in his earthly life but also the rejection of Jesus that leads to his ultimate glorification in John's gospel. The LXX of Isaiah 52:13–15 apparently figured large in John's understanding of Jesus' death as his exaltation and glorification (see commentary on glory at 1:14).

Jerusalem's rejection of Jesus in the first century should not be construed as a greater sin than that of all other peoples. For, as D. Moody Smith observes, the sin of the Jewish nation at the time of Jesus is ultimately that of every individual and of the human race as a whole: "In rejecting the messianic claims of Jesus [ultimately the sin of all] is exposed and the basis is laid for the preaching of repentance and forgiveness of sins through Jesus"[18] (see "Going Deeper into God's Sovereignty in Salvation: John 12:37–50" below).

12:43 *Praise.* "For they loved human glory [*doxa*; δόξα] more than the glory [*doxa*; δόξα] of God" (author's translation). John here invokes both meanings of the Greek word *doxa* (δόξα), first, in its sense of reputation, honor, or praise, and second in the sense of a manifestation of God. The many who rejected Jesus demonstrated that they valued the way they were perceived, especially in the synagogue, more than the manifestation of God that Jesus presented in his incarnation.

12:47–48 *I do not judge. . . . There is a judge.* Although judgment is the inevitable result of darkness, it was because of love, not judgment, that Jesus came into the world (Jn 3:16–17).[19] The judgment of darkness will be based on the acceptance or rejection of the message of Jesus, sent by God (see commentary at 5:22, 37; and 8:15–16).

12:50 *So whatever I say is just what the Father has told me to say.* These final, impassioned words of Jesus to the world at the end of his public ministry are a plea to believe his claims, lest those claims judge them at the last day. For all that Jesus said were commands of God that lead to eternal life. Jesus' words are "just what" the Father has told him to say, and so Jesus ends his public ministry with a strong defense of monotheism.

Going Deeper into God's Sovereignty in Salvation: John 12:37–50

In God's redemptive wisdom, Jesus, the divine Son of God, was born into the world to die. But Jesus did not die a peaceful, natural death in his old age. He was executed as an alleged blasphemer and as traitor to Rome, dying the violent death of a common criminal. By that horrific death, Jesus would "draw all people" to himself (12:32) so that they might not perish but have eternal life (Jn 3:16). God's greatest gift of love to the world would come through history's most tragic death of the One who was purely innocent. It was God's intent to send Jesus into the world to save it (12:47), and because that salvation would involve an atoning death at the hands of those who held the power to do it, it was, in a real sense, God's will that Jesus must die as he did (cf. Ac 4:27–28). God worked his redemptive plan providentially through the decisions and actions of people throughout history, but none so directly as those of the Jewish and Roman authorities in Jerusalem when Jesus finally appeared.

The blindness of Jerusalem's Jewish leaders in their failure to recognize Jesus as the Messiah (often referred to as *obduracy*) is perhaps the greatest irony of history. The very people chosen by God—bound to him by covenant, prepared by him through prophets and sages throughout centuries—at the crucial moment in history not only failed to recognize Jesus as the long-awaited Messiah but directly caused his execution! The apostles, especially John and Paul, pondered that profound irony and found insight in the prophet Isaiah that helped to explain it. In the wisdom of God's redemptive plan, God himself both foresaw Jesus' rejection and took responsibility for Israel's blindness (12:40; Ac 4:27–28). The Jews who rejected Jesus *could not* believe (12:39) because God, through Isaiah, had prophesied it to be so. As Craig Evans notes, both Mark and John "have cited Old Testament texts to demonstrate not simply that Jesus' rejection and death were anticipated, but that the very purpose and intention of Jesus [and hence in John's theology, the intention of God] was to foster the obduracy which would lead to the passion."[20] Bruce Metzger has further observed that "the occurrence of certain events was held to be involved in the *predetermined* plan of God revealed in the Scriptures."[21]

That God and Christ would in any sense blind eyes or harden hearts is a difficult concept indeed. As George Beasley-Murray observes, "The statement sounds like naked predestinarianism, even irresistible reprobation, but it was neither so intended nor would it have been so understood."[22] If God is truly sovereign over all things in history and on earth, then we must allow that he is also sovereign over salvation. The insistence that people must determine their own destiny in relation to God is, in fact, a symptom of the sinful autonomy that began with Adam and Eve and persists in the human race today. If God's redemptive plan was to send the Son to atone for sin, then God must have preordained all the decisions and actions that would lead history to the cross of Christ. And yet God did so in a way that leaves people completely responsible for their rejection of him in Christ. The concept of the concurrency of execution and exaltation demonstrated in Christ's crucifixion also operates in the salvation offered to people. Exodus says both that God hardened Pharaoh's heart (Ex 4:21) and that Pharaoh hardened his own heart (Ex 8:15, 32). Genesis 50:20 teaches that Joseph's brothers were responsible for the evil they did when they sold their brother into slavery in Egypt, yet concurrently (at the same time and in the same act) God swept up their evil into a greater good.

God's sovereign role in salvation might offend our modern sense of justice. If God is sovereign over salvation, and some are saved but others not, then some might claim he is arbitrary, unjust, and unfair. But that allegation is based on the presupposition that human beings are morally neutral in their relationship with God. In fact, every member of the human race is already condemned by our sin, which Jesus refers to as hatred for God (Jn 15:24). If we want God's justice, then he would consign each and every one of us to eternal separation from himself. That would be just, and the human race would be doomed. But Scripture and history show us that God dispenses mercy and grace to those whom he chooses, based not on their qualities or merit, but solely, mysteriously on his divine will. He sent Jesus to open the eyes of the blind, to transform the hearts of the hardened through nothing less than a new birth (Jn 3:5–7). By their own will some receive Christ *because* God the Father drew them (Jn 6:37, 44–45, 65; 10:29; 15:16; 17:24). We choose him only *because* he chooses us for grace and mercy rather than justice. Submission to the mystery of God's sovereignty in salvation is the hallmark of a believer who has completely surrendered his or her will to God's will.

What the Structure Means:
The Hinge of the Fourth Gospel (Jn 12)

John 12 bridges the years of Jesus' public ministry to the final week of his earthly life, and so functions as a hinge in the fourth gospel. The narrative of Jesus' public ministry consisting of miraculous signs that demonstrated his divine power would, in its original historical setting, have sat uncomfortably with the passion narrative, the story of Jesus' suffering and death, though this may be hard to imagine after two thousand years of Christian theology. Chapters 11 and 12 form the bridge between the two that also explains how it was that the Messiah was executed as part of God's providential, redemptive plan.

Following chapter 12, John's narrative of Jesus' life will shift from public displays and large crowds spanning the Jewish festivals to a private, intimate time with his closest disciples during his last week on earth, finally culminating with the cross, empty grave, and postresurrection appearances of Jesus. As Sandra Schneiders puts it, "Chapters 11 and 12 of John constitute a proleptic presentation of the 'Hour' of Jesus. The raising of Lazarus both foreshadows Jesus' resurrection and finalizes the intention of the authorities to kill him. The anointing at Bethany foreshadows Jesus' burial and exposes Judas as the one who will precipitate the Hour by his betrayal."[23] Without these crucial chapters the story of Jesus would be incomplete and enigmatic.

Quotations from the Old Testament expounding Jesus' last entry into Jerusalem show him to be the long-awaited messianic king and also explain his rejection by his own people on the basis of Old Testament prophecy. A change in the phrase used to introduce quotations, from "it is written" during Jesus' public ministry to "this was to fulfill" in the passion account, shows that in John's mind the passion story begins with this dismal closing summary of Jesus' ministry by showing that the violent death of Jesus took place according to God's will.[24] John presents no intervening years of domestic tranquility or other purposes to which Jesus devoted himself. Jesus came, revealed himself publicly to Israel as the Messiah, and was promptly executed for it, thereby securing forgiveness of sins for all who believe.

Even after Jesus performed many signs that signaled he was both the Messiah and divine, still there was unbelief (12:37). Even after Jesus entered Jerusalem in the manner and mode predicted by the prophet Zechariah, silently declaring himself to be the messianic king, he was viewed as a dangerous imposter. The division of the people based on faith and unbelief in response to Jesus was also part of God's divine plan of redemption (cf. 12:37, 42).

Chapter 12 also implies an invitation to readers of this gospel to identity themselves as believers or as rejecters, a rhetorical structure that is powerfully evangelistic. The "hour" for Jesus has come; the hour of decision has come also for the reader.

John 12 Through Old Testament Eyes

To this point in the gospel, John has used images and motifs of the Old Testament—such as Shepherd, Lamb of God, wine, exodus manna—to reveal Jesus as the Messiah and Son of God. In chapter 12 John begins to show how Jesus fulfilled specific Old Testament prophecies of the messianic Davidic king from Psalm 118, Zechariah, and Isaiah. Jesus' kingship had been implied in the Good Shepherd Discourse of chapter 10, as ancient Near Eastern kings were metaphorically cast as shepherds of their people. But with Jesus' entry into Jerusalem he is shown to be the Davidic king, predicted by Psalm 118 and Zechariah 9:9, arriving in the royal city humbly riding on a donkey to claim his throne.

But instead of the acclaim he deserved, Jesus was met with rejection by the Jewish authorities. John explains this tragic failure also as a fulfillment of Old Testament prophecy, specifically that of Isaiah who himself was met with blind eyes and hardened hearts. With the quotation of Isaiah 53:1 John evokes the description of Isaiah's Suffering Servant, which falls like a dark shadow over the story of Jesus' last week of earthly life. Through the subsequent chapters of the gospel, the violent humiliation of the Suffering Servant invoked by John 12:38 informs the reader's understanding that Jesus is the Suffering Servant whom Isaiah foretold. The cross-shaped shadow cast over chapters 13–19 foretells not only the crucifixion of Jesus but his exaltation as King of the Jews as well.

JOHN 13

13:1 *Just before the Passover Festival.* John has constructed his story of Jesus and his interpretation of the significance of Jesus' life within the framework of the Jewish festivals: Hanukkah (Feast of Dedication), Tabernacles, Sabbath, and most pointedly, Passover (see commentary at 2:13, 14; 5:1; 6:4; 7:2, 37; 9:5, 7; 10:22; 11:55; and 12:1). If John is writing after the destruction of the temple in AD 70, as most scholars believe, then there is a deep significance to John's point that the meaning of the festivals of Israel, no longer possible to celebrate with the temple rituals, has been taken up into the person of Jesus Christ. Jesus is the new temple (Jn 2:19–21), and all of the promise and hope of its sacrifices and rituals have been fulfilled, according to John, in the one, final sacrifice of Jesus on the cross. The people's relationship with God is no longer mediated through the priests of the Jerusalem temple, but through Jesus Christ God's Son. John shapes his telling of the last week of Jesus' life, "just before Passover," to underscore the associations of its rituals with the experience of Jesus.

There is a thorny debate about what evening of the week this "evening meal" (13:2) was eaten on, whether it was an actual Passover meal, and whether John's reckoning of the day agrees with or contradicts the Synoptic Gospels (see Mk 14:12; Lk 22:15). The use of different calendars may have been involved, as there were two calendars in use at that time, one that is "lunar-solar" and another that is lunar.[1] A rehearsal of the complexities of this debate is beyond the scope of this commentary, and can readily be found elsewhere.[2] But the crux is whether this evening meal was an actual Passover meal, which would place it during the early hours following sunset on Thursday evening (Nisan 15), or the evening before Passover (Nisan 14), which would entail Jesus' crucifixion occurring on Thursday at the time the Passover lambs were being sacrificed in the temple. The later bishops in Asia Minor—the region in which the gospel of John is believed to have been written—strongly supported commemorating Jesus' death on a date corresponding to Nisan 14. Eusebius and Jerome both quote the letter of Polycrates to Victor of Rome (about AD 195) which claimed that the apostle Philip, John, Polycarp of Smyrna, and Sagaris of Laodicea all "kept the fourteenth day of the passover according to the gospel" (*Hist. eccl.* 5.24.6). The gospel referred to would be the fourth gospel as opposed to the Synoptic Gospels, which put Jesus' last meal on Thursday and his crucifixion on Friday, the tradition preserved to this day in the Western church.

Christian tradition has long assumed that the Last Supper was Jesus' final Passover meal with his disciples, but there is nothing in the Synoptic accounts that compel that assumption. In fact, Mark 14:2 makes the point that the authorities did *not* want to arrest Jesus during the feast, and that preference supports John's chronology that Jesus was arrested the evening *before* Passover began. John explains that the Jewish leaders remained outside the Roman palace *because they wanted to be able to eat the Passover* (Jn 18:28), perhaps indicating that Jesus was crucified *before* the Passover meal began at sunset. If so that would mean in John's account Jesus' last meal with his disciples was not the actual Passover and no meat from a sacrificial lamb would have been on the table, suggesting the point consistent with John's theology that Jesus *himself* would be the Lamb of God slain for the sins of the world. It furthermore seems quite appropriate that Jesus' establishment of the new covenant in his blood (even though John does not explicitly mention this phrase) *not* be on the same occasion as the celebration of the old covenant Passover, even while drawing close associations with it to explain the significance of Jesus' death.

The hour had come. John has prepared his readers for the climax of Jesus' life, which he has referred to throughout as "the hour." Notably, that "hour" would be when Jesus "returns" to God the Father through the experience of death, opening the way for death to become the gateway into eternal life with God for all who follow Jesus.

He loved them to the end. "To the end" (*eis telos* [εἰς τέλος]) could mean to the ultimate extent or to the endpoint. Here, in keeping with the author's fondness for double entendre, it likely means both, for the ultimate extent of Jesus' love for his own who are in the world is most clearly shown in his excruciating death on the cross, which is also the purposeful endpoint and goal of his incarnation (Jn 12:27). At this point in the gospel story (13:1) the end is now in sight for Jesus, and this reference anticipates his final words on the cross: "It is finished!" (*tetelestai* [τετέλεσται], a form of the verb *teleō* [τελέω], "to complete"; 19:30). Jesus is the ultimate consummation of all the hopes and promises of God's covenant with his people found in the Old Testament (Jn 19:28). This is not only stated explicitly in the fourth gospel, but the gospel story in John takes its form on this premise, based so completely on the Hebrew Bible. Clearly this shows that John embraces the Scripture of Israel, and despite his stand against the Jewish leaders in Jerusalem at the time of Christ, his gospel is not anti-Semitic as the term is used today.

13:2 *The devil had already prompted Judas.* The devil, also known in Scripture as Satan (cf. 13:27), is here revealed to be the unseen opponent of the incarnate Son of God. John portrays the crucifixion as the encounter long ago predicted in the garden of Eden between Satan and Jesus (Ge 3:15; cf. Rev 12:9; 20:2). John understood the Jews of Jerusalem who rejected Jesus to have unwittingly colluded with the devil in their opposition (Jn 8:44). As predicted from the beginning in Genesis 3:15, Satan was finally and fully defeated when Jesus walked through death and rose from the grave into eternal life. The Son of God broke Satan's power that had enticed Adam and Eve to spiritual death in the garden of Eden.

13:4 *Wrapped a towel.* Jesus—who knew that God the Father had put all things under his power, and that he had come from God and would return to God through death—got up from the table that evening, took off his outer clothing, and wrapped a towel around his waist. The first lesson Jesus taught on his last evening with his disciples was an enacted parable, taking the role of a lowly servant. This common household task routinely performed before eating (Ge 18:4; 19:2; 43:24; Jdg 19:21) had apparently been neglected because none of the disciples was willing to humble himself to serve the others in this lowly task. Customarily, the position of reclining couches around a table for a meal positioned a diner's head toward the table and their feet to the outside of the circle. Jesus probably poured water over his disciples' feet catching it in the basin and then dried them with the towel.

13:7 *Later you will understand.* When viewed, as Peter did, at the level of the mundane task of footwashing, a necessary task of hygiene and cleanliness in the ancient world, Jesus' intent to wash Peter's feet was outrageous. Grown men, especially a teacher with disciples, did not do such a thing for each other. The other disciples likely felt the same way, but Peter is the one who boldly, or perhaps rashly, speaks out. We would no doubt have felt discomfort too, in such an awkward moment. But Jesus did this outrageous thing, first, as an enacted parable of the cleansing efficacy of his descent to earth in incarnation and ascent through death on the cross; and second, as a paradigm of what true service to others would look like (Jn 13:15). Only after the resurrection and ascension, and perhaps only after much reflection on their time with Jesus, would the disciples understand these things.

13:8 *Unless I wash you, you have no part with me.* Peter misses the point of the enacted parable of the towel and basin, so critical for understanding the significance of Jesus' death. "Jesus responds by making plain that this emphatic rejection of his service is tantamount to a rejection of himself."[3] Cleansing is at the heart of spiritual salvation. As Marianne Meye Thompson notes, "The footwashing does not in itself accomplish the cleansing that Jesus' death does: but it prefigures and illumines the cleansing significance of his death."[4]

13:11 *Not every one was clean.* The binary opposites of unclean and clean in the physical world had long provided the basis for its metaphorical use in a moral and spiritual sense. Washing signified forgiveness for sin (Ps 51:2, 7; Eze 36:25). The entire ritual system of the Old Testament had been based on the idea that ritual cleanliness represented an acceptable moral and spiritual state necessary when approaching the holy, whether that be a site, an altar, or God himself (see, e.g., Lev 5; 7; 10; 11; 13–16; Nu 8; 19). People could move between a state of profane commonness (that is, uncleanness) through prescribed rituals to a state of cleanness in order to worship or to satisfy the ritual requirements of the law. Animals were stated in Scripture to be either clean or unclean, and only clean animals could be consumed (Lev 11; Dt 14:1–21), and only the perfect clean animal was to be offered for religious sacrifice (Lev 9:1–4). Here Jesus creates a wordplay on the chore of making the feet clean to point out that his disciples are clean (Jn 13:10)—that is, in a state of moral and spiritual acceptability because of their faith in Jesus—yet require his service (on the cross) for that faith to be spiritually efficacious. But not everyone present in the group did, in fact, truly believe in Jesus—namely, Judas Iscariot, who saw only an opportunity for personal gain through political expediency (13:11).

13:12 *Returned to his place.* The disrobed Jesus knelt before his disciples, washed their feet, and then returned to his place. This is a picture of what John described in John 1:14 of the Word becoming flesh on earth, and is similar to Philippians 2:6–11, where Christ empties himself, takes the form of a servant, becomes obedient to death on a cross, and then returns to his rightful place as God exalted him to the highest place. The footwashing is, therefore, first an enactment of Jesus' mission in the incarnation. But the revelation of that truth is at the same time a call to those who follow Jesus to remember his willingness to physically humble himself in the activity of a servant and to do likewise for the needs of others. Francis Moloney observes, "Resuming his position at table, he asks if they 'know' what he has done for them (v. 12). The pattern of teacher and lord kneeling in self-gift for his own must continue as one of the marks of the followers of Jesus. He has given them an example they must repeat in their lives of service, no matter what their role might be."[5]

13:13 *"Teacher" and "Lord."* In Jewish culture of that day both terms referred to someone with authority over others who offered instruction. The head of such a group would never have stooped, literally or metaphorically, to wash the feet of his student and subservient disciples. But Jesus breaks that social mold, and instructs his disciples, no matter how high-ranking, to have a similar attitude. There is to be nothing beneath their dignity, for Jesus has dignified even the lowliest forms of service.

13:15 *I have set you an example.* The Greek word *hupodeigma* (ὑπόδειγμα, "example") was used to refer to behavior for moral instruction. Jesus as teacher and Lord set such an example. In the intertestamental period, this word was used specifically to refer to a noble example of how to willingly die a good death (e.g., 2 Mc 6:28, 31; 4 Mc 17:23). Certainly there is a no more noble an instance of willingly dying on behalf of others than that of Jesus, as horrible a death as his was. The principle of example is the willingness to serve others, even in the laying down of one's own life.

Going Deeper into Washing Feet and the Dignity of Menial Labor: John 13:1–17

There is no extant evidence that during their remaining years the apostles ever repeated or instituted footwashing as a ritual of Christian faith and worship as if it were a sacrament. Later it did become a traditional church ritual for the Thursday before Good Friday, Maundy Thursday (see commentary on 13:34). There is nothing wrong with that tradition as long as those participating understand the point of the example is not to repeat the basin and towel as of Christian necessity, but is instead a picture of approaching all of life with a willingness to be a servant to others regardless of one's status and role.

By doing the task of a servant as an example for his disciples, Jesus dignified even the socially lowest forms of work that serve the needs of others, for in that culture a slave or one of the younger children would perform the chore of footwashing. These days some tend to refuse to do the work that often goes to the poor and to immigrants, work that is physically difficult, dangerous, or unseemly. This includes, for instance, landscaping, farm fieldwork, and caregiving for small children, the disabled, or the elderly.[6] No doubt in every society there are assumptions and attitudes that create perceptions of the value of various kinds of work. What does it say about American culture that a baseball player is valued at multiple millions of dollars while the person who grows and harvests our food or teaches our children is so much less valued in terms of earnings?

But if we take the example of Jesus seriously, no Christian should consider any form of honest work that serves others to be below them. The highest, most powerful, most deserving person in the universe, the incarnate Son of God, did not consider his divine status something that made him ineligible, first, for becoming a human being and, furthermore, for doing lowly human work, even the work of the lowliest. Even those of us who do not make our living in the lower-paying service jobs of our social order may find seasons of our life demanding we assume the role of caregiver to someone who needs it. Through his example, Jesus has endowed with dignity and respect those who perform the most unseemly acts of care for those unable to care for themselves. It is in those unrecognized and often unrewarded acts that Jesus' love shines through in our dark and broken world.

13:18 *I know those I have chosen.* Again the theme of election surfaces in this gospel. Although election is often individualized as a matter of personal salvation, in the Old Testament it is set in the context of God's universal authority and his desire to bless all nations (Ge 12:1–3). The election of Israel was the means by which salvation would come to the human race and is part of God's commitment to work within human history.[7]

To fulfill that redemptive mission, Jesus chose twelve men through whom the message of salvation would be extended to the world. Amazingly, one of them would be the agent by whom Jesus' death would result. Jesus knew Judas' disloyal heart, and yet apparently he knelt before him and washed Judas' feet. Although the immediate reference in the story is to Judas' betrayal, Jesus may not have been thinking only of just that one instance, for it "could apply to the state of the Christian community always and everywhere" the apostles ministered.[8] The other eleven did not suspect Judas, and so we must be aware that even some who appear to follow Jesus may, nevertheless at some point, betray him. We must each be especially watchful of ourselves.

This is to fulfill. Like the other gospel writers, John believes that the events of Jesus' life, and especially those of the last week of his life, fulfilled promises and predictions found in the Old Testament (see Jn 2:22; 5:39; 19:28). The narrators of the Gospels, not the characters themselves, "speak" most of the fulfillment formulae and the quotations they introduce (e.g., Mt 4:13–14). But John 13:18 is one of two quotations from the Old Testament (see also 15:25) that are both introduced by the fulfillment formula *and* spoken by Jesus himself. (This is a good example of the distinction between the author and narrator; the author wrote the words spoken by both Jesus and other people in the story, and the author wrote the words spoken by the narrator. But in this case the distinction between quotations spoken by the narrator and those spoken by Jesus are of interest.) In 13:18 Jesus quotes Psalm 41:9, "Even my close friend, someone I trusted, one who shared my bread, has turned against me," showing that Judas' betrayal fulfilled the prediction against the messianic Davidic king, and that Jesus was aware of what Judas was about to do. Although readers of the fourth gospel know that one of the Twelve will betray Jesus, on that last evening of Jesus' life none of his other disciples knew that (see Jn 13:22), and they apparently had no suspicions of Judas (13:28–29). Jesus explains that the betrayal is a fulfillment of Scripture so that when it happens it will not shake their belief in Jesus as the Messiah and Son of God (13:19). The betrayal that led to his death was not to be understood as a tragic accident that frustrated the plan of God but as the heart of its fulfillment.

In John 15:25, Jesus quotes another psalm, Psalm 69:4, to indicate that just as the world hated him, it will hate his disciples when they have been sent out in his name (see commentary on 15:25). John 13 begins the transition that generalizes attitudes focused on Jesus into attitudes toward his disciples in their subsequent mission, representing a transfer of his presence in the world from Jesus to those who follow him. This suggests "that the Scripture citation in Jn 13.18 is functioning at two levels. To the disciples within the story it looks beyond the story, as a prophecy of betrayal in the course of their coming mission. . . . Yet to the reader the citation anticipates a fulfillment within the story, as it predicts Jesus' personal betrayal at the hands of Judas."[9]

13:20 *Whoever accepts anyone I send.* This topic of transfer is stated here where Jesus refers to, though using other words, the custom known as the *sheliach* (שָׁלִיחַ). A *sheliach* (שָׁלִיחַ) was a person who had been designated as an agent and sent with full "power of attorney," so to speak, for a given mission on behalf of the sender. Therefore, a diplomat sent by a king was to be treated as the king himself would have been. As J. Ramsey Michaels observes, "In this sense his disciples are already 'apostles.' . . . Yet the sending in the proper sense does not occur until John 20.21–22"[10] (see commentary there). As Christ's presence in the world, the disciples will be sent after his resurrection out into the world bearing the gospel truth Jesus revealed. They can expect the same kinds of responses they witnessed Jesus himself receive.

13:23 *The disciple whom Jesus loved.* This is the first appearance of this anonymous disciple who was Jesus' closest friend and the eyewitness on whose testimony the gospel of John is based (see also 19:25–27; 20:2; 21:1–14, 20–24).

The identity of this anonymous disciple is highly debated[11] (see the introduction and commentary on Jn 21:21–24). However, he is portrayed to be closer to Jesus, both physically in this moment and perhaps emotionally, than Peter, who must ask "the disciple whom Jesus loved" to ask Jesus about the identity of the betrayer.

13:26 *Dipping the piece of bread.* People who reclined for a meal typically leaned on their left elbow, leaving their right hand free for food. In the ancient Near East, meals were scooped from one or more bowls on the table using a piece of bread as the fork or spoon. Apparently the disciple whom Jesus loved was to his right, allowing him to lean back closer to Jesus (see 13:25), with Judas reclining next to Jesus on his left, the most honored seat at a banquet. The offer of food from Jesus' hand to Judas was customarily a sign of friendship and honor. Jesus is aware of Judas' impending betrayal, but he does not retaliate or abandon his love for Judas. Moloney points out that "Eucharist is a subtheme to the meal and the gift of the piece of bread . . . just as baptism is a subtheme to the footwashing."[12]

13:27 *Satan entered into him.* The transaction of bread between Jesus and Judas that initiates this dark empowerment indicates that Jesus is in control of even the events that will end his life. As Martin Luther said of Satan, "The devil is God's devil," and he can do nothing that subverts God's power.[13] Even the greatest powers of darkness cannot operate apart from God's sovereign plan and purpose. "Judas was given the right or authority to do what he was going to do" though that does not relieve Judas of responsibility for his decision.[14] As Jesus had said, "No one takes it [my life] from me, but I lay it down of my own accord. I have authority to lay it down and authority to take it up again. This command I received from my Father" (Jn 10:18). Throughout the Old Testament an accusing, slanderous power who opposed God's relationship with his creation is first referred to as the serpent in the garden of Eden (Ge 3:1–14) and later personalized as (the) Satan (e.g., 1 Chr 21:1; Job 1:6–2:7; Zec 3:1–2). In the New Testament, Satan is often referred to as the devil who works against God's plan of redemption by trying to divert Jesus from his mission (Mt 4:1, 4; Lk 4:2, 4). He is revealed to be none other than the serpent who enticed Adam and Eve at the beginning (Rev 12:9). Satan had tried to usurp the power and authority of God, but here John shows him to be completely bound by Jesus' authority. The Son of God commands Judas to act quickly on his betrayal, for the hour had come.

13:30 *And it was night.* The sun had set, and Judas no doubt went out into the darkness of a Jerusalem evening. But John's reason for including this detail was to show that even one of the Twelve, even after extended time with Jesus, was nevertheless on the side of darkness. Judas was one of the Twelve and had enjoyed the same attention, privilege, and exposure to Jesus as the others, yet his heart was hard toward the Son of God (a specific example of the introductory statement of Jn 1:10–11). His reasoning operated at the merely political level without perceiving the true significance of Jesus and why he had come. Jesus offended Judas, but only when Jesus permitted him could Judas carry out the plans of his heart, bringing the darkness of death into the light of Jesus' earthly life (see commentary at Jn 1:9).

13:31 *Now the Son of Man is glorified.* This is the last of thirteen references to the "Son of Man" in the fourth gospel. Of the Son of Man John has said the following:

> Angels ascend and descend on him. (1:51)
> He came from heaven. (3:13)
> He must be lifted up. (3:14)
> He was given authority to judge. (5:27)
> He gives food that endures to eternal life. (6:27)
> His flesh and blood must be ingested for eternal life. (6:53)
> He will ascend to where he was before. (6:62)
> He will be lifted up. (8:28; 12:34)
> He is an object of faith. (9:35)
> He will be glorified. (12:23; 13:31)

It may well be that the phrase "son of man" was used in ancient parlance almost as a reflexive idiom to refer to one's self as a mere human being, but Jesus refers to himself with that idiom as a representative of true humanity. Nevertheless, what is said of the Son of Man connotes his divinity. As Britt Leslie writes,

> Given the specific accumulation of functions of the Son of Man, it seems unlikely to me that the title is simply synonymous with "a person" or "this person" (as in me or I). It is possible that the title may be synonymous with the Son of God, but then why not simply use Son of God throughout? So, to summarize Jesus, as the Johannine Son of Man, functions as 1) *gateway to and revealer of heaven/heavenly things* (1:51; 3:13ff), 2) *bringer of life and judgment* (3:13ff; 5:26–29; 6:27, 53, 62), and 3) *one in perfect harmony with the Father's instructions* (8:28).[15]

The glorification of the Son of Man spoken of in 13:31 arises from an understanding of Jesus as the Suffering Servant of Isaiah 52:13 LXX, which says of him, he "shall be exalted [*hupsoō*; ὑψόω] and glorified [*doxazō*; δοξάζω] exceedingly," the same verbs used throughout the gospel of John to speak of Jesus and here, the Son of Man. John is unique among the New Testament writers when he spoke of the humiliation, suffering, crucifixion, and resurrection of Jesus as one event, referring to it as his exaltation or glorification. The word *glory* in Scripture often refers to a visible manifestation of God, and in John's usage it is "the visible revelation of God's character."[16] The Prologue refers to this concurrent glorification of the Son of Man and of God in this "hour" when it states, "We have seen his glory, full of grace and truth" (Jn 1:14). See also commentary on glory at 1:14.

13:34 *Love one another.* Jesus has provided an enactment of what it means to serve others; here he states his intent that his disciples love one another as the hallmark of their faith in him. This mandate, given on the last evening of his life, provides the basis for the term "Maundy Thursday" derived from the Latin word *mandatum*, which refers to the love command (i.e., mandate). Jesus instructs the disciples to love one another as Jesus has loved them—that is, expressed through self-giving service (see commentary at 15:12, 17).

13:36–38 *I will lay down my life.* As D. Francois Tolmie points out, "Peter uses exactly the same words to describe his willingness to die for Jesus, as those that Jesus used when he described himself as the Good Shepherd" in chapter 10.[17] This dialogue anticipates both Peter's denial of Jesus in John 18:15–27 and his reappointment as a shepherd of the Lord's flock in John 21:15–19.

Tolmie further points out the significant echo of the verb *follow* (*akoloutheō* [ἀκολουθέω]) in 13:36 from "chapter 10, where it is said that the sheep will *follow* the shepherd (10:4, 5) and again in 10:27, where Jesus says that his sheep hear his voice and *follow* him. Later, in 12:26, Jesus also says that whoever serves him, must *follow* him."[18] In 13:36 Jesus denies that Peter can, in fact, follow now, but will later, a statement that seems to suggest that although Peter is not yet fully a disciple of Jesus the day will come when his full faith in Jesus will result in the end of his earthly life (Jn 21:18–19, 22).

13:38 *Before the rooster crows.* Chapter 13 is a transition to the darkness gathering around Jesus. Not only has one of the Twelve gone out to betray him, but another, Peter, will also deny Jesus in order to save himself. Peter refuses to accept Jesus' declaration of his impending departure from this life and instead counters with his own offer to protect Jesus, unwittingly working against God's plan for Jesus' life. It is Jesus who will and must give up his life for Peter, the other disciples, and all who are his.

Beginning with the evening meal on the night before Jesus was crucified, the apostle Peter assumes increasing prominence in these latter chapters of the gospel of John, being mentioned by name often as the companion of the beloved disciple at crucial points of the story (13:23–24; 20:2–8; 21:7, 20–24). This suggests that John had special interest in the relationship between Peter and the beloved disciple (who I identify in the introduction as John), though scholars debate whether it was an adversarial relationship or one of mutually regarded leadership in the Johannine churches.[19]

What the Structure Means:
The Upper Room Discourse (Jn 13–17)

The apostle John has told the story of the approximately three-year public ministry of Jesus in what is often called the Book of Signs (Jn 1:19–12:50). Beginning with John 13, the apostle slows his telling of Jesus' life to focus several chapters on just the last evening of Jesus' earthly life in what is often referred to as the Farewell Discourse or Upper Room Discourse (Jn 13–17). For Jesus had retreated with his disciples to a large upstairs room (Mk 14:14; Lk 22:12) to spend a last evening together before his death. This quiet time bridges Jesus' appearances in public as a free man to his arrest, "trial," and execution (Jn 18–19). These chapters of the gospel of John provide both instructions for Christian living after Jesus is gone—primarily in the mandate to love by serving one another—and hope for the believer's life after death to resume with Jesus where he is going.

The first twelve chapters of the fourth gospel cover a period of time of about two and a half to three years; chapters 11–19 document the last week of Jesus' earthly life; and chapters 13–17 represent just his last evening with his disciples. One of this gospel's distinctive features is its lack of the institution of the Last Supper, or Eucharist, that is found in all three Synoptic Gospels. Instead, John documents the footwashing as an example of discipleship and of the love Jesus has for his disciples and the love they are to have for one another. The approaches of both the Synoptics and the fourth gospel "supply the meaning of the death of Jesus that they go on to narrate."[20] It is likely at the time the fourth gospel was written that Holy Communion had long been an established sacrament of the church, and its origin needed no further explanation than that supplied by the Synoptic Gospels. Instead, John includes instruction on the significance of Christ's death and the mandates it extends to Jesus' disciples: the mandate for servant leadership and the command to love one another. The rejection of Jesus that led to his execution is also extended to the disciples in the warning they, too, will be hated and betrayed when they are sent out in Jesus' name to be his presence in the world. The purpose of the Upper Room Discourse is to prepare those who followed Jesus to live in a world where he would no longer be present. As such, it is a precious last word from Jesus for Christian believers yet today.

John 13 Through Old Testament Eyes

The commemoration of the exodus from Egypt as celebrated in the Passover creates the frame in which John will tell the story of Jesus' last hours on earth. Jesus chooses to spend these precious hours with his disciples to inform, comfort, and motivate them as the horrendous event of his crucifixion approaches, and for the lives they must thereafter live as his agency in this world.

The footwashing indicates that the cleansing for sin previously accomplished by the death of sacrificial animals in the temple would finally and fully be accomplished by the death of Jesus, the Lamb of God (Jn 1:29, 36). Passover had established the concept of vicarious sacrifice in the religious life of Israel, as the blood of the lamb was substituted for the death of each family's firstborn son. This was followed by the continual and repeated sacrifice of animals through millennia for cleansing from sin, which had likely come to an end with the destruction of the temple in Jerusalem in AD 70 by the time John wrote his gospel at the end of the first century. Following Jesus' crucifixion, animal sacrifice would no longer be needed, for the truth to which it pointed was once-for-all accomplished by the death of the Lamb of God.

Words of the Old Testament also provided a prophecy (Ps 41:9 in Jn 13:18) that showed Judas' betrayal would not thwart Jesus' mission in the world but, to the contrary, that it had been foretold as part of messianic redemption. Even this evil instigated by Satan was being taken up within God's great plan for the mission of Jesus. The disciples are thereby to be assured that nothing is happening that lies outside the purview and purposes of the sovereign God. Furthermore, Jesus was not blindsided by his disciple's betrayal for he already knew what role Judas would play in sending him to the cross. Yet Jesus allowed Judas to do only what the Father had ordained, and loved him nevertheless.

The Old Testament, therefore, provides the context in which the significance of Jesus' vicarious death as the purpose of the incarnation in God's redemptive plan could be revealed.

JOHN 14

14:1 *Do not let your hearts be troubled.* Surely the disciples of Jesus had every reason to be troubled. After nearly three years with Jesus, it was dawning on them that all their hopes for the future were about to be shattered if Jesus' talk of imminent death was realized. No matter one's possessions, achievements, or status in this life, death ends it all. The same verb was used in 13:21, when Jesus himself was "troubled in spirit," and he prescribes to his disciples the same remedy that he had to invoke himself: Jesus trusted in God while facing his imminent death. Because of his relationship to God, Jesus can appropriately command his disciples to trust in him even though it appears everything they thought they knew was about to shatter[1] (see "Going Deeper into Untroubled Hearts in Troubling Times: John 14:1–6").

14:2 *My Father's house has many rooms.* Some readers have probably learned this verse from the King James Version, which reads, "In my Father's house are many mansions." In the most recent English translations, it looks like a major downsizing has occurred from mansions to rooms. The Greek noun *monē* (μονή), translated "mansions" or "rooms," is a cognate noun of the verb *menō* (μένω, "stay, remain, abide"), which occurs forty times in John's gospel. The Greek noun has two related senses: (1) "a state of remaining in an area"; or (2) "a place in which one stays," whether it be a hut or a palace.[2] Since *monē* (μονή) is used in the context of "the house of my Father," *rooms* is an appropriate translation, suggesting both individuality and unity of place. Jesus assures his disciples that there is a place for them with God, a place to arrive in and stay forever. The word *mansion* derives from the Latin Vulgate's *mansiones*, and at the time the King James was translated, it meant simply a place to stay without the connotation of opulence. In a good example of how English language changes—and the consequent need for the periodic revision of English Bibles—as in our times it has come to refer to a large, lavish home.

One can still ask, *When* does a follower of Jesus abide in one of these places in the Father's house? The usual understanding is that these are abodes to which one goes after death, or perhaps at the return of Christ. But in 14:23 the same Greek noun is used to refer to the abode of the Father and Son in the *present* life of those who love Jesus. As Robert Gundry explains, "The two occurrences of *monē* (μονή) in John 14 demonstrate a reciprocal relationship; as believers have abiding-places in Christ, so Jesus and the Father have an abiding-place in each believer. The plural form *monai* (μοναί) in verse 2 emphasizes the individuality of the places which all believers have in Christ. . . . The reception of believers by Jesus at his coming will not be for the purpose of taking them to their abiding-places; it is consequent on their being in those abiding-places before he comes."[3] By this understanding, the Father's house (*oikia* [οἰκία]) is not heaven but God's spiritual household, into which believers enter during this life upon faith in Christ. In John's gospel Jesus promised a reuniting with his disciples through his resurrection from death and by the sending of "another paraclete," the Holy Spirit. The Old Testament motif of the temple as God's dwelling place is fulfilled by the church in Christ, now collectively the temple of the Holy Spirit. In another example of realized eschatology pointing to future eschatology, the current spiritual position of believers portends the second coming of Christ as the "already" to the "not yet."

"In Christ the believer has the 'way' leading into the Father's presence, the 'truth' revealing the Father's inmost character, and the 'life' infusing into the believer the Father's very nature. These are the present consequences of our positions in Christ, just as reception into his immediate presence at his return is the future consequence."[4] We arrive in our *monē* (μονή), or dwelling place, upon embracing faith in Christ in this life, and will be taken to be where Christ is upon death or his return.

Nevertheless, the concept of heaven as a house with rooms is found elsewhere in Jewish writings of the time.[5] Moreover, the *monai* (μοναί) that Jesus prepares are located *where he is going*, which is clearly a reference to the place of his dwelling with God *after* his death. And so the traditional understanding is not wrong, but needs to allow that Jesus will take disciples to their eternal abode *because* they have already found their dwelling place in Jesus in this life (see "Going Deeper into the Comforting Hope of 'Heaven': John 14:1–14").

I am going there to prepare a place for you. Although it may be natural to read this statement to mean that *after* his death Jesus will prepare a place,[6] the statement continues with Jesus' explanation of why he had to die. It is *by* dying on the cross and rising in resurrection life to a new realm of existence (i.e., "going away") that Jesus prepares the place, opening the Father's "house" to those who put their trust in him.

14:5 *How can we know the way?* Thomas, the loyal but ever pragmatic disciple (cf. Jn 11:16; 20:25), asks a perfectly logical question. Without knowing Jesus' destination, how could they know the route to take? Where *is* the Father's house to which Jesus is departing?

14:6 *I am the way and the truth and the life.* As D. A. Carson points out, Jesus' reply affirms that if they trust in him and know that he *is* the way, they don't need to know precisely where it leads.[7] Jesus does not just *show* us the way; he *is* the way. Since "the way" is under discussion, it has a bit more semantic prominence than the additional two nouns, *truth* and *life*, to which it is syntactically coordinated (correlative *kai* [και]). Jesus did not come as if he were an outstanding theology professor, teaching truth *about* God; he came to show us God in a form human beings could most truly comprehend, the incarnate form (cf. 1:18). Furthermore, as Son of God his life *is* God's eternal life that the human experience of death and the grave could not overcome.

No one comes to the Father except through me. "Now that Jesus has come as the culminating revelation of the Father, it is totally inadequate to claim that one knows God, on the basis of the *antecedent* revelation of bygone epochs, while disowning Jesus Christ."[8] Therefore, while knowledge of the Old Testament is essential for understanding God's redemptive work in history, and as the primary literary and theological background for the New Testament writings, Old Testament revelation is wholly inadequate to reveal God fully. The epoch-changing event of Christ's incarnation also falsifies the often-quoted sentiment that there are "many roads to God." There is one. His name is Jesus.

Going Deeper into the Comforting Hope of "Heaven": John 14:1–14

When I was nine years old I realized for the first time that everyone dies. The thought that terrified me was not that I would one day die, but that my parents would die and leave me. As I lay in my bed one night crying at the thought, my dad, hearing my distress, came and sat on the edge of my bed to ask what was wrong. When I shyly told him, he responded by quoting Jesus from John 14:2 in the KJV: "In my Father's house are many mansions; I go to prepare a place for you." A flash of insight came into my childish mind: this made perfect sense because Jesus was, after all, a carpenter. And so he's in heaven building a new house for me and my parents and brothers to live in when we die. It was a deeply comforting thought.

Many years later I more fully understood that the preparation Jesus did to make a place for us to be with God wasn't achieved by celestial carpenter's tools, but by an excruciating death on the cross. He died to provide, not a mansion, but an eternal relationship with the triune God, so that in this life and the next we might be with Jesus and with those others who have followed him. Nevertheless, I was somewhat disappointed when I first encountered in seminary the idea that "we are not at first to regard the 'abodes' as rooms in heaven which are being constructed for us by the architect of the Celestial City."[9] While Scripture promises a future life after death, there is little to help us envision what that "place" will be like. Even if "mansion," with ten thousand square feet and gold-plated faucets, is not the right idea, the book of Revelation (whether or not authored by the same John as the gospel) does paint an opulent picture of Main Street in the new Jerusalem (see Rev 21–22) with its brilliant jeweled architecture, gold, precious stones, and luxurious landscaping.

However, as N. T. Wright has reminded the church, "heaven" if conceived of as a disembodied state is not our final destination, and the new Jerusalem comes *down* from God to the new earth inhabited by the resurrected followers of Jesus.[10] It was not as a disembodied spirit but as a resurrected human being that Jesus ascended to the Father, and his purpose is to call forth the bodies from their graves of all who trust in him (Jn 5:28; 6:54; 11:23–25).

John 14 does not develop the specifics of life after death, but having "a place in the Father's house" does suggest an intimate relationship with the Father in a place fully in his presence and purposes. It is a reunion of Jesus with his disciples, even for those of us, as also the vast majority of Christians, who did not know him during his earthly life. And because there are "many" dwelling places in the Father's house, it suggests we will not be lonely. There is room for each and every one who puts their trust in Jesus Christ.

Going Deeper into Untroubled Hearts in Troubling Times: John 14:1–6

It is sometimes said that there are things worse than death, and in some sense that is likely true. Extreme poverty, chronic painful illness, imprisonment, and separation from loved ones—such things may come to mind as possible worse-than-death scenarios. However, there is a finality to death that ends all the hopes this world can offer. In that sense, death is the worst of all possibilities that human beings face. In the face of death, Jesus prescribes trust in God, the heavenly Father, as the remedy for putting one's heart at peace. Jesus has conquered the worst life can do to us; he has dignified our suffering and promised us eternal peace and joy.

As Thomas à Kempis comments, "Follow Me: *I am the way, and the truth, and the life.* Without the way thou canst not go; without the truth thou canst not know; without the life thou canst not live. I am the Way which thou oughtest to follow; the Truth which thou oughtest to believe; the Life which thou oughtest to hope for. I am the Way unchangeable; the Truth infallible; the Life everlasting."[11]

When trouble comes, as it surely does to each of us, and when the day of our death inexorably arrives, let our hearts not be troubled, but let them rest in and trust in the Father's love for us.

14:8 *Show us the Father.* Throughout the Old Testament we find appearances of God's presence in visible earthly forms (theophanies; Gk. *theos* + *phainō* [θεός + φαίνω]), such as the burning bush, the angel of the Lord, and the chariot throne (e.g., Ex 3:2–6; 19:18–19; 20:18; 23:20–23; 32:34; 33:14–15; Dt 4:12, 15; Jos 5:13–15; Jdg 6:11–24; 13:6–7, 11–14, 20; Isa 6:1–5; 63:9; Eze 1:26–28). Philip may well have been asking for that sort of visible manifestation of God's presence. Even after extended time with Jesus, seeing his miracles, hearing his words, the disciples apparently had not yet comprehended the greatest theophany of all time, the incarnation of the Son of God. Who could blame them?

14:9 *Anyone who has seen me has seen the Father.* There is nothing about God the Father that has not been revealed in Jesus Christ, so close is their relationship. The incarnate Word has seen God face-to-face (Jn 1:1), fulfilling the promise that God would raise up another prophet like Moses "whom the Lord knew face to face" (Dt 18:18; 34:10). Here Jesus confers that status on his apostles who knew him face-to-face and would deliver the message of his gospel to the world (see commentary on Jn 1:21).

14:10 *It is the Father, living in me, who is doing his work.* John defends monotheism with the concept of the mutual indwelling of the Father and the Son. With the advent of Jesus there are not two Gods, but one God mutually present "in" the Father and in the Son. Words fail when attempting to describe the incarnation beyond saying what Scripture says, that Christ is in the Father and the Father is in Christ (14:11). The quality and nature of Jesus' "works" are such as to indicate that they are at the same time the Father's works, as the Father was understood and revealed in the theology of Judaism. With this verse the concept of the "Sent one" (*sheliach* [שָׁלִיחַ]) so prominent earlier in the fourth gospel (see commentary on 3:17, 34), is superseded by the union of two distinct identities.[12] Jesus is not just sent by God the Father; he shares the divine nature of God the Father. Everything Jesus does the Father does; everything the Father does Jesus does. The presence of God the Father is fully manifested in the man Jesus. There is nothing about God that has not been revealed by Jesus Christ, and so there can be no clearer theophany.

14:12 *They will do even greater things.* This incredible statement must give us pause (cf. Jn 1:50). Everyone who believes in Jesus will do even "greater things" (*meizona* [μείζονα]) than Jesus? Because it is almost impossible to think of doing anything greater than turning water into wine (Jn 2:1–11), or healing a man born blind (Jn 9), or raising someone to life who has been in the tomb four days (Jn 11), "greater" is sometimes understood to be quantitative, as in "more things." The rationale given is that with the coming of the Spirit, Jesus' power is multiplied by the many disciples he would gain throughout the world with the spread of the gospel as recorded in the book of Acts. But that's not what Jesus said. "Greater things" (*meizona* [μείζονα]) are not "more things" (*pleiona* [πλείονα]). Furthermore, the *reason* for Jesus' disciples doing "greater things" is *because* he is going to the Father. His death and resurrection are the basis for understanding what "greater things" mean and recognizing they usher in a new epoch.

In the Old Testament the prophets did some spectacular miracles. Moses parted the sea (Ex 14), Elisha made iron float (2 Ki 6), and the Shunammite's son was raised to life (2 Ki 4). And yet Jesus' miracles were qualitatively different from those of the Old Testament prophets because his arrival marked the inauguration of a new age of God's presence in this world. In a somewhat similar way, the greater things that followers of Christ do after his departure "will be set in the framework of Jesus' death and triumph, and will therefore more immediately and truly reveal the Son [than the signs and works Jesus did during his earthly life]. Thus *greater things* is constrained by salvation-historical realities."[13] And so the works of the disciples are greater because they are done in the context of the greater revelation that Jesus' life, death, and resurrection has brought.

This is the point in the Farewell Discourse that Jesus begins to reveal that just because he is going away doesn't mean the work he began will stop. To the contrary, this is the first hint of the Johannine commissioning of the disciples to continue the work, of Jesus passing the torch to his disciples, as flawed and fearful as they were in that moment.

14:13 *Whatever you ask in my name* (cf. 15:16; 16:23, 26). The prepositional phrase "in my name" limits "whatever you ask" to things consistent with and according to the revealed nature and purposes of Jesus. Prayers for self-serving gain or requests that oppose the work of God in Christ are therefore excluded. The "greater things" done by Jesus' disciples after his departure would, nevertheless, be done by Jesus himself ("*I will do* whatever you ask in my name"). There is no competition between what Jesus did and what his disciples will do. Jesus' death and resurrection eliminated the human limitations that constrained his work during his earthly life and contribute to our understanding of in what way the things that his disciples will do are "greater" (see commentary at Jn 15:7).

14:15 *Keep my commands*. This is the first time in the fourth gospel that Jesus speaks of his disciples' love for him, following after much talk about Jesus' love for them. The future, indicative verb as found here (*tērēsete* [τηρήσετε], "you will keep") is a way of expressing an imperative thought that also contains a hint of promise. The ancient Greek version of the Ten Commandments uses the same syntax, a future indicative where one might expect the imperative mood.

Obedience to Jesus is also the definition of the kind of love he demands, first, for him, and consequently, for others. Just as the Ten Commandments of the Old Testament defined the moral quality of ancient Israel's relationship with God, Jesus' commands transpose them into a higher key that involves inner spiritual transformation. Love for Jesus will result in, both by one's will and by the promise of one's spiritual transformation, obedience to the whole truth that Jesus reveals. This link between love for the Lord and obedience is a major theme of the Johannine writings. As Carson explains, "What the one who loves Jesus will observe is not simply an array of discrete ethical injunctions, but the entire revelation from the Father, revelation holistically conceived (*cf.* 3:31–32; 12:47–49; 17:6)."[14] Just as the commandments of the Old Testament were intended to express a relationship to God, here Jesus reveals that obedience to his commands entail the behavior of the new covenant relationship with God through Christ.

14:16 *He will give you another advocate*. The Greek term *paraklētos* (παράκλητος), sometimes translated "advocate," was used in the first century to refer to a person who came to one's aid in a situation of judgment, such as a court of law, either as counsel at law or as a friendly witness. This led to the word being translated as "advocate" or "counselor" (at law). But such a definition doesn't cohere well with the functions of the paraclete as described in this gospel as teaching, preaching, and revealing (Jn 14:26; but cf. 1 Jn 2:1, where the context is judgment for sin). Eskil Franck argues, probably rightly,

that paraclete with its legal connotation was chosen by the author to associate
the roles of the Holy Spirit with the trial motif of the gospel, in which truth is
on trial and is being judged.[15]

Within Jewish tradition, the cognate noun *paraklētos* (παράκλητος) in
the Septuagint was often used to refer to comfort or consolation (e.g., Job 21:2;
Hos 13:14; Isa 30:7). For this reason, *paraklētos* (παράκλητος) in this verse has
sometimes been translated "comforter" (KJV) or "counselor." Given the context
of Jesus' consolation of his disciples in the face of his imminent departure, the
connotation of comfort is probably apt. But considering that Jesus refers to "another paraclete," his role as a paraclete must also influence our understanding
of the term. In 1 John 2:1 the reference to Jesus as a *paraklētos* (παράκλητος) is
clearly in the context of judgment: "My dear children, I write this to you so that
you will not sin. But if anybody does sin, we have a *paraclete* with the Father—
Jesus Christ, the Righteous One." The comfort afforded by the paraclete is in its
essence *because* he intercedes on our behalf before the Father, putting right our
relationship with God at the time of the judgment of our sin.

Until chapter 14, Jesus has been the unique one sent by the Father, but
now the disciples are to be consoled by the sending of another paraclete who
will be with them, the Holy Spirit (14:26), or as Jesus first mentions him, the
Spirit of truth (14:17). Here begins the Trinitarian doctrine of God, for although John does not use the word *trinity* nor does he present the doctrine in
the fully developed form known today, the interrelationships of Father, Son,
and Spirit entail such a concept (cf. 4:17, 20).

14:17 *The Spirit of truth.* The concept of truth is an important characteristic
of God in the Old Testament, for as Creator, God is the ground of all reality
and truth (Ge 1:1–28). Truth is, furthermore, characteristic of what is said by
those who speak for God, such as the prophets (e.g., 1 Kg 17:24; Isa 48:1; Jer
7:28) and, in the fourth gospel, those who belong to God. Truth as revealed by
Jesus is a major theme in the gospel of John, occurring in twenty-five verses.
The Spirit of truth indwells the disciples of Jesus, separating them from "the
world" that does not see or know him (see also commentary at 15:26).

14:18 *I will not leave you as orphans.* This Greek predicate adjective *orphanous*
(ὀρφανούς) could be used more broadly than the English word permits,
even to refer to parents who were "bereft of a child."[16] But here the metaphor
probably draws upon the Old Testament image of "the father's house" as
"a household living a single corporate life whose center and source is the
father."[17] The disciples had lived in the company of Jesus as a family in some
sense, with him at the head. His imminent death would be so devastating to
them that their plight could be compared to that of orphans.

14:26 *The Holy Spirit . . . will teach you.* The Old Testament frequently mentions the Spirit of God or the Spirit of the Lord, beginning with the creation story in Genesis 1:2, where the "Spirit of God" was hovering over the formless void that would become the created order. Throughout the Old Testament the Spirit of God "came upon" individuals, making them God's agency in this world. The New Testament writers continue to use the phrase "Spirit of God" but far more frequently refer to the Holy Spirit, a reference found only a few times in the Old Testament (Ps 51:11; Isa 63:10–11). The New Testament writers and especially the gospel of John strongly associate the Spirit with Jesus, referring to both as paracletes, and asserting that the death and resurrection of Jesus releases the Spirit of God in a new way on followers of Jesus (Ac 2; Jn 14; 16; 20:22), making them God's agency in this world. In John 14:17 the Holy Spirit is described as the Spirit of truth, and in this second mention he is said (1) to be sent from the Father in Jesus' name, (2) to teach the disciples, and (3) to remind them of Jesus' earthly words. This promise would console the disciples that the good Jesus had begun to do in his work and words would not end with his death, but would continue in the mission of his disciples (see also commentary at 15:26).

The Father will send in my name. The Father will send anew the Spirit of God into the world on the followers of Jesus and in the name of Jesus. Because Jesus will ask the Father to send the Spirit (14:16), the Father will send the Spirit in the name of Jesus. The Spirit comes as the emissary of Jesus, which defines a new epoch in the work of the Spirit in this world. As Carson points out, "John's purpose is . . . to explain to readers at the end of the first century [and all subsequent readers] how the first witnesses, the first disciples, came to an accurate and full understanding of the truth of Jesus Christ. The Spirit's ministry in this respect was not to bring qualitatively new revelation, but to complete, to fill out, the revelation brought by Jesus himself."[18] And so the Old Testament Spirit of God who came on individuals who would accomplish God's redemptive acts is present at Jesus' request and in Jesus' name to inform and indwell those who follow Jesus.

14:27 *Peace I leave with you.* Jesus' departing gift to those who follow him is peace (*eirēnē* [εἰρήνη]), connecting him to the eschatological promises for Israel's salvation in the Old Testament, where *shalom* (שָׁלוֹם, "peace") was used to refer to the prosperity, safety, wholeness, and well-being that was grounded in God (e.g., Ps 29:11 [28:11 LXX]; 35:27 [34:27 LXX]; 85:8 [84:9]; 119:165 [118:165 LXX]; 122:6–8 [121:6–8 LXX]; Isa 9:5–6; 26:3, 12; 57:19; Eze 34:25–29; Na 1:15 [2:1 LXX]). Much more than an internal psychological state or the absence of war, the word sums up the blessings of God's presence in the Aaronic blessing in Numbers 6:24–26: "The LORD bless you and keep you; the LORD make his face shine on you and be gracious to you; the Lord turn his face toward you and give you peace." The Hebrew word for peace (*shalom* [שָׁלוֹם]) became a conventional greeting in Jewish culture, *shalom*, (cf. Jn 20:19, 21, 26) that is still used in modern Israel and by Jews around the world today. In the Old Testament God is the giver of such peace; therefore, Jesus' bestowal of peace upon those who follow him is a subtle way of identifying him with God. "Soteriologically, peace is grounded in God's work of redemption; eschatologically, it is a sign of God's new creation, which has already begun; teleologically, it will be fully realized when the work of new creation is complete."[19] Because peace is the realization of God's redemption of the world through Christ, the world cannot produce peace (see also commentary at Jn 20:19).

14:30 *The prince of this world.* Jesus prepares for the final battle with the approach of Satan who empowered Judas and the Jewish leaders (see commentary at 12:31; 13:27; 15:6).

John 14 Through Old Testament Eyes

John 14 presents teaching that would no doubt have been shocking to readers who knew only the Hebrew Scriptures, for it presents an intimate association of Jesus, God the Father, and the Spirit of God that is an embryonic form of the Trinitarian doctrine of God. Furthermore, it presents Jesus, Son of God, as the exclusive way to the Father, a concept that boggles minds even still today.

Jesus' death was not a tragic mishap, but is the essential preparation needed to prepare a place for those the Father calls into his house (14:3). As such, belief in what this reveals about God and his relationship to humankind is the only path to eternal life, for *only* Jesus has prepared that path. The exclusivity of eternal life through Christ alone was an offense to Judaism, which did not recognize Jesus as the long-awaited Messiah and the culmination of God's redemptive relationship with his people. Today, that same exclusivity is an offense to those who believe there are many equivalent ways to God, even though the religions of our times are in essence at odds with Christianity and with each other. Not every spiritual path can be true (cf. 14:6).

The closest association between Jesus and the Father is presented in 14:8–14, as mutually indwelling (14:10, 20). To see Jesus is to see the Father for, as Sinclair Ferguson puts it, "There is nothing un-Jesus-like in the heart of the Father."[20] That is, there is nothing of God the Father that has not been revealed in Jesus Christ.

John 14 introduces the Holy Spirit who is "another paraclete" (14:16) and the Spirit of truth (14:17). The activity of the Spirit will be explained in John 16, but here we learn that the Holy Spirit will be with Jesus' disciples and *in* them. This indwelling of the Spirit, along with the Father and the Son (14:23) is unheard of in the Old Testament, where the Spirit episodically "comes upon" individuals who are empowered to accomplish specific redemptive acts. The phrases "Spirit of holiness," "Spirit of the Lord," or "Spirit of God" occur frequently in the Old Testament. The distinction between the Spirit and God the Father is less clear in the Old Testament, but the Spirit is "holy" because the Spirit comes from God (e.g., Isa 63:10). The empowerment by the Spirit of specific acts of deliverance in the Old Testament (e.g., Jdg 3:10; 11:29; 14:6; 1 Sa 11:6) anticipates the redemptive work of the Spirit in the New Testament, where he is distinguished from God the Father and God the Son. The prophetic empowerment of the Spirit in the Old Testament (e.g., 2 Sa 23:2; Eze 2:2; 3:12, 14; Mic 3:8) that brought the "word of the Lord" anticipates the testifying and teaching role of the Spirit in the New Testament, especially as revealed in the gospel of John (cf. Jn 16).

John presents an intimate association of Jesus, God the Father, and the Spirit of God that nevertheless distinguishes clearly between the Father, the Son, and Holy Spirit. Jesus teaches that after his resurrection the intimacy between God and his people will be caught up in the intimacy within the Trinity itself. Even two thousand years of Christian reflection has not plumbed the depth of that mystery, or articulated it more clearly than John does here.

JOHN 15:1-25

15:1 *I am the true vine.* Read within the context of Passover (Jn 13:1), this imagery of the vine, the source of wine, probably would have alluded to the cup of wine drunk at the Passover meal, the cup which Jesus (in the Synoptic Gospels) raised and proclaimed to be "the cup of the new covenant in my blood" (Mt 26:28; Mk 14:23, 24; Lk 22:20). "I am the true vine" is the final "I am" statement in the gospel of John. The "I am" statements not only suggest an identification of Jesus with the great I AM of Exodus 3 but in predicate form as here also reveal new truth about the character and nature of I AM's relationship with humanity. Jesus identifies himself as the "true" (*alēthinē* [ἀληθινὴ]) vine, meaning the authentic, genuine, or real vine. This is possibly an allusion to Jeremiah 2:21 LXX, which also describes a vine planted by God as *alēthinē* (ἀληθινὴ), "true," in the sense of being of pure stock. Jesus' emphatic manner of expression implicitly suggests another vine that is somehow less true, less authentic.

When read through Old Testament eyes, echoes of the vine in Psalm 80 and in Ezekiel 15 immediately jump to mind (see also Hos 10:1–2; Isa 5:1–7; Jer 2:21; Eze 17:1–21; 19:10–15; see also "John 15:1–17 Through Old Testament Eyes" below). Psalm 80, especially in its LXX translation (Ps 79 LXX), "can account for the identifications of the Son, the Father, and the disciples in the vine image."[1] Passages from Ezekiel 15, 17, and 19 speak of branches (*klēma* [κλῆμα]) that seem to have a separate identity from the vine itself, and also speaks of pruning, burning, and a connection to the royal house. Because of several common elements between Psalm 80 and the Ezekiel passages, it would be inviting for an interpreter such as the apostle John to connect and merge the imagery.

As Francis Moloney observes, "Although 15:1–11 focuses upon Jesus' words to his disciples, an atmosphere of polemical contrast between Jesus' exclusive claim to be the true vine, over against Israel's claim to be a vine, is present from v. 1."[2] Jesus' declaration means that "'Jesus, the Messiah and Son of God, fulfills Israel's destiny as the true vine of God (Ps. 80:14–17).' John may be interpreting Psalm 80 as a Messianic prophecy fulfilled in Jesus: God is doing in Jesus exactly what the psalmist asked him to do."[3] Jesus' statement, therefore, has an implicit positive connection to the Davidic hope, but given Jesus' adversarial relationship to the Jerusalem authorities in the fourth gospel it is likely to also be an indictment of Israel's failure to bear the fruit God expected.

Jesus' further statement that the Father is the gardener or vinedresser reinforces the echo of Psalm 80:8–9, where after clearing the ground, God the Gardener transplants a vine from Egypt. This transplantation is a reference to the exodus from Egypt that established Israel as a nation, and so the vine is symbolic of God's people of the Sinai covenant. The clearing of the land for the vine recalls the conquest of Canaan and the establishment of Israel as a holy nation. Psalm 80:10–11 records the success of that vine, as its "branches" reached as from the Mediterranean Sea to the Euphrates River, the fullest extent of the nation of Israel at its height. As Andrew Streett asserts, "The original meaning of Psalm 80, therefore, suggests the importance of the king and the restoration of the nation, situating it solidly among the passages that would later be viewed as messianic and eschatological."[4] In Psalm 80, Israel had been "cut down" and "burned with fire" (Ps 80:16). The psalmist prays that God would nevertheless watch over the vine, and looks to "the root your right hand has planted, *the son you have raised up* for yourself" (Ps 80:15). In the Septuagint, the son is called "the man at your right hand, *the son of man*" (Ps 79:16 LXX) at whose appearing Israel would be revived (79:19 LXX) and saved (79:20 LXX). Jesus, who preferred the self-identification of "Son of Man," invokes this Psalm through the imagery of his "I am" statement, declaring himself to be the true vine, the true Israel whose branches are those who believe and obey the revelation of God he brings (Jn 15:3–5).

15:2 *He cuts off . . . he prunes.* If Jesus is the genuine vine, the branches of that vine lie under the vinedressing care of the Father, who both prunes and cuts off. There are wordplays and associations readily apparent in the Greek of these verses that are not well preserved in English translation. The verb translated "cuts off" is *airei* (αἴρει), and "he prunes" is *kathairei* (καθαίρει), which more generally means "cleanse" but in the horticultural context of cleansing a branch may be understood as pruning. A visit to California vineyards teaches that pruning the vine actually does stress it, but also forces the energy into the fruit instead of the leaves. And so while the Father's pruning suggests uncomfortable situations, it is intended to increase production of spiritual fruit.

F. F. Bruce points out, "Here is an echo of John 13:10, 'you are clean (*katharoi*), but not all.' Judas was the exception then . . . he is an unfruitful branch that has to be removed."[5] Judas may have appeared to be in the vine, but he was not, as he never received the lifegiving sustenance that flowed through its branches.

15:3 *You are already clean because of the word.* Earlier in the evening the footwashing indicated that Jesus himself is the true source of spiritual cleansing (Jn 13:2-17). Here the concept of washing is expanded to the word that he speaks—in other words, the revelation his advent brings. The remaining disciples to whom Jesus speaks are "clean" because they have believed the revelation he brings, even if ever so imperfectly and incompletely (cf. Jn 13:10-11). The Father uses the message of Jesus to cleanse (prune) the branches so that they may become more fruitful. This suggests the importance of the Scripture for the Christian in every season of life.

15:4–5 *Remain in me, as I also remain in you. . . . You are the branches. . . . You will bear much fruit.* Jesus pleads with his disciples whom he is about to leave behind in this world to continue his mission by remaining in him. But the remaining is not simply for the purpose of enjoying his fellowship; here they are told they must do something as a result of remaining. He has *shown* his love in John 13:1-38, and here he *tells* them they need to *respond* to his love.[6] Unlike Judas Iscariot, in order to bear fruit they are to continue to believe what he has told them and to receive the message his death and resurrection will speak. The fruit is not specified here, but refers to spiritual growth in all its forms that show one to be a disciple of Jesus (see commentary at 15:8). But before teaching more on the attributes of a fruitful branch, Jesus issues a severe warning that evokes the prophecy of Jerusalem as a useless vine (Eze 15). Should they not remain in Jesus, the true vine, they cannot bear fruit; they can do nothing.

At the same time, Jesus remains in us, which recalls the indwelling of the Holy Spirit mentioned in John 14:17. This also has parallels to God's promise to dwell with (in the midst of) Israel in the tabernacle (Ex 25:8; 29:45; Lev 26:11-12; Eze 37:27-28; 43:9), suggesting once more how Jesus stands in place of the temple (see also commentary at 7:37 and "John 7 Through Old Testament Eyes.")

As an interesting aside, John 15:5 was the first verse of Scripture read upon arrival on the surface of the moon by astronaut and Presbyterian elder Buzz Aldrin to acknowledge God's grace in the success of the Apollo 11 mission.[7]

15:6 *Like a branch that is thrown away . . . and withers . . . thrown into the fire.* The branches of a vine that do not bear fruit are useless for any other purpose. Because a branch is not attached to the life source of the vine, rather than producing fruit, it withers, and is good only as fuel for fire. Jesus is here echoing Ezekiel 15:1–8, where the word of the Lord asks, "Son of man, how is the wood of a vine different from that of a branch from any of the trees in the forest? Is wood ever taken from it to make anything useful? Do they make pegs from it to hang things on?" (Eze 15:2–3). Its only worth is to be fuel for a fire, which will further destroy its usefulness. In light of the vine imagery of Psalm 80, the nation of Israel is here being indicted for its failure to produce the fruit God intended. In a scathing indictment, the Sovereign Lord says, "As I have given the wood of the vine among the trees of the forest as fuel for the fire, so will I treat the people living in Jerusalem" (Eze 15:6).

Jesus is the genuine vine that *does* produce the fruit of righteousness *through* the branches that have life-giving connection to him, forming the new covenant nation of God's redeemed people. But any who fail to remain in Christ through attention and obedience to the revelation he brought into the world will, like Judas Iscariot, fail to bear fruit, and will be cut off and thrown into the fire, a metaphor for judgment and destruction. Christians must heed the history of God's old covenant people documented in the Old Testament, for judgment on a faithless rejection of God's grace remains the same now as then.

15:7 *Ask . . . and it will be done.* This promise must never be taken out of context. Note the conditional protasis ("if . . .")" "*if* you remain in me and [*if*] my words remain in you." The conditional particle *ean* (ἐάν) followed by the subjunctive verb form presents a future condition ("if ever . . .") or a present general condition ("if now . . ."). Far from a blank check, this statement requires a disciple to be drawing life from Christ and producing the fruit of justice and righteousness, out of which any prayer request flows. God invites followers of Christ to be at work with him in the redemption of the world, and answers to prayers consistent with that work will assuredly follow (cf. commentary on Jn 14:13).

15:8 *Bear much fruit.* Just as prize-winning grapes might display the skill and hard work of the vinedresser, bringing honors and glory, Jesus' followers bring glory to the Father when they bear "much fruit" and identify themselves as disciples of Jesus. In John 14:13, the Son glorifies the Father; those who are in the Son (branches in the vine) also glorify the Father. The failure to let the gospel message of Christ transform lives not only brings the threat of fire, but it also robs God of the glory due his name. John underspecifies what that fruit might be, but Isaiah 5:7 explains what God had expected of the vine he had planted: He looked for righteousness and justice but he found only bloodshed and distress. Gary Manning notes, "While the fruit does not have exactly the same meaning in Isaiah 5 and John 15, both use fruit to describe positive moral qualities expected in God's people."[8]

Jesus is the true vine that produces true justice and righteousness, and those who are organically connected to Christ through trust in him will bear that fruit. Although it is typical to read this in terms of the fruit of the individual believer, in the Old Testament the vine metaphor refers primarily to Israel as a whole (Isa 5:1–7; 27:6; Hos 14:4–8) and its mission in the world. The branches of the vine represent the church as a local, national, and worldwide body that is organically connected to the Lord in order to fulfill his purposes in every location and generation. That can happen only when the individuals bear fruit *together* in the mission and work of the church.

Interpreters debate to what the fruit metaphor specifically refers. The ninefold fruit of the Spirit listed by the apostle Paul in Galatians 5:22–23 is no doubt included, as a branch takes on more of the characteristics of the true vine, bringing glory to God. But to allow John his own voice, in the immediate context he mentions two specific fruit-bearing traits: effective prayer (15:7, 16) and love for one another (15:12–16). Faithfulness to the message of Jesus is to inform the prayer of disciples, making it effective. Prayers offered to the Father are offered in the name of Jesus, and must be compatible with his mission. Love for others, which may be Johannine shorthand for the ninefold transforming fruit of the Spirit, releases God's love into the world through the disciples of Jesus.

15:12 *Love . . . as I have loved you.* The command to love others goes back to Leviticus 19:18 under the old covenant: "love your neighbor as yourself." But here Jesus revises "as yourself" to "as I have loved you." By introducing a new standard of love he transposes the Old Testament law into the key of the gospel of grace (cf. Jn 1:16–17). See commentary on 5:46. Since Jesus' love was self-sacrificing, this seems to "demand loving them more than oneself or at least to require that 'as oneself' has a profounder meaning than the self-protective limitation that one might otherwise put on it. Thus, John's version of the command that sums up all of one's duties to others is . . . explicitly and decisively colored by Jesus' death"[9] (cf. commentary 13:34; 15:17). The disciples are given the seemingly impossible mandate "to love one another with an unconditional love, matching the love of Jesus for them."[10]

15:16 *I chose you and appointed you.* The theme of election, so prominent in the Old Testament story of God's "chosen" people, is taken up in the gospel of John to explain the disciples of Jesus as the embryonic Christian church. In the fourth gospel only Jesus is the stated subject of the verb "choose" *eklegomai*; [ἐκλέγομαι]; Jn 6:70; 13:18; 15:16, 19), but in the Old Testament it is God who has chosen Israel to be his people (e.g., Dt. 14:2, "For you are a people holy to the Lord your God, and it is you the Lord your *God has chosen* to be an exceptional people to him out of all the nations on the face of the earth" (LXX). This is a prime example of Jesus' claim that his works are the Father's works (Jn 5:17, 19; 6:38; 8:29; 9:4; 10:25; 14:10). But the sovereignty of God the Father in salvation is preserved in John's gospel, for it is the Father who draws and gives Jesus those who believe in him (Jn 6:37; 10:29).

This is the last of more than thirty times in the fourth gospel that the verb "remain" or "abide" (*menō* [μένω]) refers to discipleship and relationship with Christ and the Father. (The subsequent occurrences in 19:31; 21:22–23 are in reference to Jesus' body and the beloved disciple.) Although the word for "covenant" (*diathēkē* [διαθήκη]) is not found in the Johannine gospel or letters, the concept of "remaining" or "abiding" may be covenantal language influenced by the Septuagint. Consider Jeremiah 31:32, where the promise of a new covenant is prefaced by God's declaration, "It will not be like the covenant I made with their ancestors . . . because *they broke my covenant*," which appears in its LXX translation (Jer 38:32) as follows: "It will not be like the covenant that I made with their fathers . . . because they did not *abide* [*emmenō*; ἐμμένω] in my covenant." The LXX translator apparently understood breaking covenant as *not* abiding, a thought that is compatible with the Johannine admonition to *abide* in Christ. While the new covenant in Christ is not explicit in John's gospel, as it is in the Last Supper of the Synoptic Gospels (Mt 26:28; Mk 14:24; Lk 22:20), the extent to which John employs the Old Testament (i.e., old covenant) to speak of Jesus implies it. The contexts in which John uses *menō* (μένω) are "similar to those of the LXX: the Covenant, observance of the commandments, fraternal union, the merciful love God."[11] Certainly the concept of an ongoing relationship with God mediated through covenant is present in John's thought in the language of *remaining* or *abiding*.

Although the concept of remaining or abiding suggests a stationary status in Christ, note that Jesus' commission to his disciples is to "*go and bear fruit.*"[12] Foreshadowed in Psalm 80:11 (79:11 LXX), where the vine God planted "sent out its branches to the sea, and its shoots to the River," the sending of the branches of the true vine into all the world is a perilous mission. Jesus prepares his disciples for this mission in 15:18–25 that follows.

John 15:1–17 Through Old Testament Eyes

This familiar passage comes from Jesus in his teaching of the knowledge that would be essential for his disciples to know after his death. But when informed by the vine image as it is found in the Old Testament we learn that, before the vine imagery can teach about discipleship, its primary revelation is that Jesus is the true Israel, for he fulfills the messianic hope of the old covenant. The vine imagery is primarily echoing Psalm 80 and Ezekiel 15 (discussed above in commentary on Jn 15:1), but the image occurs also in Hosea 10:1–2; Isaiah 5:1–7; Jeremiah 2:21; Ezekiel 17:1–21; 19:10–14. The prophet Hosea indicts Israel as a spreading vine who "brought forth fruit for himself" that led God's people into idolatry. The Song of the Vineyard in Isaiah 5:1–7 speaks of God's watchful care for his beloved vineyard, the nation of Israel, that disappointed by producing bloodshed and lawlessness instead of justice and righteousness. Jeremiah 2:21 records God's lament for his chosen vine that turned against him into "a corrupt, wild vine." The extended parables of the vine in Ezekiel 17:1–21 and 19:10–14 describe the rulers of Judah in their covenant unfaithfulness at the time of exile that ended the Davidic dynasty in the land. Arguing that Ezekiel 17 and 19 are the primary Old Testament background for Jesus' vine imagery, Gary Manning writes, "Ezekiel's vine parables, like John's and unlike any other OT vine images, distinguish between vine and branches. In Ezekiel 17 and 19, the branches are individuals and the vine is the royal house of Israel."[13]

Read against this Old Testament background, John 15:1 claims that Jesus is the true (genuine, authentic) vine that will produce the fruit the divine gardener expected. In light of the Ezekiel passages, this imagery suggests Jesus' association with Davidic kingship in contrast to the faithless rulers of Israel's past. The vine metaphors in Ezekiel "announce judgment against Jerusalem and its leaders. This is perhaps one reason for John's [Jesus'?] appropriation of Ezekiel's vine metaphors. Conflict with Jerusalem and its rulers is one of the driving themes of John."[14] Furthermore, the judgment due to ancient Israel and its rulers fell finally and fully on Jesus, who becomes the true vine through bearing God's judgment on covenant unfaithfulness.

Only after perceiving the christological significance of Jesus' "I am" statement in light of the Old Testament use of the vine imagery can its application to Christian discipleship be properly understood. As Manning explains, "The individual's relationship with God had always been mediated through Israel. Individual fate was tied to the collective fate of Israel. Now Jesus calls his followers to mediate their relationship to God through himself. Their fate would no longer be dependent on Israel's faithfulness and usefulness; it would now be firmly fixed on Jesus."[15]

Jesus evokes images from Ezekiel in both the Good Shepherd discourse (Jn 10) and the true vine imagery (Jn 15), making "many of the same Christological and ecclesiological claims. In both cases, *Jesus transfers authority and privilege from Israel or its rulers to himself.* The sheep must follow the good shepherd instead of the bad; the branches must cling to the true vine instead of the false. John 15, like John 10 redefines God's people."[16] Israel is being invited to follow the Messiah and become branches in the true vine, along with Gentiles who enter the vine in the same way: faith in Jesus Christ, through whom God's covenant promises are fulfilled.

15:17 *Love each other.* Although the command to love is sometimes thought of as a New Testament idea in our popular culture, it has its roots in the Holiness Code of Leviticus 19:18, "Love your neighbor as yourself." When asked which was the greatest commandment, Jesus replied it is love for God, but then elevated the command to love one's neighbor to be the second highest (Mt 22:39; Mk 12:33; Lk 10:27), saying it is more important than all the burnt offerings and sacrifices of the Old Testament covenant (Mk 12:33), elevating how we treat others over our form of worship. As branches on the true vine, Christians are to love each other, producing the fruit of righteousness and justice. Arguably, treating others with righteousness and justice *is* the definition of Christian love. In the ancient context of Moses, one's neighbor would have been a fellow Hebrew; here John emphasizes love for fellow believers without contesting the more general principle of love for neighbor, whether the neighbor is Christian or not.

15:19 *I have chosen you out of the world.* The reason followers of Jesus are no longer *of* the world is that Christ has chosen them *out* of it (cf. 17:6), implying that all believers were once part of the world in its rebellion against God, living in the darkness of sin. Union with the true vine whose life runs through them makes believers bear fruit resembling Jesus, and so they become more alien to the world. Their transformation in becoming more like Jesus has the same effect on those of the world that Jesus himself did: rejection and hostility, at least to some extent.

15:22 *If I had not come . . . they would not be guilty of sin.* Surely the people to whom Christ came were sinners long before he appeared on the scene. His arrival did not create their guilt. Theft, murder, adultery, false witness, and a multitude of other sins have characterized human life from time immemorial, and the law given millennia before Christ's coming condemns such sins. But

Jesus makes the odd statement that if he had not come and brought revelation from God, they would not be guilty of sin (cf. 15:24). Here Jesus defines Christ-centered sin, sin that could not have existed prior to his coming. The sin of which he speaks is the rejection of his message despite the works and words of the Father through him. To all the sins the world has committed from the beginning, the rejection of Christ, the only means of divine forgiveness, is the epitome of the human history of sin.

15:23 *Hates my Father as well.* To reject Christ is to "hate" him; to hate Christ is to hate the Father who sent him. This would have been especially stinging to devout Jews of Jesus' day who felt that by their rejection of Christ they were actually upholding a proper monotheistic worship of God.

15:25 *This is to fulfill.* Five times in his gospel John introduces quotations of the Old Testament with the verb *plēroō* (πληρόω, "fulfill"; 12:38; 13:18; 15:25; 19:24, 28). Accordingly, even the rejection and hatred of Jesus is not outside of God's redemptive plan, but rather fulfills Scripture. The phrase "their Law" indicates that the term "Law" refers to the fuller canon of Hebrew Scripture beyond the Pentateuch, as here the quotation is from the Psalms. Furthermore, Jesus refers to "*their* Law" not to disavow his own embrace of the Hebrew Scriptures, but to ironically point out that the Law Jesus' opponents presume to uphold actually condemns them (see also commentary on "your law" at 8:17 and 10:34).

The phrase "hate without reason" appears in both Psalm 35:19 and in Psalm 69:4 to refer to the righteous sufferer, embodied at that time by Israel's King David. There the substantive participle "those who hate" has been paraphrased in John 15:25 as a third-person plural aorist indicative, "they hated me." Because Psalm 69:9 has already been quoted in John 2:17 (see commentary there), it is the likely source of the quotation here as well. Matthew Scott points out that "1) details from the psalm are woven without notice into the narrative of Jesus' passion; and 2) words from the psalm (John 2:17), or such as might be spoken by the psalmist (John 15:25; 19:28), are placed in the mouth of Jesus."[17]

But rather than a quotation from a specific psalm, Margaret Daly-Denton observes resonances with Psalms 109:3, 35:19, and 119:161 as well, and so considers this "a familiar phrase of David, which finds its true significance on the lips of Jesus," enabling John's readers "to see a parallel between the career of David and the events of Jesus' hour which they now see as foretold in scripture."[18] Here it functions to confirm that even the hostility toward Jesus was anticipated in Scripture and, with respect to the disciples, functions "to keep them from falling away (John 16:1), to motivate and form their reaction to the experience of persecution."[19]

JOHN 15:26-16:33

15:26 *When the Advocate [paraclete] comes.* The paraclete was introduced in John 14:16, 26, as another divine presence who would be with the disciples after Jesus' departure, whom the Father would send in Jesus' name, and who would teach and remind the disciples of the revelation Jesus brought. There, the paraclete was identified explicitly as the Spirit of truth (14:17) and as the Holy Spirit (14:26). Recall that the Spirit of God appears on the very first page of the Bible in Genesis 1:2, where he is hovering over the primordial waters during the creation of the universe. Echoing Genesis 1:1 in its opening verse, the gospel of John also associates Jesus the Word with the act of creation, apart from whom nothing that has been made was made (Jn 1:3). Here, John further associates the Spirit of God with Jesus, suggesting a Trinitarian relationship within the Godhead.

Throughout the Old Testament the Spirit is integral to the eschatological promises of Israel's covenant with God. God promised the Spirit would be upon a servant from the line of David (Isa 11:1–10; 42:1–4) and foretold a pouring out of God's Spirit that would bring transformation to the people (Isa 32:14–18; Eze 11:17–20; 36:24–27), new life after death (Eze 37:1–14), and access to a full knowledge of God (Isa 11:1–10; Jer 31:34; Joel 2:28–32). When John 16 is viewed through Old Testament eyes, the functions of the Spirit speak loudly of Jesus' fulfillment of these eschatological covenant promises made through the prophets.

The gospel of John associates the fulfillment of the eschatological promises of the Old Testament specifically with Jesus. At his baptism Jesus is identified as the one on whom the Spirit of God rests (Jn 1:32, 33). Jesus states the necessity of new birth by the Spirit, indicating spiritual transformation and a new heart for the people, in John 3:5–6, 8 (cf. Jn 4:23). The Spirit is portrayed metaphorically as flowing water that will be released when Jesus is glorified/crucified (Jn 7:37–39; 19:30; cf. Isa 44:1–5; Eze 36:24–27; cf. Ac 2:15–21), bringing a fuller knowledge of God than the people previously had known. The Father sends the Spirit (*paraclete*) in the name of Jesus (Jn 14:26), bringing the Old Testament covenantal promises to a Trinitarian fulfillment.

He will testify about me. Jesus was familiar with the work of the Spirit centering on himself, for he explained that the Spirit of truth would testify (*martyreō* [μαρτυρέω]) to the truth of the revelation that Jesus Christ brings. Divine truth is on trial throughout the gospel, but it does not end with the trial and execution of Jesus. Even today the truth of the revelation of Jesus Christ is treated with suspicion and judgment. Apart from the work of the Spirit there would be no chance of blind eyes perceiving the divine reality.

15:27 *You have been with me from the beginning.* Jesus commissions those who were with him the night before he died to speak authoritatively of him after his death, bearing witness to the significance of his life, death, and resurrection. They had been with the earthly Jesus from the beginning of his public ministry (Jn 1:29). While believers in every generation are expected to be witnesses for Christ, the apostolic witness preserved in the New Testament writings is the touchstone of truth about the Father, Son, and Holy Spirit.

16:2 *They will put you out of the synagogue.* The witness the apostles bore about Jesus would not be welcomed in the synagogues, so Jesus warns them of the cost of their witness. The gospel of John was written several decades after the death of Jesus, when the number of Jesus' followers had grown significantly and the relationship between Jewish Christians and their family and friends had grown strained to the breaking point. But the hostility Jesus experienced from the Jewish leaders during his own lifetime indicates that the revelation he brought could not be contained within the old wineskins of Second Temple Judaism. Jesus understands the good intentions of the Jewish leaders who rejected him, and recognized they believed they were protecting the truth about God. And so the truth about God is contended throughout this gospel and through the centuries of history down to us today.

16:7 *Unless I go away.* John had recognized that throughout Jesus' ministry he implicitly linked the Holy Spirit with his departure, for in 7:39 the narrator explains that before Jesus was glorified on the cross the Spirit had not yet been given. Here Jesus explicitly links his departure with the coming of the Spirit.

I will send him to you. Although the Spirit of God was present in various ways throughout the Old Testament times, Jesus spoke of a sending of the Spirit that was yet future and was contingent upon his "going away"—that is, his death and ascension. The sending of the Spirit is a vindication of the truth Jesus brought. Consider if I said to you, "I'm going to Florida soon. When I get there, I'll send you a crate of oranges." A few weeks later, a crate of oranges shows up at your door. You then know that I've arrived safely in Florida and that I'm keeping the promise made when I was with you. The pouring out of the Spirit in a new way on the followers of Jesus (Ac 2:1–13) vindicates him, assures us that he has reached his destination with the Father, that his atoning blood has been accepted, and convinces us that he will do everything that he said he would.

What the Structure Means: Sending of the Spirit—*Filioque* (Jn 16:7–15)

The sending of the Spirit in John's gospel became a source of bitter dispute that contributed to the split of the Eastern and Western churches in 1054. In this historic debate about *filioque* (Latin "and from the Son") the agent of the sending was hotly disputed. Jesus will ask the Father to send the Spirit (14:16), and the Father will send the Spirit in Jesus' name (14:26). But in 15:26 Jesus says *he* will send the Spirit from the Father, and in 16:7 he promises to send the *paraclete* after he departs. So is the Spirit sent from the Father or the Son? The Eastern church (from which Eastern Orthodoxy derives) insists that the Spirit proceeds from the Father alone, but in Western Christianity (the Roman Catholic Church and the Protestant churches that developed from it), the phrase "and from the Son" (*filioque*) was added to the Nicene Creed to insist that the Spirit proceeded from *both* the Father and the Son. This was to avoid distancing the Spirit from the Son, which would contradict verses that speak of the oneness of Christ and the Spirit. This fine point of theology combined with cultural differences and misunderstandings permanently split the global Christian church.

16:8 *He will prove the world.* The word often translated "prove" or "convict" is *elegchō* (ἐλέγχω), which means "to bring to light, expose, convict, convince, discipline."[1] In its ancient context it has a neutral connotation at best and almost never positive, but most frequently expresses the connotation of exposing guilt. Elsewhere in the gospel of John it has been translated in the NIV as "exposed" (Jn 3:20) and "prove . . . guilty" (8:46). One work of the Spirit is to bring people to recognize the guilt they have incurred by being wrong in their thinking, and therefore to raise the opportunity of repentance.

16:8–11 *Wrong . . . about sin . . . about righteousness . . . and about judgment.* Three specific corrections are mentioned: about sin (*hamartia* [ἁμαρτία]), about righteousness (*dikaiosunē* [δικαιοσύνη]), and about judgment (*krisis* [κρίσις]). Each of these words occurs hundreds of times in the Old Testament. D. A. Carson convincingly interprets the syntax of the Greek of 16:9, which is difficult, that it is the *world's* sin, the *world's* righteousness, and the *world's* judgment that is wrong.[2]

The Spirit proves the world's thinking about sin wrong because, Jesus says, people do not believe him. People may think that they are free to accept or reject Christ with impunity, but here the rejection of Christ itself is shown to be the height of sin.

In the Old Testament the rejection of God was the ultimate sin (e.g., Dt 31:20; 1 Sa 8:7; Jer 15:6), so the echo of that theme suggests the unity of the Father and the Son. To reject one is to reject the other. If people recognized the truth Jesus brought, they would recognize their sin and turn to him for atonement rather than to deny or rationalize their sin.

The Spirit proves the world's view of what constitutes righteousness is wrong because, Jesus says, he is going to the Father. At that time, there was plenty of religious righteousness—in the sacrificial system, and in the observation of the 613 Pharisaical laws, but as Isaiah had said of the people of his day, "all our righteous acts are like filthy rags" (Isa 64:6). The world's view of righteousness is wrong, and the fact that it was used as the charge *against* Jesus that led to his execution shows just how wrong it is. Yet Jesus calls his disciples to continue to live and witness to the truth as he did, to continue to expose the emptiness of the world's righteousness and call people to repentance.

The Spirit proves the world's thinking about judgment wrong because the prince of this world, Satan, has been condemned by the execution and resurrection of Jesus. Therefore, all who pass judgment based on Satan's lies also stand condemned with him. When Jesus was condemned for healing a man on the Sabbath, he exhorted the people to "stop judging by mere appearances, but instead judge correctly" (Jn 7:24). As Carson observes, "All false judgment is related to him who was a liar from the beginning, whose children we are if we echo his values (8:42–47)"[3] (see commentary at Jn 8:44).

16:13 *He will guide you into all the truth.* Jesus builds on the Old Testament idea that God leads his people into truth (Ps 25:5; 43:3; 86:11). The Spirit will guide the apostles to remember and to understand more deeply the revelation that Jesus brought through his life, death, and resurrection. Although often rightly quipped that "all truth is God's truth," the context here does not refer to knowledge more broadly but to the divine reality Jesus presents to the world. The disciples were not capable of comprehending the full truth about Jesus at that moment, both because of their grief and confusion about what was about to happen to him, and because the resurrection they would witness would change everything they thought they knew (Jn 16:12). But as his apostles, they would know the full truth that Jesus brought once they witnessed his death, resurrection, and ascension, and as the Holy Spirit inspired their witness, teaching, and preaching of the significance of what they had witnessed.

A misunderstanding of this promise may have led to problems in the Johannine churches later, as false teachers claimed new revelation from the Spirit that was inconsistent with the apostolic witness and that diminished the role of Jesus' death for salvation (see 1, 2, 3 John).[4] Jesus' promise cannot be used to justify any claim of a generic revelation from God's Spirit that excludes Christ, for the Spirit's role is to testify *about Jesus* (Jn 15:26). The Spirit does not bring new spiritual knowledge into the world, but enlightens in every place and every generation the truth already revealed in Jesus Christ.

16:21 *A woman giving birth.* Jesus comforts his confused and grief-stricken disciples by alluding to the imagery of a woman's pain in childbirth that is followed by the great joy of the birth of a child. Such imagery was used in the Old Testament to signify the coming of a messianic era (Isa 66:7–10; Mic 5:1–4; cf. Isa 9:6; 53:12–54:1; 62:5; Hos 13:13–14). Isaiah uses it to depict the experience of God's ancient people as they recognized the failure of their mission in the world. Isaiah 26:17–19 expresses both lament and promise in the imagery of a pregnant woman in the throes of labor about to give birth. J. Alec Motyer explains the pain as the national catastrophe when the Assyrians invaded: "the enslavement of northern Israel, and all the contemporary trauma" of Isaiah's time.[5] Rather than bringing God's presence to the world, the world of Isaiah's day was destroying God's nation and people. They understood that the world needed to learn righteousness (Isa 26:9) but recognized that no salvation of any sort had come into the world through them:[6]

> We were with child, we writhed in labor,
>   but we gave birth to wind.
> We have not brought salvation to the earth,
>   and the people of the world have not come to life.
>   (Isa 26:18)

Yet Isaiah affirms,
>   But your dead will live, LORD;
>   their bodies will rise—
>   let those who dwell in the dust
>   wake up and shout for joy.
>   (Isa 26:19)

In John 16:20 Jesus acknowledges the pain, grief, and mourning his imminent death will cause his disciples, but he explains it to them as the *necessary*
pains of labor from which a great joy will be born. Resurrection necessitates a
prior death. The promised resurrection will bring them great joy when they see
Jesus alive after his execution and understand his invitation to eternal life. And
that resurrection *did* accomplish God's mission in the world that brings salvation
to the earth and life to its people. By analogy, Jesus' suffering that led to glory
suggests that the hardships and sufferings the disciples will experience are also,
perhaps in inscrutable ways, a (necessary?) prelude to eternal joy with the Lord.

16:23–24 *My Father will give you whatever you ask in my name.* See
commentary at John 14:13 and 15:7.

16:32 *A time is coming and in fact has come when you will be scattered.* This
could be an allusion to the scattering of sheep in Zechariah 13:7. If so, Jesus
would be the shepherd who is struck resulting in the flock running away. The
Old Testament often portrays what happens to God's flock without a faithful
shepherd (e.g., 1 Ki 22:17; Eze 34:5–6, 12; Zec 11:16; Isa 53:6; Jer 23:1; 50:17).
Also see commentary on John 10:1–18.

16:33 *In me you may have peace.* See commentary at 14:27.

I have overcome the world. Even as he knowingly faces certain torture and
death, Jesus clearly states that he has conquered (*nikaō* [νικάω]) the world.
What the world may see as the brutal defeat of a common criminal at his
execution is in the divine reality the conquest of the world with all its pain,
evil, hatred, lies, and persecution. It will be the long-awaited moment of the
release of the Spirit in a newly powerful and effective presence of God (Jn
20:22). And with that truth and that divine presence, the followers of Jesus
will know a peace that surpasses understanding, a peace that even the worst
this world has to offer cannot overcome (Jn 14:27).

Going Deeper into the Work of the Spirit: John 14–16

Contrary to popular belief in modern spirituality, there is no generic
spirit of God. Many in modern society claim to be spiritual but not
religious, eschewing especially the organized religion of Christianity and
its churches. They appeal to God's spirit as a benevolent force for peace
and love independent of all organized religious belief. Even Christians
may have only a vague concept of the Holy Spirit and his role in the life
of the believer. (Note the unelaborated statement of the Apostles' Creed,
"I believe in the Holy Spirit.")

The Spirit of God that hovered over the primordial universe at the moment of creation is, in the New Testament and especially in the gospel of John, closely identified with God, the Father of Jesus Christ, the Son of God. He does not exist as an independent entity outside of or apart from the Trinity. John specifically reveals the Spirit as "*another paraclete*" who will be the divine presence with Jesus' disciples after his death and resurrection. Believing disciples in John's gospel receive the Spirit through the breath of Jesus Christ (Jn 20:22), implying the most intimate association of the Spirit with Christ. When the Spirit falls on God's people in Acts 2, it is not on all who were in Jerusalem for Pentecost but specifically on those who placed their faith in Jesus, marking them with signs visible to all as the newly constituted people of God on whom the promises of the ages had come. There is such intimacy between the Father, the Son, and the Spirit that what one does, the other does (Jn 14:26; 16:13, 15).

John presents a new age of the Spirit that begins with Jesus' death and resurrection. He presents the Spirit as the divine presence who will be present with Christian believers in the world until the Lord returns (14:18). He will teach all things (14:26) through a deepened and enriched remembrance of Jesus' teaching in the minds of the apostles. The role the Spirit plays in teaching is specifically tied to Jesus' teaching. As Eskil Franck observes, "The reminding function . . . is meant neither to retain the exact wording of the historical Jesus, nor to present any vaticinia ex eventu ['prophecy after the event'], but to penetrate deeper into the deeds of Jesus and the experiences the disciples had during their time together."[7] This is no generic spirituality but is wedded to the apostles' experience of the historical Jesus:

> The Spirit will testify about Jesus. (15:26)
> He will guide into all truth. (16:13)
> He will tell what is yet to come. (16:13)
> He will glorify Jesus. (16:14)
> He will receive from Jesus and make known to the apostles. (16:14)

The Spirit does not impart generic spirituality to any and all people, but reveals truth about Jesus for those who are or will become followers of Christ (15:26; 16:15).

The promise of revelation was made to the original disciples who witnessed Jesus and who were chosen to be apostles of Christ (15:27). It was likely a misunderstanding of this promise and a claim to have received new revelation from the Spirit that caused the schism in the Johannine churches as documented in 1 and 2 John (see esp. 1 Jn 2:19).[8] Popular leaders were apparently teaching a gospel that downplayed or eliminated the atoning death of Jesus and justified their own teaching, claiming that the Spirit was revealing new truth through them. But the revelation of the gospel cannot be separated from the central event of Jesus' mission: his crucifixion and resurrection. The promised revelation of "all things" (14:26) and "all the truth" (16:13) *is* comprehensive spiritual truth, but that truth is both centered on and circumscribed by Jesus Christ. The Spirit of God does not participate in creating alternative roads to God that lie outside the One who is the Way, the Truth, and the Life (Jn 14:6).

Modern spirituality is offended by the exclusive claims of Jesus Christ and therefore invents other ways of knowing God than the way revealed in Christ. Although there is no national, religious, ethnic, racial, or spiritual identity that disqualifies a person from coming to Christ through the work of the Holy Spirit, no one comes to the Father except through Jesus Christ. The invitation of the gospel is universal, but the means of the gospel by the work of the Spirit is particular and exclusive.[9]

JOHN 17

This farewell prayer that Jesus prays in the hearing of his disciples consists of three parts: (1) Jesus' prayer for his own glorification; (2) his prayer for the disciples who had followed him in his three-year ministry and whom he was now leaving; (3) his prayer for all believers in all times and places. If Jesus came into the world to make God known (1:18) this prayer represents his consecration of himself to that mission, and the consecration of his disciples to the continuing mission to make God known in the world through the gospel after his departure.[1]

17:1 *The hour has come. Glorify your Son.* Regarding "the hour" see commentary at 7:8, 30; 8:20; 12:23, 27.

The verb *doxazō* (δοξάζω, "glorify") occurs in sixteen verses in the fourth gospel, always with God the Father or the Son as the object (Jn 7:39; 8:54; 11:4; 12:16, 23, 28; 13:31, 32; 14:13; 15:8; 16:14; 17:1, 4, 5, 10; 21:19). The twenty-eight occurrences of the noun *doxa* (δόξα, "glory") indicate that the revelation of God's glory through the incarnation is a major theme of this gospel. In secular Greek, *doxa* (δόξα) meant "opinion" or "reputation." But centuries before Jesus came the translators of the Greek Old Testament chose *doxa* (δόξα) to translate the Hebrew word *kābôd* (כָּבוֹד), a word that had a larger semantic range with three senses: (1) wealth, power, importance; (2) honor, prestige, good reputation; (3) visible splendor.[2] The New Testament writers used the word *doxa* (δόξα) most often with the senses of the Hebrew word that had bled through the Greek Old Testament, primarily "honor" and "visible splendor."

When Jesus asks God to "glorify" him, he is asking God to make visible the honor and splendor he had before his incarnation as a human man (17:5; cf. 7:39; 12:16). As the Suffering Servant, he had no glory or honor (Isa 53:2,

3) as he bore the sin of God's people (Isa 53:8, 11–12). This lack of honor and glory was a necessary consequence of the incarnation of the Son. Here the Son is asking the Father to return him to that state of honor and splendor, not by shedding his human form but by transforming it in resurrection. Of course, resurrection is possible only as the sequel to death, just as the birth of a child follows the necessary pains of labor (Jn 16:21–22). So with the vision of eternal glory before him, Jesus prepares to go to his execution on the cross. As Richard Bauckham notes, John has done something "theologically remarkable" and distinctive from the other gospel writers. He has collapsed the sequence of suffering followed by glory "into what he can speak of as a single event of Jesus' exaltation ('lifting up') or glorification" (Jn 3:14; 8:28; 12:32, 34) based on the double meaning of the Greek verb *hupsoō* (ὑψόω, "physically lift up or exalt") and its use in Isaiah's prophecy.[3] This single event occurs during the "hour" toward which Jesus had lived his earthly life.

Jesus' request to be glorified in God's presence suggests that Jesus was conscious of his own shared divine nature with the Father, for the Old Testament states that God will *not* share his glory with another (Isa 42:8; 48:11). It also alludes to the immediately preceding verses, Isaiah 42:1–7, in which the Lord God does glorify his Suffering Servant, implicitly identifying Jesus as that glorified One. The Father's glorification of the Son revealing his honor and splendor in turn reveals the honor and splendor of the Father. This mutual glorification of the Father and the Son is yet another way John's gospel supports monotheism in a binitarian form (cf. Jn 13:31–32; 17:9, 10) that is shown to be Trinitarian by the divine presence of "another paraclete" (Jn 14:15–17; 16:7–15).

17:2 *You granted him authority over all people.* See comment on Daniel 7:13–14 in "John 3 Through Old Testament Eyes." Also see commentary at 5:27.

17:3 *This is eternal life.* The Son entered the world to bring true knowledge of God to a lost human race. His purpose was not simply philosophical or theological, but to give access to eternal life after death, a universal human need. Eternal life is defined here as knowledge of the only true God through Jesus Christ. "The believer comes to life by knowing the God revealed by Jesus, the Logos [Word] of God. Revelation, through which all flesh can come to eternal life (17:2–3), has taken place in Jesus' revealing words and works (see 5:36)."[4]

But this knowledge of God is not a form of gnosticism—that is, of possessing an esoteric knowledge of passwords or concepts that opened various levels of the spiritual world. Jesus refers to knowledge of God as personal relationship, of Christ in the believer and the Father in Christ (Jn 17:23). There is no esoteric knowledge or doctorate in theology needed to gain eternal life, but simple acceptance of the truth that Jesus went to the cross and was resurrected from the grave to provide eternal life for all who would believe that truth. That relationship with Christ into which the believer enters through this faith is based on the eternal fellowship of the Father and Son, into which fellowship the pinnacle of God's creation—the human race—is invited. It would fall to the disciples of Jesus to make this truth known throughout the world.

17:4 *Finishing the work.* When Jesus prayed these words on the last night of his earthly life his crucifixion and resurrection were as certain as anything could be that had not yet happened. Jesus states the purpose of his mission, to finish the work of revealing God the Father (cf. 1:18; 4:34; 5:36).

17:10 *I have been glorified in them* (NASB). After praying for the completion of his mission in the world, Jesus then prays for those who had accompanied him through the three years of his ministry, who heard his teaching and saw his miracles, and who would be devastated by his execution. They had placed their hopes in him, and here he prays that the Father would consecrate and protect them for the work of continuing his mission to make God known in the world.

Jesus states that in those disciples "I have been glorified" (NASB; *dedox-asmai* [δεδόξασμαι], perfect tense). The modifying prepositional phrase *en autois* (ἐν αὐτοῖς) could be read as instrumental (by them) or locative (in them). In context, the locative is probably the more principal sense, but it allows an understanding that *by* or *through* the disciples Jesus had been glorified. But how so? As D. A. Carson observes, "The extent to which Jesus has been glorified in the lives of his disciples is still pathetically slim compared with what will yet be (cf. 13:34–35; 14:13), but it is infinitely better than what he has received from 'the world.'"[5] These men chosen by Jesus to be his witnesses (Jn 15:27) had responded to his presence with belief in him—imperfect, faltering, and flawed as their faith was. But it was their belief in the claims of Jesus that revealed to the world around them that Jesus was who he said he was. And so our faith in the midst of an unbelieving world also brings glory to Jesus by revealing who Jesus is and showing him worthy of our worship (see "Going Deeper into Glorifying God: John 17:10"). As Edward Klink explains, "The church becomes the place where the glory of God is revealed to the world as a living testimony to God's glory and love."[6] Faith in Christ glorifies God.

17:11 *Protect them by the power of your name.* The Old Testament is full of stories of God protecting his people, such as when Lot and his visitors were threatened (Ge 19:11), when Elisha and his servant were surrounded by the Syrian army (2 Ki 6:11–23), and most iconically when Israel escaped Pharaoh's army. Jesus (here and in Jn 17:15) follows the pattern of the Psalms in praying for the protection of others (Ps 12:7; 31:20; 46:4–7) and trusting in the God who is the fortress and guard of his people (Ps 91; 121).

Jesus names God in the vocative with which he addresses him as "Holy Father." This is not an instruction to use the name of God as an incantation as if the power was in the uttering of it, a common practice in the ancient pagan world (see, e.g., Ac 19:13–16). Rather this is a Semitism where "name" refers to the attributes and character of the one named. Jesus prays to the Holy Father that he would protect the disciples who would go out bearing his message with the Father's righteous power (cf. Ps 54:1, where "name" and "might" are in synonymous parallelism). "In the name of Jesus" became the prayer of the early believers as they spread the gospel (see Acts), and still today is how many Christians end their prayers (see commentary at 1:12).

They may be one as we are one. This statement surely echoes, but also nuances, the Shema: "Hear, O Israel: The LORD our God, the LORD is one" (Dt 6:4). The concept of oneness may imply either uniqueness or unity, but in Second Temple Judaism the Shema was understood to state the *uniqueness* of the God of Israel.[7] There is no other God but the Creator God worshiped by Israel. The Shema established the principle of monotheism at the birth of the ancient nation of Israel. Jesus echoes the Shema with its principle of monotheism but here clearly refers to the *unity* of the Father with the Son, revealing the unique Creator God as both Father and Son (see "What the Structure Means" in the introduction regarding monotheism and the Shema; also Jn 17:21 where the concept of oneness is applied to those who follow Jesus).

17:12 *The one doomed for destruction* ("the son of destruction"). This appellation, *ho huios tēs apōleias* (ὁ υἱὸς τῆς ἀπωλείας), occurs in 2 Thessalonians 2:3 to describe the eschatological damnation of the man of lawlessness (*anomia* [ἀνομία]). Throughout the New Testament the words *apōleias* (ἀπωλείας; seventeen times) and *anomia* (ἀνομία; thirteen times) are used to refer to eschatological judgment. While the fate of Judas raises interesting and important theological questions that are outside the scope of this commentary, Jesus teaches that Judas was not an example of the failure of Jesus' protection, but an object of Jesus' judgment, as are all the lost.[8] Jesus extended fellowship to Judas in the last meal (13:26), but Judas had aligned himself with Satan, taking himself out of the realm of light and into the place of condemnation.

So that Scripture would be fulfilled. Jesus protected his disciples during his earthly life with the power ("name") God the Father had given him. And yet there was Judas, the disciple from all appearances who was like all the others, yet who nevertheless betrayed Jesus in a nefarious way that led to his crucifixion. Even before it happened Jesus was aware that the betrayal by one of his own disciples would be part of the plan, as was hinted at in the Old Testament (cf. Jn 13:18–30). The unspecified Scripture referred to here is most likely that same verse quoted in 13:18 (Ps 41:9), which in its entirety speaks of God's protection from enemies and a petition to God to be "raised up" (Ps 41:10), perhaps a prophetic suggestion of resurrection.

17:17 *Sanctify them.* The concept of sanctification (*hagiazō* [ἁγιάζω]; Jn 10:36; 17:17; 17:19) would have been familiar to John's original readers, for in the Old Testament animals were sanctified, or set apart, for sacrifice (Ex 29; Lev 1; 3–4; 5:6–12, 14–19; 6–7) and men were set apart for priestly work (Lev 8–9). The concept of sanctification involves both consecration and purification, making the sanctified animal, person, or object suitable for the task to which it has been dedicated. In Jesus' prayer, he asks the Father to sanctify the disciples who had been with him "by the truth"—that is, by the revelation that Jesus brought in fulfillment of the Old Testament Scriptures. Just as the disciples' faith in Jesus' message brought glory to him (see commentary above on 17:10), their faith in him set them apart from the world, which rebelled against God and Christ. Faith in Christ becomes the criterion that distinguishes the disciples from all others and is the transforming power in their lives that makes them suitable for the task of making God known in the world. The Spirit of truth (Jn 14:16–17, 26) will guide those who have been sanctified into the fuller and deeper understanding of the significance of Jesus Christ. Genuine faith in him involves obedience to his teaching (Jn 14:23) through which transformation occurs.

17:19 *I sanctify myself.* The truth by which the disciples would be sanctified would be incomplete without the death, resurrection, and ascension of Jesus, and so to that mission that he dedicates himself in the hearing of his disciples. He does not want them to think that by some tragic mistake he will be killed (cf. Jn 13:1, 3, 19) but to understand that the horror of the cross was precisely the purpose for the Son's incarnation. Nor does he want the disciples to think that he goes unwillingly to his death. He steadfastly walked toward his "hour" throughout his earthly life, and now on the last evening of it, he recommits himself to the gruesome event in the hearing of his disciples. The purposefulness of Jesus' death and his willingness to experience it are essential parts of the truth by which the disciples are to be sanctified, and by which God is made known to the world.

17:20 *For those who will believe in me through their message.* What a thrill for a Christian believer today to read that on the last night of his life, Jesus prayed for us! He has prayed for God to protect us (17:11, 15), for our unity

(17:11), for the full measure of joy (17:13), and for our sanctification by the word (17:17). Jesus extends that prayer to all who will believe in him through the message of the original apostles, implying his confidence in the assured success of the apostles' mission to the world. Almost two thousand years later, the billions of Christians throughout the centuries and around the world are an answer to Jesus' prayer.

17:22 *They may be one as we are one.* One of the eschatological hopes of ancient Israel was the reunification of the Northern and Southern Kingdoms in a regathering of God's people into one kingdom once again (e.g., Isa 43:6; Jer 24:6, 7; 29:10; Eze 34:23; 37:15–17; Hos 1:11; Am 9:11–15; Mic 2:12). In the Old Testament, we see the "correlation of one God, one temple, one law, and one people" that is based on "the idea that God's people are unified by their allegiance to one God."[9] In Johannine thought, those who followed Jesus were viewed as called out from that one people, disrupting its unity and, therefore, would have been viewed as a threat by the Pharisees and temple priests. Here Jesus applies the concept of oneness as referring to the unity of those who receive his revelation and follow him. See commentary on 17:11.

17:23 *They may be brought to complete unity.* The oneness that Jesus prays for is the unity of those bound in like-mindedness by the truth he reveals. It is a unity based on allegiance to the one, unique God who exists as Father and Son and Spirit. Organizational unity of the visible church may be an ideal, but the unity Jesus refers to here is the spiritual unity of believers who love Jesus and, therefore, love other believers. The eternal love between the Father and the Son motivated the incarnational mission of Jesus. People who embrace the gospel message will be infused with this divine love (17:26). "The loving community of believers witnesses to the love of God in Christ for all the world to see."[10] Words may be necessary for evangelism, but they will ring hollow if love is not characteristic of those who speak of Jesus Christ. The Christian church continually needs to reflect and repent of everything that destroys this unity in love for which Jesus prayed.

17:24 *I want [them] . . . to be with me where I am.* In contrast to Jesus' prayer in Gethsemane that the Father's will, not his own, be done, here Jesus clearly states what he wants. First, he wants those who believe in him to be with him where he is. Although we may have many questions about heaven, the new heavens and earth, and the afterlife, the truth that believers will be with Jesus where he is should be sufficient knowledge to make the Christian look forward to that day when earthly life is over.

To see my glory. Second, Jesus wants those who believe in him to see his full glory that he possessed before the creation of the world. Those who followed Jesus during his life witnessed his humiliation, his torture, his brutal execution accompanied by taunts and insults. Even today the world uses the Lord's name as a curse word, continues to reject him, and often insults his followers. But Jesus wants those who follow him to see his victory and his vindication. These two points, that believers will one day be where Jesus is and will see his full, glorious victory, goes far beyond the Old Testament's theophanies and provides hope and motivation for Christian belief during this life (cf. 17:5).

This is the last of the many occurrences of "glory" or "glorify" that refer to Jesus in the fourth gospel. The first occurred in John 1:14: "The Word became flesh and made his dwelling among us. We have seen his glory, the glory of the one and only Son, who came from the Father." This last reference to Jesus' glory comes at the end of his mission, when his work is about to be finished and he is about to return to the Father, forming a subtle *inclusio* around the incarnational mission of the Son.

17:25 *The world does not know you.* In the Prologue John notes that the world did not know who Jesus truly was (1:10–11). Here we see that the Father shares this same rejection the Son does.

Going Deeper into Glorifying God: John 17:10

"And glory has come to me through them." So Jesus says as he prays to the Father. He is referring to those who followed him during his public ministry, to those whom the Father gave to him out of the world (17:6, 11). Despite their weak and confused understanding of Jesus, those who followed him brought him glory. Glory is the visible manifestation of God's presence, and the belief of the earliest followers of Christ visibly manifested his identity and character. How do Christian believers today glorify God? This is how Jesus describes those who bring glory to him: (1) they *obey* God's word (17:6); (2) they *accept* the words that Jesus brought (17:7); (3) they *know* with certainty that Jesus came from God the Father (17:8); (4) they *believe* that God sent Jesus (17:8). Look at the verbs: obey, accept, know, believe. These are not mandates for grandiose acts necessary for glorifying God, but they are the means to continue the mission of making God known to the world.

The world does not obey, accept, know, and believe. And so the mere practice of going to church, so in decline in Western society, is a primary way to glorify God because attending a Christian worship service is a statement of association with Christ, of obeying, accepting, knowing, and believing him. It is something the people of the world do not do. And sadly, in increasing numbers, even those who self-identify as Christian are failing to attend church, especially among the younger generations. The *church* is the place where the invisible God is made visible in the world, and those who faithfully attend services where the church gathers are making a statement that God is real, his word is true, and his love continues to reach out.

Of course, there is more that a believer can, and should, do to make God known to the world. But all of it originates in and with the church, the body of Christ. In the church God instructs us, challenges us, and teaches us to love people we may not even like very much. There he motivates us to make his love known to each other, in our extended families, our communities, and in faraway places. There we are to find acceptance, healing, and incentive to live well in Christ. It is in the church that the sacraments of grace are administered, and by partaking we declare to the world that we do obey, accept, know, and believe.

The world competes to rob the Lord God of the glory his followers would offer. The world schedules fitness classes, children's soccer games, and other good things at traditional times of worship. Stores and restaurants beckon us to skip church and enjoy some recreational retail. Our choice to attend worship rather than the many other things that call for our time and money makes a silent but loud statement.

What the Structure Means: Jesus' Prayer (Jn 17)

While scholars may disagree on the precise boundaries of the prayer, most see in chapter 17 three concentric circles of Jesus' prayer[11] that may be patterned on the Yom Kippur prayer of the Jerusalem high priest:[12] prayer for himself, prayer for his disciples who personally knew and followed him, and prayer for all believers in all times and places (that's us!). Although Jesus doesn't explicitly mention sacrifice or priestly duty, this chapter has been referred to as the Priestly Prayer of Jesus since the days of the early church, and as the High Priestly Prayer since at least the fifth century. Francis Moloney observes, "Despite the difference in literary form, the themes of making God known to fragile disciples, and, through them, to 'the world,' . . . return in 17:1–26."[13] This is a prayer of consecration for Jesus and those who follow him before he leaves this world.

Jesus allows his disciples to hear him pray to the Father on this last night of his earthly life. As most believers who have attended prayer meetings recognize, prayer together is an intimate time of hearing each other pray. Jesus' prayer models this creation of intimacy and builds cohesion among his disciples who will soon be apostles taking the gospel to the world. We see Jesus' heart as he prays for the last time with these men who have been his closest friends for three years. Jesus' prayer for himself points the reader to what is yet to happen in the story of Jesus. His prayer for his disciples points to a future for them subsequent to the death of Jesus. And his prayer that all might be where he is and see his glory points "into a place that transcends the story time of both Jesus and his followers, beyond the in-between time" when the Lord and his disciples will be eternally reunited.[14]

In 17:1–5, Jesus prays for himself by acknowledging that the end of his earthly life and his mission has come (17:1). He asks that the Father would reveal the Son's true nature ("glorify") so that the Son can reveal God's true nature in the world. Jesus acknowledges that the Father has granted the Son authority over *all* people so that the Son can give eternal life to those the Father has chosen (17:2) (see "Going Deeper into Divine Election: John 6:37–65"). Because the provision of eternal life necessarily involved the death of Jesus, he asked the Father to restore the Son through death to the eternal glory he set aside when he took on human flesh (17:5).

In 17:6–19, Jesus prays for those God has given him out of the world, those first believers who followed Jesus, albeit who followed in confused, flawed, and incomplete faith. Jesus identifies these people as the Father's people who were given to the Son (17:6). He prays not for the world in this moment but only for those the Father has given to the Son (17:9). This is not to say that Jesus bore animosity for the world, for the incarnation itself shows his love for the world (Jn 3:16). However, in these private moments just before his death, he focuses on edifying those who would continue his mission in his physical absence. His prayer reminds them that he is returning to the Father through the experience of the death of his body (17:11), a powerful statement of death's purpose in the life of the Christian. It has become the doorway to the Father for Jesus and for those who follow him. But before death, followers of Jesus Christ must still live in a world that is basically hostile to their belief in a crucified and resurrected God. Jesus prays for the Father to protect them while they are still in this world (17:11). Jesus reminds his disciples that what was about to happen to him was not a tragic mistake, or a sign of Jesus' powerlessness, but was the fulfillment of a plan that was revealed in ages past in the Old Testament Scripture (17:12). Even its ugly details, such as the betrayal of one who was known as a disciple of Jesus, was not a surprise but had been known to Jesus before it happened. What surprised the disciples with disappointment and heartbreak was not a surprise to Jesus, a good reminder for believers today as well. Accepting this truth that Jesus brought sanctified these disciples as they were "sent . . . into the world" (17:18). Jesus consecrated himself to the horrible death he faced so that they may be sanctified by the truth of what his crucifixion accomplished.

Perhaps other readers have shared my astonishment when they read John 17:20 for the first time: Jesus prayed for *us*! If we count ourselves among those who believe in him through the message of the apostles—that is, the New Testament and the apostolic teaching of the church—then Jesus was thinking even of us as he prayed that last night of his life on earth. His prayer sweeps believers of all times and places into unity with those who were with him at his death (17:21), but even more astonishingly, into unity with the Father and Son. The Father in Jesus Christ, and Jesus Christ in those who obey, accept, know, and believe (17:6–8, 23). If the Lord Jesus has prayed for you as you live out your Christian life from birth to death, what more encouragement, motivation, or incentive could there be? With the knowledge that the prayer of Jesus still stands, we can live in the love and knowledge of the Father and Son that will make us witnesses to God's love for the world.

What the Structure Means:
Reviewing the Upper Room Discourse (Jn 13–17)

Following what is often called the Book of Signs (Jn 1:19–12:50), the apostle John slows down his telling of the story of Jesus to focus several chapters on just the last evening of Jesus' earthly life in what is often referred to as the Upper Room Discourse, or Farewell Discourse (Jn 13–17). This last night together "just before the Passover Festival" (13:1) bridges the end of Jesus' public ministry to his arrest and execution in chapters 18–20. The events of the last night begin to explain the significance of Jesus' imminent death, an explanation that will await fuller understanding until after the disciples have witnessed the resurrected Jesus and have received the Holy Spirit.

The Upper Room Discourse presents consolation for the disciples through action, explanation, exhortation, warning, and prayer that prepares them for lives that continue Jesus' mission in a dark world. The footwashing in chapter 13 is an action—a parable in motion—that explains the death of Jesus as a cleansing of those who follow him. It is also a memorable example of Jesus' humility and service that should characterize his disciples when he is no longer with them.

In chapters 13 and 14 Jesus explains his imminent departure through death not as tragedy but as his glorious transport back to the Father. Despite the ugliness of what the disciples will watch Jesus experience, the betrayal, arrest, and crucifixion were all, astoundingly, part of the Father's plan and the Son's mission. Jesus explains the coming and work of another paraclete, the Holy Spirit, who will be his divine presence with the disciples when he is no longer with them. It is the Spirit who will remind the apostles of everything Jesus taught, inspiring their understanding of Jesus, and who will be the divine agent who confronts the world. Jesus tells them of the mutual indwelling of the Father and Son who send the Spirit as the way to maintain a Trinitarian monotheism (see "What the Structure Means: Sending of the Spirit—*Filioque* (Jn 16:7–15)"). What's more, those who believe in him enter into the fellowship of the Father, Son, and Spirit.

In chapter 15 Jesus presents the metaphor of the vine and the branches to exhort his disciples to abide in the truth he has revealed, apart from which there is no life and no fruit. The abiding of which Jesus speaks is not passive, for it requires active obedience to the commands of Jesus that are summarized as "love each other as I have loved you" (Jn 15:12).

Jesus completes the evening with a prayer for the mission—that he will both be glorified by the Father and glorify the Father with successful completion of his mission that will look like defeat. He prays that his continuing future mission through his apostles will bear the fruit for which he is sending them into the world. And he prays for the completion of his mission in the lives of all who will believe through the message of the apostles. His will is that all who believe in him will be with him where he is going so that they will see him, not as a bloodied man on the cross, but in his glorious victory over sin and darkness. Only after being consoled and commissioned in the Upper Room Discourse are the disciples, and the readers of John's gospel, ready for the story of Jesus to continue with his arrest, trial, and execution.[15]

JOHN 18

18:1 *Crossed the Kidron valley.* The Kidron valley was a wadi[1] on the eastern edge of the old city of Jerusalem, separating the eastern wall of the temple from the Mount of Olives. Throughout the Old Testament it is referred to as the place where unclean items were thrown after being removed from the temple (e.g., 2 Ch 29:16; 30:14). Jesus' departure also reenacts the path David followed when he exited the city upon being rejected as king by the people (2 Sa 15:23).

There was a garden. John does not mention its name, Gethsemane, as recorded in the Synoptic Gospels. It was the furthest distance one could travel and still be considered "in" the city of Jerusalem for the Passover.[2] Jesus and his disciples had frequented the garden, and Judas knew the place (18:2). Jesus makes no attempt to hide from his betrayer or to delay or avoid the events that will follow.

18:3 *Carrying torches, lanterns and weapons.* "Armed for violence, Jesus' enemies, Romans and Jews representing 'the world,' come in search of the light of the world, carrying their own light, lanterns, and torches."[3]

18:4 *Jesus, knowing all that was going to happen to him.* John repeatedly indicates that Jesus had full knowledge of what lay ahead in his immediate future, and that Jesus unflinchingly leaned into it (cf. 13:1).

Went out and asked. Again, rather than hiding from Judas and the soldiers who had come to arrest him in the dark shadows of the garden, Jesus boldly "went out" and confronted them.

18:5 *Jesus of Nazareth.* Jesus is here identified by his hometown, Nazareth. It may carry a derogatory connotation (cf. Jn 1:46).

I am he (Gk. *egō eimi* [ἐγώ εἰμι]). Modern readers may need to be reminded that apart from previous personal contact, those sent to arrest Jesus would not have recognized his face, for there was no technology that could have been used to circulate his image. Furthermore, because it was dark and hard to see, the soldiers would have had trouble knowing which of the group was Jesus unless he was identified like this. That is why Judas was needed as a guide to lead them to Jesus and to identify him. Jesus did not try to pass himself off as someone else, but freely admitted his identity. But as is common to John, "For him [the evangelist], each several act and word of Jesus, upon any particular occasion, holds within it a meaning going beyond the particular occasion."[4] Given the immediately preceding context of this passage, an allusion to the Old Testament divine name echoes loudly in the otherwise common response: "I am [he]" (see commentary at 4:26; 6:20, 35; 8:24, 58). Judas and the soldiers had come to arrest God in the flesh (see Jn 1:1, 14).

18:6 *They . . . fell to the ground.* Only the fourth gospel mentions this unusual detail.

D. A. Carson may be right that this does not suggest a theophany but rather that "they are staggered by his open self-disclosure on a sloping mountainside in the middle of the night" and did not flee from their presence.[5] Some temple police may have recognized echoes of the prophecy of Isaiah 40–55, which mentions "I am" thirteen times in reference to God (Isa 41:4; 43:10, 25; 45:8, 18, 19, 22; 46:4, 9; 48:12, 17; 51:12; 52:6). Surely the incapacity of the soldiers sent to arrest Jesus when he shows himself highlights his voluntary surrender to the authorities in the full knowledge that they will execute him. His commanding request that his disciples be free to leave further shows the extent to which Jesus was in charge of the situation.

18:9 *This happened so that the words he had spoken would be fulfilled.* Until this point in John's gospel story, only words of Scripture are said to "be fulfilled" (Jn 12:38; 13:18; 15:25; 17:12; see also 19:24, 36). Here, Jesus is portrayed as a prophet whose words, like Scripture, are fulfilled by things that are happening. As F. F. Bruce observes, "The words of Jesus could not have *less* validity than the words of the prophets."[6] In this case, Jesus' words in John 6:39 and 17:12 are fulfilled by the release of the disciples who were with him. In those verses, however, Jesus speaks in the context of eternal life, not temporal danger as the disciples face here. Bruce further explains, "The Evangelist's thought moves on two levels, and in the Lord's intervention to save his disciples from physical harm he sees a parable of his saving them from eternal death."[7] Further to the point, Jesus' power to shield his followers from the powers of the temple authorities and the Roman guard indicates his ability to keep his other promises as well.

18:11 *Shall I not drink the cup . . . ?* Although John does not record Jesus' prayer in the garden of Gethsemane, this reference to drinking the cup suggests that he knew of Jesus' request for the cup to pass from him if possible as found in all three Synoptic Gospels (Mt 26:39; Mk 14:36; Lk 22:42). Had it been possible for another way to secure eternal life God would no doubt have answered Jesus' prayer.

The image of the cup in the Old Testament represents God's wrath on the earth's wickedness (La 4:21; Ps 75:8; Isa 51:17, 22; Jer 49:12). The prophecy of Isaiah 51:22, where the Sovereign Lord, the God who defends his people, says to his people, "from that cup, the goblet of my wrath, you will never drink again." The Lord took the cup of his wrath from the hand of his people and handed it to his Son. Because the cup did not pass from Jesus on that fateful day in Jerusalem, God's people now drink from the cup of Holy Communion instead of the cup of God's wrath.

18:13 *Annas . . . the father-in-law of Caiaphas, the high priest that year.* The Old Testament stipulated that the high priest was to be a lifetime office, after which the high priestly office would pass to a male descendant (Lev 16:32). In the Second Temple period the high priest wielded considerable political power. So at the time of the Roman occupation of Judea, the high priest served at the pleasure of the Roman occupiers, who could remove him from office at their whim. According to Josephus, Annas served as high priest from AD 6 to 15 and then the Roman governor who preceded Pontius Pilate removed him from office (Josephus, *Ant.* 18.2.1–2). Caiaphas was a son-in-law of Annas and held the office of high priest in the year Jesus died (Josephus, *Ant.* 20.9.1). But many Jews probably viewed Annas to be the true high priest for as long as he lived. Moreover, as the patriarch of the high priestly family he held substantial influence.

18:14 *Caiaphas . . . had advised the Jewish leaders.* See John 11:49–53. From the time Jesus raised Lazarus from the dead, the temple authorities had ordered that anyone who knew where Jesus was should report him so he could be arrested. This was exactly what Judas Iscariot had done, choosing the authority of the Jewish leaders over the authority of Jesus.

18:15 *Another disciple . . . known to the high priest.* Underspecification is a distinctive element of the gospel of John, so there is debate about who this disciple was. Even Mary's name goes unmentioned in this gospel, with reference to her only as "Jesus' mother" (Jn 2:1; 19:25). The disciples are also sparsely named, in preference to the reference "one of the disciples" or "one of the Twelve" (Jn 1:40; 6:8, 71; 12:4; 13:23; 18:26; 20:24). This verse presents yet another underspecified reference, "another disciple." Throughout church tradition this other disciple was often understood to be the beloved disciple, and some have argued further that he was the apostle John and author of this gospel.

In *The Beloved Disciple* James Charlesworth surveys alternative identities both for the beloved disciple (Lazarus? Nicodemus? Joseph of Arimathea? Thomas?) and for this enigmatic disciple known to the high priest and concludes that this other disciple was not "the beloved disciple" at all but Judas Iscariot, the betrayer of Jesus.[8] Although Charlesworth's theory has not found wide acceptance, it does makes some sense that Judas would have been known to the high priest, at least from arranging for Jesus' arrest, that he would have accompanied Jesus back to the high priest (if for no other reason than to get his payment), and would have been freely admitted to the courtyard of the high priest's residence because of his immediate role in the arrest of Jesus. Although history remembers Judas and Peter on different sides in reference to Jesus, in that historical moment Peter would certainly have been confused about Judas' loyalty, for until just that evening, Judas was thought to be a close disciple of Jesus who held the group's finances, and Jesus himself seems to have sent Judas out from the supper to do some task (Jn 13:27b). Judas may have requested that Peter be allowed into the courtyard of the high priest as a safe haven if he assumed Peter was also wavering in his commitment to Jesus, a premise supported by Peter's subsequent three-times denial of even having known Jesus. If Judas was the "other disciple" in this dramatic moment, both Peter the denier and Judas the betrayer are shown standing with those opposing Jesus. And yet each of them will go on to have much different destinies, with Judas going to a tragic suicide and Peter's reinstatement to become the primary leader of the church in Jerusalem and beyond.

Nevertheless, contra Charlesworth, most interpreters still identify the "other disciple" here as the beloved disciple, primarily on the basis of an interpretive tradition that goes back to Chrysostom and Jerome. Furthermore, in another instance of ambiguity, John 20:2 seems to identify someone referred to as "the other disciple" as the beloved disciple who ran to the empty tomb with Peter. Moreover, it makes sense that the one on whose testimony the fourth gospel is based (Jn 21:24) would have been one who witnessed the so-called trial of Jesus (Jn 18:15), the crucifixion (Jn 19:26), and the empty tomb (Jn 20:3). All considered, it is probably best to understand 18:15 as referring to the beloved disciple.

18:21 *Ask those who heard me.* When questioned about his disciples and about his teaching Jesus refers his interrogators to those who heard him and who know what he said—that is, to his disciples. This may be an implicit request for legitimate due process based on actual witnesses, but it also functions in the narrative to introduce the disciples as the authoritative witnesses to what Jesus said and did who will carry the gospel into the future. It presents the church as the custodian of Jesus' words.[9] Having been betrayed by a disciple, Judas, who had heard and knew Jesus, and Peter, who denied he even knew Jesus, the success of this strategy seemed improbable at this point in the narrative.

18:23 *If I said something wrong* (Gk. *ei kakōs elalēsa* [εἰ κακῶς ἐλάλησα]). The expression *kakōs lalein* (κακῶς λαλεῖν) or *legein* (λέγειν) occurs in the Septuagint in reference to unrighteous speech against God or neighbor (Lev 19:14; 20:9; Isa 8:21; 1 Mc 7:42).

18:24 *Annas sent him bound to Caiaphas the high priest.* The high priest presumably lived in the former Hasmonean palace located on the west hill of Jerusalem facing the temple.[10] Annas also likely lived in the same palace complex. Because the Torah stipulated that the high priest hold the office for life, many Jews would have considered Annas to be the rightful high priest, and Caiaphas would be unlikely to take action without Annas' approval. The fact that Annas sent Jesus bound to Caiaphas means that Annas supported the prosecution of Jesus, and was implicitly giving his approval for the events that followed. Because the high priest Caiaphas would have been sequestered in the temple for purification in preparation for Passover, he was not present when Annas interrogated Jesus.[11]

18:27 *At that moment a rooster began to crow.* This fulfills the prediction about Peter that Jesus had made just several hours before. See John 13:38. Jesus knows in advance even the details of those last hours of his life. Despite knowing how weak and frail the faith of his disciples was, he entrusts them to be his witnesses to the truth he has revealed.

18:28 *From Caiaphas to . . . the Roman governor.* All four gospel accounts of Jesus' interrogation before the high priest indicate a number of irregularities showing Jesus was denied the due process of a legitimate trial. Throughout the fourth gospel the chief priests are presented as continually opposing Jesus, and eventually join with the Pharisees to plot his death. Because the Jewish authorities had already decided to kill Jesus (Mt 26:3–4; Mk 14:55; Lk 19:47; Jn 11:53), the so-called trial's only purpose was to produce a trumped-up charge that Pilate would accept as worthy of capital punishment.

To avoid ceremonial uncleanness . . . to be able to eat the Passover. The Old Testament prescribes extensive measures for making oneself ritually clean and eligible to enter sacred space (Lev 17–26). Entering into a Gentile's abode was sufficient to make one ritually "unclean" and, therefore, disqualified to participate in certain rituals and worship. The zeal of the Jewish leaders for ritual purity contrasts sharply with the moral irony that they were about to execute an innocent man. Pilate accommodates the Jewish leaders by coming outside to them. Jesus, however, is not afforded the same religious consideration.

If "to eat the Passover" refers to the ritual meal itself, this is support for the idea that Jesus was crucified on the day the Passover meal was eaten, and so his last supper with the disciples was not formally a Passover meal. Many interpreters read the phrase as referring to any of the ritual meals during the week of the Feast of Unleavened Bread that accompanied Passover, usually also in support of the Last Supper as a formal Passover meal (see commentary on Jn 13:1).

18:29 *Pilate.* Pontius Pilate was the Roman governor of Judea (AD 26–36/37) who was in Jerusalem along with an increased number of soldiers to keep the peace during the Passover holiday. A Latin inscription discovered in Caesarea in 1961 refers to him as a "prefect," making him one of the people in the New Testament who has historical corroboration. He is known in secular Roman history for executing Jesus of Nazareth (Tacitus, *Annals* 15.44.3).[12]

18:31 *Judge him by your law.* Pilate was hesitant to get involved in what he perceived as a matter internal to Jewish law. Judged by Jewish law on the presumption of blasphemy, "he must die, because he claimed to be the Son of God" (Jn 19:7). Jewish law would have prescribed that Jesus be stoned to death, but at that moment in history, the Sanhedrin did not have the authority to execute capital punishment.

18:32 *This took place to fulfill what Jesus had said.* The unfolding of the end of Jesus' earthly life came just as he had predicted, when he had previously spoken about being "lifted up" (Jn 3:14; 8:28; 12:32, 34), which implied the Roman form of execution, crucifixion.

18:33 *King of the Jews.* This is the first of four occurrences of the title "King of the Jews" in the gospel of John (18:33; 19:3, 19, 21). In all four Gospels Pilate is the first to mention this title during his interrogation of Jesus (Mt 27:11; Mk 15:2; Lk 23:3; Jn 18:33) because to invoke Roman law as the Jewish leaders were requesting Pilate needed a political charge. Minor revolts by Jewish zealots with small bands of men attempting to imitate the previous successful Maccabean revolt against the Greeks were not infrequent in Judea (Josephus, *Ant.* 17.10.8). This title had previously been applied to the Hasmonean ruler

Alexander (Josephus, *Ant.* 14.3.1) and to Herod the Great (Josephus, *Ant.* 16.10.2), but Jesus never took this title for himself, probably to avoid its misleading political connotation.

18:36 *My kingdom is not of this world.* Jesus understood himself to be, not the king of the Jews, but eternal king of the far greater kingdom of God. Although the Old Testament often portrays God as a reigning king (e.g., Ex 15:18; Ps 10:16; 29:10; 66:7; 146:10; Jer 10:10; Mic 4:7), the phrase "kingdom of God" is found outside the New Testament only in the apocryphal Odes of Solomon 17:3: "But we will hope in God our savior; for the might of our God is forever with pity, and the kingdom of our God is forever over the nations in judgment." Jesus does not deny his kingship, but denies it to have an earthly, geopolitical character, much less an immediate threat to Rome's rule.

18:37 *The reason I was born and came into the world is to testify to the truth.* Jesus' trial forms an *inclusio* with the beginning of the gospel, in John 1:14 and 17, where he was said to come with grace and truth. Now at the end, in the most demanding of circumstances, we see this fulfilled as he speaks the truth with no hostility, but only the intent of offering mercy by his death.

18:39-40 *Your custom . . . at . . . Passover.* Through interrogating Jesus, Pilate did not find a political threat or a justification for execution. By Roman law, Jesus was innocent, and therefore Pilate looked for a way to release him that would satisfy the Jewish crowd. Pilate referred to this otherwise undocumented practice as "your practice"—that is, a Jewish practice, not Roman. But it is not a practice mentioned in the Old Testament. This suggests it may have been a practice of the previous political reign of the Hasmonean rulers that came to an end with the Roman occupation of Jerusalem. But the crowd gathered outside refused to see Jesus released on Pilate's offer and instead chose a known insurrectionist, Barabbas. The innocent would die in place of the guilty.

What the Structure Means: Peter and Jesus (Jn 18)

All four Gospels include extensive passion narratives, for the crucifixion of Jesus is the very heart of the gospel, without which there is no gospel. However, the four accounts are not identical, and each gospel writer structures the passion narrative to address the concerns and interests of the infant post-Easter church some decades after Jesus' death. The structure of John 18 presents at least two major themes: (1) a contrast between Jesus, the Good Shepherd, and Peter who will, by the time the fourth gospel is written, have become a chief shepherd of the church;

and (2) a pointer to the mission of Jesus' chosen disciples as bearers of the testimony about his words and deeds. Their testimony was eventually written down and constitutes the books of the New Testament, to which all who wish to know about Jesus must turn.

In the Good Shepherd Discourse Jesus taught that his sheep will *follow* (*akoloutheō* [ἀκολουθέω]) him (10:4, 27; 13:36–37; cf. 21:19, 22). Just hours before Jesus' arrest, Peter had declared his willingness not only to follow but also to die for Jesus (13:36–38) using "exactly the same words to describe his willingness to die for Jesus, as those that Jesus used when he described himself as the Good Shepherd."[13] And yet Jesus denies that Peter is able to follow him (13:36), thus "characterizing Peter as not being able to do what the sheep of the Good Shepherd do, i.e., to *follow* him."[14] And yet shortly after Jesus' arrest, Peter *did* follow Jesus into the courtyard of the high priest, only to promptly *deny* that he was a disciple of Jesus (18:17, 25) and that he was in the garden during the arrest (18:26–27). "Peter and the other disciple are portrayed as *following* Jesus—in keeping with the behavior expected of the sheep of the Good Shepherd. However, in Peter's case this is the only positive thing that can be said about him in this chapter."[15]

If the "other disciple" of 18:15 was Judas, as James Charlesworth suggests (see commentary on 18:15), then the betrayer was also a disciple following Jesus on that night. As Karoline Lewis observes in her reading of the Good Shepherd Discourse, the statement in 12:6 that "Judas does not care for the poor, echoes the behavior of the hireling in 10:13 who does not care for the sheep. . . . As one of Jesus' disciples, he is at one and the same time, sheep, hireling, and thief."[16] While disciples follow Jesus, apparently not all who follow Jesus are disciples. Is John warning his readers that even those who follow Jesus—namely, those in the church—can nevertheless deny and betray him? At the time the gospel of John was written, everyone knew that Judas had committed suicide in disgrace, but that Peter had been reinstated by Jesus and had become a chief shepherd of the sheep (Jn 21). The contrasting destinies of these two men stand as warnings that invite the reader to self-inspection of just how one is following Jesus.

John furthermore structures this chapter by placing Peter's denials interspersed with Jesus' interrogation by the high priest. The scene shifts back and forth between Peter's interrogation and Jesus' interrogation, giving the impression that these two exchanges were happening almost simultaneously and inviting the reader to compare and contrast Peter and Jesus. As Francis Moloney observes, "A dramatic contrast is created wherein Jesus denies nothing and Peter denies everything."[17] Jesus stands as the Good Shepherd who is about to give his life for the flock (Jn 10:11, 17), but Peter stands in the darkness among those who were opposing Jesus. But by the time John's gospel was written, Peter had become a primary apostle in the church. How did that happen? The story of Peter's darkest night explains and prepares the way for the reinstatement of Peter in chapter 21, indicating that the so-called Epilogue was an integral part of John's gospel story at its origin.

In John's version of the interrogation of Jesus by the high priest, when asked about his teaching Jesus offers no defense of himself but simply points to his disciples (Jn 18:21). *They* were the ones who had heard what Jesus taught and who had seen what Jesus did. Ask *them*. Now that Jesus is leaving this world, access to the truth about him must be through the testimony of those who were with him from the beginning (15:27) and through whom the Holy Spirit will teach and remind of everything Jesus had said (14:26). But on that dark night Jesus' disciples were not testifying. They were scattered in hiding or denying they knew him or accepting payment for betraying him, the first instance of behavior that has no doubt been repeated throughout the history of the church. "As Jesus points to the disciples as the ones who have heard him, and custodians of his word, one of them—indeed, the leading disciple—is with the powers of darkness . . . denying his association with Jesus."[18] Indeed the scene John paints makes for a very inauspicious start to the mission of making God's crucified Son known to the world. But the disciples had one more thing to see—Jesus raised from his grave.

JOHN 19

19:2–3 *A crown of thorns . . . a purple robe . . . "Hail, king of the Jews."* Purple garments were a sign of honor, and were worn by kings and rulers (Est 8:15; La 4:5; Da 5:7, 16, 29). The soldiers anticipate the charge Pilate will ultimately lay against Jesus in 19:19–22 with a mock crown and sham robe of royal purple, deriding him as they do so. In a shame-based culture, such ridicule is one of the cruelest blows others could inflict (see Ps 22:6–7; 35:16; 69:12; 74:10–11; 74:22; Isa 50:6–8).

19:7 *He claimed to be the Son of God.* The title "Son of God" was an ancient way of referring to a king as the earthly viceroy of God (e.g., Ps 2:6–7), but Jesus had claimed a sonship with God the Father that went beyond that ancient Near Eastern usage (e.g., Jn 5:25). His claims that he said only what God says and did only what God does, and his claims to be preexistent (e.g., Jn 8:58) led those who heard to accuse him of blasphemy, a charge punishable by death (see commentary on 5:18). Jesus died *because of who he was*, not in spite of it (see commentary on "One and only Son" at John 1:14 and on "Son of God" at 1:49).

19:11 *You would have no power over me if it were not given to you from above.* The Old Testament presents God as the one who rules over kings, removing them and setting them up on their thrones (Eze 31:10–11; Da 2:21; 4:30–31; 5:20).

19:15 *We have no king but Caesar.* Ironically, the chief priests here doubly condemn themselves since God's original intention was for Israel to have no king but God, much less a pagan king (1 Sa 8:6–7).

19:16 *Handed him over to be crucified.* The so-called trial has been conducted; the sentence has been delivered. Pilate, a judge who seems to doubt knowledge of truth is possible (Jn 18:38), has nevertheless ironically passed judgment on him who is the Truth. Many of the obscure proleptic references earlier in the gospel are now resolved: the lifting up (see 3:14; 8:28; 12:32), "the hour" (see 2:4; 7:6, 30; 8:20; 13:1; 17:1; 19:27), the gift of the Spirit (see 7:37–39), the revelation of a God who so loved the world that he gave his only Son (see 3:16). The crucified Jesus has been proclaimed as King (see 18:28–19:16) and has exercised his royal authority (19:16b–37). He has brought to completion the task given by the Father. He has revealed the glory of God.[1]

19:17 *Carrying his own cross.* It was common Roman practice for the criminal to carry the crossbeam to his own crucifixion (Plutarch, *The Divine Vengeance* 554A/B). Some of the church fathers saw in this a parallel to Isaac carrying the wood to the place of what would have been his own execution had God not intervened (Ge 22:6). Even some Jewish scholars familiar with the practice of crucifixion thought "Isaac carried the wood 'like one carries his stake [i.e., cross] on his shoulder' (*Genesis Rabbah* 56:3 [on Gn. 22:6])."[2]

Which in Aramaic is called Golgotha. John translates the Aramaic word *golgatha* (skull) into its Greek equivalent, *kranion* (κρανίον), for his readers. The Vulgate translated the word with the Latin equivalent *calvaria*, which was transliterated by the KJV translators, and so the place where Jesus was crucified has been known in English as Calvary ever since. The author's mention of Aramaic words that he then translates into Greek for the reader reveals he was familiar with the language of Judea but was writing for an audience who was not.

19:19–22 *Jesus of Nazareth, The King of the Jews.* Pilate ordered the charge against Jesus, as he defined it, to be fixed to the cross, where all passing by could see what happens to anyone who claimed to be a competing authority to Rome. But Jesus himself never claimed the title "King of the Jews"; it was what others had said of him, and perhaps reflected the desire of many of his followers, especially those who appreciated Jesus' ability to fill their stomachs (Jn 6:15). Since Pilate could find nothing with which to charge Jesus (Jn 18:38; 19:4), he had chosen the political charge suggested by the accusers, probably to make an example of Jesus of anyone who would threaten Roman power.

Rome had given Herod the Great the title "King of the Jews" (or King of Judea), and as his sons were called tetrarchs under the Roman governor, he was the last man to bear that title until it was forced on Jesus. Though Jesus never took the title upon himself, ironically he *was* the long-awaited theocratic king of God's kingdom, the Messiah (Jn 1:41), but that kingdom is not of this world. Jesus died under a charge of being who he was, the messianic king of Israel. Regarding Jesus as king and Messiah, see commentary on John 1:20, 41, 49; 2:17; 3:3; 6:15; 7:42; 12:13–15.

19:24 *This happened that the scripture might be fulfilled.* The executioners, by custom, could dispose of the clothing of the executed criminal as they wished. In this case, Jesus' clothing was divided among the soldiers, but the undergarment was of such quality that they decided to leave it intact and cast dice for it. The casting of dice for clothing evokes Psalm 22:18, following the wording of the Septuagint (Ps 21:19). John sees in this action a fulfillment of that Scripture.

It has been long noted that in the gospel of John two words are used in reference to the Old Testament, *graphō* (γράφω) and *plēroō* (πληρόω), the former usually as the perfect, passive, participle ("it is written") and the latter in the aorist, passive, subjunctive form ("might be fulfilled").[3] Notably, "it is written" as an introduction to an Old Testament quotation is used throughout 1:1–12:16, where "that it might be fulfilled" is found from John 12:38–19:36. Of this distinction Craig Evans writes, "The function of the Old Testament in the Fourth Gospel, as seen in the formal quotations, is not ad hoc, but is systematic and progressive, showing that Jesus' public ministry (1.29–12.36a) *conformed to scriptural expectations and requirements*, while his Passion (12.36b–19.37) *fulfilled scriptural prophecies.*"[4]

This distinction is apparently intentional on the part of the author, and sheds light on how he views the relationship between Jesus and Israel's history and Scripture. The Synoptics, especially Matthew's gospel, re-presents Israel's history in the life of Jesus as obedient Israel (e.g., Mt 2:15). In John we find a distinction between Jesus' ministry and the events surrounding his death with respect to how these two parts of his story relate to the Old Testament. The contours and expectations of the Old Testament are paralleled in Jesus' life and ministry (e.g., the feeding of the five thousand as provision of abundant life in Jn 6), whereas specific prophecies of the Old Testament are *fulfilled* in the events surrounding Jesus' *death* (e.g., the triumphal entry fulfilling Zec 9:9 in Jn 12:15). This nuanced use of the Old Testament shows that Jesus' death was a part of God's plan from the beginning, and therefore, most clearly revealed God's love for the fallen human race.

19:26 *The disciple whom he loved.* See the introduction and commentary at John 21:24 for further discussion of the "beloved disciple."

19:28 *Knowing that everything had now been finished and so that Scripture would be fulfilled.* Jesus has been arrested, accused, sentenced, and is being executed on the cross, all in accord with the Scriptures. When John's use of the Old Testament is considered as a whole, John seems to be more interested in presenting Jesus—his life, words, deeds/signs, passion, death, and resurrection—as the fulfillment of Scripture in general rather than the fulfillment of the individual passages from the Old Testament. The creative and redemptive work of God reaches its goal in Jesus Christ. As Jeannine Brown writes, "God has given Jesus the task of finishing the *divine creative work*."[5] John takes special care to underline that the whole of Old Testament Scripture points to Jesus Christ: his identity, mission, and destiny.[6]

Jesus knew that his death was the culmination of both his earthly mission and God's redemptive plan. His body was all but dead, and so he knew not only that his "hour" had come (see 13:1) but also that he had accomplished all that the Father had sent him to accomplish.

19:29 *A jar of wine vinegar.* This is likely a fulfillment of Psalm 69:21: "they . . . gave me vinegar for my thirst" (but cf. Ps 22:15). At the start of his public ministry as John tells it in 2:13–17 (see commentary there), Jesus acted in the temple in such a way that called to mind Psalm 69:9: "zeal for your house consumes me" (Jn 2:17, and see commentary there). That happened during the first Passover that John mentions Jesus attending. During the third and final Passover of Jesus' ministry, another action evokes Psalm 69:21, when he announces his thirst and is given vinegar. Psalm 69, a psalm of the Davidic king, therefore "bookends" the ministry of Jesus.

Hyssop plant. Hyssop was a bushy plant that grew throughout the ancient Middle East, but is not confidently identified with any modern plant. It is mentioned several times in the Old Testament in association with purification rites, beginning in Exodus 12:22–23, where Moses instructs the Hebrews to use hyssop as a sort of brush to sprinkle the blood of the Passover lamb on their doorposts. In addition to this reference in John 19:29, Hebrews 9:19 refers again to its use by Moses to sprinkle the scroll and the people with the blood of the sacrifice at a covenant ratification ceremony (Ex 24:6–8).

Therefore, the allusion to Psalm 69 associates the execution of Jesus with the righteous suffering of the Davidic king, and the reference to hyssop associates his death with the blood sacrifice of the Sinai covenant. Later his disciples associated the sheep metaphor in Isaiah 53:1–12 with the death of Jesus, understanding him to have sacrificially borne our sins on the cross (cf. John 1:29).

Matthew Scott observes,

> Though not as daringly read for Christology as Ps 21 [Ps 22 Heb. and Eng.], Ps 68 [Ps 69 Heb. and Eng.] enjoyed popularity in early Christian exegetical attempts to ground the suffering and death of Jesus in scripture. . . . In the case of this psalm, such attempts take two forms: 1) details from the psalm are woven without notice into the narrative of Jesus' passion; and 2) words from the psalm (John 2:17),

or such as might be spoken by the psalmist (John 15:25; 19:28), are placed in the mouth of Jesus.[7]

19:30 *It is finished.* The mission of the incarnation of the Son of God is now complete as Jesus' earthly life ends (cf. Jn 4:34; 5:36; 17:4). He not only has identified himself with human beings in his birth and life but also has joined us in the experience of death—and an excruciating death at that. John has consistently referred to the crucifixion as Jesus' exaltation. As C. H. Dodd observes, "His crucifixion may signify in the fullest possible way His glory and His exaltation, but in historical actuality it remains a miserable and humiliating end to a gallant struggle."[8]

The verb *teleō* (τελέω, "complete, fulfill") occurs three times in the perfect tense in verses 28 (twice) and 30. In John 19:28 Jesus, knowing that "all things have been fulfilled" (*panta tetelestai* [πάντα τετέλεσται], author's translation) and so that Scripture, too, would be fulfilled (*hina teleiōthē he graphē* [ἵνα τελειωθῇ ἡ γραφή]), announces his thirst. The fulfillment of Scripture, as the record of God's redemptive work, comes to its completion at the same time as Jesus' incarnate life. With the fulfillment of Scripture, Jesus can then pronounce "it is finished" (*tetelestai* [τετέλεσται]) in 19:30 as his final words before dying. The ancient Scriptures have reached their *telos* in the death of Jesus.

Martin Hengel has taken the fulfillment idea even further by observing that the fourth gospel begins with *en archē* (ἐν ἀρχῇ), "the very beginning, before the six days of creation. . . . God's work of creation and salvation, which begins with *en archē* (ἐν ἀρχῇ) in Gen 1.1 and Jn 1.1, is 'finished' in the death of the Son of Golgotha at evening of the sixth day."[9]

Gave up his spirit. The death of Jesus is closely associated in John's gospel with the giving of the Holy Spirit to the infant church (see 7:39; 20:22), but here the reference is to Jesus' spirit as a human being. It denotes that Jesus was truly dead, for when a human being dies their spirit departs from the body (Ps 146:4; Php 1:22–24). John reports that Jesus "gave up" his spirit—no one took it from him—suggesting his control over the voluntary act of his death (cf. Jn 10:15, 17, 18).

19:31, 33 *It was the day of Preparation* (cf. 19:42). Jesus was crucified on the Day of Preparation for the Passover (cf. 18:28), in a year when, by John's reckoning, the Passover fell on a Sabbath, making it "a special Sabbath." Observance of the Torah's prohibition against leaving an executed criminal exposed (Dt 21:22, 23) would have been especially important to the Jewish authorities.

Have the legs broken. Crucifixion usually took a long time, sometimes days, to bring the mercy of death, as its victim suffered a long, slow asphyxiation.

The ability of the legs to push up a bit on the nails through the feet, even though extremely painful, allowed shallow breathing. To speed death, the soldiers would break the legs of the crucified, hastening asphyxia. The corpse was most often left on the cross until birds of prey had devoured it.

Did not break his legs. Jesus had already died when the soldiers came with an iron mallet to break his legs. This circumstance, too, evoked associations with the Passover lamb slain without a bone broken (Ex 12:46; Nu 9:12; Ps 34:20).

19:34 *A sudden flow of blood and water.* Modern medical science can explain the buildup of hemorrhagic fluid around the lungs under these extreme circumstances of suffering torture, but such understanding was not available to those who witnessed Jesus' death. There is no doubt that Jesus has died. Jesus' wound suggested to John a symbolic connotation of water/Spirit and blood/atonement that may be in mind in John 7:37–39 and 1 John 5:6. As Gerry Wheaton explains, "Since verse 39 [7:39] both defines the water symbolism with the Holy Spirit and expressly links the coming of the Spirit with the cross of Jesus, the report of the flow of water (and blood) in 19:34 seems calculated to recall Jesus' words in 7:38 in order to indicate the *symbolic* fulfillment of this promise at the moment of his death."[10]

It is less likely that John directly alludes here to baptism and to the Eucharist, although both Christian sacraments point to the spiritual realities "that are focused in the sacraments but always exceed the sacraments."[11] The "blood symbolizes Jesus' sacrificial death (or his life poured out in death), and water the Spirit of life (connecting especially with 7:37–39)."[12]

19:35 *The man who saw it.* The beloved disciple, who is the source of this gospel (21:24), includes this third-person self-reference to underscore the truth that Jesus truly died on the cross. Later when claims of resurrection were circulating, skeptics offered the theory that Jesus had not died but had somehow survived the cross. Here we find a statement by an eyewitness of the crucifixion whose testimony is documented in what became the fourth gospel. This is his affidavit, so to speak, that he saw Jesus truly dead.

So that you also may believe. The author, who was an eyewitness to the crucifixion, partially steps out from behind the narrator by using a second-person plural pronoun "you" (*humeis* [ὑμεῖς]), bringing his testimony from that distant day of the crucifixion into the present of his readers, calling "you" to faith (see commentary on John 21:25).

19:36 *These things happened so that the scripture would be fulfilled: "Not one of his bones will be broken."* The wording does not exactly match any of the Old Testament verses with similar reference (Ex 12:46; Nu 9:12; Ps 34:20) and may be a paraphrase sufficient for associating Jesus both with the Passover lamb and with God's protective care of the righteous sufferer (though note that God's care does not relieve Jesus from pain and death).

19:37 *They will look on the one they have pierced.* This final quotation of the Old Testament is of Zechariah 12:10, showing that Jesus' unbroken bones fulfills the prophecy found there. The quotation is of the Hebrew text, with its strange syntax that mixes the first- and third-person pronouns: "They shall look on me, on him whom they have pierced" (ESV). Zechariah 13 is in the immediate context of Zechariah 12:10, which predicts in 13:7 that the shepherd will be struck, a theme that resonates with John's Good Shepherd Discourse (Jn 10). Therefore, D. A. Carson reads the mix of pronouns "that God is pierced when his representative, the Shepherd . . . is pierced."[13]

The opening verse of Zechariah 13:1, "On that day a fountain will be opened to the house of David and the inhabitants of Jerusalem, to cleanse them from sin and impurity," should probably also be included in John's interpretation of the crucifixion. John apparently sees the otherwise improbable convergence of the unbroken bones (Ex 12:46; Nu 9:12; Ps 34:20) with the consequential piercing of Jesus' side (Zec 12:10) to be the striking of the Shepherd (Zec 13:7), which results in cleansing and purification (Zec 13:1).

Zechariah 12:10 is also applied in Revelation 1:7 as a prophecy of the yet-future event of the parousia, when the nations of earth who have opposed him will weep when they see the pierced Christ coming in glory.

19:40 *This was in accordance with Jewish burial customs.* Torah prescribed not only the removal of corpses from public display on the day of execution but also burial on the same day as death so the land would not be desecrated (Dt 21:22, 23). Knowing the importance of this Jewish custom and wanting to keep the peace for Passover, Pilate releases Jesus' body to two members of the Jewish Sanhedrin, Joseph of Arimathea, who had become a secret disciple of Jesus, and Nicodemus, who has appeared several other times in John's story of Jesus (Jn 3:1, 4, 9; 7:50; 19:39).

The burial of Jesus, an executed criminal, in a private garden tomb was an extraordinary turn of events. Corpses of those executed for treason against Rome were usually consigned to a mass grave outside the city walls, if they were buried at all. Pilate may have assumed that would be the destiny of Jesus' body as well, but either the expediency of time since sundown was nearing or the respect of secret disciples led to a nearby garden tomb in which no one had yet been buried. There they laid the body of Jesus after anointing it with about seventy-five pounds of aromatic spices, as was the custom in the ancient Near East (cf. Jn 12:3). John gave this explanation to his original readers, apparently not expecting they would know, which suggests readers in a provenance outside Palestine, such as Ephesus, the traditional place of writing. A dignified burial according to Jewish law and custom implicitly proclaims the innocence of Jesus, despite his execution as a criminal. Although John does not explicitly point to it, the action of Joseph and Nicodemus fulfill the prophecy of Isaiah 53:9: "He was assigned a grave . . . with the rich in his death" (see also commentary at 19:31, 33).

John 19 Through Old Testament Eyes

The New Testament writers boldly proclaim that the crucified Jesus of Nazareth is the culmination of the Old Testament covenant(s) and the fulfillment of its promises and prophecies. The author of the gospel of John is no exception to this, but further elaborates that the crucified Jesus was none other than the incarnate Son of God who shared God's divine power and purpose and eternal life. The Old Testament promises of Israel's God were not to be fulfilled simply in the geopolitical space of human history, but were to have a transcendent, universal result of eternal life after physical death for all who believed.

In the gospel of John, the connection between Jesus' life and death and the Old Testament is presented in two ways: first, by consistently identifying Jesus with the Passover lamb that had provided protection from death at the Egyptian exodus; second, by showing that the details of Jesus' life and death fulfilled specific prophecies and promises.[14] When Jesus is introduced in John's gospel story, he is labeled as "the lamb of God" (Jn 1:29, 36), invoking allusions to both the Suffering Servant, who was led like a lamb to the slaughter (Isa 53:7), and to the sacrificial Passover lamb whose blood on the doorposts protected from the angel of death (Ex 12). The idea of Jesus as the Passover lamb developed early in Christian thought, as it is found explicitly stated by the apostle Paul (1 Co 5:7). Further explanation is provided by John the Baptist in John 1:29 that Jesus, as lamb of God, "takes away the sin of the world." Jesus the Passover Lamb protects from death *by* taking away the sin of the world for those who come to him in faith. The association of Jesus with Passover is alluded to throughout his ministry in the gospel of John. His visit to the Jerusalem temple, narrated early in John's gospel, is "when it was almost time for the Jewish Passover" (Jn 2:13), the first of three Passovers mentioned in this gospel. Jesus strides into the temple, clearing it of those who sold sacrificial animals as well as the moneychangers who facilitated their business (Jn 2:14–17), and in so doing implicitly announces that animals will no longer be needed for sacrifice because the true Lamb of God is here. Furthermore, Jesus announces that the temple itself has become obsolete, because his own body is the new temple where sacrifice is to be made and where God meets humankind (Jn 2:18–22). The understandably hostile response of the Jewish leaders to that announcement is the harbinger of the violence that will eventually end Jesus' life in chapter 19.

The miracle of the feeding of the five thousand, documented in all four Gospels, also occurs when "the Jewish Passover Festival was near" (Jn 6:4). After producing bread and fish to satisfy the people's hunger (Jn 6:5–15), Jesus announces himself to be the bread of eternal life that comes down from heaven, much superior to the manna from heaven that filled Israel's stomachs in the wilderness during the exodus (Ex 16:4; Ne 9:15; Ps 78:24, 25).

John 13:1 introduces the last night of Jesus' earthly life, and frames the events that transpired with the reference "It was just before the Passover Festival" when Jesus realized that his hour had come to leave this world and return to the Father through physical death. Throughout the passion narrative, Passover is mentioned explicitly (Jn 18:28; 19:14) and implicitly, as Jewish readers of that time would recognize that Jesus is sentenced to death at the very hour when the slaughter of Passover lambs would have begun in the temple (19:14) (see discussion of John's chronology in comparison to the Synoptic Gospels at 13:1).

Stanley Porter notes that certain details of the crucifixion echo the Passover story of Exodus.[15] Hyssop was used at the crucifixion (Jn 19:29), perhaps echoing the hyssop used to paint the blood of the Passover lamb on the doorposts (Ex 12:22).[16] Throughout the Old Testament, hyssop is used in rites of purification (Lev 14:4, 49, 52; Nu 19:18; Ps 51:7; cf. Heb 9:19), so the connotation of purification is present in the details of the crucifixion (Jn 19:29). Jesus' body was not to be left on the cross overnight, just as the remains of the Passover lamb were not to be left until the next day (Ex 12:10). Moreover, Moses, that great leader of the exodus, is mentioned more times in the gospel of John than in the other three Gospels, starting with a contrast between Moses and Jesus Christ in John 1:17.[17]

There has been "sustained and consistent use of recognizable Passover language throughout" the gospel of John to interpret the significance of Jesus' ministry.[18] In addition to this culmination of the final Passover in the death of Jesus, the quotation of three Old Testament quotations within the crucifixion story indicates that Jesus' death was not a tragic accident but the fulfillment of prophecy. The Old Testament quotations in John 19:36 and 37 follow the demise of Jesus and are the last Old Testament quotations in the gospel of John, suggesting that Jesus' death fully and finally closes the revelation of the Old Testament as far as John is concerned. The reference to none of Jesus' bones being broken, despite Pilate's direct order to do so (Jn 19:31–33), is understood by John to further identify the body of Jesus as a Passover lamb and a righteous sufferer protected by God in fulfillment of Exodus 12:46 and Numbers 9:12 (cf. Ps 34:20). Therefore, John identifies Jesus as the Lamb of God at both the very start of Jesus' ministry (Jn 1:29) and the very end just after his death (Jn 19:36). Jesus is shown, therefore, as constituting a new exodus that puts an end to animal sacrifice in the temple.

There are, notably, no Old Testament quotations associated with the resurrection of Jesus in John's gospel. Perhaps this reflects the unprecedented and absolute newness of the new creation inaugurated by Jesus' resurrection, a concept not fully anticipated by ancient Israel.

JOHN 20

20:1 *Early on the first day of the week.* And so begins the story of the dawn of the day a new epoch began for the human race. The Jewish Sabbath was the seventh day, established at the foundation of ancient Israel by what we know as the fourth of the Ten Commandments (Ex 20:8–11; Dt 5:12–15). The Sabbath commemorated the day following God's creation of the universe described in Genesis 1 within a six-day span. In the year Jesus died, according to John, Passover fell on a Sabbath day (19:31), or Saturday.

Saw that the stone had been removed. Mary Magdalene observed the Passover Sabbath, waiting to go to the tomb until the first day of the new week, Sunday. The tomb into which Joseph of Arimathea and Nicodemus had placed Jesus' body was a cave-like space cut into a rock face (Jn 19:41–42). After the placement of the body, a large stone would be placed to cover the opening of the tomb, keeping the corpse safe from scavenging animals and casual tomb robbers. A year later, the family of the deceased would reenter the tomb to collect the remaining bones for placement in an ossuary, a stone box fashioned to hold the disassembled skeleton of the deceased. The tomb would then be reused for the remains of the next family member to die. Against all expectations, Mary Magdalene found the tomb open, the stone removed from the entrance. This was the first evidence of the resurrection of Jesus, creating a new realm of being, a *new* creation for the human race. How appropriate that the resurrection be discovered on the *first* day after the Sabbath celebration of the old creation order. This is why Christians from the earliest times celebrate Sunday as the Lord's Day instead of the Jewish Sabbath, Saturday (see commentary on 20:19, 26).

20:2 *Simon Peter and the other disciple, the one Jesus loved.* See the introduction and the commentary on John 21:24 for discussion of the "beloved disciple," the ideal witness on whose testimony this gospel is based. As Francis Moloney observes, "The reader senses that there is a tension between these two figures. One is the disciple whom Jesus loved in a special way (see 20:2), while the other is the bearer of authority."[1] By the time this gospel was written, there may have been some tension between what has come to be called the Great Church centered in Rome and the more parochial Johannine churches of Asia Minor. But this does not mean that decades earlier there was necessarily personal tension between Peter and John or any of the other disciples.

This incident may portray the beloved disciple (20:8) in a more favorable light in comparison to Peter, who denied Jesus. At the time the fourth gospel was written, the apostle Peter likely had been martyred and the beloved disciple's eyewitness to Jesus gave him great standing as a witness to the truth.

20:5 *Strips of linen lying there.* See 20:6–7. Burial custom called for the corpse to be wrapped in strips of linen with aromatic spices between the layers, much as mummies were wrapped in Egypt. Had Jesus' body been moved to another location or stolen by grave robbers, the valuable linen and spices would have gone with it. Even grave robbers would not likely have unwrapped the body, leaving the linen behind, as they would more likely have taken the linen and left the body. Therefore, this detail attests to something more unusual. The strips of linen apparently fell from the resurrected body of Jesus or the body passed through them unimpeded. As Richard Bauckham observes, "The resurrection appearance stories show, among other things, that he did not simply pass through death as though it was in the nature of death to be a universal gateway into postmortem immortality. Rather, he nullified death. What led the Beloved Disciple to believe that Jesus had risen from death was the sight of Jesus' grave clothes lying abandoned in the empty tomb (20:5–8). Jesus had left death behind."[2]

20:7 *As well as the cloth that had been wrapped around Jesus' head . . . separate from the linen.* The syntax of the Greek is ambiguous whether the neuter perfect participle *entetuligmenon* (ἐντετυλιγμένον, "wrapped") refers to the cloth (*soudarion* [σουδάριον]) positioned around Jesus' head as a chin strap still lying where his head had been (e.g., NIV) or as having been removed and folded in another place (e.g., ESV). In either case Moloney's observation is apt: "Not only is the tomb empty, but the trappings of death are also empty. Lazarus was raised from the dead, but he came forth bearing the clothing of death. The risen Jesus has no such trappings."[3]

20:9 *Did not understand from Scripture that Jesus had to rise from the dead.* In the moment, Peter and the beloved disciples saw the evidence of resurrection, but did not have a full understanding of what God had revealed by it. Some scholars have proposed a specific Old Testament verse in mind here, such as Psalm 16:10 or Hosea 6:2, but John probably refers to the entirety of the Old Testament revelation as the context in which to understand Jesus' resurrection.[4] By the time John wrote this gospel, the apostles had worked out and subsequently preached the significance of Jesus' life, death, and resurrection from the Old Testament (cf. 1 Co 15:3–7). Consequently, the original readers would have the advantage of that fuller understanding.

20:12 *Saw two angels in white seated where Jesus' body had been.* Mary Magdalene, who had apparently returned to the scene, can make sense of the empty tomb only by thinking Jesus' body had been removed to another location. Perhaps Peter and the beloved disciple had taken the linen cloths with them so Mary did not observe that additional evidence.[5]

20:15 *Who is it you are looking for?* "The reader senses the irony as the one whom she seeks asks her whom she is seeking."[6] She is seeking the corpse of Jesus, but must learn that his bodily being has now been transformed. As Sandra Schneiders puts it, "She is seeking 'the Lord' whom she equates with his corpse. The equation of person with body and body with flesh, therefore of person with flesh, is precisely what Easter faith must transcend."[7]

20:16 *Jesus said to her, "Mary."* Mary recognized Jesus when he called her by name, reminding the reader that the Good Shepherd "calls his own sheep by name" (10:3–4), and his sheep recognize his voice. As Bauckham observes, this encounter "echoes the parable of the good shepherd. Like the sheep in the parable (10:3, 14), Mary recognizes Jesus' voice when he says her name. She is one of his own who knows him personally, as he knows her. For her he has laid down his life and received it again. His love for her has not been extinguished by death but has proved stronger than death."[8]

Cried out in Aramaic, "Rabboni!" (which means "[my] Teacher"). This title first occurs in John 1:38, when Jesus makes contact with his first disciples. There it is also translated from Aramaic to Greek for the original readers. This linguistic evidence suggests the author of the fourth gospel was a native of Palestine but those to whom he writes were not.

This title was also used to refer to John the Baptist (3:26), who was preaching and baptizing when Jesus first appeared on the scene. Jesus may have been identified as a great religious teacher at the start of his ministry, but here after the resurrection, that title does not do him justice. As delighted as Mary was with the reinstatement of her relationship with Jesus, he must reveal to her that their relationship has far outgrown that of rabbi-disciple. He does this by refusing her hold on him (20:17).

20:17 *I have not yet ascended to the Father.* Jesus was not resurrected merely to resume his earthly life, as Lazarus had been (Jn 11:44). This epoch-making break in the way Jesus will relate to his disciples should probably be understood to "instruct her that she must desist from her attempt to reestablish the relationship she once had with him. The hour is still in progress, and Jesus not only forbids her to cling to him, but explains why all clinging should cease."[9] Mary, like Thomas later in the chapter, lives during the transition from Jesus' earthly life to his resurrection life. While she nostalgically wishes for a return of their previous relationship, Jesus is establishing a new type of relationship with her, perhaps not unlike that which one day resurrected believers will have to reestablish with their resurrected loved ones.

Instead of picking up their previous relationship, Mary is now sent forth as one of those witnessing to the truth of his resurrection. Going against the cultural convention that a woman's testimony is not to be received, Jesus sends her to his "brothers." In the fourth gospel, twelve of the fourteen occurrences of *adelphos* (ἀδελφός, "brother") refers to familial siblings, but here *adelphos* (ἀδελφός) is used clearly to refer not to siblings but to disciples of Jesus (20:18; cf. 21:23). The resurrection of Jesus changes everything, making his followers children of the family of God (cf. Jn 1:12) and, therefore, siblings to him and one another.

To my Father and your Father, to my God and your God. Jesus does not say he is ascending to "our Father" and "our God" but identifies with the children of God while yet preserving the uniqueness of his own Sonship to the Father. "The hour of Jesus, shortly to culminate in Jesus' ascension to the Father, will create a new situation where the God and Father of Jesus will also be the God and Father of Jesus' brethren."[10]

20:18 *I have seen the Lord!* Women play a surprising role in the gospel story given the culture of the day. Mary, the mother of Jesus, was present when Jesus began his public ministry (Jn 2:1–11); it was the witness of a woman that took the gospel beyond the Jews to the Samaritans (Jn 4:39); and here a woman, Mary Magdalene, is the first person to see the risen Jesus.

20:19 *On the evening of that first day of the week.* On the evening of the same day Jesus rose from the dead, Jesus mysteriously entered a locked room and stood among his disciples. His resurrected human body clearly had been transformed in ways hard to imagine. His first order of business was to show himself to those who were grieving his death. Notably, the location of his appearing is simply "among his disciples" without other reference to place, inviting the image of Jesus being wherever his disciples are gathered (cf. 20:26, "among them").

Just as the grave could not keep Jesus from rising, the ordinary material barriers of this reality in which we live, such as locked doors and walls, could not restrict his resurrected body. Note that the text does not say that Jesus came *through* the door or walls, just that they were not a barrier to his materialization, for want of a better word, in the midst of his disciples. His bodily presence, while real, was not a physical presence as physicality is defined in this world.

The phrase "first day of the week" "appears to contribute to his [John's] theology" of the new creation. "We read in Genesis 2:2–3 that God rested on the seventh day of creation (the final day of the week). For John, a new 'week' has begun . . . signaling that the re-creation begins at the resurrection of Jesus Christ."[11]

Peace be with you! Never was the traditional Jewish greeting *shalom* (שָׁלוֹם; Gk. *eirēnē* [εἰρήνη], "peace") uttered with such profound significance, fulfilling Jesus' promise of peace in John 14:27. Throughout its hundreds of occurrences in the Old Testament *shalom* (שָׁלוֹם) referred to much more than the absence of war. The cognate Hebrew verb *shalom* (שָׁלוֹם) means "to be completed"[12] and in the biblical context referred to the peace of God's presence for blessing, bringing whole, abundant life to God's people. It came to have connotations of prosperity, safety, and health. The appearance of Jesus, the beloved teacher sent from God, alive and well after his torturous death, was the most significant instance of shalom. Jesus here offers that peace to his frightened disciples, in the phrase "peace be to you" (*eirēnē humin* [εἰρήνη ὑμῖν]). When the finality of death has been conquered in the redemptive plan of God, people are set free to live a whole and abundant life both now and eternally (see also commentary at Jn 14:27).

20:21 *I am sending you.* The sending of the Son, who descended from the Father and ascended back to the Father through death and resurrection, is a major theme of the fourth gospel. The Son of Man came into this world to make God known (Jn 1:18), and here he commissions his disciples to continue his mission by being bearers of that revelation of his incarnation to the world. The fourth gospel ends before that commission is fulfilled, but by the time it was written, the gospel of Jesus Christ had reached around the Roman world. The Johannine churches in Asia Minor, far from Jerusalem, were living fruit of that commission fulfilled. And so the readers of the story may see themselves as the continuing fruit of the story, as they also become bearers of its message. Their historical experience has direct connection back to Jesus' apostles.

20:22 *He breathed on them and said, "Receive the Holy Spirit."* John here shows the fulfillment of the giving of the Spirit promised to happen when Jesus was glorified (Jn 7:39), completing the teaching about the Spirit within the fourth gospel. Modern reference to this incident as "the Johannine Pentecost" has invited issues concerning the relationship of this narrative with Acts 2, which recounts the coming of the Holy Spirit with wind and tongues of fire on the day of Pentecost in the year Jesus died. To understand the symbolic role of John's association of the Spirit with the exhalation of Jesus, the literary artistry of the fourth gospel must be remembered, especially as it would have been read decades after the event of Pentecost. There were not two "givings" of the Spirit, nor is John 20:22 in any conflict with Acts 2.

First, despite most modern English translations, the verb *emphysaō* (ἐμφυσάω, "breathe") does not in itself connote breathing *into* or *on* an object unless there is a dative object or prepositional phrase, which is absent here.[13] In the original bestowal of life in Genesis 2:7, both the Hebrew and the Septuagint include a prepositional phrase making it clear that God breathed "into his [Adam's] face" (Heb. *bet* [בְּ]; Gk. *eis* [εἰς]). Because both the Hebrew *rûaḥ* (רוּחַ) and Greek *pneuma* (πνεῦμα) have three distinct senses—breath, wind, spirit—it is apt to describe the endowment of the Holy Spirit with that verb denoting a movement of air. But the verb does not occur in Acts 2 (where the Spirit is "poured out") or elsewhere in the New Testament. The concept of the *indwelling* of the Spirit in the believer comes from other texts (e.g., Job 32:8; Eze 36:27; 37:14; Rom 8:11; 1 Co 6:19; 2 Co 1:22; Eph 3:16; 2 Ti 1:14).

To make a theological point, John identifies the exhaled breath, or spirit, of the resurrected Jesus with the Holy Spirit to signal the new life that Jesus' resurrection has inaugurated (cf. Jn 5:24). This portrayal of the re-creation of life echoes the original endowment of human life in Genesis 2:7, suggesting perhaps an *inclusio*: "John begins and ends with Jesus as the source of life, the agent of the first creation and the new creation."[14] Jesus' exhalation may also echo the promise of life out of death pictured in the restoration of life to the dry bones of Ezekiel 37:9 (which also includes a prepositional phrase following the verb, "breath into these corpses" (Heb. *bet* [בְּ]; Gk. *eis* [εἰς]). As D. A. Carson explains, "John 20:22 is not mere symbolism anticipating an endowment of the Spirit that is nowhere mentioned, it is symbolism anticipating the endowment of the Spirit that the church at the time of writing has already experienced."[15] This symbolic reference is consistent with John's portrayal of Jesus' actions as enacted parables that have anticipatory reference, for instance, the footwashing as anticipating the cleansing of the disciples by the cross (Jn 13:1–17), and the coming of the Greeks to signal the imminent arrival of Jesus' "hour" (Jn 12:20–27).

The fourth gospel uses verbal artistry to portray theological truth even as it describes events that really happened (see "John's Use of the Old Testament:

Verbal Artistry" in the introduction). As an analogy consider the center panel of the triptych *The Fall and Redemption of Man*, painted by Lucas Cranach the Younger (1515–1586), which graphically portrays the crucifixion with a stream of blood and water from Jesus' side pouring out on the head of the artist who is standing next to Martin Luther![16] This is a theological statement whereby the artist is claiming the salvation provided by Christ's crucifixion as interpreted by Luther, and is not meant to be understood as if it were a photograph portraying historically the presence of the artist and the Reformer at the foot of the cross in the first century. Similarly in 20:22 John provides an interpretation of Jesus' glorification in the resurrection as being the necessary antecedent to the release of the Spirit. This neither contradicts nor denies the Acts 2 account of the Spirit's descent on the church on the day of Pentecost but provides John's theological emphasis linking Jesus' death to the giving of the Spirit.

The Spirit is breathed out with the imperative to "receive the Holy Spirit" as part of the commission to continue the mission of Jesus, the giving of a new heart promised in Jeremiah 31:33; Ezekiel 36:26–27; 37:5. As Carson notes, other imperative verbs in the fourth gospel are proleptic, such as Jesus' request that the Father glorify him (Jn 17:5). "But that does not mean the glorification takes place even as Jesus speaks."[17] Jesus' postresurrection outbreathing proleptically links the future work of the Spirit to his incarnational mission, and "thus, the disciples, empowered by the Spirit, in the midst of their fear and joy, will be the agents for the future sanctification of generations of believers."[18]

20:23 *If you forgive anyone's sins . . . if you do not forgive.* Jesus, the Son of God, has come into the world to reveal God's love as expressed in the atonement for sin on the cross. That atonement has now been accomplished, as Jesus has risen from the grave, the first human being to be forevermore freed from death. In the Old Testament, atonement for sin that resulted in God's forgiveness was based on prescribed animal sacrifices performed by priests (e.g., Lev 4:20, 26, 31, 35). These sacrificial rituals could be effective only because of the coming sacrificial atonement of Jesus that God had planned (1 Pe 1:20). The death of Jesus Christ on the cross accomplished fully and finally the atonement that the Old Testament animal sacrifices foreshadowed. Now that Jesus had come, God would forgive sin based on the acceptance or rejection of this new message that full forgiveness of sins is open to all because of Jesus' death and resurrection (cf. Ac 13:38–39). Here the gospel of John very clearly commissions the disciples of Jesus—namely, the church, for this task based on the presence of the Holy Spirit. It is not that the apostles could subjectively decide who would receive God's forgiveness and who would not; rather, forgiveness is bestowed or not based on the apostolic declaration that anyone who repents and believes in Jesus will be forgiven and anyone who does not will not be forgiven. Christian witnesses empowered by the Holy Spirit would declare and live out that message in their own lives.

The preaching of the gospel is a speech-act that both proclaims and judges those who hear it because the authority of the Son of God operates through the Christian church. The church has been given the authority to proclaim the gospel: the forgiveness of sin because of the death and resurrection of Jesus. All Christians, but especially Christian clergy, have the authority to assure others of the forgiveness of their sin because of Jesus and the presence of the Holy Spirit in the church. When an agent of the Christian church proclaims forgiveness of sin in Christ ("If you forgive anyone's sins . . ."), it is God who forgives, for only God can forgive sin ("their sins have been forgiven to them"). The verb *apheōntai* (ἀφέωνταί) is in the perfect tense and passive voice, suggesting God's role.

In the parallel phrase, the translation "if you do not forgive [anyone's sins] . . ." is an interpretation that anticipates the opposite of forgiveness, but the verb is *kratēte* (κρατῆτε), to hold or retain, a verb not otherwise found in the context of sin. And so the phrase reads, "if you retain [anyone's sins, their sins] have been retained." The result is expressed again in the perfect tense and passive voice of the verb *kekratēntai* (κεκράτηνται), "they have been retained."[19] This suggests that the persistence of sin is the state that pertains until one hears the church proclaiming the gospel of forgiveness. If as a result of the gospel message one does not seek forgiveness but rejects Christ, the sin of that person "has been retained"—that is, is not forgiven. As Johannes Beutler explains it, "From a Johannine perspective, all individual sins are rooted in and culminate in the one sin of rejecting Jesus and his message of salvation. Thus, the authority to forgive sins may not always achieve its goal. In some cases, the lack of readiness to accept the message may have to be pointed out, and this means 'retaining sins.'"[20]

While the syntax of John's expression is difficult, the point of 20:23 is clear: Jesus has vested the Christian church with his authority through the presence of the Holy Spirit to proclaim forgiveness of sin. But apart from the acceptance of Christ's gospel upon its hearing, there is no forgiveness of sin, and the rejection of Christ is itself the most fundamental sin.

John 20 Through Old Testament Eyes

Although a few people in the stories of the Old Testament were resurrected from death in the sense of being restored to mortal life, the resurrection of Jesus into a new state of being is unprecedented. The widow's son at Zarephath (1 Ki 17:17–24), the son of the Shunammite

(2 Ki 4:32–37), and the man whose corpse was thrown into Elisha's grave (2 Ki 13:21) were restored by God's prophets to life in this world, only to have to die again eventually. Jesus was resurrected not as a return to his earthly life, but in a transformed body that transcends this mortal life and the physical limitations of this world. This went far beyond anything known in the Old Testament.

As Sandra Schneiders explains, "Early Israelite eschatology was a collectivist, national, and this-worldly expectation of Israel's ongoing prosperity if it remained faithful to the covenant."[21] From its establishment as a nation, God set before Israel "life and prosperity, death and destruction" (Dt 30:15). He also promised that he was the source of life and would bring the dead to life (Dt 32:39; 1 Sa 2:6; Isa 25:8; 26:19; Eze 37:1–10; Da 12:2; Hos 13:14). But these references to life for the dead could be understood as a restoration of national Israel as a geopolitical power for a long (eternal?) time of peace and prosperity as a continuation of this worldly state of being.

When Jesus raised Lazarus from death, Lazarus joined the ranks of those few who had experienced death and a restoration to this mortal life (see commentary on Jn 11). In so doing Jesus revealed his power to raise the dead, a power apparently similar to that of Elijah and Elisha. For all three men, this power accredited their message to speak for God. But Jesus' message was far greater than that of any Old Testament prophet and, together with the other signs he did, revealed that with him the messianic age had dawned. Jewish expectation would therefore assign a role of political and national power to Jesus, which is certainly what his disciples expected immediately following his resurrection, when they asked if he was now going to restore the kingdom to Israel (Ac 1:6). But Jesus' resurrection achieved a far greater good than the restoration of Israel's national sovereignty and power. He achieved the opening of eternal life after death for the entire human race, irrespective of national, racial, or ethnic associations.

When the Old Testament references to God's ability to restore life out of death are read in the hindsight of Jesus' resurrection, we can see that those intriguing hints were pointing to the eternal life that Jesus would bring. That resurrection life would far exceed the expectation of the people who read these promises before Jesus came, revealing that resurrection would be individual and personal, as Abraham reasoned that God could bring his own son Isaac back to life (Heb 11:19), and Job declared his faith in a "redeemer" who would live, and that Job himself, and not another, would see God "in my flesh" after his flesh had been destroyed (Job 19:25–27). The resurrection to life after death will be everlasting, as Isaiah promised the destruction of death itself for all nations—not just for Israel—and so broadens God's redemptive beyond the geopolitical nation of Israel (Isa 25:6–8). The universal nature of the resurrection was foreseen by Daniel, who wrote, "Multitudes who sleep in the dust of the earth will awake: some to everlasting life, others to shame and everlasting contempt" (Da 12:2), and so introduced the element of judgment into the concept of resurrection.

God revealed eternal life through Christ only gradually through the millennia of the Old Testament times, and his people made sense of each stage of revelation as best they could, not fully understanding the extent and transcendence of the promises. When Jesus came he did not simply make more promises of a more explicit nature; as a human being who had died, he was resurrected to the new state of being of eternal life, thus demonstrating for all time what God's redemptive promises truly meant.

20:26 *A week later.* The phrase idiomatically translates "after eight days" (*meth' hēmeras oktō* [μεθ᾽ ἡμέρας ὀκτὼ]; cf. 20:19), which by the conventional inclusive counting refers again to Sunday, a week after Jesus arose from the grave. Jesus again makes his appearance to be with his disciples, again through locked doors, and again greets them, "Peace be with you." In John's recollection, Jesus himself set the precedent for Sunday to be the day Christians gather to be with Jesus, which became known as the Lord's Day (cf. Rev 1:10). "Scholars have rightly suggested that the rhythmic reference to 'the first day of the week' ([Jn 20] v. 1), 'the evening of that same day' (v. 19), and 'eight days later (v. 26) deliberately situates all these events on the day of the Lord."[22]

The weekly gathering of the church to meet with the Lord has continued throughout the centuries and around the world since. The traditional congregational greeting in many churches, "the peace of the Lord be with you," with its expected response, "and also with you," may have found its origin in this postresurrection appearance of Jesus to his disciples.

And Thomas was with them. Just as Mary had to learn that her previous way of relating to Jesus was over, Thomas was also a disciple living between the earthly presence of Jesus and his resurrection presence. Rather than believe what the other disciples told him, that they had seen Jesus alive (Jn 20:25), Thomas refused to believe on the basis of their testimony. "He insists that he will believe only if he can touch the very wounds of Jesus, only if he can return to the dispensation of pre-Easter faith, only if he can continue to relate to Jesus in the flesh."[23] But that would never again be possible. For the post-Easter generations it would be on the basis of the apostolic testimony of those who had seen the resurrected Jesus that the gospel mission would go forth in the world. The demand made on Thomas to believe, having not seen, would be the demand made on all who would subsequently come to faith in the risen Christ.

Going Deeper into Why We Worship Every Week: John 20:19, 26

In the Greco-Roman world, and in most societies throughout human history, there was no such thing as the weekend. The concept of a five-day workweek arose in both Great Britain and the United States during labor movements in the early 1900s. Because Sunday was the day of worship for Christians and Saturday for Jewish people, those two days were designated as the "weekend," when the responsibility of one's daily job would cease. In those societies both at the time of Jesus and in many places still today where Sunday is not a day off, Christians gathered for worship very early in the morning before going to work, or perhaps on Sunday evening.

The designation of Sunday as the Christian day of worship originated with Jesus' resurrection from the grave on that day of the week. God could have appointed the Jewish Sabbath as the day of Jesus' resurrection, but the day following it connotes the new covenant and new epoch represented by a new day of worship. Although Easter Sunday is the preeminent Christian day commemorating the resurrection of Jesus, every Sunday is a memorial to the Lord's resurrection (cf. Rev 1:10, "the Lord's day") and has appropriately been observed as a day of worship since the gathering of Jesus' disciples on that first Easter Sunday.

Although Christians need not be legalistic about the day of worship, weekly worship on Sunday should not be easily abandoned in favor of simply a more convenient time, as Jesus himself established his weekly meeting with his disciples on Sunday. This is not to say that Jesus is not always present with his people, but that he himself chose Sunday as the day to meet in his postresurrection state with his disciples. Many Christians may have essential work that must be done on Sunday, such as medical personnel and first responders. Others may be too frail or ill to attend at the Sunday hour. But the exceptions to Sunday worship should be just that—exceptions.

Jesus also set the precedent for a *weekly* gathering for worship by appearing the second time also on a Sunday a week later (Jn 20:26). Probably following the weekly schedule of Jewish synagogue worship, Jesus changed the day of worship but not its frequency. And yet so many Christians in modern society have abandoned the weekly practice of going to church on Sunday.[24] A 2017 Gallup survey reported that "in 2017, 38% of adults said they attended religious services weekly or almost every week," representing a decline in recent decades.[25] Instead, there has been an upswing in the number of people who consider themselves to be "spiritual" but not religious, and who express disdain for organized religion such as the Christian church. Even Christians seem too often drawn to an individual, privatized form of worship that keeps them from attending church on Sunday.

Followers of Jesus should heed the precedent he set for a *weekly* gathering in his presence on the first day of the week as a matter of spiritual obedience. While there is no "law" in the Bible that says, "Thou shalt worship weekly," there is centuries-old tradition under both the old and new covenants that call for the practice. Making worship a priority on the *first* day of the week starts afresh a new seven-day cycle of the life of God's shalom.

20:27 *Put your finger here.* Although "doubting Thomas" is seen as resistant to the kind of faith that Jesus demands, this episode is of essential importance for the theological significance of the resurrection because, as Bauckham explains, "it shows that Jesus had nullified death *in* his own human and corporal identity. As he was incarnate in flesh (1:14) and gave his flesh in death for the life of the world (6:51), so his fleshly humanity was raised. Only this makes his death and resurrection life-giving for fleshly and mortal humans. For those not privileged to see this, as only Thomas and the other disciples who met the risen Christ could, it is entirely essential that those disciples *did see.*"[26] John does not allow us to think that Jesus experienced only some "spiritual" resurrection that believers can absorb into their hearts through faith. The resurrection of Jesus was a fleshly resurrection, albeit flesh of a different and extraordinary kind. The survival of the wounds he suffered is evidence of the continuity between earthly and resurrection life.

20:29 *Blessed are those who have not seen and yet have believed.* Jesus has future believers in mind as he departs this life on earth, becoming invisible. The goal of his mission is to redeem and reconcile people through a faith that is not based on knowing the *man* Jesus (as essential as his manhood was) but on believing the *risen* Christ. This will come through the testimony of those apostles who did have eyewitness knowledge of Jesus as their testimony is passed down through time. Jesus has prayed for all who take their place in the ranks of those who have not seen, as Thomas saw, and yet have believed (Jn 17:20). Here he underscores the essential role of faith.

20:30 *Jesus performed many other signs.* A statement about the abundance of materials about the protagonist was not uncommon in the ancient literary tradition.[27] It is certainly believable that Jesus, throughout his earthly life, did many other things than the four Gospels taken together record. The proliferation of later apocryphal gospels and stories may have been a response to what was read in this statement as an implicit invitation.

But of greater relevance, the performance of signs was an important accreditation of those who had been sent from God, beginning with Moses at the start of the nation of Israel in the exodus (Ex 4:9, 17, 28, 30; 7:3; 10:1–2; Nu 14:11, 22; Dt 4:34; 6:22; 7:19; 11:3; 26:8; 29:3; 34:11). God formed for himself a nation (Dt 4:34), performing signs in Egypt and in the wilderness that revealed his glory (Nu 14:22; cf. Jn 2:11), leading Israel to faith under the old covenant. But the people refused to believe in God and treated him with contempt, in spite of all the signs he performed (Nu 14:11). When the Word became flesh to reveal God, it was with the same tactic and goal: Jesus performed many signs, some recorded in Scripture and many others not, so that people may believe that Jesus is the Messiah, the Son of God, and have both abundant life now and eternal life after death (Jn 20:31).

The evangelist apparently wishes to put the faith of those who knew Jesus during his earthly ministry on equal footing with those who like us, and even most people at the time of Jesus, have had no opportunity for such an encounter. John shows that seeing does *not*, in fact, lead to believing the truth. For Mary Magdalene, Peter, and the beloved disciple all saw the resurrected Jesus and yet left their encounters with no *true* understanding of what they were seeing. Thomas was invited to faith through the words of the disciples who *had* seen the Lord, but refused to believe *on that basis*. And yet the words of the disciples who became apostles are the only testimony we have on which to base faith. John's gospel itself is here presented as another "sign" intended to lead to faith, just as the changing of water to wine, the healing of the blind man, and the feeding of the five thousand were so intended. Authentic faith in Christ comes not by physical sight but by believing the significance of his life, death, and resurrection as offered in the words of those who did see and were chosen to bear witness.[28] Believing the words of the commissioned witnesses is how all come to faith, whether during the time of Jesus and the apostles or in the twenty-first century.

20:31 *Believe that Jesus is the Messiah.*[29] With this statement John describes Jesus as the Messiah, bringing all of ancient Israel's redemptive hope to its culmination. As Beth Stovell concludes, "Jesus' identity as messiah and Davidic king did not emerge in a vacuum and were not a wholly new invention by Jesus' followers, but rather were weaved from the fabric of existing conceptions of messianism already present in Second Temple Judaisms."[30] While this is without doubt true, the nature and definition of the kind of Messiah that Jesus is must be read from John's gospel itself, and probably does not match exactly *any* of the strands of Jewish messianism that predated Jesus. John's personal friendship with Jesus, especially if he is the disciple whom Jesus loved, must have reshaped his understanding of what it would mean to declare that "Jesus is the Messiah" in light of the crucifixion and resurrection.

The Old Testament developed its messianic concept through Scriptures such as Psalm 2:2 and Isaiah 11:1–10, rooted in faith that God keeps covenant with his people. But the fulfillment of the messianic hope that God had planned from eternity burst every expectation of the Old Testament promises. The Messiah was not to be just a descendent of King David who would restore national sovereignty and dignity to a theocratic geopolitical nation of Israel. The Son of God, the Word of God, himself would step into human history becoming flesh to reveal the glory of God as not just a king but a Savior. And not just a Savior who delivered his people from the threat of war and conquest, but a Savior who would defeat the most powerful enemy, death itself. Such unprecedented ideas reached far beyond the Old Testament concept of the Messiah, in a fulfillment of redemptive history in Jesus Christ that inaugurates nothing less than a new creation.

By believing you may have life in his name. The formula "in [a person's] name" in the Old Testament is a claim of delegated authority, as in battle (1 Sa 17:45; 2 Ch 14:11; Ps 20:5, 7; 118:10–12), or as in formal communications from a leader (1 Sa 25:5; 1 Ki 21:8; Est 3:12; 8:8). Significant for this context especially is authority to bless or curse (Dt 10:8; 2 Sa 6:18; 2 Ki 2:24; Ps 129:8). Here life is bestowed on the basis of faith by the authority of Jesus, the resurrected Messiah and Son of God, of whom there is no greater authority (see Jn 1:12–13).

The gospel of John is powerfully effective as a witness that brings people to faith in Christ. (See my testimony of coming to faith by reading it in the introduction.) Literary analysis gives us some perspective on why this is so. The fourth gospel is full of dramatic irony that, as Britt Leslie explains, is particularly powerful because it depends on superior audience knowledge in comparison to the characters in the narrative.[31] In reference to the healing of the blind man in John 9 as an example, Leslie explains,

Because the audience knows something that the other characters (who are usually the target of the irony) do not, they have a bond with the narrator and stand in a superior position over the target characters. The audience's knowledge of Jesus' origins (from hearing the prologue) equips them to judge the Pharisees in agreement with Jesus' final verdict. . . . When the Pharisees claim to "know" Jesus is a sinner, the audience already knows he is not because they are "in-on" the secret revealed in the prologue. When the healed man argues what the audience already knows, they are bonded together by that common knowledge and the Pharisees are excluded, even as they ironically sought to exclude the man (v. 34). In this way the narrative itself *creates* insiders.[32]

By the end of the gospel of John, readers have such attained shared insider knowledge forming a bond "that extends from the story world into the real world of the audience."[33] Many readers identify with the author, narrator, Jesus, and the disciples over against the world and all who oppose God as revealed in Christ. This literary phenomenon provides a mental context for the spiritual work of conversion to faith. Those who come to believe in the glory and power of God that Jesus has revealed in his crucifixion and resurrection are born again into that new creation to live eternally in God's presence and power.

And so in some sense, the written text of the gospel of John itself becomes a sign. Just as people saw the works of Jesus, perceived their significance as signs, and came to faith, readers of the fourth gospel recognize that its documentation of Jesus' life and its significance is itself a sign that calls them to faith.[34]

Going Deeper into the Resurrection as New Creation: John 20

Imagine telling someone who had never heard of Jesus that there was a man who died about two thousand years ago in Jerusalem and that three days later he was resurrected into a transformed body. They might look at you and say, "Wow! That's amazing! He was one lucky dude." One perspective on the resurrection of Jesus is that, even if it happened, it happened to just one person out of the more than a hundred billion who have been born on this earth, and so what? What's *that* got to do with me? The gospel of John teaches that the resurrection of Jesus didn't just happen inexplicably to one lucky, random guy, but that Jesus' resurrection inaugurates a new universe into which those who are reconciled to God will also be resurrected to eternal life. Rather than being a once-in-a-hundred-billion event, it is an event relevant to every living human being. The resurrection of Jesus Christ is the touchstone on which human destiny, both collectively as well as individually, is struck.

In his seminal book *Surprised by Hope: Rethinking Heaven, the Resurrection, and the Mission of the Church*, N. T. Wright points out how the New Testament's teaching on human destiny has been so widely misunderstood.[35] Resurrection "is not an absurd event within the old world but the symbol and starting point of the new world. The claim advanced in Christianity is of that magnitude: Jesus of Nazareth ushers in not simply a new religious possibility, not simply a new ethic or a new way of salvation, but a new creation."[36] And, Wright argues, there is greater continuity between this life on this earth and eternal life after death than most of us have dared imagine.

This is important because what one believes about the future largely determines how one lives today. I used to ask my undergraduate students, "If you knew for sure that Jesus would return before your graduation, would you still come to class?" The question led to some interesting discussions about eschatology, Christian life, and ethics. A hopeless future leads to meaningless lives, but the resurrection of Jesus provides a hope and significance to human life that ushers the coming of the rule and reign of God into life today. The eternal life of the Christian has indeed already begun as Jesus explains (Jn 5:24).

The New Testament teaches that believers pass at death into the presence of the Lord (Lk 23:43; Php 1:23), but the New Testament also indicates that postmortem state is not the eternal destination but a temporary, intermediate state until the resurrection of all at the end of the age (1 Th 4:13–16; Rev 21). And resurrected people need "a new heavens and earth" in which to live that is commensurate with their new bodies—continuous with the earthly person they were yet discontinuous with the mortality and limitations of this physical universe. As we read in Revelation 21—written also by an author named John—the new heaven and earth *comes down from heaven.* John did not see a temple in that place because the Lord God Almighty and the Lamb *are* its temple (Rev 21:22). It is the place where God will dwell among resurrected human beings eternally (Rev 21:3).

The resurrection of his body from death was the proof of principle that human beings can exist in some new state that preserves individuality. Believers will be resurrected in our bodies, albeit transformed—made like him (or he like us), like him we rise. How then should we now live a resurrection life in light of this eternal future in a resurrected body in the new heavens and earth?

In this life the significance of the resurrection appearances of Jesus in John 20 speak to two questions: Where is the Lord, and how can the risen Lord be experienced now?[37] While Jesus was raised bodily—his corpse was absent from the tomb—the resurrection body was not physical as physical is defined in this world. Jesus retained his personal identity that distinguishes him from others—he was not absorbed into some cosmic consciousness or energy, not an impersonal experience of light or beauty. His fully human, resurrected body continues to be the locus of his interactions with others, and therefore allows him to maintain relationships with others.[38] Because of this, Jesus is not merely the founding leader of a religious movement in the way Muhammad or Buddha are thought to be. Although the Christian church has its earthly leaders, Jesus was, is, and will always be the living head of the universal church, which derives its life from him. Although the relationships of Mary Magdalene and Thomas with Jesus had to be radically transformed, they both experienced Jesus alive in his new state of being. He was not just a memory. The resurrection of his full humanity gave them assurance not only of his living presence *now* but also a certain hope of their own transformed state of being after death

The resurrection appearances of John 20 show that the bodily, though not physical, presence of Jesus continues in the midst of his disciples, the Christian church. On two consecutive Sundays he appeared in the midst of the disciples (Jn 20:19, 26), but he is never said to have departed or ascended in John's gospel, the ascent to the Father being understood as concurrent with his death. Faith is no longer grounded in seeing and hearing the earthly Jesus but on receiving the testimony of the apostles he appointed to bear witness to what they saw and heard. One encounters the risen Lord in our day in the midst of his people, the Christian church, with its sacraments, Scripture, and divine love.

JOHN 21

What the Structure Means: The Epilogue (Jn 21)

This final chapter in the gospel of John is most frequently called the "Epilogue" and is believed by many scholars to have been added sometime after the original gospel ended at 20:31, perhaps by the same author or by another. This belief was founded primarily on source criticism, made famously applicable to the fourth gospel by Rudolf Bultmann in the twentieth century. However, subsequent literary studies have defended the idea that the so-called Epilogue has always been an integral part of the gospel of John from its origin, a view that is becoming the dominant view.[1] This understanding is supported by the lack of *any*—zero—manuscript evidence that the gospel ever circulated without the "Epilogue."

Although John 20, especially verse 31, may read like an apt ending for the ministry of Jesus, there are threads in John's gospel that have not been tied up by the end of John 20. John 21 is forward-looking into the time subsequent to the end of the narrative time, the time when the disciples must carry on Jesus' mission without his physical presence, and yet with his real, living presence through the Holy Spirit. This structure is significant for the reader, who also lives in that time outside of the narrative time of John's story of Jesus.

Chapter 21 identifies the person whose written testimony forms the gospel of John, the beloved disciple (Jn 21:24). While we wish we knew more specifically who the beloved disciple was, almost certainly the original readers would have known his name and been familiar with him (see commentary on Jn 21:24). This identification of the disciple who had been with Jesus the last evening of his life, who had probably accompanied

Jesus into his interrogation by the high priest, who had stood at the foot of the cross and had accepted responsibility for Jesus' mother, who had witnessed the empty tomb and the grave cloths, and who first recognized the risen Jesus standing on the beach—this identification accredited the testimony of the beloved disciple as one who knew the truth about Jesus and whose words should be received and believed (Jn 20:31; 21:24).

The apostle Peter, a prominent figure in the fourth gospel, but one whose faith was never truly certain within the narrative and who denied Jesus in his darkest hour, had become a great leader of the early church in the decades following Jesus' death. His reinstatement as a shepherd of the Lord's sheep as described in John 21:15–21 accredited Peter to be worthy of his leadership role. The apostle Peter and the beloved disciple—as a shepherd of the church and as witness to the truth of the gospel, respectively—are accredited for their respective roles by connecting each of them to the direct will of the risen Jesus, establishing the primary leaders of the early church as it moved forward to continue the mission of Jesus.

For the original readers of the fourth gospel, the focus on the relationship between the beloved disciple and the apostle Peter comes to its head in chapter 21, pointing "strongly toward a concern for unity both among Johannine Christians and between them and other believers," such as those in churches shepherded by Peter.[2] But because Jesus emphasized the unity of his followers as an important witness to his mission (Jn 17:20–23), the message of chapter 21 is relevant to readers through all generations of time.

Beverly Gaventa has argued cogently that chapters 20 and 21 are dual endings to the story of Jesus that bring closure to the story in two necessary ways by relating each ending differently to the body of the fourth gospel: John 20 completing the story of Jesus' resurrection by taking the reader back to the Prologue, in which the Word who had become flesh was introduced, and John 21 completing the story by referring to events from within the gospel story and speaking of the future as well.[3] Gaventa explains, "It is Jesus' descent from the Father that created the opportunity for narration. A reasonable form of closure in this instance would be for Jesus to return to the Father and leave behind a stable group of followers, and that is the closure John 20 provides. . . . Chapter 21 offers another kind of closure, or perhaps it is anti-closure, one that opens up the futures of Peter and the Beloved Disciple (futures directly connected with Jesus' own will), one in which the community authoritatively asserts the reliability of its traditions, and one that knows that Jesus' story will never close." For "just as the Prologue goes back in time to creation, so the Epilogue previews the future mission of the disciples, symbolized by the miraculous catch of fish, and focuses especially on the different roles that Peter and the Beloved Disciple are to play in it. The time projected by the Epilogue runs to the parousia. Its last words, in v. 23, are Jesus' words 'until I come,' corresponding at the other end of time to the first words of the Prologue: 'In the beginning.'"[4]

Therefore, while it is perhaps correct to consider John 21 an "Epilogue," it is an Epilogue that most likely was included originally to complete the author's purposes.

21:1 *Simon Peter, Thomas . . . Nathanael . . . the sons of Zebedee, and two other disciples.* The number of followers of Jesus at this encounter was seven. The group was a mix of those who would later be known as apostles (Peter and John, son of Zebedee), those of the Twelve, and otherwise anonymous disciples. In other words, these seven (the number of completion) perhaps represent all followers of Jesus.

21:7 *It is the Lord!* True to his role as the ideal witness, it is the beloved disciple who first recognizes the risen Jesus in this encounter. Obviously, the beloved disciple was in the boat with Peter, and 21:1 lists all those who were present. The traditional author, John, was one of the sons of Zebedee mentioned as present. It seems improbable that the eyewitness on whom this gospel is based would be one of two other disciples unnamed in 21:1.

21:9 *A fire of burning coals there with fish on it and some bread.* The specific mention of a charcoal fire calls to mind John 18:18, where Peter stood with the opponents of Jesus warming himself on the night Jesus was arrested. That scene certainly alludes to Peter's three-times denial of even knowing Jesus. Here, Peter is invited to stand among Jesus' disciples and partake of a meal of fish and bread, just prior to being asked three times if he loves Jesus. This scene shows Jesus' will to reinstate Peter specifically as a shepherd of the Lord's flock, a role that all would recognize he in fact held at the time this gospel was written.

Long before this gospel was written, the fish was a multivalent symbol for life and immortality in several ancient near eastern cultures.[5] It is debatable whether the author of the fourth gospel here provided the impetus for the later eucharistic fish symbolism for Jesus. ΙΧΘΥΣ is the Greek word for fish and became an acronym for the phrase "Jesus Christ, Son of God, Savior." By the end of the second century this symbol often designated Christian graves as a sign of the resurrection, especially in Asia Minor, where tradition says the fourth gospel was written. If John intends the breakfast on the beach to have deeper significance, the disciples—including Peter—are being invited to partake of the benefits of Jesus' resurrection as food for their task to continue the mission of Jesus.

21:11 *It was full of large fish, 153.* The specificity of the description of the fish caught in the net, and the explicit point that the net did not tear, have caught interpreter's attention through the centuries. Some interpreters see no further significance than the historical fact that there were actually 153 fish in the net, though it is debatable whether Galilean fishermen counted their catch so accurately. There are other numbers in the fourth gospel that seem to have no further significance than their arithmetic meaning, such as the thirty-eight year illness of the lame man (5:5) or the five thousand miraculously fed by Jesus (6:10) or the five colonnades of the pool (5:2).

But many interpreters throughout church history have seen a deeper significance to the number, even if it was the actual number of fish caught.[6] For throughout the fourth gospel, metaphor and symbolism have been used to reveal the significance of Jesus' actions. In this case, many interpreters consider this fishing expedition blessed by the risen Jesus to be a metaphor for the preaching ministry of the church through which Jesus will "draw" (Gk. *helkō* [ἕλκω]) people to himself. This verb was used in two other places to refer to the Father drawing followers to Jesus (Jn 6:44) and Jesus' prophecy that his crucifixion will draw all people to himself (Jn 12:32). In subsequent Christian tradition the net was understood to be the preaching ministry that drew people into the boat, a metaphorical reference to the church. This understanding is consistent with the immediate context and purpose of John 21 as a preview of the church's future mission to the world through the work of the disciples, especially Peter and the beloved disciple.

So if the numeral 153 has symbolic meaning, what could it be? The number does not occur elsewhere in Scripture, and it is not an obvious reference to anything in the culture of that time. The many various interpretations are ancient and fascinating,[7] but most are based on complex schemes of factoring 153, which is a triangular number,[8] or on converting numbers to Hebrew or Greek letters or vice versa—schemes that are alien to a modern understanding. The number of the name of the beast, 666, in Revelation 13:18 is perhaps the most famous and familiar example for modern readers.

Using triangular numbers, John Emerton proposed one explanation linking the number 153 and the context of John 21:3–11 to Ezekiel 47:10.[9] A numerical allusion to Ezekiel 47 may be supported by another possible allusion to Ezekiel

47:1, where the prophet "saw water coming out from under the threshold of the temple toward the east." The fourth gospel understands Jesus to be the new temple (Jn 2:19–21) from which living water will flow (Jn 7:37–39).

None of the attempts to plumb the meaning of 153 in John 21:11 have brought scholars to a consensus, but the context of John 21 as a preview of the disciples' life after Jesus leaves does suggest more than a purely arithmetic function. In the Synoptics Jesus called his disciples to be fishermen for human souls (Mt 4:19; Mk 1:17). This abundant catch, the untorn net signifying the strength and efficacy of the preached gospel, and Peter's role in drawing the net to the resurrected Jesus all suggest that the episode is an enacted parable of the future ministry of the church.

What the Structure Means: Same Question, Three Times (Jn 21:15–19)

The scene after breakfast shifts from a resurrection appearance to focus on two prominent disciples: first Peter, called here by his given name Simon son of John (21:15–19), and then on the disciple Jesus loved (21:20–24). Peter had failed in his calling to an apostolic role when at the first challenge to his witness he denied even knowing Jesus—three times no less (Jn 18:17, 25, 27). Nevertheless, it was Peter who had accompanied the beloved disciple to the empty tomb, and who still hung out with Jesus' disciples (Jn 21:2). Despite Peter's failure of courage, Jesus willed to reinstate him to the mission for which he had been prepared, the continuation of Jesus' mission in the world. Without directly referring to the denial, which the other disciples probably had not witnessed and of which they may not have been aware, Jesus repeats the question "Do you love me?" three times to allude to Peter's three-times denial. In fact, Jesus asks Peter if he loves him more than the other disciples present do. This comparison may have been intended to draw Peter's attention to the bravado with which he previously had presumptuously shined the spotlight on himself—for instance, his refusal to let Jesus wash his feet (Jn 13:8) and his bold claim that he would lay down his life for Jesus just hours before denying he ever knew Jesus (Jn 13:37).

Much ink has been given to the variation of the verb in the repeated questions. Jesus asks if Peter loves him (Gk. *agapaō* [ἀγαπάω]; 21:15–16) and Peter affirms that he does love Jesus (Gk. *phileō* [φιλέω]; 21:15–17). Finally, in the third repetition of the question, Jesus switches to the same verb used by Peter, *phileō* (φιλέω). Too much has been made of the distinction between these verbs, probably based more on C. S. Lewis' use of the four Greek verbs for love as an organizing principle in *The Four Loves* than on lexical semantics of Hellenistic Greek. The variation between *agapaō* (ἀγαπάω) and *phileō* (φιλέω) is but one of three pairs of lexical alternation in these verses: between verbs for shepherding (*boskō* [βόσκω] in 21:15, 17; *poimainō* [ποιμαίνω] in v. 16) and between the nouns for sheep (*arnion* [ἀρνίον] in 21:15; *probaton* [πρόβατον] in vv. 16, 17).

Jesus has established himself as the Good Shepherd who lays down his life for his sheep (Jn 10:11, 14–15) and that to be in Jesus' flock means that one must follow Jesus as a sheep follows the shepherd (Jn 10:4). The metaphor of Jesus as the Shepherd alludes to King David, who was the Shepherd of Israel (2 Sa 5:2; 24:17; 1 Ch 11:2; 21:17), in accordance with the ancient Near Eastern practice of referring to rulers as shepherds (see 2 Sa 7:7; 1 Ki 22:17; 1 Ch 17:6). The metaphor identifies Jesus as the long-awaited Davidic king who would inherit the promises of the covenant and reestablish God's people (Ps 23:1; Ps 28:9; Isa 40:11; Jer 31:10). But Gary Manning is probably correct that "Jn 21:15–17 should therefore be treated as a resumption of John's shepherd symbolism, not as an allusion to any OT passage."[10]

After the resurrection, Jesus appoints Peter to "shepherd" Jesus' sheep, not through ruling but through pastoral nurture based on Peter's own following of Jesus (Jn 21:19).[11] Peter never saw this role as exclusive to himself (contra the Roman Catholic doctrine of papal succession), for in 1 Peter 5:2 he charges all elders in the church to be "shepherds of God's flock." Jesus is the Good Shepherd of John 10, but he also involves his disciples in shepherding his sheep, the church, and in so doing takes the promises he makes beyond the story of his own life and into the world beyond the narrative.[12]

Jesus understood that Peter's courage had failed in the face of mortal threat on the night Jesus was arrested. He reinstates Peter (see commentary at 1:40) but warns him that to accept his apostolic role means eventual martyrdom by the same method of execution Jesus suffered (Jn 21:18–19). Although Peter would live to be an old man, his love for and loyalty to Jesus would again be tested. Having fully informed Peter of the cost, the Lord charges him to nevertheless, "Follow me!" And, as they say, the rest is history.

21:21 *Lord, what about him?* Peter's question is a less-than-reassuring response to his reinstatement, for he immediately wants to know what Jesus has to say about the beloved disciple. But readers already knew that Peter had risen to apostolic prominence as he shepherded the church for the rest of his life. This is how the gospel of John extends the story of Jesus into the life of the church far beyond that day of breakfast on the beach. The reader is made aware of Peter's past failures, and yet of his reinstatement by Jesus himself. This is an encouragement to all, especially church leaders, who have in their various ways denied the Lord. Grace and mercy exceed the sin of denial. It is never too late to follow Jesus.

21:22 *What is that to you?* Peter is roundly told to mind his own business. It is of no importance what other disciples do or do not do; the perennial command is to follow Jesus.

Going Deeper into Following Jesus: John 21:20–23

"Lord, what about him?" I have no idea if John intended this to be humorous, but I find it amusing that, after being reconciled in his relationship with Jesus and appointed to shepherd Jesus' followers, Peter's first words were to get into another person's business. There is an implicit comparison intended in the information Peter seeks. How does his relationship with Jesus stack up against Jesus' relationship with the beloved disciple? How like human nature! We all seem interested in the question, "But what about him?" Jesus was quick to nip the direction of Peter's thoughts in the bud. "What is that to you?" (Jn 21:23) is a rebuke that tells Peter to mind his own business. And his business was to follow Jesus (Jn 21:22) regardless: "*You* must follow me" (with the emphatic Greek singular pronoun *su*; σύ, "you") emphasizing Peter's charge in contrast to that of others. Peter apparently got the point, for many years later he instructs his own readers in 1 Peter 4:15 not to meddle in the business of others.

In the immediate context of the prediction that Peter would meet martyrdom as an old man, Peter was probably wondering whether a similar fate awaited the disciple whom Jesus loved and within what timeframe. He was no doubt trying to evaluate his own worth in comparison to that of the beloved disciple. But that is none of a sheep's business whose only charge is to follow the Good Shepherd. Jesus makes it clear that his will for this other disciple had nothing to do with Peter's relationship to Jesus. Peter was simply to keep his eyes on Jesus and to follow.

Throughout the Christian life, most of us probably ask, "Lord, what about him?" many times in various ways. "Lord, why does so-and-so live on the edge and seem to suffer nothing bad for it?" "Lord, why did so-and-so live such a long life and my parent/spouse/child get cancer at such a young age?" "Lord, why did this have to happen to *me*?" "Lord, aren't I a better Christian than *she* is?" In fact, social scientists theorize that "the desire to learn about the self through comparison with others is a universal characteristic of humans" though the frequency and extent varies from person to person.[13] Therapists suggest that habitual comparison of oneself with others is a quick path into disillusionment and depression. Even comparing our older selves to our younger selves can at times be discouraging. Since comparison is often automatic and subconscious, such questions may not surface to our consciousness, but it is hard to go through life without some sense of comparison, some sense of questioning our relationship with God based on our observation of others.

Pastors and other church leaders may be especially susceptible to wondering about God's blessing on their ministry when compared to other churches with larger congregations, bigger budgets, more staff, and expansive square footage. Although most of us know that size is no indicator of God's favor or a ministry's effectiveness, the "what about him, Lord?" question is almost unavoidable, at least below the surface. Is God blessing us as much as he "should" in comparison to others? That line of questioning is theologically unsound and psychologically damaging.

Comparing oneself to others, though a common way of evaluating our own worth (especially with the help of social media), is a poor basis for self-worth. Most often comparison with others leads to a loss of joy, a lack of appreciation for who we are in the unique life God has given us, and a distraction from our own values and goals when the grass looks greener elsewhere. For Christians, putting our eyes on Jesus and following him through thick and thin in all the circumstances of life for all the years of one's life is the Lord's overarching will for us. We are to keep our eyes on the Shepherd, not on other sheep. And so what other sheep are doing or where they are going should be irrelevant to us.

Peter and the beloved disciple—whether he was John the son of Zebedee or another man—were two great apostles of the early Christian church. And yet as the fourth gospel tells it, they were quite different from one another, had different gifts and abilities, different roles in the Lord's work, and different destinies in life. There may have been an element of competition between them. The worth of Peter could not be measured by comparison to the perceived worth of the beloved disciple, or vice versa.

Sheep are not all the same, but they are called to unity in the flock when they all follow the same Good Shepherd.

21:23 *The rumor spread.* The risen Son of God could without doubt sustain someone in this life until he returns. Of course, that rumor would have been more plausible were the Lord's return expected within a normal lifespan of that time, and this verse is sometimes offered as evidence that the earliest Christians did indeed expect the Lord's return in their lifetimes. (Although the fourth gospel is known for its realized eschatology, this is a notable reference to the future parousia of the Lord.) This correction of the rumor based on an erroneous understanding of what Jesus had said and meant would be acutely relevant if the beloved disciple had in fact died, and that is often an inference drawn from it. But the remaining verses with the shift to the first-person singular leaves the impression that the beloved disciple may have still been alive at the time the fourth gospel was written, perhaps as a very elderly man.

21:24 *This is the disciple who testifies to these things and who wrote them down.* The author here wishes to reveal something of the identity of the one who has borne witness to Jesus in his life, ministry, death, and resurrection. The antecedent of the demonstrative pronoun "this" (Gk. *houtos* [οὗτος]) is found in 21:23, which in turn finds its antecedent in 21:20: "the disciple whom Jesus loved." First introduced in 13:23 as the disciple who was sitting closest to Jesus at the Last Supper, he appears in six verses but is never explicitly identified in the fourth gospel (Jn 13:23; 19:26; 20:2; 21:7, 20, 24) (see commentary on 21:25). In the extensive scholarly discussion of his identity, he is conventionally referred to as "the beloved disciple" though this is a paraphrase of the fuller subordinate phrase "the disciple, the one whom Jesus loved," found in the Greek. "It is now generally agreed that the Beloved Disciple was a real historical person who has representative, paradigmatic, or symbolic significance in John."[14]

The beloved disciple is vitally important to the gospel of John and its reception because it is on his testimony that the story of Jesus ("these things") is based, and it is he who originally wrote (or caused to have written) the story that we have as the gospel of John. This raises the question about this third-person self-reference. While it was not unusual for an ancient author to refer to himself in the third person (see commentary on 21:25), it does seem a bit odd that he would claim such a place in Jesus' affections. The form of the relative clause ("whom Jesus loved") seems more plausibly added posthumously by a later editor to replace the author's original third-person self-references, and so this honorific title may not have been the author's own choice.

Furthermore, in chapters 13–21, the beloved disciple is consistently presented in contrast to the apostle Peter, who by the time this gospel was written had come to pastoral prominence shepherding the church and probably giving Rome its initial claim to ecclesiastical authority. But the disciple whom Jesus loved takes precedence over Peter in the fourth gospel. This may be driven by a tension between the Johannine churches and the Great Church centered at Rome at the time this gospel was written, perhaps a tension not unlike that mentioned in 1 Corinthians 1:12, where some follow Paul, others Apollos, and yet others Cephas (i.e., Peter). But it is probably an exaggeration to project such conflict back several decades into the personal lives of Peter and John during their time with Jesus. Along with James, who was martyred decades before the fourth gospel was likely written, these three formed Jesus' inner circle of close friends who were present at all the key events of Jesus' ministry. Whatever tensions and conflicts developed among their later disciples does not imply conflict between them. If, however, the apostle John did author the fourth gospel, then his portrayal of his relationship with Peter takes on greater value for understanding their interpersonal dynamic.[15]

Despite Peter's prominence in the first-century church, he did not himself pen a gospel that bears his name, though of course tradition claims that Mark's gospel is based on Peter's memories. Richard Bauckham is probably right that "the disciple whom Jesus loved" is not to be read as an idealized *disciple* of Jesus, but an idealized *witness* who was present even at those times and places where Peter was not but which are essential to the story of Jesus, such as at Jesus' trial (assuming he was the "other disciple" in 18:15), at the crucifixion (19:26), and at the empty tomb (20:2).[16] The intent of the fourth gospel "is not to denigrate Peter but to show him as the disciple who through failure and grace is enabled by Jesus to become the chief pastor of the church."[17] The disciple whom Jesus loved is given precedence in those respects that make him a superior *witness* to key events in Jesus' life and ministry, and therefore an ideal authority for writing a gospel. Bauckham sees both Peter and the disciple whom Jesus loved as representing "two different kinds of discipleship: active service and perceptive witness"[18] (cf. Jn 5:31). But the fourth gospel was likely written after Peter's death, and may have been a means of transferring his ecclesiastical authority to another surviving eyewitness of Jesus' life, death, and resurrection—the beloved disciple.[19]

This is the disciple who testifies . . . and who wrote. The antecedent of "this" goes back to 21:20, when Peter saw the disciple whom Jesus loved following. The beloved disciple is contrasted with Peter but given priority concerning the story of Jesus that as an eyewitness he has preserved, or caused to be preserved, in writing.[20]

We know that his testimony is true. The author makes here the claim that what he has written is to be understood as testimony (*martyria* [μαρτυρία]). Kevin Vanhoozer argues the point that "testimony is as reliable a means of knowing as perception and memory. Indeed, testimony makes the past and present perceptions of others available to those who could or did not perceive for themselves" (cf. Jn 20:31).[21] Because of the nature of human communication, a hermeneutic of suspicion is not the first stance one should take when reading testimony. A witness must be presumed a credible source of truth until proven otherwise. The author probably uses an associative "we" here, drawing his (ideal) readers into the embrace of his testimony and acceptance of its truth about Jesus Christ. The reader is therefore put on the spot by the demand to decide whether the beloved disciple is a credible witness and whether they will accept or reject Jesus Christ. It is powerful evangelistic rhetoric.

21:25 *Jesus did many other things as well.* A similar statement is found in John 20:30, but with some important difference. There Jesus "performed many other signs in the presence of his disciples," summarizing the earthly ministry of Jesus that has been told in the framework of "signs" in chapters 2–12. Here Jesus "did many other things," a more general reference that embraces the postresurrection setting of John 21 and, perhaps, even beyond. The reader is invited to think of what things Jesus has promised to those who follow him. He is still doing things today.

I suppose. This is a startling statement, not just because it provokes the imagination to think of the many other things Jesus did that are unknown to us, but because here, and only here, does the author speak directly to his readers in the first-person verb "I suppose" (Gk. *oimai* [οἶμαι]). First-person verbs and pronouns occur hundreds of times in the fourth gospel, most often on the lips of Jesus (e.g., the "I am" statements) but also in the mouths of several characters, such as the Samaritan woman (Jn 4) and the man born blind but given sight by Jesus (Jn 9). In contrast, the authorial self-references are narrated in third person through the voice of the narrator. This is likely because a first-person reference disrupts the past timeframe of the narrative by making "the reader/hearer aware of him as the one now telling the story, and so the character in the story is at the same time acting in the narrative and addressing the reader/hearer."[22] In 19:35 the author partially steps into the world of the reader using a third-person self-reference "the man who . . ." and the second-person plural, "you" (*humeis* [ὑμεῖς]): "*The man* who saw it has given testimony, and his testimony is true. He knows that he tells the truth, and he testifies so that *you* [second-person plural, i.e., the readers] also may believe." But here in this final statement of the fourth gospel, the author fully steps out from behind the narrator, not to call attention to himself, but to testify to the other manifold words and actions of Jesus, bringing them into the present where the reader is called to faith.

The author's use of an anonymous, third-person self-reference in ancient historiography is well attested. It allows the author to focus the reader's attention on the role played in the events being narrated, which are perceived as being of greater import than the author himself. It signals a distinction between biography (first-person) and reported historiography (third-person).[23] In anticipation of the climatic reveal in 21:24 that the beloved disciple's own testimony is the eyewitness basis for this story of Jesus, his role is marked out by the unusual moniker used to refer to him within the story. Had his personal name been used in third person (for instance, "John"), he would have just blended into the group of named disciples without distinction. But one of the main points of the fourth gospel is to establish the gospel on the eyewitness authority of the beloved disciple, and especially in comparison to Peter's role. As Edward Klink points out, "In short, anonymity allows the Beloved Disciple to function as both a character within the narrative and an 'agent' over it—a witness in the fullest sense."[24]

The sudden switch to the first-person "I" is also understandable as an ancient convention, when authors would sometimes narrate their stories in the third person and then switch to first person, as we see here, to authenticate an epistolary postscript. Here the authentication invites others who have not seen what the beloved disciple has seen nevertheless to still believe on the basis of his testimony.[25] As Bauckham notes, "The basis of the Gospel in eyewitness testimony is already indicated in the Prologue, but in such a way that empirical observation and theological perception are inextricable. It is the testimony of those who saw the glory of God in the flesh of Jesus Christ, as *neither* Jesus' unbelieving contemporaries *nor* later Christian believers did."[26]

The whole world would not have room for the books that would be written. This is striking hyperbole—or is it hyperbole? If the truth be known about what the risen Jesus Christ has done in every age and every part of the world, one could imagine that the world's bookshelves and libraries could not contain the pages that could be written. The beloved disciple may have been referring to just the time of Jesus' activity of which he was aware, but his statement extends the mission of Jesus beyond the time and understanding of the beloved disciple into the world of each reader, calling us to embrace the story of Jesus' mission today.

The Johannine Jesus Through Old Testament Eyes

It is not an overstatement or hyperbole to claim that Jesus' identity and role cannot be rightly understood apart from the interpretive context of

Israel's Scriptures. The texts and the traditions of Israel are thoroughly woven throughout John's telling of the story of Jesus, and those extensive associations could not have been understood as they relate to Jesus until after he rose from the dead (see Jn 2:22). This is what Richard Hays refers to as "reading backwards"—of reading the Old Testament "in light of a new revelation imparted *by* Jesus and focused *on* the person of Jesus himself."[27] While historical-grammatical exegesis seeks to read the texts of the Hebrew Bible within their original historical context in order to understand what God was saying at that moment, the resurrection of Jesus Christ is a hermeneutical lens through which the Hebrew Bible must be reread in light of what God has revealed in Christ.

In his understanding of Jesus' life and death, John shares with the other Gospels the identification of Jesus as the Messiah, the Christ, the Davidic King, the Son of God, and Son of Man, all of which have strong associations with the Old Testament and must be understood within that context. To avoid making this section a summary of New Testament Christology, it will focus on those categories unique to or distinctive of the fourth gospel that find their significance in the Scriptures of Israel. For the same reason, only the "I am" statements with a personal predicate will be discussed here, though each of them has deep connections with the Old Testament (but see the commentary for a discussion of each of them *in situ*).

The Word become flesh (Jn 1:14). Perhaps the most famous statement of the gospel of John with respect to Jesus is its very first sentence that "in the beginning was the Word, and the Word was with God, and the Word was God" (Jn 1:1). After explaining the Word as the agent of creation, apart from whom "nothing was made that has been made" (Jn 1:3), John makes the incredible claim that "the Word became flesh and dwelt among us" (Jn 1:14), identifying the enfleshed word with the man Jesus.

The two (Greek) words "in the beginning" (Gk. *en archē* [ἐν ἀρχῇ]) form a direct allusion to Genesis 1:1, where the same words are found (Heb. *bərēʾšît* [בְּרֵאשִׁית]; LXX, *en archē* [ἐν ἀρχῇ]) in the same opening position of that book. Furthermore, the topic of creation in John 1:1–3 joins the Word to the Genesis account, the first book of the Hebrew Scriptures. The author himself invites us to read Jesus' story in engagement with Israel's Scriptures. Furthermore, John presents Jesus' power to create through the first miraculous "sign": the changing of water into wine.

But where was the Word at creation? For the word "word" (Heb. *dabar* [דָּבָר]) is not found in the creation account. Instead we see God *speaking* the universe into existence ("And God said . . . and there was"; Ge 1:3, 6, 9, 11, 14, 20, 24, 26), *naming* creation (Ge 1:5, 8, 10), and *blessing* the living creatures (Ge 1:22, 28). All of these verbal actions—speaking, naming, and blessing—involve words, God's words. A person's words are a unique, intimate expression of the person's thoughts, will, intents, purposes, and yet are distinguishable from the person. The Word that was with the God of Genesis in the beginning is the closest thing to God that could be distinguished from God's person. It was through God's spoken Word that the universe came into being, avoiding implications that attend creation stories from other ancient cultures. For instance, pantheism is avoided because the universe was not made from a body part of any divine being, such as is common in other creation stories. The Word was neither a created being nor part of the created order (contra the later heresy of Arianism), but stood apart from creation in a most profound unanimity with God the Father.

But with the embodiment of that divine Word, the issue of monotheism, the hallmark of Israel's religion, is brought sharply into play within John's story of Jesus. With this identification of the Word with God, and yet distinguishable from God, John begins his defense of monotheism: the existence of both Jesus Christ and God the Father does not constitute two Gods. John will further explicate the relationship between Jesus Christ and the Father throughout the fourth gospel in defense of and in transformation of Israel's monotheism.

John's gospel alone refers to Jesus Christ as the Word, and that only in the Prologue. Of all the things said about Jesus in the New Testament, identifying him as the Word who was in the beginning with God and who was God is certainly the most incredible and the "highest" of the christological claims made in the New Testament. It necessarily implies the eternal preexistence and divine power of the being who descended to humanity from the Father through human birth (though John does not speak of the nativity), and who will ascend back to the Father through human death.

Lamb of God (Jn 1:29, 36). The concept that Jesus is the Lamb of God was probably already a part of Christian tradition when John wrote this gospel, assuming as most scholars do that Paul's letter of 1 Corinthians is earlier than the fourth gospel. For in 1 Corinthians 5:7, Paul refers to

"Christ, our Passover lamb." The association of Jesus with a sacrificial lamb most likely developed from an early identification of Jesus with the Suffering Servant of Isaiah 53, especially 53:7, "he was led like a lamb to the slaughter, and as a sheep before its shearers is silent, so he did not open his mouth."

Although John uses the more general phrase "Lamb of God" when he introduces Jesus (Jn 1:29, 36), he frames the life of Jesus and especially his death in terms of Passover. Jesus makes his first appearance at the temple in Jerusalem at Passover (Jn 2:13, 23), where he announces himself as the new and true temple (Jn 2:21). He drove the sacrificial animals from the temple because he, the true Lamb of God, had appeared. The miraculous feeding of the five thousand was about the time of Passover (Jn 6:4) and recalls the provision of manna in the wilderness during the exodus. As that bread sustained Israel's life, Jesus offers his own body as the sustenance of eternal life (6:35, 48). Most significantly, Jesus' last days of earthly life were lived during the week before Passover (Jn 12:1) and the "hour" that culminates his life coincided with the Passover rituals. John's chronology of Jesus' passion is distinctive for locating the crucifixion on the same day that the Passover lambs were being slaughtered (Jn 18:28). And so while John does not use the title "Passover Lamb" of Jesus, he interprets Jesus' ministry and death through the framework of that most important of Israel's feasts.

True temple (Jn 2:13–22). The temple of Jerusalem was the center of Israel's religion throughout its history. It was the place were heaven and earth met, with the Holy of Holies representing the footstool on earth of God's throne in heaven. It was the place where God had put his name and where he was to be worshiped (cf. Jn 4:19–24). It was the location where the priesthood functioned in accordance with God's law, offering the sacrifice of animals for the sins of the people. It was the place where the high holy prayers were offered on behalf of all Israel.

But Jesus announced himself to be the new temple, though only after his death did his disciples understand the claim. In the fourth gospel, "Jesus now takes over the temple's function as a place of mediation between God and human beings."[28] John presents Jesus as the place where God truly dwells among people (Jn 1:14) and as the full and final sacrifice for sin (Jn 3:14–18). As the new temple, John shows that Jesus is the source of the abundant living water that Ezekiel envisioned would flow from the temple threshold (Eze 47:1–2), a vision that was reenacted each year at the Festival of Tabernacles. Against the backdrop of the water and illumination rituals of Tabernacles at the Jerusalem temple, Jesus proclaimed himself to be the source of living water (Jn 7:37–39) that would flow from the temple of his body. John explained that the living water was a metaphor for the Holy Spirit, who would flow from the death of Jesus' body to be present in the world in a new way.

The Good Shepherd (Jn 10:1–18). Before John 10 was written, the idea of a shepherd over God's people was a political thought that alluded to the renewal of the Davidic kingship. Ezekiel (34:23–24) speaks of God appointing over his people one shepherd, David, who will feed them and be a prince among them. In the pre-Christian ancient Near East the shepherd was a metaphor for a ruler, and so when Jesus announces himself as the Good Shepherd (Jn 10:11, 14) and then attends the Festival of Dedication (Hanukah) in Jerusalem (10:22), the question of whether he is the Messiah would be natural (10:24). Hanukah celebrates a miracle that occurred about two centuries earlier, when the Maccabees reclaimed the temple from the Seleucids and rededicated it. It was a feast that raised high nationalistic hopes for the reclamation of Jerusalem from under Roman rule. John includes the detail that Jesus was walking in Solomon's Colonnade, a structure that commemorated the Davidic king who had brought ancient Israel to its peak of national glory. Given this Old Testament and political background, when Jesus identified himself as the Good Shepherd who would lay down his life for the sheep (Jn 10:11) it *was* a claim to be a new Davidic king, the Messiah. For the people of Jerusalem it would inevitably evoke messianic hopes of a political nature. But Jesus' kingship exceeded the geopolitical hopes of first-century Jerusalem, and it is in the context of Hanukah that he presses the point that he is not just the son of David, but the Son of God.

Jesus is presented in similar terms in the other Gospels and throughout the New Testament, but the gospel of John most clearly presses the point of Jesus' divinity, making the issue of monotheism most acute. The Old Testament categories used as metaphors and images for the identity of Jesus make the point that Jesus Christ, the incarnate Son of God, speaks and works in complete concert with God the Father, for he came to reveal the unseen God (Jn 1:18). Whoever has seen Jesus has seen the Father, for they mutually indwell (Jn 14:8–11). John's presentation of the relationship between Jesus Christ and God the Father is more fully developed than is the relationship of the Holy Spirit with Christ and the Father. But there are not two (or three) Gods; John presents a threefold concept of monotheism, three persons of the *one* Godhead. The fourth gospel is the epitome of the beloved disciple's divinely inspired creative genius.

Going Deeper into the Difference the Old Testament Makes

One of the central principles of the New Testament writers is that Israel's Scriptures are, in some sense, about Jesus. In the gospel of John Jesus himself expressed this principle when he says to the Jewish leaders of Jerusalem, "You study the Scriptures diligently because you think that in them you have eternal life. These are the very Scriptures that testify about me" (Jn 5:39); and, "If you believed Moses, you would believe me, for he wrote about me" (Jn 5:46). Therefore, the Old Testament makes all the difference in understanding who Jesus is.

And yet, paradoxically, the call to belief in the fourth gospel can be clearly understood by even those who have no knowledge of the Old Testament. As a college student I made a commitment to Christ after reading the gospel of John but at that time had virtually no knowledge of the Old Testament, except for some of its well-known characters. As I mentioned in the preface to this commentary, when I read John 2, where Jesus changes water to wine, I had no knowledge of the rich background that the Old Testament imagery of wine and vineyard provide, or their association with the messianic age. But I did know from the organic chemistry class I had recently taken that changing H_2O to wine involved at least the introduction of carbon and a rearrangement of the molecular structure of the liquid in those stone water pots. I recognized that Jesus was performing the work of God, and that drew me to faith in him for eternal life.

The beloved disciple expresses a mind saturated with the metaphors, imagery, and theology of Israel's Scriptures, and he employed them with a creative genius that makes the fourth gospel a remarkable piece of literature to this day. The more deeply we know the books of the Old Testament in their historical context and their place in redemptive history, the more delight and irony we will find in the story of Jesus as the beloved disciple uniquely presents it.

The Scriptures of Israel are woven throughout the gospel of John, though with a technique different from the other Gospels. Richard Hays counts twenty-seven quotations and direct allusions in the gospel of John, a relative paucity compared to Matthew with 124, Luke with 109, and

Mark with 70.[29] The Psalms are heavily represented in John's gospel, with more than 60 percent of its quotations coming from its verses, especially those that express the suffering and exaltation of Jesus.[30] Even John's manner of alluding to the Old Testament texts is not heavily dependent on extensive, explicit lexical links. For example, the allusion to Genesis 1 in John 1:1 consists of only two Greek words (*en archē* [ἐν ἀρχῇ]) and depends instead on the same positioning of those words in both Genesis 1:1 and John 1:1. A very significant allusion to Isaiah 52:13 LXX is created by simply one word, *hupsōthēsetai* (ὑψωθήσεται, "will be lifted up"). The fourth gospel exploits the double meaning of that word, both exaltation and physical lifting, to make the major theological point that Jesus' crucifixion *was* his exaltation, for it was the perfect accomplishment of his incarnational mission in which God's love for humanity was most clearly revealed.

Instead of quotations and direct allusions to the texts of the Old Testament, the beloved disciple employs images, metaphors, and the traditions of Israel that originated in the Hebrew Bible, especially those of the temple and the feasts. Using these images and metaphors John paints a narrative portrait of Jesus "analogous to the visual artistry of Rembrandt's portraits" that reward sustained meditation[31] (see "John's Use of the Old Testament: Verbal Artistry" in the introduction). The replacement of the Jerusalem temple by Jesus' own body, the sustenance of manna replaced by Jesus' flesh, the self-sacrifice of the Good Shepherd King who leads his sheep in paths of righteousness as they follow Jesus, and the vine sustaining life to its branches are but a few of the gripping images that are fueled by the Old Testament. The major point in all of John's use of Israel's Scripture in his various techniques is that all the prophecy and promise of the old covenant has been fulfilled in Jesus Christ and his establishment of the Christian church.

While a reader such as myself can come to faith through the gospel of John without reference to the Old Testament, it remains true, as Hays puts it that "John . . . simply and steadily presupposes the law of Moses and the words of Israel's Scripture as the essential hermeneutical matrix for recognizing and understanding Jesus' testimony."[32] Reading the gospel of John through Old Testament eyes makes all the difference.

ACKNOWLEDGMENTS

Perhaps "it takes a village to raise a child," but the same could be said about writing a book. I gratefully acknowledge that this commentary is the result of the work or influence of many. I am grateful to Andy Le Peau, the series editor of Through Old Testament Eyes for inviting me to contribute a volume to the commentary series. How propitious to have an editor who published *Write Better: A Lifelong Editor on Craft, Art, and Spirituality* (IVP, 2019). His counsel and suggestions have made this a better commentary than it otherwise would have been.

I also acknowledge with appreciation the anonymous (to me) peer reviewer whose questions and comments helped me to sharpen and improve the content of this commentary at many points.

I thank the folks at Kregel who have supported this project, especially Laura Bartlett, Shawn Vander Lugt, Robert Hand, Jeff Reimer, and perhaps others unknown to me whose work has shepherded this book to print.

The writing of a book involves the reading of many others, and I have enjoyed the resources of the libraries at Wheaton College, Westminster Theological Seminary, Princeton Theological Seminary, and Oreland Evangelical Presbyterian Church. I thank the librarians who have supported my requests for materials and assistance, especially Greg Morrison at Wheaton College's Buswell Library. I gratefully recognize the benefits I enjoy as the Gerald F. Hawthorne Professor Emerita of New Testament Greek and Exegesis (Wheaton College) which have expedited access to needed resources. Thank you to my Wheaton colleague Dr. Dan Treier for checking a citation in Buswell Library on my behalf.

My first academic course on the fourth gospel was under the teaching of Professor Moisés Silva, Westminster Theological Seminary, in Spring 1991, who later supervised my doctoral dissertation (though not on the gospel of John). I still recall many of his insights that deepened my understanding of and love for John's gospel. To him I dedicate this commentary with gratitude for his influence in my life as professor, colleague, mentor, and friend these many years.

I fondly remember the students I taught at Westmont College and at Wheaton Graduate School, whose probing questions and shared insights have enriched my understanding of this gospel, pushing me to new inquiries. My former Westmont student Dr. Ben Reynolds (Tyndale University) is now himself a Johannine scholar, and this commentary enjoys benefits from his published work and from conversations with him.

And finally my love and appreciation to Roland and Susan (Ellis) Wills, friends from my teenage years, who first invited me to read the newly published tract of the *New International Version* gospel of John as they shared with me their newfound faith in Jesus Christ. Their witness those many years ago changed my life.

My husband, Dr. Forrest (Buzz) Jobes, has been, as always, exemplary of Ephesians 5:25 in support of my work, for which I am grateful.

I thank all who have made this commentary a better work than it would have otherwise been, but its deficiencies remain mine alone.

Soli Deo gloria!

LIST OF TABLES

LIST OF WHAT THE STRUCTURE MEANS

LIST OF THROUGH OLD TESTAMENT EYES

LIST OF GOING DEEPER

ABBREVIATIONS

1 Mc	1 Maccabees
2 Mc	2 Maccabees
4 Mc	4 Maccabees
AB	Anchor Bible Commentary
Alex.	Plutarch, *Life of Alexander the Great*. Translated by John Dryden. New York: Modern Library, 2004.
Ant.	Josephus, *Antiquities of the Jews*. Translated by William Whiston. Lynn, MA: Hendrickson, 1980.
BECNT	Baker Exegetical Commentary on the New Testament
CBQ	*Catholic Biblical Quarterly*
EvQ	*Evangelical Quarterly*
FAT	Forschungen zum Alten Testament
Gk.	Greek
Haer.	Irenaeus, *Against Heresies*. Translated by Alexander Roberts and William Hautenville Rambaut. *Ante-Nicene Fathers* 1. Edinburgh: T&T Clark, 1885.
Heb.	Hebrew
Hist. eccl.	Eusebius, *Ecclesiastical History*. Loeb Classical Library. Translated by Kirsopp Lake and J. E. L. Oulton. 2 vols. Cambridge, MA: Harvard University Press, 1926–1932.

JBL	*Journal of Biblical Literature*
JETS	*Journal of the Evangelical Theological Society*
JSNTSup	Journal for the Study of the New Testament Supplement Series
JTS	*Journal of Theological Studies*
KJV	King James Version
LXX	Septuagint
NICNT	New International Commentary on the New Testament
NIDNTTE	*New International Dictionary of New Testament Theology and Exegesis.* Edited by Moisés Silva. Rev. ed. Grand Rapids: Zondervan 2014.
NIV	New International Version of the Holy Bible
NTL	New Testament Library commentary series
PNTC	Pillar New Testament Commentary
RelStB	*Religious Studies Bulletin*
SBLDS	Society of Biblical Literature Dissertation Series
SNTSMS	Society of New Testament Studies Monograph Series
s.v.	*sub verbis* (under the word)
WBC	Word Bible Commentary
ZECNT	Zondervan Exegetical Commentary on the New Testament
ZNW	*Zeitschrift für die Neutestamentliche Wissenschaft*

SELECT BIBLIOGRAPHY

Attridge, Harold E. *Essays on John and Hebrews*. Tübingen: Mohr Siebeck, 2010.

Bailey, Kenneth E. *The Good Shepherd: A Thousand-Year Journey from Psalm 23 to the New Testament*. Downers Grove, IL: IVP Academic, 2014.

Bauckham, Richard. *Gospel of Glory: Major Themes in Johannine Theology*. Grand Rapids: Baker Academic, 2015.

_____. *Jesus and the God of Israel: God Crucified and Other Studies on the New Testament's Christology of Divine Identity*. Grand Rapids: Eerdmans, 2009.

_____. "The Fourth Gospel as the Testimony of the Beloved Disciple." In *The Gospel of John and Christian Theology*, edited by Richard Bauckham and Carl Mosser, 120–39. Grand Rapids: Eerdmans, 2008.

_____. *The Testimony of the Beloved Disciple: Narrative, History, and Theology in the Gospel of John*. Grand Rapids: Baker Academic, 2007.

_____. "The 153 Fish and the Unity of the Fourth Gospel." *Neotestamentica* 36 nos. 1–2 (2002): 77–88.

_____. *God Crucified: Monotheism and Christology in the New Testament*. Grand Rapids: Eerdmans, 1999.

_____. "The Throne of God and the Worship of Jesus." In *The Jewish Roots of Christological Monotheism: Papers from the St. Andrews Conference on the Historical Origins of the Worship of Jesus*, edited by Carey C. Newman, James R. Davila, and Gladys S. Lewis, 43–69. Leiden: Brill, 1999.

_____. "Jesus' Demonstration in the Temple." In *Law and Religion: Essays on the Place of the Law in Israel and Early Christianity*, edited by Barnabas Lindars, 72–89. Cambridge: James Clarke, 1988.

Bauckham, Richard, and Carl Mosser, eds. *The Gospel of John and Christian Theology*. Grand Rapids: Eerdmans, 2008.

Beale, G. K. *We Become What We Worship: A Biblical Theology of Idolatry.* Downers Grove, IL: IVP Academic, 2008.

Beasley-Murray, George R. *John.* WBC 36. Waco, TX: Word, 1987.

Beutler, Johannes, "Resurrection and the Forgiveness of Sins: John 20:23 against Its Traditional Background." In *The Resurrection of Jesus in the Gospel of John*, edited by Craig K. Koester and Reimund Bieringer, 237–51. Tübingen: Mohr Siebeck, 2008.

Beutler, Johannes, and Robert T. Fortna. *The Shepherd Discourse of John 10 and Its Context.* Cambridge: Cambridge University Press, 1991.

Blomberg, Craig L. *The Historical Reliability of John's Gospel: Issues and Commentary.* Downers Grove, IL: InterVarsity Press, 2001.

Boyarin, Daniel. "Logos, a Jewish Word: John's Prologue as Midrash." In *The Jewish Annotated New Testament*, edited by Amy-Jill Levine and Marc Zvi Brettler, 688–91. 2nd ed. Oxford: Oxford University Press, 2011.

Brown, Jeannine K. *The Gospels as Stories. A Narrative Approach to Matthew, Mark, Luke, and John.* Grand Rapids: Baker Academic, 2020.

––––––. "Creation's Renewal in the Gospel of John." *CBQ* 72 (2010): 275–90.

Brown, Raymond E. *The Gospel according to John I–XII.* AB 29. Garden City, NY: Doubleday, 1966.

Bruce, F. F. *The Gospel of John: Introduction, Exposition and Notes.* Grand Rapids: Eerdmans, 1983.

Buch-Hansen, Gitte. *"It Is the Spirit That Gives Life": A Stoic Understanding of Pneuma in John's Gospel.* Berlin: de Gruyter, 2010.

Cahill, P. Joseph. "Narrative Art in John IV." *RelStB* 2 (1982): 41–47.

Calvin, John. *The Gospel according to St. John 1–10.* Translated by T. H. L. Parker. Edited by David W. Torrance and Thomas F. Torrance. Grand Rapids: Eerdmans, 1959.

––––––. *John.* Crossway Classic Commentaries. Wheaton, IL: Crossway, 1994.

Carson, D. A. "John and the Johannine Epistles." In *It Is Written: Scripture Citing Scripture; Essays in Honour of Barnabas Lindars*, edited by D. A. Carson and H.G.M. Williamson, 245–64. Cambridge: Cambridge University Press, 1988.

––––––. *The Gospel according to John.* PNTC. Grand Rapids: Eerdmans, 1991.

Charlesworth, James H. *Jesus as Mirrored in John: The Genius in the New Testament.* London: T&T Clark, 2019.

––––––. *The Beloved Disciple: Whose Witness Validates the Gospel of John?* Valley Forge, PA: Trinity Press International, 1995.

––––––. "The Dead Sea Scrolls and the Gospel According to John." In *Exploring the Gospel of John in Honor of D. Moody Smith.* edited by R. Alan Culpepper and C. Clifton Black, 65–97. Louisville: Westminster John Knox, 1996.

Chennattu, Rekha M. "Scripture." In *How John Works: Storytelling in the Fourth Gospel*, edited by Douglas Estes and Ruth Sheridan, 171–86. Resources for Biblical Study 86. Atlanta: SBL Press, 2016.

Coloe, Mary L. "Witness and Friend: Symbolism Associated with John the Baptist." In *Imagery in the Gospel of John: Terms, Forms, Themes, and Theology of Johannine Figurative Language*, edited by Jörg Frey, Jan G. Van der Watt, and Ruben Zimmermann, 319–32. WUNT 200. Tübingen: Mohr Siebeck, 2006.

Conway, Colleen M. *Men and Women in the Fourth Gospel: Gender and Johannine Characterization*. SBLDS 167. Atlanta: Society of Biblical Literature, 1997.

Culpepper, R. Alan. *Anatomy of the Fourth Gospel. A Study in Literary Design*. Philadelphia: Fortress Press, 1983.

———. "Designs for the Church in the Imagery of John 21:1–14." In *Imagery in the Gospel of John: Terms, Forms, Themes, and Theology of Johannine Figurative Language*, edited by Jörg Frey, Jan G. Van der Watt, and Ruben Zimmermann, 370–401. WUNT 200. Tübingen: Mohr Siebeck, 2006.

Culpepper, R. Alan, and C. Clifton Black, eds. *Exploring the Gospel of John in Honor of D. Moody Smith*. Louisville: Westminster John Knox, 1996

Culpepper, R. Alan, and Jörg Frey, eds. *The Opening of John's Narrative (John 1:19–2:22): Historical, Literary, and Theological Readings from the Colloquium Ioanneum 2015 in Ephesus*. Tübingen: Mohr Siebeck, 2017.

Daly-Denton, Margaret. "Singing Hymns to Christ as God." In *The Jewish Roots of Christological Monotheism: Papers from the St. Andrews Conference on the Historical Origins of the Worship of Jesus*, edited by Carey C. Newman, James R. Davila, and Gladys S. Lewis, 277–92. Leiden: Brill, 1999.

———. *David in the Fourth Gospel: The Johannine Reception of the Psalms*. Leiden: Brill, 2000.

Day, Janeth Norfleete. *The Woman at the Well: Interpretation of John 4:1–42 in Retrospect and Prospect*. Leiden: Brill, 2002.

Derrett, J. Duncan M. "John 9:6 Read with Isaiah 6:10; 20:9." *EvQ* 66, no. 3 (1994): 251–54.

Dodd, C. H. *The Interpretation of the Fourth Gospel*. 1953. Repr., Cambridge: Cambridge University Press, 1988.

Du Rand, Jan A. "A Syntactical and Narratological Reading of John 10 in Coherence with Chapter 9." In *The Shepherd Discourse of John 10 and Its Context*, edited by Johanne Beutler and Robert T. Fortna, 94–115. Cambridge: Cambridge University Press, 1991.

Estes, Douglas, and Ruth Sheridan, eds. *How John Works: Storytelling in the Fourth Gospel*. Atlanta: SBL Press, 2016.

Evans, Craig A. "The Hermeneutics of Mark and John: On the Theology of the Canonical 'Gospel,'" *Biblica*, 64/2 (1983):153–172.

———. "Obduracy and the Lord's Servant: Some Observations on the Use of the Old Testament in the Fourth Gospel." In *Early Jewish and Christian Exegesis. Studies in Memory of William Hugh Brownlee*, edited by Craig A. Evans and William F. Stinespring, 221–36. Atlanta: Scholars Press, 1987.

———. *Word and Glory: On the Exegetical and Theological Background of John's Prologue.* JSNTSup 89. Sheffield: JSOT Press, 1993.

Ferguson, Sinclair B. *Lessons from the Upper Room.* DVD. Sanford, FL: Ligonier Ministries, 2014.

Fletcher-Louis, Crispin. *Jesus Monotheism.* Vol. 1, *Christological Origins: The Emerging Consensus and Beyond.* Eugene, OR: Cascade, 2015.

Franck, Eskil. *Revelation Taught: The Paraclete in the Gospel of John.* Coniectanea Biblica New Testament Series 14. Lund, Sweden: CWK Gleerup, 1985.

Frey, Jörg, Jan G. Van der Watt, and Ruben Zimmermann, eds. *Imagery in the Gospel of John: Terms, Forms, Themes, and Theology of Johannine Figurative Language.* WUNT 200. Tübingen: Mohr Siebeck, 2006.

Gaventa, Beverly Roberts. "The Archive of Excess: John 21 and the Problem of Narrative Closure." In *Exploring the Gospel of John in Honor of D. Moody Smith*, edited by R. Alan Culpepper and C. Clifton Black, 240–52. Louisville: Westminster John Knox, 1996.

Grindheim, Sigurd. "The Work of God or Human Beings: A Note on John 6:29." *JETS* 59, no. 1 (2016): 63–66.

Gundry, Robert H. "'In My Father's House Are Many Μοναί' (John 14 2)." *ZNW* 58 (1967): 68–72.

Haenchen, Ernst. *John I: A Commentary on the Gospel of John Chapters 1–6.* Translated by Robert W. Funk. Hermeneia. Philadelphia: Fortress, 1984.

Hanson, A. T. "John's Use of Scripture." In *The Gospels and the Scriptures of Israel*, edited by Craig A. Evans and W. Richard Stegner, 358–79. JSNTSup 104. Sheffield: Sheffield Academic, 1994.

Harstine, Stan. *Moses as a Character in the Fourth Gospel: A Study of Ancient Reading Techniques.* JSNTSup 229. London: Sheffield Academic, 2002.

Hays, Richard B. "Christ Prays the Psalms: Paul's Use of an Early Christian Exegetical Convention." In *The Future of Christology: Essays in Honor of Leander E. Keck*, edited by Abraham J. Malherbe and Wayne A. Meeks, 122–36. Minneapolis: Fortress, 1993.

———. *Echoes of Scripture in the Gospels.* Waco, TX: Baylor University Press, 2016.

———. *Echoes of Scripture in the Letters of Paul.* New Haven, CT: Yale University Press, 1989.

_____. *Reading Backwards: Figural Christology and the Fourfold Gospel Witness.* Waco, TX: Baylor University Press, 2014.

Heilmann, Jan. "A Meal in the Background of John 6:51–58?" *JBL* 137 (2018): 481–500.

Hengel, Martin. "The Old Testament in the Fourth Gospel." In *The Gospels and the Scriptures of Israel,* edited by Craig A. Evans and W. Richard Stegner, 380–95. JSNTSup 104. Sheffield: Sheffield Academic, 1994.

_____. "The Prologue of the Gospel of John as the Gateway to Christological Truth." In *The Gospel of John and Christian Theology,* edited by Richard Bauckham and Carl Mosser, 265–94. Grand Rapids: Eerdmans, 2008.

Himmelfarb, Martha. "Afterlife and Resurrection." In *The Jewish Annotated New Testament,* edited by Amy-Jill Levine and Marc Zvi Brettler, 691–95. 2nd ed. Oxford: Oxford University Press, 2011.

Holloway, Paul. "Left Behind: Jesus' Consolation of His Disciples in John 13, 21–17, 26." *ZNW* 96 (2005): 1–34.

Hurtado, Larry. "The Binitarian Shape of Early Christian Worship." In *The Jewish Roots of Christological Monotheism: Papers from the St. Andrews Conference on the Historical Origins of the Worship of Jesus,* edited by Carey C. Newman, James R. Davila, and Gladys S. Lewis, 187–213. Leiden: Brill, 1999.

_____. *How on Earth Did Jesus Become a God? Historical Questions about Early Devotion to Jesus.* Grand Rapids: Eerdmans, 2005.

_____. *Lord Jesus Christ: Devotion to Jesus in Earliest Christianity.* Grand Rapids: Eerdmans, 2003.

_____. *One God, One Lord: Early Christian Devotion and Ancient Jewish Monotheism.* 3rd ed. New York: Bloomsbury T&T Clark, 2015.

Hylen, Susan. *Allusion and Meaning in John 6.* Berlin: de Gruyter, 2005.

Jackson, Howard M. "Ancient Self-Referential Conventions and Their Implications for the Authorship and Integrity of the Gospel of John," *JTS* 50ns (1999): 1–34.

Jensen, Matthew D. "John Is No Exception: Identifying the Subject of εἰμί and Its Implications, *JBL* 135, no. 2 (2016): 341–53.

Jobes, Karen H. *1, 2, & 3 John.* ZECNT. Grand Rapids: Zondervan, 2014.

_____. "Sophia Christology: The Way of Wisdom?" In *The Way of Wisdom: Essays in Honor of Bruce K. Waltke,* edited by J. I. Packer and Sven K. Soderlund, 79–103. Grand Rapids: Zondervan, 2000.

Keener, Craig. *The Gospel of John: A Commentary.* 2 vols. Peabody, MA: Hendrickson, 2003.

Kempis, Thomas à. *The Imitation of Christ.* Westwood, NJ: Barbour, 1984.

Klink, Edward W., III. *John.* ZECNT. Grand Rapids: Zondervan, 2016.

Koester, Craig R. *Symbolism in the Fourth Gospel. Meaning, Mystery, Community.* Minneapolis: Fortress Press, 2003.

_____. "What Does It Mean to Be Human? Imagery and the Human Condition in John's Gospel." In *Imagery in the Gospel of John: Terms, Forms, Themes, and Theology of Johannine Figurative Language*, edited by Jörg Frey, Jan G. Van der Watt, and Ruben Zimmermann, 403–20. WUNT 200. Tübingen: Mohr Siebeck, 2006.

Koester, Craig R., and Reimund Bieringer, eds. *The Resurrection of Jesus in the Gospel of John*. Tübingen: Mohr Siebeck, 2008.

Köstenberger, Andreas J. *John*. BECNT. Grand Rapids: Baker Academic, 2004.

_____. "John." In *Zondervan Illustrated Bible Backgrounds Commentary*, edited by Clinton E. Arnold, 2:2–216. Grand Rapids: Zondervan, 2002.

Kovacs, Judith L. "'Now Shall the Ruler of This World Be Driven Out': Jesus' Death as Cosmic Battle in John 12:30–36." *JBL* 114 (1995): 227–47.

Kysar, Robert. *John*. Minneapolis: Augsburg, 1986.

Lang, David. *The Accordance Dictionary of Place Names*. 5.2.2. OakTree Software, 2000.

Lee, Dorothy A. *The Symbolic Narratives of the Fourth Gospel: The Interplay of Form and Meaning*. JSNTSup 95. Sheffield: JSOT Press, 1994.

Leslie, Britt. *One Thing I Know: How the Blind Man of John 9 Leads an Audience Toward Belief*. Eugene, OR: Pickwick, 2015.

Lett, Jonathan. "The Divine Identity of Jesus as the Reason for Israel's Unbelief in John 12:36–43." *JBL* 135, no. 1 (2016): 159–73.

Levine, Amy-Jill, and Marc Zvi Brettler, eds. *The Jewish Annotated New Testament*. 2nd ed. Oxford: Oxford University Press, 2011.

Lewis, Karoline M. *Rereading the "Shepherd Discourse": Restoring the Integrity of John 9:39–10:21*. Studies in Biblical Literature 113. New York: Peter Lang, 2008.

Lightfoot, J. B. *St. John's Gospel: A Commentary*. Oxford: Clarendon, 1956.

Lincoln, Andrew T. "The Lazarus Story: A Literary Perspective." 211–232 in *The Gospel of John and Christian Theology*. edited by Richard Bauckham and Carl Mosser. Grand Rapids: Eerdmans, 2008.

_____. *Truth on Trial: The Lawsuit Motif in the Fourth Gospel*. Peabody, MA: Hendrickson, 2000.

Lindars, Barnabas. *Behind the Fourth Gospel*. London: SPCK, 1971.

Linforth, Katherine C. *The Beloved Disciple: Jacob the Brother of the Lord*. Freemantle, Australia: VIVID, 2014.

Loader, William. "John 1:51 and Johannine Christology." In *The Opening of John's Narrative (John 1:19–2:22): Historical, Literary, and Theological Readings from the Colloquium Ioanneum 2015 in Ephesus*, edited by R. Alan Culpepper and Jörg Frey, 119–32. Tübingen: Mohr Siebeck, 2017.

Malatesta, Edward. *Interiority and Covenant: a Study of "einai en" and "menein en" in the First Letter of Saint John.* Analecta Biblica 69. Rome: Biblical Institute Press, 1978.

Manning, Gary T. *Echoes of a Prophet: The Use of Ezekiel in the Gospel of John and in Literature of the Second Temple Period.* JSNTSup 270. London: T&T Clark International, 2004.

Maritz, Petrus, and Gilbert Van Belle. "The Imagery of Eating and Drinking in John 6:35." In *Imagery in the Gospel of John: Terms, Forms, Themes, and Theology of Johannine Figurative Language,* edited by Jörg Frey, Jan G. Van der Watt, and Ruben Zimmermann, 333–52. WUNT 200. Tübingen: Mohr Siebeck, 2006.

Martyn, J. Louis. *History and Theology in the Fourth Gospel.* New York: Harper & Row, 1968.

McDermott, Gerald R. "How the Trinity Should Govern Our Approach to World Religions." *JETS* 60, no. 1 (2017): 49–64.

Metzger, Bruce M. "The Formulas Introducing Quotations of Scripture in the NT and the Midrash." *JBL* 70 (1951): 297–307.

Michaels, J. Ramsey. "Betrayal and the Betrayer: The Uses of Scripture in John 13.18–19." In *The Gospels and the Scriptures of Israel,* edited by Craig A. Evans and W. Richard Stegner, 459–74. JSNTSup 104. Sheffield: Sheffield Academic, 1994.

_____. *The Gospel of John.* NICNT. Grand Rapids: Eerdmans, 2010.

Moloney, Francis J. "Can Everyone Be Wrong? John 11.1–12.8." *New Testament Studies* 49 (2003): 505–27.

_____. *Glory Not Dishonor: Reading John 13–21.* Minneapolis: Fortress, 1998.

_____. *The Gospel of John: Text and Context.* Leiden: Brill Academic Publishers, 2005.

_____. *Love in the Gospel of John: An Exegetical, Theological, and Literary Study.* Grand Rapids: Baker Academic, 2013.

_____. *Signs and Shadows: Reading John 5–12.* Minneapolis: Fortress, 1996.

Morris, Leon. *The Gospel according to John.* NICNT. Grand Rapids: Eerdmans, 1995.

Motyer, J. Alec. *The Prophecy of Isaiah: An Introduction & Commentary.* Downers Grove, IL: InterVarsity Press, 1993.

Moyise, Steve, and Maarten J. J. Menken. *Isaiah in the New Testament.* London: T&T Clark International, 2005.

Murray, John. *The Collected Writing of John Murray.* Vol. 2. Carlisle, PA: Banner of Truth Trust, 1977.

Nielsen, Jesper Tang. "The Lamb of God: The Cognitive Structure of a Johannine Metaphor." In *Imagery in the Gospel of John: Terms, Forms, Themes, and Theology of Johannine Figurative Language,* edited by Jörg Frey, Jan G.

Van der Watt, and Ruben Zimmermann. 218–56. WUNT 200. Tübingen: Mohr Siebeck, 2006.

Newman, Carey C., James R. Davila, and Gladys S. Lewis, eds. *The Jewish Roots of Christological Monotheism: Papers from the St. Andrews Conference on the Historical Origins of the Worship of Jesus.* Leiden: Brill, 1999.

Newman, John. "Eating and Drinking as Sources of Metaphor in English." *Cuadernos de Filología Inglesa* 6, no. 2 (1997): 213–31.

Nickelsburg, George. *Resurrection, Immortality, and Eternal Life in Intertestamental Judaism.* Cambridge, MA: Harvard University Press, 1972.

O'Day, Gail R. *The Word Disclosed: John's Story and Narrative Preaching.* St. Louis: CBP, 1987.

Painter, John. "Tradition, history and Interpretation in John 10." In *The Shepherd Discourse of John 10 and Its Context,* edited by Johanne Beutler and Robert T. Fortna, 53–74. Cambridge: Cambridge University Press, 1991.

Parsenios, George L. "The Testimony of John's Narrative and the Silence of the Johannine Narrator." In *The Opening of John's Narrative (John 1:19–2:22): Historical, Literary, and Theological Readings from the Colloquium Ioanneum 2015 in Ephesus,* edited by R. Alan Culpepper and Jörg Frey, 1–16. Tübingen: Mohr Siebeck, 2017.

_____. *Departure and Consolation: The Johannine Farewell Discourses in Light of Greco-Roman Literature.* Leiden: Brill, 2005.

Plummer, Richard. *The Samaritans: A Profile.* Grand Rapids: Eerdmans, 2016.

Porter, Stanley E. "Can Traditional Exegesis Enlighten Literary Analysis of the Fourth Gospel? An Examination of the Old Testament Fulfillment Motif and the Passover Theme." In *The Gospels and Scriptures of Israel,* edited by Craig A. Evans and W. Richard Stegner, 396–428. JSNTSup 104. Sheffield: Sheffield Academic, 1994.

_____. "Exodus 12 and the Passover Theme in John." In *Sacred Tradition in the New Testament: Tracing Old Testament Themes in the Gospels and Epistles,* 127–51. Grand Rapids: Baker Academic, 2016.

_____. *John, His Gospel, and Jesus. In Pursuit of the Johannine Voice.* Grand Rapids: Eerdmans, 2015.

Porter, Stanley E., and Ron C. Fay, eds. *The Gospel of John in Modern Interpretation.* Milestones in New Testament Scholarship. Grand Rapids: Kregel, 2019.

Reinhartz, Adele. *Befriending the Beloved Disciple. A Jewish Reading of the Gospel of John.* New York: Continuum, 2001.

_____. "The Gospel according to John." In *The Jewish Annotated New Testament,* edited by Amy-Jill Levine and Marc Zvi Brettler, 177. 2nd ed. Oxford: University Press, 2017.

_____. "John 8:31–59 from a Jewish Perspective." In *Remembering for the Future: The Holocaust in an Age of Genocide*, edited by John K. Roth and Elisabeth Maxwell, 2:787–97. New York: Palgrave, 2001.

Rensberger, David. *Johannine Faith and Liberating Community*. Philadelphia: Westminster, 1988.

Reynolds, Benjamin E. "Reading the Gospel of John's Christology as Jewish Messianism: Challenges and Possibilities." In *Reading the Gospel of John's Christology as Jewish Messianism: Royal, Prophetic, and Divine Messiahs*, edited by Benjamin E. Reynolds and Gabriele Boccaccini, 13–42. Leiden: Brill, 2018.

_____, ed. *The Son of Man Problem: Critical Readings*. London: T&T Clark, 2018.

Reynolds, Benjamin E., and Gabriele Boccaccini, eds. *Reading the Gospel of John's Christology as Jewish Messianism: Royal, Prophetic, and Divine Messiahs*. Leiden: Brill, 2018.

Ridderbos, Herman. *The Gospel of John: A Theological Commentary*. Translated by John Vriend. Grand Rapids: Eerdmans, 1992.

Ryle, J. C. *Expository Thoughts on the Gospels: John*. Vol. 1. Edinburgh: Banner of Truth Trust, 1887. Repr., Carlisle, PA: Banner of Truth Trust, 1997.

Sanders, James A. "A New Testament Hermeneutic Fabric: Psalm 118 in the Entrance Narrative." In *Early Jewish and Christian Exegesis: Studies in Memory of William Hugh Brownlee*, edited by Craig A. Evans and William F. Stinespring, 177–90. Atlanta: Scholars Press, 1987.

Schnackenburg, Rudolf. *The Gospel according to John*. Vol. 1. New York: Herder and Herder, 1968.

Schneiders, Sandra M. *Jesus Risen in Our Midst: Essays on the Resurrection of Jesus in the Fourth Gospel*. Collegeville, MN: Liturgical Press, 2013.

_____. "Women in the Fourth Gospel." *Biblical Theology Bulletin* 12 (1982): 35–45.

Scott, Matthew. *The Hermeneutics of Christological Psalmody in Paul: An Intertextual Inquiry*. SNTSMS 158. New York: Cambridge University Press, 2014.

Selvaggio, Anthony T. *The Seven Signs: Seeing the Glory of Christ in the Gospel of John*. Grand Rapids: Reformation Heritage Books, 2010.

Smith, D. Moody. "The Setting and Shape of a Johannine Narrative Source." *JBL* 95, no. 2 (1976): 231–41.

Stovell, Beth M. *Mapping Metaphorical Discourse in the Fourth Gospel: John's Eternal King*. Leiden: Brill, 2012.

_____. "Son of God as Anointed One? Johannine Davidic Christology and Second Temple Messianism." In *Reading the Gospel of John's Christology as Jewish Messianism: Royal, Prophetic, and Divine Messiahs*, edited by Benjamin E. Reynolds and Gabriele Boccaccini, 151–77. Leiden: Brill, 2018.

Streett, Andrew. *The Vine and the Son of Man: Eschatological Interpretation of Psalm 80 in Early Judaism.* Minneapolis: Fortress, 2014.

Tenney, Merrill C., and Moisés Silva, eds. *The Zondervan Encyclopedia of the Bible.* 5 vols. Grand Rapids: Zondervan, 2009.

Thompson, Marianne Meye. "Baptism with Water and with Holy Spirit: Purification in the Gospel of John." In *The Opening of John's Narrative (John 1:19–2:22): Historical, Literary, and Theological Readings from the Colloquium Ioanneum 2015 in Ephesus,* edited by R. Alan Culpepper and Jörg Frey, 59–78. Tübingen: Mohr Siebeck, 2017.

_____. "'Every Picture Tells a Story': Imagery for God in the Gospel of John." In *Imagery in the Gospel of John: Terms, Forms, Themes, and Theology of Johannine Figurative Language,* edited by Jörg Frey, Jan G. Van der Watt, and Ruben Zimmermann, 259–77. WUNT 200. Tübingen: Mohr Siebeck, 2006.

_____. *John: A Commentary.* NTL. Louisville: Westminster John Knox, 2015.

_____. "The Raising of Lazarus in John 11: A Theological Reading." In *The Gospel of John and Christian Theology,* edited by Richard Bauckham and Carl Mosser, 233–44. Grand Rapids: Eerdmans, 2008.

Tolmie, D. Francois. "The (Not So) Good Shepherd: The Use of Shepherd Imagery in the Characterisation of Peter in the Fourth Gospel." In *Imagery in the Gospel of John: Terms, Forms, Themes, and Theology of Johannine Figurative Language,* edited by Jörg Frey, Jan G. Van der Watt, and Ruben Zimmermann, 353–67. WUNT 200. Tübingen: Mohr Siebeck, 2006.

Tsutserov, Alexander. *Glory, Grace, and Truth: Ratification of the Sinaitic Covenant According to the Gospel of John.* Eugene, OR: Pickwick, 2009.

Turner, John D. "The History of Religions Background of John 10." In *The Shepherd Discourse of John 10 and Its Context,* edited by Johannes Beutler and Robert T. Fortna, 33–52. Cambridge: Cambridge University Press, 1991.

Van der Watt, Jan G. "Angels in John 1:51." In *The Opening of John's Narrative (John 1:19–2:22): Historical, Literary, and Theological Readings from the Colloquium Ioanneum 2015 in Ephesus,* edited by R. Alan Culpepper and Jörg Frey, 133–63. Tübingen: Mohr Siebeck, 2017.

_____. "Ethics Alive in Imagery." In *Imagery in the Gospel of John: Terms, Forms, Themes, and Theology of Johannine Figurative Language,* edited by Jörg Frey, Jan G. Van der Watt, and Ruben Zimmermann, 421–48. WUNT 200. Tübingen: Mohr Siebeck, 2006.

_____. *Family of the King: Dynamics of Metaphor in the Gospel According to John.* Leiden: Brill, 2000.

Vanhoozer, Kevin. "The Hermeneutics of I-Witness Testimony: John 21.20–24 and the 'Death' of the 'Author.'" In *Understanding Poets and Prophets: Essays in Honour of George Wishart Anderson,* edited by A. Graeme Auld, 366–87. JSOTS 152. Sheffield: Sheffield Academic, 1993.

Westcott, Brooke Foss. *The Gospel According to St. John*. London: John Murray, 1908.

Wheaton, Gerry. *The Role of Jewish Feasts in John's Gospel*. SNTSMS 162. Cambridge: Cambridge University Press, 2015.

Whitenton, Michael R. "The Dissembler of John 3: A Cognitive and Rhetorical Approach to the Characterization of Nicodemus." *JBL* 135, no. 1 (2016): 141–58.

Williams, Catrin H. "Johannine Christology and Prophetic Traditions: The Case of Isaiah." In *Reading the Gospel of John's Christology as Jewish Messianism*, edited by Benjamin E. Reynolds and Gabriele Boccaccini, 92–123. Leiden: Brill, 2018.

———. "Isaiah in John's Gospel." In *Isaiah in the New Testament*, edited by Steve Moyise and Maarten J. J. Menken, 101–16. London: T&T Clark International, 2005.

Willitts, Joel. "David' Sublation of Moses: A Davidic Explanation for the Mosaic Christology of the Fourth Gospel." In *Reading the Gospel of John's Christology as Jewish Messianism: Royal, Prophetic, and Divine Messiahs*, edited by Benjamin E. Reynolds and Gabriele Boccaccini, 203–25. Leiden: Brill, 2018.

Witherington, Ben, III. *Biblical Theology: The Convergence of the Canon*. Cambridge: Cambridge University Press, 2019.

———. *John's Wisdom: A Commentary on the Fourth Gospel*. Louisville: Westminster John Knox, 1995.

Wright, N. T. *Surprised by Hope: Rethinking Heaven, the Resurrection, and the Mission of the Church*. San Francisco: HarperOne, 2008.

Wright, William. *Rhetoric and Theology: Figural Reading of John 9*. Berlin: de Gruyter, 2009.

Zimmermann, Ruben. "Jesus—the Lamb of God (John 1:29 and 1:36): Metaphorical Christology in the Fourth Gospel." In *The Opening of John's Narrative (John 1:19–2:22): Historical, Literary, and Theological Readings from the Colloquium Ioanneum 2015 in Ephesus*, edited by R. Alan Culpepper and Jörg Frey, 79–96. Tübingen: Mohr Siebeck, 2017.

———. "The Narrative Hermeneutics of John 11: Learning with Lazarus How to Understand Death, Life and Resurrection." In *The Resurrection of Jesus in the Gospel of John*, edited by Craig K. Koester and Reimund Bieringer, 75–101. Tübingen: Mohr Siebeck, 2008.

———. "Imagery in John: Opening Up Paths into the Tangled Thicket of John's Figurative World." In *Imagery in the Gospel of John: Terms, Forms, Themes, and Theology of Johannine Figurative Language*, edited by Jörg Frey, Jan G. Van der Watt, and Ruben Zimmermann, 1–43. WUNT 200; Tübingen: Mohr Siebeck, 2006.

ENDNOTES

INTRODUCTION

1. Yasmine Hafiz, "The Moon Communion of Buzz Aldrin That NASA Didn't Want to Broadcast," *Huffington Post*, July 19, 2014, https://www.huffpost.com/entry/moon-communion-buzz-aldrin_n_5600648.
2. This description is attributed to a variety of scholars, but I have been unable to determine who originally said it.
3. Eskil Franck, *Revelation Taught: The Paraclete in the Gospel of John* (Malmö, Sweden: CWK Gleerup, 1985), 43.
4. Jeannine K. Brown, *The Gospels as Stories. A Narrative Approach to Matthew, Mark, Luke, and John* (Grand Rapids: Baker Academic, 2020), 160–62; ibid., "Creation's Renewal in the Gospel of John," *CBQ* 72 (2010): 275–90, esp. 284–86; Rekha M. Chennattu, "Scripture," in *How John Works: Storytelling in the Fourth Gospel*, ed. Douglas Estes and Ruth Sheridan, Resources for Biblical Study 86 (Atlanta: SBL Press, 2016), 171–86.
5. Much of Johannine scholarship in the last century followed Bultmann's seminal work and focused on source criticism and redaction of the fourth gospel from its various assumed sources. The Prologue and Epilogue have been thought to be additions to the original gospel with the Book of Signs and Book of Glory coming from two separate sources. More recently, scholars have turned to analysis of the gospel assuming its unity from essentially one author because (1) there is no manuscript evidence that the gospel of John ever circulated without the Prologue and Epilogue or in any other form than we have it today, (2) the syntax and vocabulary of the Prologue and Epilogue are consistent with that in the rest of the gospel, and (3) literary themes found throughout the gospel are also present in both the Prologue and Epilogue. Defense of this study's interpretation of the unity of the fourth gospel as it now stands is beyond the scope of this book, but discussion of the unity and the redaction of John can be found in most commentaries and introductions. For a recent study of the issues, see Stanley E. Porter, *John, His Gospel, and Jesus: In Pursuit of the Johannine Voice* (Grand Rapids: Eerdmans, 2015); for a history of modern Johannine scholarship see Stanley E. Porter and Ron C. Fay, eds., *The Gospel of John in Modern Interpretation*, Milestones in New Testament Scholarship (Grand Rapids: Kregel, 2019).
6. Edward W. Klink III, *John*, ZECNT (Grand Rapids: Zondervan, 2016), 84.
7. Barnabas Lindars, *Behind the Fourth Gospel* (London: SPCK, 1971), 66, 78.

8. See Benjamin E. Reynolds and Gabriele Boccaccini, eds., *Reading the Gospel of John's Christology as Jewish Messianism: Royal, Prophetic, and Divine Messiahs* (Leiden: Brill, 2018).

9. Gerry Wheaton, *The Role of Jewish Feasts in John's Gospel*, SNTSMS 162 (Cambridge: Cambridge University Press, 2015), 188.

10. Benjamin E. Reynolds, "Epilogue: The Early Jewish Messiah of the Gospel of John," in Reynolds and Boccaccini, *Reading the Gospel of John's Christology*, 437–49, quotation on 438.

11. Larry Hurtado, *One God, One Lord: Early Christian Devotion and Ancient Jewish Monotheism*, 3rd ed. (New York: Bloomsbury T&T Clark, 2015); Hurtado, *Lord Jesus Christ: Devotion to Jesus in Earliest Christianity* (Grand Rapids: Eerdmans, 2003); Hurtado, *How on Earth Did Jesus Become a God? Historical Questions About Early Devotion to Jesus* (Grand Rapids: Eerdmans, 2005); Richard Bauckham, *Jesus and the God of Israel: God Crucified and Other Studies on the New Testament's Christology of Divine Identity* (Grand Rapids: Eerdmans, 2009); Bauckham, *God Crucified: Monotheism and Christology in the New Testament* (Grand Rapids: Eerdmans, 1999).

12. Crispin Fletcher-Louis, *Jesus Monotheism*, vol. 1, *Christological Origins: The Emerging Consensus and Beyond* (Eugene, OR: Cascade, 2015).

13. Carey C. Newman, James R. Davila, and Gladys S. Lewis, eds., *The Jewish Roots of Christological Monotheism: Papers from the St. Andrews Conference on the Historical Origins of the Worship of Jesus.* (Leiden: Brill, 1999).

14. Richard Bauckham, "The Throne of God and the Worship of Jesus," in Newman, Davila, and Lewis, *Jewish Roots of Christological Monotheism*, 43–69, esp. 45 (emphasis added).

15. Marianne Meye Thompson, "'Every Picture Tells a Story': Imagery for God in the Gospel of John," in *Imagery in the Gospel of John: Terms, Forms, Themes, and Theology of Johannine Figurative Language*, eds. Jörg Frey, Jan G. Van der Watt, and Ruben Zimmermann, WUNT 200 (Tübingen: Mohr Siebeck, 2006), 259–77, esp. 263.

16. Thompson, "'Every Picture Tells a Story,'" 263.

17. Chennattu, "Scripture," 183.

18. D. A. Carson, *The Gospel According to John*, PNTC (Grand Rapids: Eerdmans, 1991), 24.

19. Quoted in Craig L. Blomberg, *The Historical Reliability of John's Gospel: Issues and Commentary* (Downers Grove, IL: InterVarsity Press, 2001), 24–25.

20. Aorist tense, translated as a perfect ("had said") by Kirsopp Lake in the Loeb Classical Library series.

21. Blomberg, *Historical Reliability*, 22–35.

22. Richard Bauckham, *The Testimony of the Beloved Disciple: Narrative, History, and Theology in the Gospel of John* (Grand Rapids: Baker Academic, 2007), 35; also Bauckham, *Jesus and the Eyewitnesses: The Gospels as Eyewitness Testimony* (Grand Rapids: Eerdmans, 2006), 12–21, 384–471.

23. Martin Hengel, *The Johannine Question*, trans. John Bowden (Philadelphia: Trinity Press International, 1989).

24. Craig Keener, *The Gospel of John: A Commentary* (Peabody, MA: Hendrickson, 2003), 1:95–98.

25. James H. Charlesworth, *Jesus as Mirrored in John: The Genius in the New Testament* (London: T&T Clark, 2019), 61–77; Charlesworth, *The Beloved Disciple: Whose Witness Validates the Gospel of John?* (Valley Forge, PA: Trinity Press International, 1995), xii, citing Pierson Parker, "John the Son of Zebedee and the Fourth Gospel," *JBL* 81 (1962): 35–43.

26. See Blomberg, *Historical Reliability*, 31–37, for a critique of such assumptions; Andreas J. Köstenberger, *John*, BECNT (Grand Rapids: Baker Academic, 2004), 6–7; Klink, *John*, 45.

27. Charlesworth, *The Beloved Disciple*; Charlesworth, *Jesus as Mirrored in John,* 72–73.
28. Blomberg, *Historical Reliability,* 37.
29. Bauckham, *Testimony of the Beloved Disciple,* 91.
30. Stanley E. Porter and Ron C. Fay, conclusion to Porter and Fay, *The Gospel of John in Modern Interpretation,* 242.
31. Brooke Foss Westcott, *The Gospel according to St. John* (London: John Murray, 1908), lii (emphasis original).
32. For an extensive discussion of issues of authorship, see Craig Keener, *Gospel of John,* 1:81–139.
33. Köstenberger, *John,* 18.
34. For instance, Ben Witherington III, *John's Wisdom: A Commentary on the Fourth Gospel* (Louisville: Westminster John Knox, 1995); Witherington, *Biblical Theology: The Convergence of the Canon* (Cambridge: Cambridge University Press, 2019), 81.
35. For instance, George L. Parsenios, *Departure and Consolation: The Johannine Farewell Discourses in Light of Greco-Roman Literature* (Leiden: Brill, 2005).
36. Karen H. Jobes, "Sophia Christology: The Way of Wisdom?," in *The Way of Wisdom: Essays in Honor of Bruce K. Waltke,* eds. J. I. Packer and Sven K. Soderlund (Grand Rapids: Zondervan, 2000), 79–103.
37. Richard B. Hays, *Echoes of Scripture in the Gospels* (Waco, TX: Baylor University Press, 2016), 284; also Hays, *Reading Backwards: Figural Christology and the Fourfold Gospel Witness* (Waco, TX: Baylor University Press, 2014), 78.
38. Hays, *Echoes of Scripture in the Gospels,* 343.

JOHN 1

1. Jeannine K. Brown, *The Gospels as Stories. A Narrative Approach to Matthew, Mark, Luke, and John* (Grand Rapids: Baker Academic, 2020), 135; idem., "Creation's Renewal in the Gospel of John," *CBQ* 72 (2010): 275–90.
2. Contra Gitte Buch-Hansen, *"It Is the Spirit That Gives Life": A Stoic Understanding of Pneuma in John's Gospel* (Berlin: de Gruyter, 2010).
3. Daniel Boyarin, "Logos, a Jewish Word: John's Prologue as Midrash," in *The Jewish Annotated New Testament,* ed. Amy-Jill Levine and Marc Zvi Brettler, 2nd ed. (Oxford: Oxford University Press, 2011), 688–91.
4. Martin Hengel, "The Prologue of the Gospel of John as the Gateway to Christological Truth," in *The Gospel of John and Christian Theology,* eds. Richard Bauckham and Carl Mosser (Grand Rapids: Eerdmans, 2008), 266.
5. Hengel, "Prologue," 272 (emphasis original).
6. Britt Leslie, *One Thing I Know: How the Blind Man of John 9 Leads an Audience toward Belief* (Eugene, OR: Pickwick, 2015), 82–83 (emphasis original).
7. Catrin H. Williams, "Johannine Christology and Prophetic Traditions: The Case of Isaiah," in *Reading the Gospel of John's Christology as Jewish Messianism,* eds. Benjamin E. Reynolds and Gabriele Boccaccini (Leiden: Brill, 2018), 92–123, quotation on 92.
8. Richard Bauckham, *Gospel of Glory: Major Themes in Johannine Theology* (Grand Rapids: Baker Academic, 2015), 72.
9. Richard Bauckham, "The Fourth Gospel as Testimony of the Beloved Disciple," in Bauckham and Mosser, *Gospel of John and Christian Theology,* 120–39, quotation on 135.
10. Bauckham, *Gospel of Glory,* 52; Stan Harstine, *Moses as a Character in the Fourth Gospel: A Study of Ancient Reading Techniques,* JSNTSup 229 (London: Sheffield Academic, 2002); Alexander Tsutserov, *Glory, Grace, and Truth: Ratification of the Sinaitic Covenant according to the Gospel of John* (Eugene, OR: Pickwick, 2009).
11. Gerry Wheaton, *The Role of Jewish Feasts in John's Gospel,* SNTSMS 162 (Cambridge: Cambridge University Press, 2015), 79; as also D. A. Carson, "John and the Johannine

Epistles," in *It Is Written: Scripture Citing Scripture; Essays in Honour of Barnabas Lindars*, eds. D. A. Carson and H. G. M. Williamson (Cambridge: Cambridge University Press, 1988), 245–64, esp. 256.

12. Richard B. Hays, *Echoes of Scripture in the Gospels* (Waco, TX: Baylor University Press, 2016), 296–300.

13. Hengel, "Prologue," 288.

14. Bauckham, *Gospel of Glory*, 50.

15. Bauckham, *Gospel of Glory*, 50.

16. Brown, *Gospels as Stories*, 115.

17. Catrin H. Williams, "Isaiah in John's Gospel," in *Isaiah in the New Testament*, ed. Steve Moyise and Maarten J. J. Menken (London: T&T Clark International, 2005), 101–16.

18. Williams, "Isaiah in John's Gospel," 102.

19. Marianne Meye Thompson, "Baptism with Water and with Holy Spirit: Purification in the Gospel of John," in *The Opening of John's Narrative (John 1:19–2:22): Historical, Literary, and Theological Readings from the Colloquium Ioanneum 2015 in Ephesus*, eds. R. Alan Culpepper and Jörg Frey (Tübingen: Mohr Siebeck, 2017), 59–78, quotation on 64.

20. Merrill C. Tenney and Moisés Silva, eds., *The Zondervan Encyclopedia of the Bible* (Grand Rapids: Zondervan, 2009), vol. 1, s.v. "Bethany."

21. For discussion of the various options see Ruben Zimmermann, "Jesus—the Lamb of God (John 1:29 and 1:36): Metaphorical Christology in the Fourth Gospel," in Culpepper and Frey, *Opening of John's Narrative,* 79–96; also Jesper Tang Nielsen, "The Lamb of God: The Cognitive Structure of a Johannine Metaphor," in *Imagery in the Gospel of John: Terms, Forms, Themes, and Theology of Johannine Figurative Language*, ed. Jörg Frey, Jan G. Van der Watt, and Ruben Zimmermann, WUNT 200 (Tübingen: Mohr Siebeck, 2006), 218–56, esp. 225–26.

22. Margaret Daly-Denton, *David in the Fourth Gospel: The Johannine Reception of the Psalms* (Leiden: Brill, 2000), 233.

23. Brown, *Gospels as Stories,* 129.

24. Stanley E. Porter, "Exodus 12 and the Passover Theme in John," in *Sacred Tradition in the New Testament: Tracing Old Testament Themes in the Gospels and Epistles* (Grand Rapids: Baker Academic, 2016), 133–37.

25. The term *inclusio* refers to a literary structure that frames a span of text created by the repetition of the same word, phrase, or motif.

26. Zimmermann, "Lamb of God," 94.

27. *Dictionary of Biblical Imagery*, ed. Leland Ryken, James C. Wilhoit, and Tremper Longman III (Downers Grove, IL: InterVarsity Press, 1998), *s.v.* "dove."

28. Or, as in many manuscripts, *Son of God.*

29. See, e.g., Benjamin E. Reynolds and Gabriele Boccaccini, eds., *Reading the Gospel of John's Christology as Jewish Messianism: Royal, Prophetic, and Divine Messiahs* (Leiden: Brill, 2018).

30. Quoted by Benjamin E. Reynolds, "Reading the Gospel of John's Christology as Jewish Messianism: Challenges and Possibilities," in Reynolds and Boccaccini, *Reading the Gospel of John's Christology*, 13–42, quotation on 23.

31. David Lang, *The Accordance Dictionary of Place Names*, 5.2.2 (OakTree Software, 2000), s.v. "Galilee."

32. Lang, *Accordance Dictionary of Place Names, s.v.* "Bethsaida."

33. Stan Harstine, *Moses as a Character in the Fourth Gospel: A Study of Ancient Reading Techniques*, JSNTSup 229 (London: Sheffield Academic, 2002), 52–53.

34. Stephen Dempster, "The Prophets, the Canon and a Canonical Approach: No Empty Word," in *Canon and Biblical Interpretation*, eds. Craig G. Bartholomew et al., Scripture and Hermeneutics Series 7 (Grand Rapids: Zondervan, 2006), 296; Stephen Chapman, *The Law and the Prophets: A Study in Old Testament Canon Formation*, FAT 27 (Mohr Siebeck, 2000), 276.

35. Edward W. Klink III, *John*, ZECNT (Grand Rapids: Zondervan, 2016), 154 (emphasis original); William Loader, "John 1:51 and Johannine Christology," in Culpepper and Frey, *Opening of John's Narrative*, 119–32.

36. Loader, "John 1:51 and Johannine Christology," 131.

37. Jan G. Van der Watt, "Angels in John 1:51," in Culpepper and Frey, *Opening of John's Narrative*, 133–63, quotation on 155; also, Van der Watt, *Family of the King: Dynamics of Metaphor in the Gospel according to John* (Leiden: Brill, 2000), 157 (emphasis original).

38. For a survey of the various ways scholars understand "Son of Man," see Benjamin E. Reynolds, ed., *The Son of Man Problem: Critical Readings* (London: T&T Clark, 2018). The Introduction provides an excellent, brief survey of the interpretive options.

39. Adele Reinhartz, "The Gospel according to John," in Levine and Brettler, *Jewish Annotated New Testament*, 177; see also Crispin Fletcher-Louis, *Jesus Monotheism*, vol. 1, *Christological Origins: The Emerging Consensus and Beyond* (Eugene, OR: Cascade, 2015).

JOHN 2

1. Richard B. Hays, *Echoes of Scripture in the Gospels* (Waco, TX: Baylor University Press, 2016), 289.

2. *Midrash Rabbah Esther*, trans. Maurice Simon (London: Soncino, 1939), 112. A midrash is commentary on biblical passages that has accumulated through the centuries among Jewish rabbis.

3. James H. Charlesworth, *Jesus as Mirrored in John: The Genius in the New Testament* (London: T&T Clark, 2019), x, 164–209.

4. See James H. Charlesworth, *The Old Testament Pseudepigrapha*, vol. 1, *Apocalyptic Literature and Testaments* (Garden City, NY: Doubleday, 1983), 630.

5. Gerry Wheaton, *The Role of Jewish Feasts in John's Gospel*, SNTSMS 162 (Cambridge: Cambridge University Press, 2015), 58.

6. See also Ruben Zimmermann, "Jesus—the Divine Bridegroom? John 2–4 and Its Christological Implications," in *Reading the Gospel of John's Christology as Jewish Messianism: Royal, Prophetic, and Divine Messiahs*, eds. Benjamin E. Reynolds and Gabriele Boccaccini (Leiden: Brill, 2018), 358–86.

7. Richard Bauckham, *Gospel of Glory: Major Themes in Johannine Theology* (Grand Rapids: Baker Academic, 2015), 55.

8. St. Augustine, *Tractates on the Gospel according to St. John* 8.1, e-Catholic 2000, https://www.ecatholic2000.com/fathers/untitled-679.shtml.

9. Tacitus, *The Annals*, trans. A. J. Woodman (Indianapolis: Hackett, 2004), 325.

10. Bauckham, *Gospel of Glory*, 72.

11. Jeannine K. Brown, *The Gospels as Stories: A Narrative Approach to Matthew, Mark, Luke, and John* (Grand Rapids: Baker Academic, 2020), 141; idem., "Creation's Renewal in the Gospel of John," *CBQ* 72 (2010): 287.

12. Francis J. Moloney, *Love in the Gospel of John: An Exegetical, Theological, and Literary Study* (Grand Rapids: Baker Academic, 2013), 82 (emphasis added).

13. J. C. Ryle, *Expository Thoughts on the Gospels: John* (Edinburgh: Banner of Truth Trust, 1887; repr. Carlisle, PA: Banner of Truth Trust, 1997), 1:99.

14. Stanley E. Porter, *Sacred Tradition in the New Testament: Tracing Old Testament Themes in the Gospels and Epistles* (Grand Rapids: Baker Academic, 2016), 137–38. In addition to this pericope, Porter identifies seven passages in John's gospel as Passover pericopes: Jn 1:29–36; 2:13–25; 6:1–14, 22–71; 8:31–47; 11:47–12:8; 13:1–17:26; 19:13–42 (esp. vv. 14, 29, 31, 36–37, 42).

15. Porter, *Sacred Tradition in the New Testament*, 133–37.

16. Hays, *Echoes of Scripture in the Gospels*, 318.

17. Andreas J. Köstenberger, "John" in *Zondervan Illustrated Bible Backgrounds Commentary*, ed. Clinton E. Arnold (Grand Rapids: Zondervan, 2002), 2:32.

18. Richard Bauckham, "Jesus' Demonstration in the Temple," in *Law and Religion: Essays on the Place of the Law in Israel and Early Christianity*, ed. Barnabas Lindars (Cambridge: James Clarke, 1988), 72–89, quotation on 88.

19. Margaret Daly-Denton, *David in the Fourth Gospel: The Johannine Reception of the Psalms* (Leiden: Brill, 2000).

20. Margaret Daly-Denton, "Singing Hymns to Christ as God," in *The Jewish Roots of Christological Monotheism: Papers from the St. Andrews Conference on the Historical Origins of the Worship of Jesus*, eds. Carey C. Newman, James R. Davila, and Gladys S. Lewis (Leiden: Brill, 1999), 277–92, quotation on 287.

21. Daly-Denton, *David in the Fourth Gospel*; Daly-Denton, "Singing Hymns to Christ," 277–92; Richard B. Hays, "Christ Prays the Psalms: Paul's Use of an Early Christian Exegetical Convention," in *The Future of Christology: Essays in Honor of Leander E. Keck*, eds. Abraham J. Malherbe and Wayne A. Meeks (Minneapolis: Fortress, 1993), 122–36, but see Hays' bibliography in *Echoes of Scripture in the Gospels* for a different source. A more recent version is found at Richard B. Hays, "Christ Prays the Psalms: Israel's Psalter as Matrix of Early Christianity," in *The Conversion of the Imagination: Paul as Interpreter of Israel's Scripture* (Grand Rapids: Eerdmans, 2005), 101–18.

22. Joel Willitts, "'David' Sublation of Moses: A Davidic Explanation for the Mosaic Christology of the Fourth Gospel," in *Reading the Gospel of John's Christology as Jewish Messianism: Royal, Prophetic, and Divine Messiahs*, eds. Benjamin E. Reynolds and Gabriele Boccaccini (Leiden: Brill, 2018), 203–25.

23. Daly-Denton, *David in the Fourth Gospel*, 128.

24. Daly-Denton, *David in the Fourth Gospel*, 122.

25. Quoted by Porter, *Sacred Tradition in the New Testament*, 138.

26. Daly-Denton, *David in the Fourth Gospel*, 241.

27. Matthew Scott, *The Hermeneutics of Christological Psalmody in Paul: An Intertextual Inquiry* (Cambridge: Cambridge University Press, 2014), 64.

28. Daly-Denton, "Singing Hymns to Christ," 277–92, quotation on 288.

29. Hays, *Echoes of Scripture in the Gospels*, 358.

30. Hays, *Echoes of Scripture in the Gospels*, 358.

31. Hays, *Echoes of Scripture in the Gospels*, 310.

32. J. B. Lightfoot, *St. John's Gospel: A Commentary* (Oxford: Clarendon, 1956), 115.

33. Lightfoot, *St. John's Gospel*, 112.

34. Hays, *Echoes of Scripture in the Gospels*, 312 (emphasis original).

35. Lightfoot, *St. John's Gospel*, 114.

JOHN 3

1. For discussion of the human condition as John presents it, see Craig R. Koester, "What Does It Mean to Be Human? Imagery and the Human Condition in John's Gospel," in *Imagery in the Gospel of John: Terms, Forms, Themes, and Theology of Johannine Figurative Language*, eds. Jörg Frey, Jan G. Van der Watt, and Ruben Zimmermann, WUNT 200 (Tübingen: Mohr Siebeck, 2006), 403–20.

2. Koester, "What Does It Mean to Be Human?," 405–8.

3. Andreas J. Köstenberger, *John*, BECNT (Grand Rapids: Baker Academic, 2004), 123.

4. If there is any direct reference to the sacrament of water baptism in John's gospel, this is probably the best possibility. See Richard Bauckham, *Gospel of Glory: Major Themes in Johannine Theology* (Grand Rapids: Baker Academic, 2015), 82, for further discussion.

5. D. A. Carson, *The Gospel according to John*, PNTC (Grand Rapids: Eerdmans, 1991), 195.

6. D. A. Carson, "John and the Johannine Epistles," in *It Is Written: Scripture Citing Scripture; Essays in Honour of Barnabas Lindars*, eds. D. A. Carson and H. G. M. Williamson (Cambridge: Cambridge University Press, 1988), 245–64, quotation on 253.

7. Bauckham, *Gospel of Glory*, 90.
8. Stan Harstine, *Moses as a Character in the Fourth Gospel: A Study of Ancient Reading Techniques*, JSNTSup 229 (London: Sheffield Academic, 2002), 56.
9. James H. Charlesworth, *Jesus as Mirrored in John: The Genius in the New Testament* (London: T&T Clark, 2019), 399–433, 449, 455.
10. Bauckham, *Gospel of Glory*, 74.
11. Richard B. Hays, *Echoes of Scripture in the Gospels* (Waco, TX: Baylor University Press, 2016), 335.
12. Bauckham, *Gospel of Glory*, 71.
13. Frederick W. Danker, Walter Bauer, William F. Arndt, and F. Wilbur Gingrich, *A Greek-English Lexicon of the New Testament and Other Early Christian Literature*, 3rd ed. (Chicago: University of Chicago Press, 2000), *s.v.* οὕτως.
14. Jan Van der Watt, *Family of the King: Dynamics of Metaphor in the Gospel according to John* (Leiden: Brill, 2000), 178, 202.
15. The NIV (2011) and NET Bible end Jesus' words at 3:15; the NIV (1984), ESV, NLT, NASB, NRSV, NKJV, and NJB continue the quotation through 3:21.
16. J. B. Lightfoot, *St. John's Gospel: A Commentary* (Oxford: Clarendon, 1956), 118.
17. For discussion that Nicodemus was convinced by Jesus see Michael R. Whitenton, "The Dissembler of John 3: A Cognitive and Rhetorical Approach to the Characterization of Nicodemus" *JBL* 135, no. 1 (2016): 141–58.
18. The quotation is from the "Did You Know?" paragraph in the Merriam-Webster online dictionary, https://www.merriam-webster.com/dictionary/plenipotentiary.
19. NIDNTTE, *s.v.* ἀποστέλλω; Jacobus Kok, "The Plenipotentiary Idea as Leitmotiv in John's Gospel," *In die Skriflig* 49, no. 2 (2015): art. 1923, http://dx.doi.org/10.4102/ids.v49i2.1923; Van der Watt, *Family of the King*, 296–302.
20. Larry W. Hurtado, *One God, One Lord: Early Christian Devotion and Ancient Jewish Monotheism*, 2nd ed. (Edinburgh: T&T Clark, 1998), 115–16.
21. Lightfoot, *St. John's Gospel,* 119.
22. See also Ruben Zimmermann, "Jesus—the Divine Bridegroom? John 2–4 and Its Christological Implications," in *Reading the Gospel of John's Christology as Jewish Messianism: Royal, Prophetic, and Divine Messiahs*, eds. Benjamin E. Reynolds and Gabriele Boccaccini (Leiden: Brill, 2018), 358–86.
23. For an extension discussion of this metaphor, see Mary L. Coloe, "Witness and Friend: Symbolism Associated with John the Baptist," in Frey and Van der Watt, *Imagery in the Gospel of John*, 319–32.
24. Herman Ridderbos, *The Gospel of John: A Theological Commentary*, trans. John Vriend (Grand Rapids: Eerdmans, 1992), 147.
25. George L. Parsenios, "The Testimony of John's Narrative and the Silence of the Johannine Narrator," in *The Opening of John's Narrative (John 1:19–2:22): Historical, Literary, and Theological Readings from the Colloquium Ioanneum 2015 in Ephesus*, eds. R. Alan Culpepper and Jörg Frey (Tübingen: Mohr Siebeck, 2017), 1–16, esp. 3, 7.
26. Parsenios, "Testimony," 7–8.

JOHN 4

1. Marianne Meye Thompson, *John: A Commentary*, NTL (Louisville: Westminster John Knox, 2015), 98.
2. Colleen M. Conway, *Men and Women in the Fourth Gospel: Gender and Johannine Characterization*, SBLDS 167 (Atlanta: Society of Biblical Literature, 1997), 108; P. Joseph Cahill, "Narrative Art in John IV," *RelStB* 2 (1982): 41–47, esp. 44–47.
3. Gerry Wheaton, *The Role of Jewish Feasts in John's Gospel*, SNTSMS 162 (Cambridge: Cambridge University Press, 2015), 66.
4. Janeth Norfleete Day, *The Woman at the Well: Interpretation of John 4:1–42 in Retrospect and Prospect* (Leiden: Brill, 2002), 161–62.

5. Conway, *Men and Women in the Fourth Gospel*, 104.
6. Conway, *Men and Women in the Fourth Gospel*, 106.
7. For an in-depth discussion of the interpretation of this story throughout church history, see Day, *Woman at the Well*.
8. Wheaton, *Role of Jewish Feasts in John's Gospel*, 69 (emphasis original).
9. George R. Beasley-Murray, *John*, WBC 36 (Waco, TX: Word, 1987), 61.
10. John Calvin, *The Gospel according to St. John 1–10*, trans. T. H. L. Parker, ed. David W. Torrance and Thomas F. Torrance (Grand Rapids: Eerdmans, 1959), 94.
11. Raymond E. Brown, *The Gospel according to John I–XII*, AB 29 (Garden City, NY: Doubleday, 1966), 175.
12. Day, *Woman at the Well*, 171.
13. Robert Kysar, *John* (Minneapolis: Augsburg, 1986), 65. As also, Ernst Haenchen, *John I: A Commentary on the Gospel of John Chapters 1–6*, trans. Robert W. Funk, Hermeneia (Philadelphia: Fortress, 1984), 221b; Rudolf Schnackenburg, *The Gospel according to John* (New York: Herder and Herder, 1968), 1:432.
14. Conway, *Men and Women*, 118.
15. There is a small sect in Israel that claims descent from the Samaritans who continue to practice animal sacrifice on Mt. Gerizim even today, but there is no temple standing. Richard Plummer, *The Samaritans: A Profile* (Grand Rapids: Eerdmans, 2016), 289.
16. Richard B. Hays, *Echoes of Scripture in the Gospels* (Waco, TX: Baylor University Press, 2016), 296.
17. Catrin H. Williams, "Johannine Christology and Prophetic Traditions: The Case of Isaiah," in *Reading the Gospel of John's Christology as Jewish Messianism: Royal, Prophetic, and Divine Messiahs*, eds. Benjamin E. Reynolds and Gabriele Boccaccini (Leiden: Brill, 2018), 93.
18. Cahill, "Narrative Art in John IV," 42.
19. Day, *Woman at the Well*, 39, citing Elisabeth Schüssler Fiorenza, *In Memory of Her: A Feminist Theological Construction of Christian Origins* (New York: Crossroad, 1983), 327–28.
20. D. A. Carson, *The Gospel according to John*, PNTC (Grand Rapids: Eerdmans, 1991), 230.
21. Wheaton, *Role of Jewish Feasts*, 74–78, esp. 78 (emphasis original).
22. Dorothy A. Lee, *The Symbolic Narratives of the Fourth Gospel: The Interplay of Form and Meaning*, JSNTSup 95 (Sheffield: JSOT Press, 1994), 66.
23. Lee, *Symbolic Narratives*, 83.
24. Conway, *Men and Women in the Fourth Gospel*, 125.
25. Thompson, *John*, 109 (emphasis original).
26. Lee, *Symbolic Narratives*, 93.
27. Lindsay Olesberg, *The Bible Study Handbook* (Downers Grove, IL: InterVarsity Press, 2012), 116.
28. Thompson, *John*, 114.

JOHN 5

1. Gerry Wheaton, *The Role of Jewish Feasts in John's Gospel*, SNTSMS 162 (Cambridge: Cambridge University Press, 2015), 117.
2. Not within the biblical canon, these books are among those known as the Apocrypha or as deuterocanonical.
3. Adele Reinhartz, "The Gospel According to John," in *The Jewish Annotated New Testament*, ed. Amy-Jill Levine and Marc Zvi Brettler, 2nd ed. (Oxford: Oxford University Press, 2017), 186; James H. Charlesworth, *Jesus as Mirrored in John: The Genius in the New Testament* (London: T&T Clark, 2019), 174, 186–98; Andreas Köstenberger, "John," in *Zondervan Illustrated Bible Backgrounds Commentary*, ed. Clinton E. Arnold (Grand Rapids: Zondervan, 2002), 2:54; Marianne Meye Thompson, *John:*

A Commentary, NTL (Louisville: Westminster John Knox, 2015), 120; James H. Charlesworth, "The Dead Sea Scrolls and the Gospel according to John," in *Exploring the Gospel of John in Honor of D. Moody Smith*, eds. R. Alan Culpepper and C. Clifton Black (Louisville: Westminster John Knox, 1996), 67.

4. Köstenberger, "John," 54.
5. Dorothy A. Lee, *The Symbolic Narratives of the Fourth Gospel: The Interplay of Form and Meaning*, JSNTSup 95 (Sheffield: JSOT Press, 1994), 111–12.
6. Thompson, *John*, 125; also Richard B. Hays, *Echoes of Scripture in the Gospels* (Waco, TX: Baylor University Press, 2016), 282.
7. Thompson, *John*, 127.
8. Larry W. Hurtado, "The Binitarian Shape of Early Christian Worship," in *The Jewish Roots of Christological Monotheism: Papers from the St. Andrews Conference on the Historical Origins of the Worship of Jesus*, eds. Carey C. Newman, James R. Davila, and Gladys S. Lewis (Leiden: Brill, 1999), 187–213, esp. 191, 213.
9. Thompson, *John*, 130–31.
10. Marianne Meye Thompson "'Every Picture Tells a Story': Imagery for God in the Gospel of John," in *Imagery in the Gospel of John: Terms, Forms, Themes, and Theology of Johannine Figurative Language*, eds. Jörg Frey, Jan G. Van der Watt, and Ruben Zimmermann, WUNT 200 (Tübingen: Mohr Siebeck, 2006), 259–77, esp. 262, 266.
11. Lee, *Symbolic Narratives*, 118.
12. Jan Van der Watt, *Family of the King: Dynamics of Metaphor in the Gospel according to John* (Leiden: Brill, 2000), 202–3.
13. Van der Watt, *Family of the King*, 178.
14. Carson, *Gospel according to John*, 266; see also Stan Harstine, *Moses as a Character in the Fourth Gospel: A Study of Ancient Reading Techniques*, JSNTSup 229 (London: Sheffield Academic, 2002), 57–59.
15. Harstine, *Moses as a Character*, 57–59.
16. Lee, *Symbolic Narratives*, 107.
17. Lee, *Symbolic Narratives*, 99.

JOHN 6

1. Marianne Meye Thompson, *John: A Commentary*, NTL (Louisville: Westminster John Knox, 2015), 140.
2. E.g., Albert Schweitzer, *The Quest of the Historical Jesus*, trans. W. Montgomery (Mineola, NY: Dover, 2005), 52.
3. Francis J. Moloney, *Signs and Shadows: Reading John 5–12* (Minneapolis: Fortress, 1996), 39.
4. For more on this allusion to crossing the Red Sea see Susan Hylen, *Allusion and Meaning in John 6* (Berlin: de Gruyter, 2005), 131–34.
5. Hylen, *Allusion and Meaning*, 131–34.
6. Or, "It is I; do not be afraid."
7. Richard B. Hays, *Echoes of Scripture in the Gospels* (Waco, TX: Baylor University Press, 2016), 321. For further discussion of Isaiah as a background for John 6 see Catrin H. Williams, "Isaiah in John's Gospel," in *Isaiah in the New Testament*, ed. Steve Moyise and Maarten J. J. Menken (London: T&T Clark International, 2005), 101–16; Gerry Wheaton, *The Role of Jewish Feasts in John's Gospel*, SNTSMS 162 (Cambridge: Cambridge University Press, 2015), 106–8.
8. Jan Van der Watt, *Family of the King: Dynamics of Metaphor in the Gospel According to John* (Leiden: Brill, 2000), 220.
9. NIDNTTE, *s.v.* "βρῶμα."
10. Jan Heilmann, "A Meal in the Background of John 6:51–58?," *JBL* 137 (2018): 481–500, quotation on 487.
11. Van der Watt, *Family of the King*, 220.

12. Sigurd Grindheim, "The Work of God or Human Beings: A Note on John 6:29," *JETS* 59, no. 1 (2016): 63–66.

13. For a discussion of other possible source verses see Hylen, *Allusion and Meaning*, 135–36.

14. Andreas J. Köstenberger, *John*, BECNT (Grand Rapids: Baker Academic, 2004), 210.

15. Francis J. Moloney, *Signs and Shadows: Reading John 5–12* (Minneapolis: Fortress, 1996), 50.

16. R. A. Culpepper, *Anatomy of the Fourth Gospel* (Philadelphia: Fortress, 1983), 196.

17. Not within the biblical canon, these books are among those known as the Apocrypha or as deuterocanonical.

18. Moloney, *Signs and Shadows*, 48.

19. Edward W. Klink III, *John*, ZECNT (Grand Rapids: Zondervan, 2016), 331.

20. Moloney, *Signs and Shadows*, 46, 48.

21. Moloney, *Signs and Shadows*, 55.

22. Richard Bauckham, *Gospel of Glory: Major Themes in Johannine Theology* (Grand Rapids: Baker Academic, 2015), 104.

23. Moloney, *Signs and Shadows*, 57.

24. Heilmann, "A Meal in the Background of John 6:51–58?," 481.

25. Bauckham, *Gospel of Glory*, 103.

26. Wheaton, *Role of Jewish Feasts*, 123 (emphasis original).

27. Thompson, *John*, 151; Stan Harstine, *Moses as a Character in the Fourth Gospel: A Study of Ancient Reading Techniques*, JSNTSup 229 (London: Sheffield Academic, 2002), 61.

28. Wheaton, *Role of Jewish Feasts*, 108 (emphasis original).

29. Herman Ridderbos, *The Gospel of John: A Theological Commentary*, trans. John Vriend (Grand Rapids: Eerdmans, 1992), 248.

30. For further reflection, see Anthony T. Selvaggio, *The Seven Signs: Seeing the Glory of Christ in the Gospel of John* (Grand Rapids: Reformation Heritage Books, 2010), 65–75.

JOHN 7

1. Richard B. Hays, *Echoes of Scripture in the Gospels* (Waco, TX: Baylor University Press, 2016), 301.

2. Francis J. Moloney, *Love in the Gospel of John: An Exegetical, Theological, and Literary Study* (Grand Rapids: Baker Academic, 2013), 84.

3. For a discussion of the ethical dimensions of what some see as duplicity, see Harold E. Attridge, *Essays on John and Hebrews* (Tübingen: Mohr Siebeck, 2010), 106–9.

4. Andreas J. Köstenberger, *John*, BECNT (Grand Rapids: Baker Academic, 2004), 231.

5. Stan Harstine, *Moses as a Character in the Fourth Gospel: A Study of Ancient Reading Techniques*, JSNTSup 229 (London: Sheffield Academic, 2002), 60.

6. Harstine, *Moses as a Character*, 66.

7. Adele Reinhartz, "The Gospel according to John," in *The Jewish Annotated New Testament*, eds. Amy-Jill Levine and Marc Zvi Brettler, 2nd ed. (Oxford: Oxford University Press, 2011), 192nn27–28.

8. Hays, *Echoes in the Gospels*, 301.

9. D. A. Carson, *The Gospel according to John*, PNTC (Grand Rapids: Eerdmans, 1991), 321–22.

10. Gary T. Manning, *Echoes of a Prophet: The Use of Ezekiel in the Gospel of John and in Literature of the Second Temple Period*, JSNTSup 270 (London: T&T Clark International, 2004), 182.

11. Carson, *John*, 321.

12. Jan Van der Watt, *Family of the King: Dynamics of Metaphor in the Gospel according to John* (Leiden: Brill, 2000), 233.

13. Craig Koester, *Symbolism in the Fourth Gospel: Meaning, Mystery, Community* (Minneapolis: Fortress, 2003), 205.
14. Gerry Wheaton, *The Role of Jewish Feasts in John's Gospel*, SNTSMS 162 (Cambridge: Cambridge University Press, 2015), 158.
15. John Newman, "Eating and Drinking as Sources of Metaphor in English," *Cuadernos de Filología Inglesa* 6, no. 2 (1997): 213–31.
16. Manning, *Echoes of a Prophet*, 186.
17. See Ruben Zimmermann, "Imagery in John: Opening Up Paths into the Tangled Thicket of John's Figurative World," in *Imagery in the Gospel of John: Terms, Forms, Themes, and Theology of Johannine Figurative Language*, eds. Jörg Frey, Jan G. Van der Watt, and Ruben Zimmermann, WUNT 200 (Tübingen: Mohr Siebeck, 2006), 1–43, quotation on 23.
18. Francis J. Moloney, *Signs and Shadows: Reading John 5–12* (Minneapolis: Fortress, 1996), 142.

JOHN 8

1. D. A. Carson, *The Gospel according to John*, PNTC (Grand Rapids: Eerdmans, 1991), 333.
2. C. S. Lewis, *Mere Christianity* (New York: Macmillan, 1958), 41.
3. Herman Ridderbos, *The Gospel of John: A Theological Commentary*, trans. John Vriend (Grand Rapids: Eerdmans, 1992), 297.
4. Ridderbos, *John*, 298.
5. John Murray, *The Collected Writings of John Murray* (Carlisle, PA: Banner of Truth Trust, 1977), 2:162.
6. Craig R. Koester, "What Does It Mean to Be Human? Imagery and the Human Condition in John's Gospel," in *Imagery in the Gospel of John: Terms, Forms, Themes, and Theology of Johannine Figurative Language*, eds. Jörg Frey, Jan G. Van der Watt, and Ruben Zimmermann, WUNT 200 (Tübingen: Mohr Siebeck, 2006), 403.
7. Koester, "What Does It Mean," 420.
8. Jan G. Van der Watt, "Ethics Alive in Imagery," in Frey and Van der Watt, *Imagery in the Gospel of John*, 421–48, esp. 435.
9. Carson, *John*, 349.
10. Edward W. Klink III, *John*, ZECNT (Grand Rapids: Zondervan, 2016), 421.
11. Adele Reinhartz, *Befriending the Beloved Disciple: A Jewish Reading of the Gospel of John* (New York: Continuum, 2001), 94.
12. Klink, *John*, 421, quoting Adele Reinhartz, "John 8:31–59 from a Jewish Perspective," in *Remembering for the Future: The Holocaust in an Age of Genocide*, eds. John K. Roth and Elisabeth Maxwell (New York: Palgrave, 2001), quotation on 2:793 (emphasis original).
13. Richard B. Hays, *Echoes of Scripture in the Gospels* (Waco, TX: Baylor University Press, 2016), 284, 289.
14. John Calvin, *The Gospel According to St John 1–10*, trans. T. H. L. Parker, eds. David W. Torrance and Thomas F. Torrance (Grand Rapids: Eerdmans, 1959), 235 (emphasis added).
15. Calvin, *John*, 235.

JOHN 9

1. Britt Leslie, *One Thing I Know: How the Blind Man of John 9 Leads an Audience toward Belief* (Eugene, OR: Pickwick, 2015), 120, 125–28.
2. George R. Beasley-Murray, *John*, WBC 36 (Waco, TX: Word, 1987), 154–55; Raymond E. Brown, *The Gospel according to John I–XII*, AB 29 (Garden City, NY: Doubleday, 1966), 371.
3. Beasley-Murray, *John*, 155; J. Ramsey Michaels, *The Gospel of John*, NICNT (Grand Rapids: Eerdmans, 2010), 541–42; Leon Morris, *The Gospel according to John*, NICNT (Grand Rapids: Eerdmans, 1995), 425.

4. Sigurd Grindheim, "The Work of God or Human Beings: A Note on John 6:29," *JETS* 59, no. 1 (2016): 63–66.
5. Beasley-Murray, *John*, 155.
6. Morris, *John*, 425.
7. David Rensberger, *Johannine Faith and Liberating Community* (Philadelphia: Westminster, 1988), 44.
8. Leslie, *One Thing I Know*, 138.
9. Ludwig Koehler, Walter Baumgartner, and Johann J. Stamm, *The Hebrew and Aramaic Lexicon of the Old Testament*, trans. and ed. under the supervision of Mervyn E. J. Richardson. (Leiden: Brill, 1994), vol. 1, *s.v.* "שׁוע." Carmen Imes first brought this to my attention in her unpublished paper "Eyes Besmeared: Jesus' Re-enactment of Isaiah's Mission in John 9." See J. Duncan M. Derrett, "John 9:6 Read with Isaiah 6:10; 20:9," *EvQ* 66, no. 3 (1994): 251–54.
10. The Greek version is preserved in the sixth-century manuscript Q (Marchalianus). See Charles C. Torrey, *The Lives of the Prophets: Greek Text and Translation* (Philadelphia: Society of Biblical Literature and Exegesis, 1946), quotation on 3.
11. Gk., Σιλωάμ; Heb., שִׁלֹחַ.
12. Leslie, *One Thing I Know*, 105.
13. Leslie, *One Thing I Know*, 176.
14. J. Louis Martyn, *History and Theology in the Fourth Gospel* (New York: Harper & Row, 1968).
15. William Wright, *Rhetoric and Theology: Figural Reading of John 9* (Berlin: de Gruyter, 2009), 196.
16. Leslie, *One Thing I Know*, 17.
17. Craig R. Koester, "What Does It Mean to Be Human? Imagery and the Human Condition in John's Gospel," in *Imagery in the Gospel of John: Terms, Forms, Themes, and Theology of Johannine Figurative Language*, eds. Jörg Frey, Jan G. Van der Watt, and Ruben Zimmermann, WUNT 200 (Tübingen: Mohr Siebeck, 2006), 416.
18. Leslie, *One Thing I Know*, 178.
19. Leslie, *One Thing I Know*, 108.
20. Stan Harstine, *Moses as a Character in the Fourth Gospel: A Study of Ancient Reading Techniques*, JSNTSup 229 (London: Sheffield Academic, 2002), 70.
21. William Wright, *Rhetoric and Theology: Figural Reading of John 9* (Berlin: de Gruyter, 2009), 165.
22. J. Alec Motyer, *The Prophecy of Isaiah: An Introduction and Commentary* (Downers Grove, IL: IVP Academic, 1993), 78 (emphasis original).
23. Motyer, *Prophecy of Isaiah*, 78.

JOHN 10

1. Britt Leslie, *One Thing I Know: How the Blind Man of John 9 Leads an Audience toward Belief* (Eugene, OR: Pickwick, 2015), 93–94; Beth M. Stovell, *Mapping Metaphorical Discourse in the Fourth Gospel: John's Eternal King* (Leiden: Brill, 2012), 253; Karoline M. Lewis, *Rereading the "Shepherd Discourse": Restoring the Integrity of John 9:39–10:21*, Studies in Biblical Literature 113 (New York: Peter Lang, 2008); Jan A. Du Rand, "A Syntactical and Narratological Reading of John 10 in Coherence with Chapter 9," in *The Shepherd Discourse of John 10 and Its Context*, eds. Johanne Beutler and Robert T. Fortna (Cambridge: Cambridge University Press, 1991), 94–115.
2. John Painter, "Tradition, History and Interpretation in John 10," in *The Shepherd Discourse of John 10 and Its Context*, eds. Johanne Beutler and Robert T. Fortna (Cambridge: Cambridge University Press, 1991), 53–74, esp. 54.
3. Leslie, *One Thing I Know*, 132.
4. William Wright, *Rhetoric and Theology: Figural Reading of John 9* (Berlin: de Gruyter, 2009), 106.

5. Kenneth E. Bailey, *The Good Shepherd: A Thousand-Year Journey from Psalm 23 to the New Testament* (Downers Grove, IL: IVP Academic, 2014), 213.

6. Bailey, *Good Shepherd*, 31–32.

7. Bailey, *Good Shepherd*, 212–18.

8. Herman Ridderbos, *The Gospel of John: A Theological Commentary*, trans. John Vriend (Grand Rapids: Eerdmans, 1992), 356 (emphasis original).

9. George R. Beasley-Murray, *John*, WBC 36 (Waco, TX: Word, 1987), 170.

10. See Stovell, *Mapping Metaphorical Discourse*, 253.

11. Richard Bauckham, *Gospel of Glory: Major Themes in Johannine Theology* (Grand Rapids: Baker Academic, 2015), 66.

12. Bauckham, *Gospel of Glory*, 29.

13. Bauckham, *Gospel of Glory*, 29–30.

14. Bailey, *Good Shepherd,* 238.

15. Rekha M. Chennattu, "Scripture," in *How John Works: Storytelling in the Fourth Gospel*, eds. Douglas Estes and Ruth Sheridan, Resources for Biblical Study 86 (Atlanta: SBL Press, 2016) 171–86, esp. 173.

16. Gerry Wheaton, *The Role of Jewish Feasts in John's Gospel*, SNTSMS 162 (Cambridge: Cambridge University Press, 2015), 164; Ruben Zimmermann, "Imagery in John: Opening Up Paths into the Tangled Thicket of John's Figurative World," in *Imagery in the Gospel of John: Terms, Forms, Themes, and Theology of Johannine Figurative Language*, eds. Jörg Frey, Jan G. Van der Watt, and Ruben Zimmermann, WUNT 200 (Tübingen: Mohr Siebeck, 2006), 1–43, esp. 23.

17. Gary T. Manning, *Echoes of a Prophet: The Use of Ezekiel in the Gospel of John and in Literature of the Second Temple Period*, JSNTSup 270 (London: T&T Clark International, 2004), 114.

18. Manning, *Echoes of a Prophet*, 115.

19. Manning, *Echoes of a Prophet*, 115. See also 112–13 for further verbal parallels between the shepherd images in John and Ezekiel.

20. Margaret Daly-Denton, *David in the Fourth Gospel: The Johannine Reception of the Psalms* (Leiden: Brill, 2000), 264.

21. Larry W. Hurtado, *Lord Jesus Christ: Devotion to Jesus in Earliest Christianity* (Grand Rapids: Eerdmans, 2003), 375.

22. Edward W. Klink III, *John*, ZECNT (Grand Rapids: Zondervan, 2016), 479.

23. D. A. Carson, *The Gospel according to John*, PNTC (Grand Rapids: Eerdmans, 1991), 395.

24. Bauckham, *Gospel of Glory*, 32 (emphasis original).

25. Klink, *John*, 479.

26. Carson, *John*, 399.

27. Carson, *John*, 399.

28. Bauckham, *Gospel of Glory*, 34.

29. Larry W. Hurtado, "The Binitarian Shape of Early Christian Worship," in *The Jewish Roots of Christological Monotheism: Papers from the St. Andrews Conference on the Historical Origins of the Worship of Jesus*, eds. Carey C. Newman, James R. Davila, and Gladys S. Lewis (Leiden: Brill, 1999), 187–213, esp. 211.

30. William Knight, *Colloquia Peripatetica: Deep-Sea Soundings Being Notes of Conversations with the Late John Duncan* (Edinburgh: David Douglas, 1879), 109.

31. C. S. Lewis, *Mere Christianity* (New York: Macmillan, 1958), 41.

32. John Dart, "Seminar Rules Out 80% of Words Attributed to Jesus: Religion: Provocative Meeting of Biblical Scholars Ends Six Years of Voting on Authenticity in the Gospels," *LA Times*, March 4, 1991, https://www.latimes.com/archives/la-xpm-1991-03-04-mn-77-story.html.

33. C. S. Lewis, "Christ Has No Parallel in Other Religions," in *Readings for Meditation and Reflection*, ed. Walter Hooper (New York: Harper Collins, 1992), 25–27, quotation on 26.

34. John Painter, "Tradition, History and Interpretation in John 10," in *The Shepherd Discourse of John 10 and Its Context*, eds. Johanne Beutler and Robert T. Fortna (Cambridge: Cambridge University Press, 1991), 53–74.

JOHN 11

1. Colleen M. Conway, *Men and Women in the Fourth Gospel: Gender and Johannine Characterization*, SBLDS 167 (Atlanta: Society of Biblical Literature, 1997), 138.
2. Beth M. Stovell, *Mapping Metaphorical Discourse in the Fourth Gospel: John's Eternal King* (Leiden: Brill, 2012), 172–73, 177.
3. For instance, Francis J. Moloney argues that none of the siblings had adequate understanding of Jesus in the terms of Johannine faith in "Can Everyone Be Wrong? John 11.1–12.8," *New Testament Studies* 49 (2003): 505–27.
4. For the diversity of Jewish beliefs, see Martha Himmelfarb, "Afterlife and Resurrection," in *The Jewish Annotated New Testament*, eds. Amy-Jill Levine and Marc Zvi Brettler, 2nd ed. (Oxford: Oxford University Press, 2011), 691–95; George Nickelsburg, *Resurrection, Immortality, and Eternal Life in Intertestamental Judaism* (Cambridge, MA: Harvard University Press, 1972).
5. Another interpretation understands that Jesus is indeed angry with the mourners. As Moloney puts it, "Jesus, the resurrection and the life, is angered, deeply moved, and he weeps, as all his attempts to lead his disciples, Martha and Mary into a true understanding of life and death meet failure." Moloney, "Can Everyone Be Wrong?," 519.
6. Marianne Meye Thompson, "The Raising of Lazarus in John 11: A Theological Reading," in *The Gospel of John and Christian Theology*, eds. Richard Bauckham and Carl Mosser (Grand Rapids: Eerdmans, 2008), 233–44, quotation on 243.
7. Ruben Zimmermann, "The Narrative Hermeneutics of John 11: Learning with Lazarus How to Understand Death, Life and Resurrection," in *The Resurrection of Jesus in the Gospel of John*, eds. Craig K. Koester and Reimund Bieringer (Tübingen: Mohr Siebeck, 2008), 75–101, quotation on 93.
8. Gail R. O'Day, *The Word Disclosed: John's Story and Narrative Preaching* (St. Louis: CBP, 1987), 91, cited by Conway, *Men and Women in the Fourth Gospel*, 148.
9. Francis J. Moloney, *The Gospel of John: Text and Context* (Leiden: Brill, 2005), 263.
10. Andrew T. Lincoln, "The Lazarus Story: A Literary Perspective," in Bauckham and Mosser, *The Gospel of John and Christian Theology*, 211–32, quote on 217.
11. Richard Bauckham, *Gospel of Glory: Major Themes in Johannine Theology* (Grand Rapids: Baker Academic, 2015), 67.
12. Zimmerman, "Narrative Hermeneutics of John 11," 77.
13. Thompson, "Raising of Lazarus," 238.
14. Thompson, "Raising of Lazarus," 242.
15. Zimmermann, "Narrative Hermeneutics of John 11," 101.
16. Moloney, "Can Everyone Be Wrong?," 522.
17. Andreas J. Köstenberger, "John," in *Zondervan Illustrated Bible Backgrounds Commentary*, ed. Clinton E. Arnold (Grand Rapids: Zondervan, 2002), 118a.
18. Conway, *Men and Women in John*, 135.
19. Lincoln, "The Lazarus Story," 211.
20. Thompson "The Raising of Lazarus," 236.
21. Lincoln, "The Lazarus Story," 217.

JOHN 12

1. Andreas J. Köstenberger, *John*, BECNT (Grand Rapids: Baker Academic, 2004), 363–64.
2. James A. Sanders, "A New Testament Hermeneutic Fabric: Psalm 118 in the Entrance Narrative," in *Early Jewish and Christian Exegesis: Studies in Memory of William Hugh*

      Brownlee, eds. Craig A. Evans and William F. Stinespring (Atlanta: Scholars Press, 1987), 177–90.

3. Sanders, "A New Testament Hermeneutic Fabric," 188.
4. Edward W. Klink III, *John*, ZECNT (Grand Rapids: Zondervan, 2016), 539.
5. Herman Ridderbos, *The Gospel of John: A Theological Commentary*, trans. John Vriend (Grand Rapids: Eerdmans, 1992), 424.
6. Jan G. Van der Watt, "Ethics Alive in Imagery," in *Imagery in the Gospel of John: Terms, Forms, Themes, and Theology of Johannine Figurative Language*, eds. Jörg Frey, Jan G. Van der Watt, and Ruben Zimmermann, WUNT 200 (Tübingen: Mohr Siebeck, 2006), 440.
7. Richard Bauckham, *Gospel of Glory: Major Themes in Johannine Theology* (Grand Rapids: Baker Academic, 2015), 73–74.
8. Klink, *John*, 555, quoting Judith L. Kovacs, "'Now Shall the Ruler of This World Be Driven Out': Jesus' Death as Cosmic Battle in John 12:30–36," *JBL* 114 (1995): 227–47, quotation on 246.
9. Catrin H. Williams, "Johannine Christology and Prophetic Traditions: The Case of Isaiah," in *Reading the Gospel of John's Christology as Jewish Messianism: Royal, Prophetic, and Divine Messiahs*, eds. Benjamin E. Reynolds and Gabriele Boccaccini (Leiden: Brill, 2018), 107.
10. D. Moody Smith, "The Setting and Shape of a Johannine Narrative Source," *JBL* 95, no. 2 (1976): 231–41, quote on 236; n20 gives extant evidence of the claim.
11. Bauckham, *Gospel of Glory*, 53–54. The operation of intertextuality created by the use of Old Testament quotations by the New Testament writers is a vast and interesting topic of biblical hermeneutics. Almost always a quotation of the Old in the New is intended to evoke the larger immediate context of the Old Testament passage, in which additional important connections are often found.
12. Jonathan Lett, "The Divine Identity of Jesus as the Reason for Israel's Unbelief in John 12:36–43," *JBL* 135, no. 1 (2016): 159–73; Craig A. Evans, "Obduracy and the Lord's Servant: Some Observations on the Use of the Old Testament in the Fourth Gospel," in Evans and Stinespring, *Early Jewish and Christian Exegesis*, 221–36.
13. George R. Beasley-Murray, *John*, WBC 36 (Waco, TX: Word, 1987), 216.
14. G. K. Beale, *We Become What We Worship: A Biblical Theology of Idolatry* (Downers Grove, IL: IVP Academic, 2008), 180–81.
15. Beale, *We Become What We Worship*, 181.
16. Catrin H. Williams, "Isaiah in John's Gospel," in *Isaiah in the New Testament*, eds. Steve Moyise and Maarten J. J. Menken (London: T&T Clark International, 2005), 101–16, quotation on 111.
17. Williams, "Johannine Christology and Prophetic Traditions," 97.
18. Smith, "Setting and Shape," 237.
19. Klink, *John*, 562.
20. Craig A. Evans, "The Hermeneutics of Mark and John: On the Theology of the Canonical 'Gospel,'" *Biblica* 64, no. 2 (1983): 153–72, quotation on 163.
21. Bruce M. Metzger, "The Formulas Introducing Quotations of Scripture in the NT and the Midrash," *JBL* 70 (1951): 297–307, quotation on 306–7 (emphasis added).
22. Beasley-Murray, *John*, 216.
23. Sandra Schneiders, "Women in the Fourth Gospel," *Biblical Theology Bulletin* 12 (1982): 35–45, quotation on 42–43. See also Conway's discussion of Schneider's point in Colleen M. Conway, *Men and Women in the Fourth Gospel: Gender and Johannine Characterization*, SBLDS 167 (Atlanta: Society of Biblical Literature, 1997), 151–53.
24. Craig A. Evans, "Obduracy and the Lord's Servant: Some Observations on the Use of the Old Testament in the Fourth Gospel," in Evans and Stinespring, *Early Jewish and Christian Exegesis*, 221–36, esp. 228; Smith, "Setting and Shape," 237; also Martin

Hengel, "The Old Testament in the Fourth Gospel," in *The Gospels and the Scriptures of Israel*, eds. Craig A. Evans and W. Richard Stegner, JSNTSup 104 (Sheffield: Sheffield Academic, 1994), 392, 402.

JOHN 13

1. James H. Charlesworth, *Jesus as Mirrored in John: The Genius in the New Testament* (London: T&T Clark, 2019), 140.
2. See D. A. Carson, *John*, PNTC (Grand Rapids: Eerdmans, 1991), 455–58; Edward W. Klink III, *John*, ZECNT (Grand Rapids: Zondervan, 2016), 757–60.
3. Colleen M. Conway, *Men and Women in the Fourth Gospel: Gender and Johannine Characterization*, SBLDS 167 (Atlanta: Society of Biblical Literature, 1997), 171.
4. Marianne Meye Thompson, "Baptism with Water and with Holy Spirit: Purification in the Gospel of John," in *The Opening of John's Narrative (John 1:19–2:22): Historical, Literary, and Theological Readings from the Colloquium Ioanneum 2015 in Ephesus*, eds. R. Alan Culpepper and Jörg Frey (Tübingen: Mohr Siebeck, 2017), 59–78, quotation on 68.
5. Francis J. Moloney, *Love in the Gospel of John: An Exegetical, Theological, and Literary Study* (Grand Rapids: Baker Academic, 2013), 106.
6. Krystal D'Costa, "What Are the Jobs That Immigrants Do?," *Anthropology in Practice* (blog), *Scientific American*, August 9, 2018, https://blogs.scientificamerican.com/anthropology-in-practice/what-are-the-jobs-that-immigrants-do.
7. Christopher J. H. Wright, *The Mission of God* (Downers Grove, IL: IVP Academic, 2006), 262–64.
8. J. Ramsey Michaels, "Betrayal and the Betrayer: The Uses of Scripture in John 13.18–19," in *The Gospels and the Scriptures of Israel*, eds. Craig A. Evans and W. Richard Stegner, JSNTSup 104 (Sheffield: Sheffield Academic, 1994), 459–74, esp. 473.
9. Michaels, "Betrayal and the Betrayer," 463.
10. Michaels, "Betrayal and the Betrayer," 461.
11. See James H. Charlesworth, *The Beloved Disciple: Whose Witness Validates the Gospel of John?* (Valley Forge, PA: Trinity Press International, 1995); Katherine C. Linforth, *The Beloved Disciple: Jacob the Brother of the Lord* (Freemantle, Australia: VIVID, 2014); D. Francois Tolmie, "The (Not So) Good Shepherd: The Use of Shepherd Imagery in the Characterisation of Peter in the Fourth Gospel," in *Imagery in the Gospel of John: Terms, Forms, Themes, and Theology of Johannine Figurative Language*, eds. Jörg Frey, Jan G. Van der Watt, and Ruben Zimmermann, WUNT 200 (Tübingen: Mohr Siebeck, 2006), 353–67.
12. Moloney, *Love*, 112.
13. Paul Althaus, *The Theology of Martin Luther*, trans. Robert C. Schultz (Philadelphia: Fortress, 1966), 165.
14. Edward W. Klink III, *John*, ZECNT (Grand Rapids: Zondervan, 2016), 596.
15. Britt Leslie, *One Thing I Know: How the Blind Man of John 9 Leads an Audience toward Belief* (Eugene, OR: Pickwick, 2015), 87 (emphasis original).
16. Richard Bauckham, *Gospel of Glory: Major Themes in Johannine Theology* (Grand Rapids: Baker Academic, 2015), 72.
17. Tolmie, "(Not So) Good Shepherd," 364.
18. Tolmie, "(Not So) Good Shepherd," 365 (emphasis original).
19. See Conway, *Men and Women in John*, 169.
20. Bauckham, *Gospel of Glory*, 67.

JOHN 14

1. The ambiguity of the mood (indicative or imperative) of the present-tense verb πιστεύετε (believe, trust) in its two occurrences here is familiar to those who read the Greek

New Testament text. In the context of a major point of chapter 14, that God is in Jesus and Jesus in God, two imperatives—"trust" in God, "trust also in me"—seems most apt. But for a fuller discussion of the four possible syntactical combinations, see D. A. Carson, *The Gospel according to John*, PNTC (Grand Rapids: Eerdmans, 1991), 487–88.

2. BDAG, *s.v.* μένω.
3. Robert H. Gundry, "'In My Father's House Are Many Μοναί' (John 14 2)," *ZNW* 58 (1967): 68–72, quotation on 70.
4. Gundry, "In My Father's House," 70.
5. Gundry, "In My Father's House," 71–72.
6. As a child I thought it made perfect sense for Jesus, the carpenter, to go build a new house for his disciples.
7. Carson, *John*, 490–91.
8. Carson, *John*, 491.
9. Gundry, "In My Father's House," 70.
10. N. T. Wright, *Surprised by Hope: Rethinking Heaven, the Resurrection, and the Mission of the Church* (San Francisco: HarperOne, 2008).
11. Thomas à Kempis, *The Imitation of Christ* (Westwood, NJ: Barbour and Company, 1984).
12. Cf. Britt Leslie, *One Thing I Know: How the Blind Man of John 9 Leads an Audience Toward Belief* (Eugene, OR: Pickwick, 2015), 140; Jan G. Van der Watt, "Ethics Alive in Imagery," in *Imagery in the Gospel of John: Terms, Forms, Themes, and Theology of Johannine Figurative Language*, eds. Jörg Frey, Jan G. Van der Watt, and Ruben Zimmermann, WUNT 200 (Tübingen: Mohr Siebeck, 2006), 436.
13. Carson, *John*, 496 (emphasis original).
14. Carson, *John*, 498.
15. Eskil Franck, *Revelation Taught: The Paraclete in the Gospel of John* (Malmö, Sweden: CWK Gleerup, 1985. For a discussion of the fourth gospel as a trial of truth, see Andrew T. Lincoln, *Truth on Trial: The Lawsuit Motif in the Fourth Gospel* (Peabody, MA: Hendrickson, 2000).
16. NIDNTTE, *s.v.* ὀρφανός.
17. NIDNTTE, *s.v.* ὀρφανός.
18. Carson, *John*, 505.
19. NIDNTTE, *s.v.* εἰρήνη.
20. Sinclair B. Ferguson, "Troubled That You May Not Be," lesson 5 of *Lessons from the Upper Room*, DVD disc 1 (Ligonier Ministries, 2014), about 22:00.

JOHN 15:1–25

1. Andrew Streett, *The Vine and the Son of Man: Eschatological Interpretation of Psalm 80 in Early Judaism* (Minneapolis: Fortress, 2014), 214.
2. Francis J. Moloney, *The Gospel of John: Text and Context* (Leiden: Brill, 2005), 269.
3. Streett, *The Vine and the Son of Man*, 215–16, quoting Andreas J. Köstenberger, *John*, BECNT (Grand Rapids: Baker Academic, 2004), 450.
4. Streett, *The Vine and the Son of Man*, 47.
5. F. F. Bruce, *The Gospel of John: Introduction, Exposition and Notes* (Grand Rapids: Eerdmans, 1983), 308–9.
6. Francis J. Moloney, *Love in the Gospel of John: An Exegetical, Theological, and Literary Study* (Grand Rapids: Baker Academic, 2013), 117.
7. Yasmine Hafiz, "The Moon Communion of Buzz Aldrin That NASA Didn't Want to Broadcast," *Huffington Post*, July 19, 2014, https://www.huffpost.com/entry/moon-communion-buzz-aldrin_n_5600648.
8. Gary T. Manning, *Echoes of a Prophet: The Use of Ezekiel in the Gospel of John and in Literature of the Second Temple Period*, JSNTSup 270 (London: T&T Clark International, 2004), 137.

9. Richard Bauckham, *Gospel of Glory: Major Themes in Johannine Theology* (Grand Rapids: Baker Academic, 2015), 65.
10. Moloney, *Love in John's Gospel*, 117.
11. Edward Malatesta, *Interiority and Covenant: A Study of "einai en" and "menein en" in the First Letter of Saint John*, Analecta Biblica 69 (Rome: Biblical Institute Press, 1978), 64.
12. Richard B. Hays, *Echoes of Scripture in the Gospels* (Waco, TX: Baylor University Press, 2016), 336–40 (emphasis added).
13. Manning, *Echoes of a Prophet*, 141.
14. Manning, *Echoes of a Prophet*, 142.
15. Manning, *Echoes of a Prophet*, 138.
16. Manning, *Echoes of a Prophet*, 145 (emphasis added).
17. Matthew Scott, *The Hermeneutics of Christological Psalmody in Paul: An Intertextual Inquiry* (Cambridge: Cambridge University Press, 2014), 64.
18. Margaret Daly-Denton, *David in the Fourth Gospel: The Johannine Reception of the Psalms* (Leiden: Brill, 2000), 204, 289.
19. Daly-Denton, *David in the Fourth Gospel*, 206.

JOHN 15:26–16:33
1. NIDNTTE, *s.v.* ἐλέγχω.
2. D. A. Carson, *The Gospel according to John*, PNTC (Grand Rapids: Eerdmans, 1991), 534–39.
3. Carson, *John*, 538.
4. See Karen H. Jobes, *1, 2, & 3 John*, ZECNT (Grand Rapids: Zondervan, 2014).
5. J. Alec Motyer, *The Prophecy of Isaiah: An Introduction and Commentary* (Downers Grove, IL: IVP Academic, 1993), 218.
6. Motyer, *Prophecy of Isaiah*, 218.
7. Eskil Franck, *Revelation Taught: The Paraclete in the Gospel of John* (Malmö, Sweden: CWK Gleerup, 1985), 48.
8. Jobes, *1, 2 & 3 John*.
9. For one discussion of the Spirit in relation to other world religions, see Gerald R. Mc-Dermott, "How the Trinity Should Govern Our Approach to World Religions," *JETS* 60, no. 1 (2017): 49–64.

JOHN 17
1. Edward W. Klink III, *John*, ZECNT (Grand Rapids: Zondervan, 2016), 728.
2. Richard Bauckham, *Gospel of Glory: Major Themes in Johannine Theology* (Grand Rapids: Baker Academic, 2015), 44.
3. Bauckham, *Gospel of Glory*, 73.
4. Francis J. Moloney, *Love in the Gospel of John: An Exegetical, Theological, and Literary Study* (Grand Rapids: Baker Academic, 2013), 125.
5. D. A. Carson, *The Gospel according to John*, PNTC (Grand Rapids: Eerdmans, 1991), 561.
6. Klink, *John*, 717, 726.
7. Bauckham, *Gospel of Glory*, 23–24.
8. Klink, *John*, 719.
9. Bauckham, *Gospel of Glory*, 29.
10. Bauckham, *Gospel of Glory*, 40.
11. Moloney, *Love*, 121.
12. Sinclair B. Ferguson, "Father, Glorify Your Son," lesson 11 of *Lessons from the Upper Room*, DVD disc 2 (Ligonier Ministries, 2014).
13. Moloney, *Love*, 123.
14. Francis J. Moloney, *Glory Not Dishonor: Reading John 13–21* (Minneapolis: Fortress, 1998), 124.

15. For a discussion of the Upper Room Discourse in light of ancient Greco-Roman consolatory texts, see Paul Holloway, "Left Behind: Jesus' Consolation of His Disciples in John 13, 21–17, 26," *ZNW* 96 (2005): 1–34.

JOHN 18

1. A wadi is a dry stream bed that floods and flows only during the rainy season.
2. Andreas J. Köstenberger, *John*, BECNT (Grand Rapids: Baker Academic, 2004), 505.
3. Francis J. Moloney, *Glory Not Dishonor: Reading John 13–21* (Minneapolis: Fortress, 1998), 130.
4. C. H. Dodd, *The Interpretation of the Fourth Gospel* (1953; repr., Cambridge: Cambridge University Press, 1988), 432.
5. D. A. Carson, *The Gospel according to John*, PNTC (Grand Rapids: Eerdmans, 1991), 578.
6. F. F. Bruce, *The Gospel of John: Introduction, Exposition, and Notes* (Grand Rapids: Eerdmans, 1983), 342 (emphasis original).
7. Bruce, *John*, 342.
8. James H. Charlesworth, *The Beloved Disciple: Whose Witness Validates the Gospel of John?* (Valley Forge, PA: Trinity Press International, 1995), 336–59, esp. 359.
9. Francis J. Moloney, *The Gospel of John: Text and Context* (Leiden: Brill, 2005), 326.
10. Köstenberger, *John*, 514.
11. James H. Charlesworth, *Jesus as Mirrored in John: The Genius in the New Testament* (London: T&T Clark, 2019), xi.
12. Tacitus, *The Annals*, trans. A. J. Woodman (Indianapolis: Hackett, 2004), 325.
13. D. Francois Tolmie, "The (Not So) Good Shepherd: The Use of Shepherd Imagery in the Characterisation of Peter in the Fourth Gospel," in *Imagery in the Gospel of John: Terms, Forms, Themes, and Theology of Johannine Figurative Language*, eds. Jörg Frey, Jan G. Van der Watt, and Ruben Zimmermann, WUNT 200 (Tübingen: Mohr Siebeck, 2006), 353–67, quotation on 364.
14. Tolmie, "(Not So) Good Shepherd," 365 (emphasis original).
15. Tolmie, "(Not So) Good Shepherd," 366 (emphasis original).
16. Karoline M. Lewis, *Rereading the "Shepherd Discourse": Restoring the Integrity of John 9:39–10:21*, Studies in Biblical Literature 113 (New York: Peter Lang, 2008), 149.
17. Moloney, *Gospel of John*, 314.
18. Moloney, *Gospel of John*, 324.

JOHN 19

1. Francis J. Moloney, *Glory Not Dishonor: Reading John 13–21* (Minneapolis: Fortress, 1998), 150–51.
2. D. A. Carson, *The Gospel according to John*, PNTC (Grand Rapids: Eerdmans, 1991), 608–9.
3. Craig A. Evans, *Word and Glory: On the Exegetical and Theological Background of John's Prologue*, JSNTSup 89 (Sheffield: JSOT Press, 1993), 174–76; Stanley A. Porter, "Exodus 12 and the Passover Theme in John," in *Sacred Tradition in the New Testament: Tracing Old Testament Themes in the Gospels and Epistles* (Grand Rapids: Baker Academic, 2016), 146–50.
4. Evans, *Word and Glory*, 174 (emphasis added).
5. Jeannine K. Brown, *The Gospels as Stories. A Narrative Approach to Matthew, Mark, Luke, and John* (Grand Rapids: Baker Academic, 2020), 140; idem., "Creation's Renewal in the Gospel of John," *CBQ* 72 (2010): 285.
6. Rekha M. Chennattu, "Scripture," in *How John Works: Storytelling in the Fourth Gospel*, ed. Douglas Estes and Ruth Sheridan, Resources for Biblical Study 86 (Atlanta: SBL Press, 2016), 186.

7. Matthew Scott, *The Hermeneutics of Christological Psalmody in Paul: An Intertextual Inquiry* (Cambridge: Cambridge University Press, 2014), 64.

8. C. H. Dodd, *The Interpretation of the Fourth Gospel* (1953; repr., Cambridge: Cambridge University Press, 1988), 439.

9. Martin Hengel, "The Old Testament in the Fourth Gospel," in *The Gospels and the Scriptures of Israel*, eds. Craig A. Evans and W. Richard Stegner, JSNTSup 104 (Sheffield: Sheffield Academic, 1994), 393–94.

10. Gerry Wheaton, *The Role of Jewish Feasts in John's Gospel*, SNTSMS 162 (Cambridge: Cambridge University Press, 2015), 157 (emphasis original).

11. Richard Bauckham, *Gospel of Glory: Major Themes in Johannine Theology* (Grand Rapids: Baker Academic, 2015), 107.

12. Bauckham, *Gospel of Glory*, 106; But see Francis J. Moloney, *The Gospel of John: Text and Context* (Leiden: Brill, 2005), 505–6, for a sacramental interpretation.

13. Carson, *John*, 627–28.

14. Stanley E. Porter, "Can Traditional Exegesis Enlighten Literary Analysis of the Fourth Gospel? An Examination of the Old Testament Fulfillment Motif and the Passover Theme," in Evans and Stegner, *Gospels and Scriptures of Israel*, 396–428; also Porter, "Exodus 12 and the Passover Theme in John," in *Sacred Tradition in the New Testament: Tracing Old Testament Themes in the Gospels and Epistles* (Grand Rapids: Baker Academic, 2016), 127–52.

15. Porter, "Can Traditional Exegesis," 419–20.

16. Porter, "Can Traditional Exegesis," 419–20.

17. Matthew mentions Moses by name seven times; Mark, nine; Luke, ten; John, thirteen times.

18. Porter, "Can Traditional Exegesis," 421.

JOHN 20

1. Francis J. Moloney, *Glory Not Dishonor: Reading John 13–21* (Minneapolis: Fortress, 1998), 160.

2. Richard Bauckham, *Gospel of Glory: Major Themes in Johannine Theology* (Grand Rapids: Baker Academic, 2015), 70.

3. Moloney, *Glory Not Dishonor*, 161.

4. D. A. Carson, *The Gospel according to John*, PNTC (Grand Rapids: Eerdmans, 1991), 639.

5. Subsequent tradition claims that the shroud of Jesus survived as what is now known as the Shroud of Turin (Italy) so named because of the cathedral in which a shroud bearing an enigmatic image of crucified man is housed. Some associate its location in Italy with the apostle Peter, who is said to have been the leader of the church of Rome at the time he was martyred. Since John says the cloth for the head was separate from the cloth wrapping the body (20:7), some argue this speaks against the authenticity of the Shroud of Turin, which is one cloth that covered head and body.

6. Moloney, *Glory Not Dishonor*, 165.

7. Sandra M. Schneiders, *Jesus Risen in Our Midst: Essays on the Resurrection of Jesus in the Fourth Gospel* (Collegeville, MN: Liturgical Press, 2013), 85.

8. Bauckham, *Gospel of Glory*, 69.

9. Moloney, *Glory Not Dishonor*, 166, 67.

10. Moloney, *Glory Not Dishonor*, 167.

11. Jeannine K. Brown, *The Gospels as Stories. A Narrative Approach to Matthew, Mark, Luke, and John* (Grand Rapids: Baker Academic, 2020), 138; idem., "Creation's Renewal in the Gospel of John," *CBQ* 72 (2010): 283.

12. *New International Dictionary of Old Testament Theology and Exegesis*, ed. Willem A. Van Gemeren, 5 vols. (Grand Rapids: Zondervan, 2012), *s.v.* שָׁלַם.

13. Carson, *John*, 651.

14. Gary T. Manning, *Echoes of a Prophet: The Use of Ezekiel in the Gospel of John and in Literature of the Second Temple Period*, JSNTSup 270 (London: T&T Clark International, 2004), 167.

15. Carson, *John*, 655.

16. Werner Schade, *Cranach: A Family of Master Painters*, trans. Helen Sebba (New York: G. P. Putnam's Sons, 1980). Originally published as *Die Malerfamilie Cranach* (Dresden, German Democratic Republic: VEB Verlag der Kunst, 1974). The plate of this painting is found on p. 229.

17. Carson, *John*, 653.

18. Moloney, *Glory Not Dishonor*, 174.

19. For more discussion of this difficult syntax see standard commentaries as well as Schneiders, *Jesus Risen in Our Midst*, 115–18; Johannes Beutler, "Resurrection and the Forgiveness of Sins: John 20:23 against Its Traditional Background," in *The Resurrection of Jesus in the Gospel of John*, eds. Craig K. Koester and Reimund Bieringer (Tübingen: Mohr Siebeck, 2008), 237–51, esp. 241.

20. Beutler, "Resurrection and the Forgiveness of Sins," 243.

21. Schneiders, *Jesus Risen in Our Midst*, 71.

22. Moloney, *Glory Not Dishonor*, 176.

23. Schneiders, *Jesus Risen in Our Midst*, 51.

24. Jeffrey M. Jones, "U.S. Church Membership Down Sharply in Past Two Decades," Gallup, April 18, 2019, https://news.gallup.com/poll/248837/church-membership-down-sharply-past-two-decades.aspx.

25. Frank Newport, "Church Leaders and Declining Religious Service Attendance," Gallup, September 7, 2018, https://news.gallup.com/opinion/polling-matters/242015/church-leaders-declining-religious-service-attendance.aspx.

26. Bauckham, *Gospel of Glory*, 70 (emphasis original).

27. Craig S. Keener, *The Gospel of John: A Commentary* (Peabody, MA: Hendrickson, 2003), 2:1214, 1240–42.

28. For a fuller discussion, see Craig R. Koester, "Jesus' Resurrection, the Signs, and the Dynamics of Faith in the Gospel of John," in *The Resurrection of Jesus in the Gospel of John*, eds. Craig R. Koester and Reimund Bieringer, WUNT 222 (Tübingen: Mohr Siebeck, 2008), 47–74.

29. Or, "The Messiah is Jesus." For a discussion of the syntax of the Greek and its implications see Matthew D. Jensen, "John Is No Exception: Identifying the Subject of εἰμί and Its Implications," *JBL* 135, no. 2 (2016): 341–53; as also D. A. Carson, who argues that the statement answers the question, "Who is the Messiah?" not "Who is Jesus?" See D. A. Carson, "John and the Johannine Epistles," in *It Is Written: Scripture Citing Scripture; Essays in Honour of Barnabas Lindars*, eds. D. A. Carson and H. G. M. Williamson (Cambridge: Cambridge University Press, 1988), 258.

30. Beth M. Stovell, "Son of God as Anointed One? Johannine Davidic Christology and Second Temple Messianism," in *Reading the Gospel of John's Christology as Jewish Messianism: Royal, Prophetic, and Divine Messiahs*, eds. Benjamin E. Reynolds and Gabriele Boccaccini (Leiden: Brill, 2018), 151–77, quotation on 173.

31. Britt Leslie, *One Thing I Know: How the Blind Man of John 9 Leads an Audience toward Belief* (Eugene, OR: Pickwick, 2015), 178.

32. Leslie, *One Thing I Know*, 178 (emphasis original).

33. Leslie, *One Thing I Know*, 195.

34. Schneiders, *Jesus Risen in Our Midst*, 83–84.

35. N. T. Wright, *Surprised by Hope: Rethinking Heaven, the Resurrection, and the Mission of the Church* (San Francisco: HarperOne, 2008).

36. Wright, *Surprised by Hope*, 67.

37. Schneiders, *Risen in Our Midst*, 46–53.

38. Schneiders, *Risen in Our Midst*, 21–23.

JOHN 21

1. R. Alan Culpepper, "Designs for the Church in the Imagery of John 21:1–14," in *Imagery in the Gospel of John: Terms, Forms, Themes, and Theology of Johannine Figurative Language*, eds. Jörg Frey, Jan G. Van der Watt, and Ruben Zimmermann, WUNT 200 (Tübingen: Mohr Siebeck, 2006), 370–401, esp. 370.

2. R. Alan Culpepper, *Anatomy of the Fourth Gospel: A Study in Literary Design* (Philadelphia: Fortress, 1983), 66.

3. Beverly Roberts Gaventa, "The Archive of Excess: John 21 and the Problem of Narrative Closure," in *Exploring the Gospel of John in Honor of D. Moody Smith*, eds. R. Alan Culpepper and C. Clifton Black (Louisville: Westminster John Knox, 1996), 240–52, quotation on 248–49; See also Culpepper, "Designs for the Church," 370–401, esp. 370; Richard Bauckham, "The Fourth Gospel as Testimony of the Beloved Disciple," in *The Gospel of John and Christian Theology*, eds. Richard Bauckham and Carl Mosser (Grand Rapids: Eerdmans, 2013), 126.

4. Bauckham, "Fourth Gospel as Testimony," 127.

5. Culpepper, "Designs for the Church," 395.

6. Culpepper, "Designs for the Church," 395.

7. But see Culpepper, "Designs for the Church," 386–94; also Richard Bauckham, "The 153 Fish and the Unity of the Fourth Gospel," *Neotestamentica* 36, nos. 1–2 (2002): 77–88.

8. Triangular numbers are numbers that are the sum of the preceding integers. For instance the first triangular number is 3, because it is the sum of 2 + 1. The next triangular number would be the sum of 1 + 2 + 3, or 6. The name derives from the visual scheme:

Three is the triangular number of 2:
```
  *
 * *
```

Six is the triangular number of 3:
```
  *
 * *
* * *
```

Ten is the triangular number of 4:
```
   *
  * *
 * * *
* * * *
```

153 is the eighteenth triangular number, the sum of 17 + 16 + 15 + ... + 1. Triangular numbers were recognized in the ancient world as mystical and figured largely in various methods of interpretation. Ancient Christian interpreters may have been attracted to triangular numbers because of their suggestion of the Trinity.

9. Cited in Bauckham, "The 153 Fish," 82.

10. Gary T. Manning, *Echoes of a Prophet: The Use of Ezekiel in the Gospel of John and in Literature of the Second Temple Period*, JSNTSup 270 (London: T&T Clark International, 2004), 132; see also Jan G. Van der Watt, *Family of the King: Dynamics of Metaphor in the Gospel according to John* (Leiden: Brill, 2000), 153–54.

11. D. Francois Tolmie, "The (Not So) Good Shepherd: The Use of Shepherd Imagery in the Characterisation of Peter in the Fourth Gospel," in Frey, Van der Watt, and Zimmerman, *Imagery in the Gospel of John*, 355.

12. Karoline M. Lewis, *Rereading the "Shepherd Discourse": Restoring the Integrity of John 9:39–10:21*, SBL 113 (New York: Peter Lang, 2008), 153.

13. Abraham P. Buunk and Frederick X. Gibbons, "Social Comparison Orientation: A New Perspective on Those Who Do and Those Who Don't Compare with Others," in *Social Comparison and Social Psychology: Understanding Cognition, Intergroup*

Relations, and Culture, ed. Serge Guimond (Cambridge: Cambridge University Press, 2006), 15.

14. Culpepper, *Anatomy of the Fourth Gospel,* 121.

15. See Martin Hengel, *Saint Peter: The Underestimated Apostle* (Grand Rapids: Eerdmans, 2010).

16. Richard Bauckham, *The Testimony of the Beloved Disciple: Narrative, History, and Theology in the Gospel of John* (Grand Rapids: Baker Academic, 2007), 82–91.

17. Bauckham, *Testimony of the Beloved Disciple,* 84.

18. Bauckham, *Testimony of the Beloved Disciple,* 84.

19. Kevin Vanhoozer, "The Hermeneutics of I-Witness Testimony: John 21.20–24 and the 'Death' of the 'Author,'" in *Understanding Poets and Prophets: Essays in Honour of George Wishart Anderson,* ed. A. Graeme Auld, JSOTSup 152 (Sheffield: Sheffield Academic, 1993), 366–87, citing Bultmann on 373.

20. Vanhoozer, "Hermeneutics," 366–87.

21. Vanhoozer, "Hermeneutics," 380.

22. Bauckham, *Testimony of the Beloved Disciple,* 91; also Harold W. Attridge, "The Restless Quest for the Beloved Disciple," in *Essays on John and Hebrews* (Tübingen: Mohr Siebeck, 2010), 137–59.

23. Howard M. Jackson, "Ancient Self-Referential Conventions and Their Implications for the Authorship and Integrity of the Gospel of John," *JTS* n.s. 50 (1999): 1–34, esp. 25–30.

24. Edward W. Klink III, *John,* ZECNT (Grand Rapids: Zondervan, 2016), 922.

25. Jackson, "Ancient Self-Referential Conventions," 7–8.

26. Bauckham, "Fourth Gospel as Testimony," 135.

27. Richard B. Hays, *Echoes of Scripture in the Gospels* (Waco, TX: Baylor University Press, 2016), 283.

28. Hays, *Echoes of Scripture in the Gospels,* 312.

29. Richard B. Hays, *Echoes of Scripture in the Gospels* (Waco, TX: Baylor University Press, 2016), 284; see also A. T. Hanson, "John's Use of Scripture," in *The Gospels and the Scriptures of Israel,* eds. Craig A. Evans and W. Richard Stegner, JSNTSup 104 (Sheffield: Sheffield Academic, 1994), 358–79; Martin Hengel, "The Old Testament in the Fourth Gospel," in Evans and Stegner, *Gospels and the Scriptures of Israel,* 380–95.

30. Hays, *Echoes of Scripture in the Gospels,* 286–87.

31. Hays, *Echoes of Scripture in the Gospels,* 284.

32. Hays, *Echoes of Scripture in the Gospels,* 300.

SCRIPTURE INDEX

374

SCRIPTURE INDEX